10:

CW00665934

Questions Answered When Separating With Children

Editors
Rebecca Giraud and Bob Greig

Consulting editor
Dr Angharad Rudkin

Published January 2019

ISBN 978-1-9164315-1-5

Bath Publishing Limited
27 Charmouth Road, Bath
BA1 3LJ
Tel: 01225 577810

email: info@bathpublishing.co.uk

www.bathpublishing.co.uk

Bath Publishing is a company registered in England: 5209173

Registered Office: As above

This book is dedicated to

Saskia Giraud-Reeves

Priya Greig

Anya Greig

Three outstanding young women

.

Introduction from the editors

Parents not agreeing what happens to the children when separating is normal. Since setting up our not-for-profit social enterprise, OnlyMums & OnlyDads ten years ago, we've had parents come to us with the issue - what happens with the children - at the centre of most of the concerns we hear about. Do they live with one parent or both? How long do they spend with the other parent? How are handovers best arranged? Concerns about the welfare of the child when staying with the other parent too are frequent.

This is our response to these questions; for us there seems to be three core themes that will help parents find answers and ultimately resolution to these problems.

1. Improving relationship and communication skills with their ex partner.

2. Determining (often with the help of external advice and support) just what is best for their child(ren).

3. The processes and actual mechanics of the mediation, family law support services, family courts and the law itself.

Dr Angharad Rudkin, Bob Greig and Rebecca Giraud

The web is replete with "advice" on these subject matters. Some of it reliable, much of it not. The issues at stake are too important to get wrong. Collating the best professional advice together in one book seemed a timely intervention when legal aid has all but gone, family courts are over stretched, and funding has been withdrawn from many of the charities and organisations that supported parents through difficult times. By using the latest research and evidence, we hope to provide objective yet relevant information and support for all stages of separation.

This book brings together guidance from many of the UKs leading family mediators and solicitors. Not only are they on the OnlyMums & OnlyDads Family Law Panel (see Page 32) which offers parents that all important initial direction but they are also all members of Resolution (see Page 223). Resolution members follow a code of practice that promotes an approach to family law that is most likely to result in an agreement.

We have been privileged to work with many parents over the last decade. Keeping children at the heart of the decision-making is everyone's biggest challenge when family life is in turmoil.

Whatever your situation, it is our hope is that this book will bring you direction and clarity.

We wish you and your family well.

Rebecca Giraud

Bob Greig

Angharad Rudkin

January 2019

Foreword by The Rt. Hon. Sir Andrew McFarlane
President of the Family Division

The publication of these '101 Questions', and more particularly the 101 Answers which follow and are aimed at those who are facing the daunting and at times bewildering prospect of picking up and reforming their lives, parenting and finances after separation, could not be more welcome, coming, as it does, at a time when more and more are having to cope with these major life-challenges without professional advice or guidance.

For many, separation from a spouse or long-term partner sufficient to trigger the need to engage with the issues covered in this book will be a once in a lifetime event. They will be facing the significant challenges that separation generates for the first time and without any experience or understanding of what may be involved. Expectations of entitlement and of what is 'right' and 'just' may run high; emotions may well be both raw and powerful. A common view amongst the judiciary is that there is a need for a range of interventions aimed at assisting those who come to the Family Court by managing their expectations at an early stage as to what the court can and cannot do for them. This book is therefore both welcome and timely simply because it is most likely to succeed in meeting this very need.

A parent in a family case who is hungry for hard information, sound realistic advice and a 'feel' for the court process will find much to feed on in these pages; they may also consume them knowing that they have been compiled from a gender-neutral perspective, with the aim simply of providing practical and legally accurate information without any underlying agenda.

Most 'self-help' books seem to be penned by a single author or a small team. In contrast, each of these '101 Questions' is answered by a different expert. This, obviously, has the benefit of enhancing the quality of the individual answers, but, in my view, there is a greater value when the book is read a whole. Each specialist contribution, like a pixel, builds up to a bigger picture. Whether the question is about pension sharing or a worry about the alcohol consumption of the other parent, the author, being experienced in working with families and the Family Court across the board, when describing how best to approach the micro-issue is also contributing to an overall understanding of how the legal system engages with the issues generated by separation more generally. It is this latter aspect, which is, in my view, of great value and marks this work out from others. Irrespective of the current pressing problem that may have caused a parent to pick this book up, any reader would be well advised to invest the time in reading it from cover to cover, thereby gaining a real 'feel' for the approach of family law professionals and the courts in general to these important and difficult problems.

The Rt. Hon. Sir Andrew McFarlane

President of the Family Division

4th January 2019

Acknowledgements

We would like to acknowledge the thousands of parents who have come through our organisation. We have learnt so much from their experiences and this book would not be on the shelves without them:

- Our first thank you goes to Dr Angharad Rudkin, Adele Ballantyne & Mike Flinn and the OnlyMums & OnlyDads Family Law Panel for their contributions and enthusiasm for this book.

- Norman Hartnell (The Family Law Company) for his Chairmanship of our Steering Group and for always being there with wise words.

- Jo Edwards (Forsters) for Chairing our Westminster Dialogues, providing timely G&Ts and unerring loyal friendship.

- Gillian Bishop (Family Law in Partnership) and Kat McTaggart (Woolley & Co) for long-term support and friendship.

- Alan Larkin (Family Law Partners), Mary Shaw (David Gray) and Chris Fairhurst (McAlisters) blend friendship, professionalism, encouragement and humour in a unique way.

- Colin Jones and Claire Easterman and their colleagues at Resolution have been invaluable in helping us steer the work of the OnlyMums & OnlyDads Family Law Panel. Thanks also to Matt, Ida, Lisa and Victoria for all their encouragement.

- Duncan Fisher and the Voices in the Middle Charity have kindly provided us with the quotations from children and young people.

- A special thank you to Sir Andrew McFarlane and Judge Stephen Wildblood QC for their contributions.

- Helen and David (Bath Publishing) - two and a half thousand email exchanges build a friendship!

Over the last ten years we have engaged with many people who have helped and inspired us in different ways:

- Julia Thackray, James Pirrie, Harjit Sarang, Russell Conway, Roger Bamber and the team at Mills & Reeve, Jolyon Maughan, Jeremy Ford and Simon Bethel, Simon Thomas, Richard Wain, Dr Sarah Wollaston MP, Nina Smith, Richard Paris, Adrian & Claire, Sophie Young, Fleur Brooke, Ruth Sutherland, Keri Tayler, Rosie Ferguson, Steven Ritson, Lisa Hall, Alison Greig, Shaun George, Siobhan Baillie, Elizabeth Coe, Camilla Choudhury-Khawaja, Lucy Mead, Polly Neate, Lucy Reed, Matthew Richardson and Anna Girdlestone. Thank you all.

- And finally to Catherine Tate for providing much needed laughter...

Bob's personal bit

My own separation was, like many others, complex. I was lucky to be surrounded by some wonderful people:

- Two totally supportive "big" brothers, Rod and Gareth could have been blessing enough. Over the years though, I have gained a new "sister"in Bethan and I think of you all every day.

- Chris Moss was there in the difficult days. I should say we met at King's College, London in 1984. Truth is, we met over the road in the Lyceum Tavern. The choice was between a two-hour lecture on Patristics or Sam Smith's Best on draught. Friendship won.

- Dave Barker for introducing me to the very best of colleagues.

Rebecca's personal bit

It has been a privilege to work with Bob over the last 10 years. His commitment to supporting parents, in particular dads, has been inspiring.

My two sisters, Bridie and Rosalie; we have supported each other in navigating that rocky road of having

separated parents and are closer as a result of it.

My dear friends Hilary, Lucy and Sarah who have always been there. In particular, Hilary for her words after my own separation: 'children of divorced parents often make for the most interesting adults'; Lucy for her wisdom and 5* B&B; and Sarah for the steaks and red wine.

And to Luke for all his support, patience and for sharing his own professional insights - thank you.

How to use this book

As the title suggests, this book contains 101 questions that have been asked of or emailed to OnlyMums & OnlyDads CIC. All the questions have been answered by our team of experts; solicitors, barristers, mediators and other professionals.

As well as the 101 questions and answers, a number of Must Read articles are included to provide more background to various issues such as pre-nups and cohabitation.

The book also has information about 15 useful organisations including Samaritans, NSPCC and Relate.

Dotted throughout the book are quotes, one-liners and top tips from parents, solicitors, children and therapeutic personnel.

A useful list of organisations has been included at the back and finally, we are indebted to Mills & Reeve who have allowed us to replicate their glossary from Divorce.co.uk.

This advice has been written by Adele Ballantyne (Family Consultant, MA Relationship Therapy, Director at Eleda Consultancy), Mike Flinn (Counsellor and Family Therapist) and Dr Angharad Rudkin (Programme Tutor / Child Clinical Psychologist within Psychology at the University of Southampton)

A number of solicitors, barristers and paralegals have contributed dozens of handy tips and helpful nuggets of wisdom throughout the book

The main priority for separating parents is their children. We have collected together some real life quotes from children who have accessed Voices in the Middle (see Page 70)

Rebecca and Bob work with separating parents every day and they have added in their top tips

Some words of wisdom from parents who've been through the separating journey. There are some regrets, words of advice and hopes for the future.

Contents

Housing & Finance

Mediation

Arbitration

Court & 'fighting' for the children

ONLY
Mums & Dads
parents meet professionals

What does it mean to put children first?

About the author

Dr Angharad Rudkin

Angharad is a Clinical Psychologist and a Clinical Tutor in Psychology at the University of Southampton.

It is so easy to be told that you need to put your children first, but what does that mean exactly?

We need to return to the notion proposed by Winnicott in the 1950s that the best kind of parents is the "good enough parent". This doesn't mean being a perfect parent - it means being a parent who trundles along doing an adequate job for most of the time, who sometimes messes up and occasionally outdoes themselves. This, of course, is not quite so straightforward before, during and after a separation for two reasons. Firstly, your child is dealing with an enormous change and therefore needs a lot more from you at the very time that, secondly, you are dealing with an enormous change and just getting out of bed is difficult enough. Being a good enough parent during a separation can feel like a superhuman effort.

Caring quota

Imagine everyone has a 'caring quota' i.e. an amount of love, care, organising, listening to, feeding and nurturing you can give (to yourself, your child and others in your family). Let's say the absolute maximum you can give is 100%. On an average kind of day your child may need about 25% and you may need about 25% for yourself. The rest is free to give if anyone needs it. When your child is in the middle of exams or being bullied at school, they may need 75% of your caring quota, which leaves less for you and anyone else around you. When your parent is very ill or you've just been made redundant, you need a lot of your own caring quota to get through each day (say, 80%) leaving just 20% for your child and everyone else. During a separation your child may need 100% of your caring, at the very same time you need 100% in order to function. You don't have to be a mathematician to realise that 200% isn't possible.

Getting the balance right

The key to getting through this time is balance. Getting a balance between caring for you and caring for your child. Remember, there is no such thing as a perfect parent, and there is definitely nothing like perfection during separation. To get the balance, we need to think about another area of research looking at parenting. Studies have shown that being a 'responsive' parent is one of the most important keys to a contented child. Being responsive means that you are open to, and aware of, your child's needs. It doesn't mean that you always have the answer or that you know exactly what to do. But it does mean listening, watching and communicating with your child in a flexible way, so that you are moving with your child's changing needs. This may be where the concept of putting your child first can be useful - responding to your child as they are right now may mean letting go of your expectations about how they *should* be. If they're not upset when you expect them to be, then respond to their happiness. If they're upset when you really don't expect them to be, then respond to their sadness rather than your belief that they should be absolutely fine.

Don't compare your family to others. It makes it seem like your family is completely broken but in reality a new family can be made again. Cerys-Sophie (16)

Some people are better at being responsive than others, but what is universal is that we find it easier to respond appropriately to others when we are being cared for. Talk to friends and family about your feelings, spend time with people who make you feel happy. Being able to relax and download some of your feelings will mean that you have more head and heart space to respond to your children.

Child's point of view

The final aspect of putting your child first is to imagine how things feel from their point of view. Remembering our own childhood can help us to understand our own children. If you find it hard to tap into memories of your childhood, read books about children so that you can understand how

they see the world. And if you are in doubt, ask them how it feels to be them right now. They may not give you an answer, but the fact that you're asking will help them feel valued.

Conclusion

So, should you put your child first? There are no 'shoulds' at a time like this. Instead, aim to be responsive to your child. Try to understand how they are feeling while accepting that their feelings and needs will change rapidly. Look for a balance between what you require to get yourself through, and what they need. Listen, watch and communicate with openness. The rest will then take care of itself.

Putting Children First is a phrase you will hear a lot. It trips off the tongue. It sounds obvious and straightforward. We have found that parents who recognise that they might not always know what is in their children's best interest and are willing to question their own instincts are probably those who end up really making the best decisions for their children. Don't be afraid to ask for help/advice. Separating with children is rarely easy or straightforward.

Notes

Parenting

About the author

Judge Stephen Wildblood

His Honour Judge Stephen Wildblood QC is the most senior family court judge at Bristol Civil Justice Centre.

In my time I have contributed to more than twenty legal text books but it is with particular trepidation that I write this. I have been asked to make four points about parenting in no more than 1,500 words. As the father of a large number of children I know how much better many others are at the task of parenting than me. The fact that I have been a family lawyer for over 38 years and am now a Designated Family Judge does not make me a better parent. I suppose that it does mean, however, that I am a more frequent witness than most to some of the pitfalls and tribulations that parenting can bring. So, that is the basis upon which I write this.

Parenting is tough

The first thing I want to say is this. Parenting is tough. Really tough. Those who think that it is all chocolate boxes and roses are kidding themselves. Remember those sleepless nights with a crying baby and work ticking towards you on the bedroom clock? Remember the challenges that the teenage years can bring? Now imagine that you are in your late teens or early twenties, have had a difficult childhood yourself and are trying to parent alone with limited finances and little support. All too often that is the situation that I witness in court and ask myself: 'if this were you, Stephen, how would you cope?'. I know the answer to that all too well. There are no shaded corners in family life, we live in an electronic age of very high material expectation where it is increasingly difficult to set firm but loving boundaries and those who are closest to us know us best. At work we can put on an image, at home we can't. But not only is parenting tough, it is also the most important job that we do. All life is temporary, at the end of the day and when our lives end, we will be remembered most for how we have treated other people - especially our children, because they are the next generation. So, parenting and our treatment of other people, especially those who are closest to us, matter more than anything else. They will be the people who carve our headstones and fit us into our coffins, all of which are the same size whatever we may have done in our public lives. As to my job - when I retire I am sure that someone will replace me and do it better than I have. So, first point - parenting is tough but it really matters.

Help with parenting

My second point. We all need help with parenting if we are to get it right and, if it goes wrong, we need help putting it right. Help may come from extended families, grandparents, uncles, aunts, cousins and the rest. But help may also need to come from outside agencies because sometimes the problems are simply too entrenched or complex for things to be kept in the family. There are some truly excellent initiatives that are geared to the provision of support and guidance for parents - the group for whom I am writing this is a very good example. We all need to be able to swallow our pride more and turn to them when difficulties arise, rather than wait for the emotional car crash to happen before trying to resolve things. Parenting works best when it is not an isolated affair, no one owns their children and everyone needs help at times with the things that matter on life's rocky journey.

Extended families

My third point. Both parents and both extended families matter. I have spent years developing a single sentence that I try to cram into judgments: 'Nature, law and common sense require that it be recognised that the best place for a child to live is with a natural parent unless proven and proportionate necessity otherwise demands.' Just as I believe that to be true, so I believe it to be true that nature, law and common sense require

that it be recognised that it is in the best interests of a child to have a relationship with both parents and with both extended families unless the same adverse criteria are genuinely and demonstrably made out in a way that cannot be put right. When I started at the bar 38 years ago it would often be said in messy divorce cases 'well, the children are better off without him.' Now that seems absurd in a truly toe-curling way. We know better now…I hope. However, I wonder what will make people's toes curl in 38 years time when they recollect our current views about parenting. As I write this, I can hear a cascade of replies in my head in answer to that point.

Resolving issues without court

Finally, although we each think, no doubt, that we have stunning insights to bring to how parents should function, especially when commenting on other people's children, there is no monopoly on common sense or perception - there was a song about that to which I used to listen in the punk rock era when I was at university with a curtain ring painfully clasped to my ear because my father had told me I would never be a barrister if I had an ear pierced. So, if you do bring your case to court please don't think that the judge will be able to identify an absolute answer to the problem. Judges are highly trained and will do their best to find a solution that puts the welfare of your child first. However, a judge is not a parent to your child, does not have absolute perception or immaculate insight, must decide the facts of a case on evidence and does not have the same connection with your child as you

do. The judge does not have parental responsibility for your child and, in many situations, two different judges may reach different decisions on the same set of facts because that is how human affairs work. My fourth point, therefore, is this. Only come to court if you really have to. There are so many ways to resolve your family difficulties other than having a court impose a solution on everyone. Mediation (which is still under-used in this country), arbitration (the importance of which has recently been given strong and further recognition by Sir James Munby), counselling, family therapy, buddying, parenting classes (such as those run by the excellent National Parenting Initiative) and many other initiatives are available and are better ways of resolving family issues than doffing the jousting gear of litigation. You only know the true cost of the battle after it has been fought. Surely it is far better to say, unlike the two characters in the well-known children's book, 'let's agree not to have a battle.'

The 'Pearly Gates test'

A fellow judge and I developed what we called the 'Pearly Gates test' in life. Two seconds after you are doing whatever it is that you are doing, you find yourself at the Pearly Gates - and no, I do not believe that there is a such a thing or place, but please bear with me. There, the saint looks over half moon glasses and asks: 'What have you got to say for yourself?' Suddenly the things that appeared to matter, don't. 'Well', you say, 'I wrote a cracking judgment in a case last year.' 'Yes, but you've just been overturned by the Court of Appeal', the reply whizzes back.

Trying not to curse, because that is hardly the done thing in such a sanctified place, you try to dredge up something worth saying. Perhaps the best that any of us might hope to say is: 'I did my best for the generations that follow me and for those who turned to me for help.'

I never did learn to précis. So my really final point is this. Enjoy it. Kids are fun. Challenging, but fun. I thought about that as I dived from a high sea wall in Portugal into clear, deep water with my three youngest children bombing into the sea around me last week. Parenting really is two way emotional traffic and I certainly have got back far more than I have ever given. I have no doubt at all about that one.

When considering arrangements for children remember that every family is different. What works for someone you know may not be the most appropriate option for your children. Think about what is best for them in your own particular circumstances. This may mean shared care, alternate weekends, every Friday night or school holidays. Flexibility is always helpful.

Kate Barton, Boyce Hatton

Effects on children of marital discord

About the author

Dr Angharad Rudkin

Angharad is a Clinical Psychologist and a Clinical Tutor in Psychology at the University of Southampton.

Before having children, we dream of a family home full of love, harmony and peace. Sadly, reality often doesn't work out that way. Two parents, running a busy house together while keeping their own work and social lives going, is a difficult task and one which can lead to high tension and stress. Children can deal with their parents making the odd snipe at one another, a short sulk in the front of the car, or a shirty comment or two. Children can even deal with relatively heated arguments that arise from a forgotten holiday suitcase, a car running out of petrol or a burnt dinner. What children really struggle with though is chronic, nasty arguments between their parents.

Arguing in front of children

In children's black and white worlds, arguing is bad and being nice is good. Parents and teachers reinforce this message when they guide children through friendships. However, it is not quite so clear cut. Arguments that are quickly and generously made up don't necessarily harm children. They can, in fact, help children to understand that parents can have a difference of opinion, feel cross, but can then resolve the issue. However, when children hear their parents arguing regularly, their view of the world changes. Disagreement becomes risky, they view conflict as dangerous and happy relationships seem impossible.

Children's levels of the stress hormone cortisol rises when they witness arguments. Seeing an argument is one thing, but witnessing the two people you love most shouting at one another, and yet be completely helpless to change this, can lead to sadness, worry and stress. Think back to a time you've been with adults who are arguing. The rational part of your brain tells you that this isn't a major problem, that everyone's different and that part of being an adult is not having to think something just because someone else does. But the emotional part of your brain switches into high alert. It automatically sends signals of escape or avoidance in order to get you out of the situation. In response, you look at the floor, play with your phone, anything instead of having to watch the argument playing out in front of you. Children are just the same. However many times you tell them it was just a little argument and that it doesn't mean anything, your child will still feel the automatic surge of anxiety and panic that comes with witnessing conflict.

Conflict and relationships

Arguments between parents not only affects the parent's relationship, it also affects their relationship with their child. Before and after divorce, conflict between parents will be high. Caught up in the vicious cycle of resentment, anger and frustration, parents struggle to find the resources to bear in mind their child's needs. Parents who live with a high amount of conflict are likely to be colder and use harsher discipline with their children. Perhaps it's become so normal to argue that they don't even notice they are also arguing with their children. Or it may be that parents dealing with high conflict just don't have the capacity to understand their

It felt like my whole world was falling down. Georgia (17)

ONLY
Mums & Dads
parents meet professionals

children need a different approach. Children living in families with high levels of arguments are also more likely to experience "minimal parenting" where parents don't set routines, structures or boundaries. They can go to bed when they want or eat whatever they want. While this may feel fun to the child in the short term, it can quickly make children feel unsettled and uncared for. This can lead to low self-esteem and low mood.

1 or 2-parent households?

Children usually fare better living in a single-parent low conflict house than remaining in a two-parent high conflict house. However, the long-term psychological impact of parental discord on a child has been well established, and adults who remember their parent's relationship as being an unhappy one are more likely to describe their own marital relationship as unhappy too. Research suggests that boys struggle more in the aftermath of a divorce. Boys tend to be more impulsive and defiant by nature, but these characteristics are exacerbated when they live with parents in conflict.

After a divorce, boys are left trying to cope with few coping skill and limited resources. While most children's school work will suffer as a result of divorce, boy's school work suffers most. Boys also receive less emotional support than girls after a divorce, which just maintains the false belief that boys are not affected, don't need to talk about it and aren't overwhelmed with emotions.

Minimising the impact of conflict

Returning to my first point, no one aims to bring their children up in unhappy households. While witnessing conflict is stressful and life changing for children, there are things parents can do to minimise the impact.

- Maintain a loving relationship with your child, which involves pouring understanding, interest and consistency into your time and communication with them.

- Seek support from friends and family to help manage your stress so that you are less likely to unwittingly take your frustration and sadness out on your child.

> 2 happy homes [for children] are better than 1 unhappy home.
>
> *Deborah Agus, Thorpe & Co*

- Work with your child's school to ensure that relevant people know and understand your child's needs, so that they feel understood and contained.

- Being emotionally close to parents is one of the most important protective factors for a child as they move through life. Do all you can to create and maintain yours, and your ex-partners, relationship with your child.

- Most importantly, try as hard as you can to be civil to your ex-partner in front of your children. If this means acting "as if" you really like them, then this is a role play worth doing.

Notes

The first days

Humans are designed to cope with many onslaughts, but change continues to prove extremely challenging. Especially when that change is unexpected or out of your control. Uncertainty is one of the hardest experiences, and can paralyse you from action. Take small steps, understand that waves of emotions will pass and write things down so that you're not relying on memory at the very time when it is least effective.

Is it over?

About the author

Adele Ballantyne, MA Relationship Therapy

Adele is a Family Consultant, member of Resolution Parenting After Parting committee and founder of Eleda Consultancy. She has experience in helping a variety of individuals, couples and families and specialises in providing help for separating couples and their children.

Deciding to end a relationship is a complex and difficult process and is not arrived at easily. Equally, being told your relationship is at an end is often a shocking and emotionally traumatic event.

It is common for those leaving and for those being left to experience similar feelings despite how it might look on the outside.

Depending on what has been happening in the relationship, and every couple relationship is unique, the ending might feel inevitable and expected or a complete surprise.

Some might describe the initial event as if they were in or witnessing a car crash. Life speeds up and thoughts run away turning life upside down. Others might say it's like everything is in slow motion and they are devastated.

Loss & uncertainty

There are, however, certain processes that couples go through when a relationship is over - both experience *loss* and both are 'pushed' into a period of *uncertainty*.

"So, is it really over?"

"I can't believe it's over"

"I didn't see it coming"

"Why didn't you tell me you were this unhappy?"

"I'll do anything, let's just try again"

"I tried to tell you, you wouldn't listen"

"You know we haven't been happy"

"We've been arguing for ages, you just storm off"

As a therapist I hear these questions again and again from couples who are about to separate or have already separated.

Coming to terms with losing someone whom you thought you would be with forever is one of the most difficult journeys a mum or dad can take; knowing that you will never again be the love of their life; that they no longer 'want' you; and they have already found someone, or will go on to find someone, who will have what you no longer have, is one of the hardest things to acknowledge. How long it takes to accept and move on depends on the individual.

Mums and dads often find it difficult to separate their couple relationship feelings from their parenting feelings and it is this dichotomy that invariably gets in the way of allowing continued relationships with the children for the non-residential parent.

So, let's talk about the two processes you will both have in common; loss and living with uncertainty.

The loss cycle

Whether you are a mum or a dad, whether you have initiated the separation or not, you will both go through loss. It is the same process that you might go through if a loved one dies and it is common for one of you to be at a different stage than the other.

Imagine this. You are in a relationship, it's been good, then OK and now it's not working. You

THE FIRST DAYS

can't talk to each other, you might feel unloved, criticised, disrespected, not wanted or needed, taken advantage of. Maybe you feel like something is going on but are afraid to ask. You've tried to talk but got nowhere. Sound familiar?

When issues like this occur in a relationship, if they are not resolved then each of you begins to exhibit different behaviour. Sometimes it's subtle, sometimes it's obvious.

Usually for one person the loss cycle begins. There are 5 stages:

- denial/shock
- anger
- bargaining
- depression/sadness
- acceptance

As one person begins to make their way through the 5 stages, the relationship may continue to deteriorate. After a time, there is often a catalyst that will force a major change. Commonly when this occurs the relationship has ended for one person. The mum or dad is at stage 5 and accepts that, for them, it is over.

Then comes the car crash for the other person and they begin their journey through the loss cycle. No wonder it's difficult for them to accept that it's ended.

Uncertainty

Once this has happened both mum and dad are thrown into a period of uncertainty.

Identities are changing from couple to single, from mum and dad together as a family unit to mum with children and dad with children. Depending on the circumstances and who decides to leave the family home, there are many questions that arise during this time.

"Will we have to sell our home?"

"I haven't worked since we had children - how will we manage financially?"

"What will our friends and family think?"

"How much will divorce cost?"

"Will I cope on my own?".

There seems to be so much to sort out both practically and emotionally and it comes at a

time when at least one of you will be 'all over the place' emotionally due to the loss you are experiencing. This can make decision-making seem impossible. Who wants to agree the practicalities of legal issues and more importantly organise the children when they are devastated, angry and confused by loss? It can turn otherwise rational, clear-thinking mums and dads into what appears to be belligerent, stubborn, unreasonable people.

Being honest with yourself about the relationship whilst you are emotionally upset is, for many extremely hard. It is important when struggling to accept that a relationship is over to get some help. There are many professionals out there who can help you on this journey.

A mum once said to me;

"So he dropped this bombshell two weeks ago, he's leaving. Ever since then we've been talking more than we have in years and we seem to be closer than ever; but, he's still leaving. I'm so confused".

This is not uncommon, often the relief for the partner who's leaving is so great that they become more amenable to conversation. Sometimes the guilt of leaving creates an atmosphere of understanding and even closeness that may have been absent for years.

A mum or dad who wants to leave knows they have hurt their partner and this initial toing and froing seems to be a way, for many to limit that hurt. However it is usually short lived as the reality sinks in.

Adele Ballantyne

Relate

About Relate

Relate, the UK's leading relationship support charity, supports families before, during and after separation to part in the least painful way possible and to maintain a positive co-parenting relationship if there are any children involved.

Good quality relationships are fundamental to our health and wellbeing, as well as our children's long-term life chances. The reality is that one in five UK adults are in a distressed relationship, 42% of marriages end in divorce and a large number of couples separate.

Relate, the UK's leading relationship support charity, supports families before, during and after separation to part in the least painful way possible and to maintain a positive co-parenting relationship if there are any children involved.

We've been around for 80 years and during that time we've been constantly adapting to meet the needs of society. We began providing relationship counselling to married couples and many people think that's still all that we do. But whilst relationship counselling does remain a core part of our work we also provide a range of other services which may be useful to anyone going through divorce, separation or any relationship issue. We work with individuals, couples and families at all stages of relationships and see people of all backgrounds, ages, sexual orientations and gender identities.

It's worth noting that our services are delivered via several mediums. Face-to-face is the most popular way of accessing support but we also offer services via webcam, telephone and instant messaging.

Now, a bit more about the services we offer for families going through divorce and separation.

Relationship counselling

Relate's relationship counselling is available to couples and individuals. Perhaps things have reached crisis point in your relationship and you and your partner are considering divorce or separation. If this is the case, it may be worth attending counselling as a couple to help you find a way forward. It may well be that you decide to go your separate ways, but talking it through with somebody objective such as a counsellor can be really beneficial. Maybe one of you has already moved out but you are wondering now if divorce is the next step for you or if a reconciliation could be possible.

According to research by Relate, 10% of divorcees said that, with the right support, "we would have been able to save the relationship and stay together" (5% definitely, 5% probably). 18% said that, with the right support, "we would have been able to make the ending of the relationship easier to deal with" (8% definitely, 10% probably). So it's really worth exploring this option even if you don't intend to stay together.

Relationship counselling can also be a really useful tool for individuals who are going through divorce or separation. It's a way of unpacking what went wrong in your relationship so that you can change any behaviours that weren't working for you, build self-esteem and move on with your life, building healthy relationships in the future.

Whichever services you access you can be assured they are confidential and delivered by trained, non-judgemental

I wish I had taken more time to introduce my new partner to my daughter.

Bridie, Mum

professionals.

Mediation

Mediation is different from relationship counselling as most couples tend to go down this route when they haven't been able to reach an agreement. Mediators help to make arrangements either to plan for separation or divorce or for after the separation or divorce has taken place, depending on the circumstances.

Mediation can help with disputes about contact and living arrangements, property, finances and child maintenance. One of the reasons many couples decide to attend mediation is that it avoids long, drawn-out court processes. It offers a neutral environment for each to put forward their point of view and be heard, helping them to strengthen communication and make informed decisions about the future.

Family counselling

Family counselling can help when parents and children are going through a divorce or separation as well as helping at other tricky times. Forming a new family can be a challenge and it's often at this point that parents contact Relate for some support to help everyone settle. The great thing about family counselling is that it helps to build stronger relationships between all the family members and support each other through what can be a difficult time.

Children and young people's counselling

Children and Young People's Counselling is for any child or young person who's having problems. These problems could be to do with bullying at school, a mental health issue such as depression or struggling to cope with their parent's separation or

divorce. Many of our young clients tell us that they feel happier after they see a Relate counsellor and are better able to deal with their problems. In some cases, the Relate counsellor can help them to concentrate better at school or college, or get on better with their friends and family.

What does it cost?

Relate is a charity but to cover our costs we do usually have to charge for our services. Each Relate Centre sets their own charges so to find out the cost of counselling in your area, please contact your local Relate. Some are able to offer free or subsidised counselling but this depends on your circumstances and the funding available. We also have a network of individual counsellors who work in private practice, but are licensed by Relate - they set their own fees too. When you contact them via our website, they will provide you with information about their own charges.

We hope this gives you a useful overview of the services we offer. If you'd like to find out more, we'd suggest visiting the Relate website (www.relate.org.uk), finding your nearest Centre and getting in touch. They can talk you through the services available locally and provide you with an initial assessment to help you decide what kind of support you would benefit from most.

Humans have developed various ways of adapting to change, but it still takes up a lot of energy, resources and time. When an unexpected, traumatic event occurs such as being told that your partner is leaving, your body and brain responds with fight, flight response or freeze response. During these responses, the brain ensures that you are in optimum survival mode. It shuts off certain aspects of functioning and heightens others, with adrenaline cortisol surging through the body. To counteract this natural physiological reaction, you need to stay as calm and relaxed as possible. Now is not the time to make any major decisions and you will need all the support from family and friends you can. Once you start to feel safe and contained, your brain will stop sending alarm signals. Having recovered from the acute stress, you can take small steps in thinking about the future, planning and making decisions. As with any loss, you will move through stages of different feelings - numbness, anger, depression, acceptance. There are no time limits, so trust that you will work your way through these stages at your own pace.

Angharad Rudkin

How did we get here?

About the author

Dr Rachel Davies, Senior Practice Consultant for Relate

Rachel is a Senior Practice Consultant for Relate. She is a Chartered Counselling Psychologist and has extensive experience of working with couples and families and providing clinical supervision to counsellors and psychotherapists in this field.

If you are looking at a book on separation then you are likely to have reached a point where it seems to be the answer, maybe the inevitable or the only way you can see out of how things currently are. The six areas of focus below will look at whether that is actually the case, consider how you can work out if the relationship is over or not and steps you can take to turn a potential separation around.

What got you to this point? Identifying the relationship 'ouches'

First it is important to say that some people are in relationships that are emotionally, physically or sexually abusive. If you are in this situation then your safety and that of your children should be your first priority and there

are people who can support you to separate safely. It may not be safe to do this alone, so seek help and support from friends, family and professional services that help people to separate safely (add links that authors approve of the obvious ones being National Domestic Abuse Helpline, Safelives and Womens Aid).

The rest of this article will consider non-abusive situations that can still leave people considering separating. When relationships aren't going well it hurts - sometimes people describe it like a physical pain and it certainly is an emotionally bruising time. There are many reasons that relationships can go wrong so for ease these are going to be referred to as the 'ouch' moments; the moments and incidents that you know have hurt you/your partner and your relationship.

You may be all too aware of a major ouch that precipitated thinking of separation, for example an affair. But sometimes it appears to come out of the blue and you have to dig a bit harder to identify what the ouches have been. It may be hard to do this but pretending an ouch isn't there is like ignoring a pain as you are worried to go to the doctor; it doesn't tend to sort it out and the delaying can make things more serious.

How did you get here - relationship journey/ couple fit

If you are struggling to identify the ouch moments or say things

like 'we drifted apart' or 'stopped feeling in love' it can be helpful to consider the journey of your relationship. Think back over the time you have been together, maybe even draw it out and note the high points where you recall feeling happy and strong together. What about the other times? Frequently there are crunch points when relationships are tested, for example just after a new baby or when one of you is made redundant or gets ill or when the children leave home. Transitions in relationships at different periods of our life are normal but for some people the transitions have become real ouches that have left a mark. Mapping the journey will help you to clarify your highs and your ouches.

> Although it is hard and we all want to be "right" when an issue comes up with the other parent, try instead to think beyond that in terms of what will make your children happy in the long term and be that "bigger person" for their sake.
>
> *Sheena Adam, Children First Family Mediation*

Two key relationship skills - communication and conflict resolution

How many ouches you can weather and what you do about them is a very individual thing. While it's impossible to give one size fits all advice, Relate generally recommends the value of talking to your partner about things that have upset you. Sharing an ouch with each other as soon as it happens and with kindness can stop it becoming a problem. Ouches that are left unspoken can build up and become resentments that are harder to address as time goes by. So try to talk about the ouches even if that seems difficult.

The good news is it's never too late to learn to communicate better. Simple things like choosing the best time when neither of you is tired, listening as much as talking and taking turns can really help. Using non face-to-face methods can also help if you have a lot you want to say. You may want to look at the relationship journey together - do their highs and their ouches match with yours?

Dealing with the ouches - what needs to happen?

Ahead of talking to your partner think about what you want in order to get past an ouch. This is a solution-focussed approach as it helps you to avoid a moan but be clear on your needs. For example, you may want your

partner to hear your side about something where you felt misunderstood or you may want them to say sorry for something they said that hurt you. The past can't be changed but couples can re-edit the story of their relationship by how they talk about an issue from the past, for example, by talking about how a period of your lives was for each of you and hearing, maybe for the first time, how it was for your partner. This can reduce the impact an ouch has in your relationship.

If you find you are holding on to an ouch or several ouches ask yourself: are you really prepared to lose your relationship over them? Do you want to give the ouches this amount of power over your potential happiness?

Equally important - designing a better relationship

When the ouches have a stranglehold on you it's hard to remember the good stuff and even to recall why you were together in the first place. Make an effort to do this though and you will see the benefits. Perhaps the passion you had for kayaking or films got you together but your kayak is hidden under debris in the garage and you go to see films with mates now. Realising this is the key to making changes. You can decide to bring some of these things back into your life. You have choices.

A diary and/or a notebook can be really helpful when separating. Throughout this book you will see the benefits of keeping a careful record of events. Who, what, when, and where are so much easier to recall when you have written them down.

Everyone responds to positive strokes from another person. Ask yourself what you loved, or still love, about your partner and then ask when you last told them or showed them you love this about them. Don't fall into the trap of waiting for them to appreciate your first. Model the partner you want to have, appreciate them and often the appreciating habit will be caught by your partner.

Learning lessons/future proofing your relationship

Ironically one of the comments people who have nearly split up sometimes make is that the most rocky patch made them stronger. Some people describe it as a wake-up call where they have realised that they have let ouches have a stranglehold in their relationship and stopped them noticing the good stuff. Use the early times after a near separation to put things in place that help rather than hinder the health of your relationship. For

I went years not speaking to anyone about what happened because I thought nobody would ever understand. Emily (16)

example, if over-working was leading to stressed based arguments then work a bit less. You may be financially poorer but your relationship health will be richer. Or if the conversation about the ouches brought up things from ten years ago, set up an annual relationship MOT where you talk to each other about what's been going on. Don't forget the noticing and appreciating.

None of this is easy and doing it well will take effort and commitment but consider the investment you have already given to the relationship, especially giving a part of your life. If it feels overwhelming or you doubt if you can do it alone then seek help. Relate regularly works with couples considering separation. After attending counselling 95% of our clients say their communication is "a bit better" or "much better" and 86% feel able to cope with any difficulties they may face in the future. What we do works and we're here for you should you need it.

Divorce and separation doesn't damage children. Parental conflict does. Staying in conflict 'for the kids' is not the answer - separating well for the kids is.

Kathryn McTaggart, Woolley & Co

The first few days of coping with the aftermath of a bombshell are challenging and are often fuelled by reactive, emotionally driven decisions. Below are some tips for coping:

- Reflect rather than react. Friends, family and social media can be great for letting off steam but what you say in the heat of the moment might be regretted later.

- Do things that help you to relax and stay calm - a walk, exercise or watching a film. And keep eating - you need fuel.

- Use your courage so that you can have useful conversations, where you are listening as well as talking.

- Write things down.

- The first reaction is not always the best reaction. Sleep on it, then consider your reply.

- Seek advice; information can be reassuring.

Adele Ballantyne

We are separating

The early days of separation can feel hazy, fast and yet, at the same time, painfully slow. The world as you knew it is changing, and you have to take your life and your children's lives into an unfamiliar future. No one stands at the altar expecting to divorce. The worlds of finance, law and mediation can feel intimidating. As with any major crises, now is the time to lean on the support of your friends and family. Look after you own needs as well as you possibly can so that you can then look after those who are dependent on you. Remember that even a few days can make a big difference, so keep your focus on the short-term. The long-term will then look after itself.

Separating: are there any practical steps I should take?

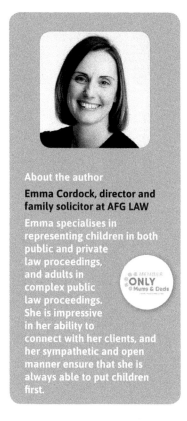

About the author

Emma Cordock, director and family solicitor at AFG LAW

Emma specialises in representing children in both public and private law proceedings, and adults in complex public law proceedings. She is impressive in her ability to connect with her clients, and her sympathetic and open manner ensure that she is always able to put children first.

For many people it can feel overwhelming when a relationship comes to an end. This checklist is not legal advice but a list of practical steps designed to try and make things a little easier and help you during this difficult time.

End of the relationship

Firstly, make a note of the date that you decided the relationship was over, even if you are still living in the same property. This date will be needed by different agencies and by your lawyers.

Children

How are you going to tell your children about your separation? Discuss this with your partner and reach an agreement on what the children should be told and how. Remember that it is a difficult time for your children as well as for you and your partner; it is important that they are not put in a position where they are aware of parental conflict or feel they have to choose between their parents. This can have a lasting impact on children's emotional welfare and development. Try to put the children's needs first.

On a practical basis think about:

- who the children will live with;

- how the children will share their time between the parents;

- whether it is possible for the children to stay in the family home so they have stability;

- whether the arrangements for the children are practical;

- getting the children to school, employment or other commitments.

If it is not possible to reach agreement, then consider getting legal advice or trying mediation.

Living arrangements

This can be a really difficult, emotional decision. Ask yourself:

- What will happen to the family home?

- Are you married or cohabiting? The legal position is different, so you might need to think about taking legal advice.

- Can you afford to stay in the house? Think about the rent or mortgage as well as the running costs.

Dividing your belongings

Sometimes this can be straightforward if it is clear you own an item, but if you have purchased things together think about making a list and try and reach a compromise. Think about what the children will need.

Managing money

This needs to be carefully approached and as always you need to think about your children's needs first. For most

I couldn't believe that my father, the man that taught me to love and to care, could leave my mother. I cried and cried for hours. Isaac (15)

separating couples the priority is trying to maintain the family home for the children. This may involve the person leaving contributing to mortgage or rent payments. Separating finances can be complicated and you may need to take legal advice.

- Think about your banking arrangements. Do you have sole or joint accounts? Do you need to set up a separate account? Think about which account the bills and rent / mortgage are paid from and be careful you don't cause any problems with missed payments or any overdrafts.

- It may be worth speaking to your mortgage provider to see if they can offer any help whilst you sort out the details e.g. moving to an interest only mortgage or taking a payment break.

- If you have joint debts such as credit cards or loans think about how you will meet these obligations between you.

- Do you need to consider maintenance?

- Are pensions involved? If you are married or in a civil partnership an ex-partner could be entitled to a share of the other person's pension(s).

- Has your benefit position changed? Do you need to speak to the DWP or HMRC? You could be entitled to further benefits.

Updating your personal information

Think about the practicalities involved and update your information now that you are no longer a couple:

- Update your emergency contacts.

- Decide on your next of kin for medical purposes.

- Review passwords and PIN numbers for banking purposes, email accounts, social media, online accounts or apps.

- Organise mail redirection for the person who leaves the shared home.

Informing people that you've separated

Think about who needs to know you have separated or moved address:

- Children's School;

- GP / Health Professionals;

- Employers;

- Bank or Building Society, credit card or loan companies;

- HMRC;

- DVLA;

- Insurance policies;

- Council Tax;

- Telephone / broadband providers;

- Utility providers.

Getting legal advice

Solicitors can help during this difficult time. It is important to know your legal rights at the start to ensure that you achieve the best outcome for yourself and your children.

We understand that our clients worry about legal costs spiralling. You can keep legal costs down by agreeing matters through negotiation and attending mediation rather than going to court. Solicitors can then

formalise the final agreement by creating a legal document so you are protected.

A lot of our clients prefer to get some initial advice prior to entering into discussions and many solicitors (as I do) offer competitive fixed fee services to help keep your costs down.

Remember that you won't both approach a separation at the same pace. If it was your decision to permanently separate, you'll be much further ahead in grieving for your broken relationship than your ex-partner. Be mindful of this and allow them the space and time they need to come to terms with the relationship breakdown. Don't rush.

Louise Buttery, Birketts Solicitors

I have decided to leave the family home. Does this have implications?

About the authors

Jessica Palmer & Hannah Sisk, Streathers

Jessica has experience with a range of private family law matters including issues arising out of divorce, child contact/residence disputes and domestic violence.

Hannah is a consultant at Streathers. She has expertise in all areas of family law including Divorce, Financial Relief, pre-nuptial agreements and Children including parenting arrangements and applications for leave to remove children from the jurisdiction.

Upon separation, it can often be tempting to leave the family home to avoid tension and conflict but there are a number of reasons why you should think very carefully before doing so. It can cause various issues financially, practically and emotionally which you should always consider before deciding to leave.

Economy of scale

Unless you are able to stay with friends or family, you will have to pay rent and utilities on a second property which for many people is unaffordable and the money spent will not be recoverable at a later stage. This situation could continue for a prolonged period of time which could lead to significant debts being incurred. This is not in anyone's best interests as it decreases the amount of assets available to meet both parties' needs.

Practical and emotional consequences

If you have children and they remain with your spouse in the family home then in some cases it can lead to difficulties with contact arrangements. You are no longer seeing your children every day and the parent they are living with is likely to automatically be seen as the primary carer which could put you at a disadvantage should there ever be a dispute about who the children should live with. The children will also have emotional ties to the family home so it can lead to them preferring to spend more time there than in temporary accommodation they are not used to.

If your spouse has a new partner, there is a danger that they could end up moving into the home or spending a significant amount of time there. This could create an increased level of hostility between you and your spouse which in turn impacts upon the children.

You will lose control over the practical care of the home which could lead to it deteriorating into a state of disrepair and there being a decrease in value of the property, the loss of which you

Allow your children to have a different opinion to your own. In fact, allow anyone (friends, family and your children) to have their own opinion on both your ex-partner and the circumstances of your separation. They can't share your hurt and trying to make them do so will only harm them as well as your relationships.

Diane, Mum

21

would struggle to recover in the long run. As well as the deterioration in value, it could also make the property more difficult to sell leaving you in a state of limbo for a longer period of time.

If the property is to be sold as part of the financial settlement, the spouse living there could cause difficulties with arranging viewings and presenting the property for sale which can create further delay.

Many people leave the property without taking all of their personal belongings with them. This is usually for practical reasons such as lack of storage or the means to transport them. However, you may find that it becomes tricky to get these items back as they are no longer in your possession. Although legally you own them, you could face yourself being denied access to obtain them or they could be disposed of without your permission. Often these items have sentimental value and cannot be replaced.

Tactical implications

Often you can end up being 'out of sight out of mind.' The spouse remaining in the property can lose all incentive and impetus to resolve the longer term financial issues because they remain comfortable where they are.

If this is the case, you could find

yourself having to make an application to court for the property to be sold or transferred which is not only a long process but can also costs thousands of pounds. If you are in the home still, you are more likely to ensure that your spouse has the same desire to resolve matters sooner rather than later for the benefit of everyone involved.

Are there other options?

It is important to consider whether there are any other options available to you first before moving out of the home. For example, is there a spare room? Are you able to shift the living arrangements around to accommodate sleeping somewhere else?

If you are thinking of leaving the home as a result of your spouse's abusive behaviour then you should seek advice first on whether you could apply for an occupation order which forces them to leave and allows you to stay in the home.

Steps to take if you feel you have no option but to move out

Be sure of your legal standing with the property. If your name is not on the legal title then you must register your matrimonial home rights over the property.

Gather any documents for you and the children that you think

> Manipulation and mistruths are common - get proper advice to make informed decisions.
>
> *Carol-Anne Baker, Bridge Law Solicitors Limited*

you may need going forward such as your marriage certificate, birth certificates, bank statements etc. It is also useful to take an inventory of items that are there when you leave and you should take any personal items, particularly those of sentimental value, in case your spouse disposes of them without consent. If you are an international couple then it is also important to consider where the children's passports should be kept.

Before leaving, try and begin putting in place a pattern of time you spend with the children i.e. certain days at the weekend or during the week. This will then make the transition when you have left easier and be more natural for the children.

Ensure that your new accommodation is attractive and adequate for the children to stay in or it could create difficulties with contact going forward.

To go from having a full, 'normal' family to a completely different lifestyle is enormous and should never be taken lightly. Don't ever think that your emotions and how you feel aren't valid. Don't ever stay silent. Jess (17)

How do I choose a solicitor and what should I be looking for?

About the author

Mandeep Gill, Venters Solicitors

Mandeep is a specialist family law solicitor whose particular specialism for a number of years has been complex international children cases such as child abduction under the Hague Convention. She undertakes other children work such as applications for Child Arrangements Orders and Prohibited Steps Orders and relocations within the jurisdiction.

I nvolvement in any legal matter can be very daunting. When that legal matter relates to a family issue, it is understandably even more overwhelming and frightening as it is as personal as it can really get. Choosing the right solicitor becomes a crucial

part of somewhat easing the initial and ongoing worries that come with being involved in a legal dispute.

So how do you choose a solicitor?

You may seek recommendations from family and friends because you trust them and feel more comfortable with a professional that has already been endorsed by a familiar figure in your life. Another way of finding a solicitor is to visit the Law Society website (lawsociety.org.uk).

You will need to feel comfortable about instructing a solicitor after telling them what is significant to you in your case. Most solicitors will expect that a prospective client would want to have an initial telephone chat with them before instructing them. This would be your opportunity to gain a sense of whether you would be happy with the solicitor acting for you.

It is important that you ultimately have trust and confidence in your solicitor to do the very best possible for you and that they have the requisite experience - this is likely to be the overriding factor when selecting a solicitor. This is particularly so in family law

cases given that these cases can be delicate, and your solicitor is likely to need to know some quite personal details about you and your family to work on your case. You will need to feel sufficiently at ease with your solicitor to provide them with this personal information.

It is a good idea to read the biography of the solicitor you are considering as this will often summarise the sorts of cases that they have expertise in. Commonly, solicitors have their biographies on their firm's website and you can often find articles your solicitor has written online.

Specialist solicitors

There are a wide range of legal areas and therefore it is necessary to consider whether you require a specialist solicitor for your particular legal issue. More and more solicitors now specialise in particular areas of law rather than doing a bit of everything. Even within family law itself, many solicitors have a specialist area - for example, some solicitors will only undertake relationship breakdown and financial cases whereas others may only undertake cases involving

Life changed drastically and I'm still adjusting. It's harder than people realise. Lauren (15)

children disputes.

International family law is a niche within family law and very few solicitors have expertise in this area. If your case has an international element, then you really do require a specialist international family solicitor. You can ask the solicitor you are considering whether they belong to any specialist groups or associations and whether their firm has any relevant professional accreditations.

Legal costs

Legal costs are an important consideration when selecting a solicitor. The solicitor will tell you about their charges at the outset, usually at the first interview. Often solicitors will charge for their time on an hourly rate basis; therefore, the longer it takes to work on your case, the higher the legal costs will be. Hourly rates vary between solicitors depending on a number of factors including their seniority and experience. Therefore, if you choose a junior solicitor for your case, their supervising solicitor will have a higher hourly rate and as they are likely to undertake work on your case as well, it is important you understand their rate too.

Alternatively, some solicitors work on the basis of fixed fees which means that you will know exactly how much you will be charged however long your case takes.

Legal aid

Whilst the legal aid budget has been drastically reduced in recent years, legal aid is still available for some areas of family law if you meet certain criteria so it is worth finding out

if the firm of the solicitor you would like to instruct undertakes legal aid work and whether you qualify for it.

Location

Another factor that can be relevant to you when choosing a solicitor is the location of their offices to your home or to the court, particularly if there is likely to be quite a few face-to-face meetings in your case and you find travel difficult. Nowadays, however, a lot of solicitors are flexible with this and can make themselves available at alternative venues if needed.

Alternatives to a solicitor

Finally, you should ask yourself whether there are any alternatives to instructing a solicitor. Whilst it is legally possible to represent yourself, this brings with it the obvious disadvantages, not least of which is a lack of knowledge and experience, which could place you at a disadvantage particularly if the other party is

> It's your life; be careful who you take advice from as others may have their own agenda.
>
> *Carol-Anne Baker, Bridge Law Solicitors Limited*

represented. Whilst in theory the family courts should assist unrepresented parties, in practice this has proved to be ineffective and difficult given the other pressures under which the family justice system is working.

Some solicitors will provide a limited service to assist and guide you through the process whilst you retain conduct of your own case and some barristers offer a direct access service so that you can instruct them directly without going through a solicitor. However, this service is very limited because barristers may only undertake court preparation and representation.

Do you need help with your situation? Understanding your legal and mediation options could save time, money and unnecessary stress. Check the OnlyMums/Dads Panel www.thefamilylawpanel.co.uk (see Page 32) to find the leading family law and mediation specialists and a range of pricing options and free family law clinics. The Panel member will set out your options and stop you taking the M6 when you could be on the M4!

THE FIRST CHAT ABOUT SEPARATION

This is a life changing moment; give it, and more importantly your partner, the time and respect they deserve.

- Pick a time and place where you can have an uninterrupted conversation.

- Prepare your partner by explaining that the conversation is important and essential.

- Try not to 'blurt it out' during a heated conversation. If possible choose a time when both of you are calm.

- Ensure that you have thought about what you want to say beforehand.

- Keep calm and breathe slowly, it will help!

- Try not to interrupt each other, wait until the other person has spoken.

- Really listen to each other.

- Check you have heard correctly by repeating what you thought you heard.

- Correct if it's not accurate.

- If either person becomes heated or angry call a time out and try again once you are both calm.

- Give your partner some space, allow the information to sink in, expect an outrage or silence.

- Talk again when they are ready to talk.

Adele Ballantyne

Org ●━━

OnePlusOne

About OnePlusOne

OnePlusOne is a research charity dedicated to strengthening relationships in couples, families, communities and workplaces using evidence-based training and digital resources.

Parents can access the full range of OnePlusOne's resources and programmes by creating an account on www.clickrelationships.org and from there, they will be guided through the options online. This means that parents can learn to improve their relationships and how to help their children at any time that is convenient to them from the comfort of their own home.

For parents who do not want to create an account and just want practical quick guidance, they can use www.clickrelationships.

org to find a wide range of evidence-based information as there are multiple short articles and quizzes available under the headings: Making it work; Sex; Lies and trust; Big changes; Breakups; Personal struggles; Parenting together; and Parenting apart.

OnePlusOne does not offer face-to-face counselling sessions. OnePlusOne recognised that people often search for information online before they seek more formal help and many parents do not have time to arrange appointments with counsellors. OnePlusOne therefore created the 'listening room' where parents can book an appointment to speak to a relationship expert online. The listening room can be used to raise questions, queries or just to be heard about relationship matters that are on their mind.

Parents have consistently turned to OnePlusOne for decades. They were founded in 1971 and are a trusted charity who are constantly working with Government Ministers, Members of Parliament, civil servants, local authorities, other charities, court services, the legal community and family-focused groups.

> *Look after yourself, ask for help, make friends with other single parents, do new things.*
>
> *Moestak, Dad*

OnePlusOne was integral to the creation of the Separating Parenting Information Programme (SPIP) (see Question 71) that is used in the family justice system and created the follow up online programme, Getting it Right for Children. The charity continues to work closely with CAFCASS, lawyers and mediators.

OnePlusOne understands that poor quality relationships can damage mental and physical health, with destructive and acrimonious parental conflict putting children at greater risk of emotional problems such as depression and anxiety. It is clear that the skills that create healthy relationships can be learned, and early intervention is crucial to success. OnePlusOne reaches couples as early as possible by training the professionals that they turn to for help with all issues in their lives, including parenting and health, together with providing online services accessible to all.

Supporting parents will always be a key part of OnePlusOne's work and the charity urges parents to visit www.clickrelationships.org.

Talking with friends about the latest in your separation dramas is something we all do. It's always worth looking out for those friends who don't automatically approve of everything you do or say. The "critical friend" is worth their weight in gold!

What is the law relating to the unmarried/cohabiting family?

About the author

Paul Summerbell, Head of Family Law (Sussex), Warren's Law & Advocacy

Paul is an Advanced Member of the Family Panel and an Accredited Specialist with Resolution.

There is a common public misconception that the unmarried/cohabiting couple enjoy similar rights to married couples. This is sometimes referred to as 'common law marriage' or 'common law husband/wife'. This is not the case and has no foundation in law. In financial terms those couples who marry and subsequently divorce have the benefit of the legal protections of the Matrimonial Causes Act 1973. Same sex couples enjoy the protections of the Civil Partnership Act 2004. There is no equivalent coherent body of law available to cohabitants. The law relating to cohabiting couples has developed in a piece meal fashion to deal with their arrangements on relationship breakdown.

The legal position of a cohabitant on relationship breakdown *in financial terms* is as follows:

- There is no legal process to end the relationship.

- There is no legal duty to provide financial support (maintenance).

- Property issues (home) are addressed by taking civil proceedings in property and trust law (see below).

- There is no statutory right to occupy the home.

- Cohabiting couples do not inherit each other's property under the intestacy rules.

- Transfer of tenancy orders can be made in some circumstances under the Family Law Act 1996.

- Occupation of the home can be obtained by establishing a contractual licence or obtaining a property order in favour of children under the Children's Act 1989 or temporarily by an occupation order under the Family Law Act 1996.

- If a partner becomes bankrupt the sale of the home can be delayed only if there are dependent children and only for 12 months.

The legal position of a cohabitant on relationship breakdown *regarding children* is as follows:

- At birth the natural mother will have automatic parental responsibility for the children but the father does not unless he is named on the child's birth certificate, or by agreement with the mother or through a court order.

- Either parent can issue proceedings under the Children Act 1989 for an order relating to the children if they are the natural parent.

- Both parents have a duty to maintain the children and can make an application to the Child Support Agency or Child Maintenance Service and Schedule 1 of the Children Act 1989 for financial support.

The main issue for many cohabitants, and the children, is what happens to the family home on the relationship breakdown. This depends on how the property is owned. If the property is held by both parties jointly as legal co-owners then the property cannot be sold or transferred without the consent of both parties. If it is not owned equally a declaration of trust should be used to specify the respective shares in the property. The TR1 form completed to convey the property can be crucial as it requires details of how the property is to be owned. It should be completed to reflect that ownership and the parties should be fully advised about how the property is to be held

before completing this document. This is often referred to as an **express trust** as the details are fully or expressly documented.

The ownership of property is in two parts:

- Legal title - the person in whom the legal estate is vested.

- Beneficial interest - the person with co-ownership rights even though their name may not appear on the legal title of the property.

If the property is owned by one party the non-owning party must then establish a **constructive trust, resulting trust** or **proprietary estoppel**. In the **constructive trust** the non-owning party must establish by both words and conduct that they were led to believe that they had a beneficial interest in the property and that the non-owning party acted in reliance on this to their detriment. This could be by way

of mortgage payments or improvements to the home. It can also be by deferring home security in the completion of the "occupier" form for the mortgage company financing the purchase of the home that allows the non-owning party to postpone those rights as against the mortgage company. This is a common form required by mortgage companies.

If a financial contribution was made to the purchase of the property the beneficial interest in the property will be allocated accordingly. This is known as a **resulting trust**.

Proprietary estoppel has been used to grant property rights in the past. Three preconditions apply:

- An assurance of an interest in property;

- Reliance on that assurance;

- Detriment suffered as a result.

This must be such as to allow the court to make an additional

finding that it would be unconscionable to deny the claimant the relief sought. It is said to be easier to establish than a constructive common intention trust as it relies on a mere assurance rather than a common intention.

In deciding the share of the property which both parties may be entitled to in circumstances where a trust is found to exist there is wide discretion to look at the whole course of the dealings between the parties and to concepts of what is fair.

If legal action is required to determine an issue concerning the property of cohabitants i.e. where they cannot agree what is to happen to the property, proceedings are issued under section 14 of the Trusts of Land and Appointment of Trustees Act 1996. In reaching any decision the court will consider:

- The intention of the parties who created the trust;

- The purpose of the trust;

When relationships go wrong and arguments occur it can be worrying for both parents, especially when children are around.

Deciding to leave is a big upheaval but for some it is the only option, especially if there is violence or emotional abuse.

There are a few strategies to try if there is no violence/abuse, before you move out;

- Agree not to argue when the children are around

- If you are talking and things begin to escalate, agree to take a 'time out'

- Perhaps relationship therapy might help you to have the most difficult conversations

Reassure your children that although you are not getting on at the moment you are trying to resolve things. Remind them it's not their fault and that you both love them.

Adele Ballantyne

- The welfare of any minor who occupies the property as his home;

- The interest of any secured creditor.

It is worthy of note that in case law it has been stated that:

"The onus is on the person seeking to show that the beneficial ownership is different from the legal ownership. So in the non-owner cases, it is upon the non-owner to show that he had any interest at all".

How to protect the cohabitant (and children)

1. Enter into a Declaration of Trust when the property is purchased, specifying the shares in the property.

2. Make sure the TR1 form conveying the property is properly completed to reflect the ownership of the property.

3. Enter into a living/ cohabitation agreement at the time of cohabitation to specify property ownership.

4. Negotiate to execute a transfer of property to properly reflect ownership of property.

5. If disagreements arise, negotiate the ownership of the property prior to using legal proceedings.

6. Ensure what life insurance provisions exist and that the cohabitant is catered for.

7. Ensure that each cohabitant has an up to date will.

Death

If the property is owned as joint tenants the property will pass to the other joint owner and the survivor becomes the sole owner of the property.

If there is no will the cohabitant has no rights to inherit under the intestacy rules. However, if the survivor can show that they were maintained by the deceased before death a claim can be brought under the Inheritance (Provision for Family and Dependants) Act 1975.

Notes

ONLY
Mums & Dads
parents meet professionals

Common law marriage is a common myth

About the author

Catherine Bell, Partner at Taylor Vinters

Catherine advises on all aspects of family law, specialising in the financial complexities of divorce and acting for high net worth individuals and advising on the separation of non-married couples. Catherine is a qualified collaborative lawyer.

MEMBER
ONLY
Mums & Dads

Many people believe that 'common law marriage' is a legally binding entity. Sadly, it's just a myth, and the reason that's sad is because many unmarried couples rely on it.

The truth is that unmarried couples who live together have few rights in relation to each other's property, regardless of how long they've been cohabiting. If a couple in a marriage or civil partnership have a relationship breakdown, the courts will aim to divide the party's assets 'fairly'. This isn't the case when an unmarried cohabiting couple separate. In

this situation, the person who owns the property in their name will be entitled to it (subject to some limited situations where the other person could make a claim).

If you separate, and the property you share with your partner is not in your name, then you could find yourself homeless. This would be particularly devastating if you've been with your partner for many years and you have children together. You could be left with very little.

Yet there is a solution.

A cohabitation agreement can give you security

The solution is to make a cohabitation agreement in case you ever separate. People often don't think about what could happen to them if their relationship were to break down until it's too late. That's why it's a good idea for both of you to make a cohabitation agreement now, while you're still enjoying a good relationship. Think of it as an insurance policy; it covers something you don't want to happen but means you'll be protected if it does.

A cohabitation agreement records what you and your cohabiting partner have agreed should happen if your relationship ends and you no longer want to live together. The agreement will be unique to you and your partner and it should at least cover property ownership, finances and arrangements for

any children from your relationship. Provided you both agree, you can include whatever matters to you - including who keeps the pets!

For the agreement to be legally binding, it's important that each of you has independent legal advice in case the other person later alleges the agreement was made under duress.

Incidentally, you don't have to be in a relationship with the person you are living with to have a cohabitation agreement. If you're simply sharing a house with someone, it's still a practical safeguard.

Other ways to protect your future

Making a cohabitation agreement is not the only step you can take to ensure both you and your partner are protected if you separate. It's worth thinking about a declaration of trust and your wills.

A declaration of trust concerns property ownership. It sets out who owns what and in what proportion, and can be very important if you and your partner are buying a property but not both contributing the same amount.

The reason each of you should make a will is because the intestate rules (which apply when someone dies without a will) don't provide any right of inheritance for a cohabitee. So, if you want your estate, which includes your property, to pass to your partner on death, you need to specifically state this in your will. And of course, your partner will need to do the same.

Happy ever after

Cohabiting couples are often unaware they have fewer rights than their married counterparts. However, I hope this has shown you that there are safeguards you can put in place.

The lack of public awareness about the limited rights of cohabiting couples, and what can be done to provide peace of

mind, led Resolution to spearhead a national campaign. During **Cohabitation Awareness** (27 November 2017 - 1 December 2017) some of my colleagues at Taylor Vinters wrote articles you might find interesting:

Cohabiting couples - your questions answered on legal rights and avoiding disputes.

Cohabiting couples - your questions answered on protecting your assets.

Cohabiting couples - your questions answered on property ownership.

All parents dread telling their children that they are separating. "Tell them the truth and what they need to know " is good advice. So too is acknowledging that this will be a process and that you may have the same or similar conversations with your children over the forthcoming weeks and months as they discover for themselves what this really means.

Notes

Family Law Panel

About The Family Law Panel

The Family Law Panel is a network of leading solicitors and mediators supporting the work of OnlyMums & OnlyDads. All are Resolution members. Many hold accredited specialisms.

The Family Law Panel is a UK-wide network of leading family law professionals (solicitors and mediators).

It is particularly useful for those parents who might need some professional advice and/or are looking to appoint a professional for the first time

The Family Law Panel (www. thefamilylawpanel.org) offers:

- Easy navigation
- Clearly laid out profiles of all members

- Specialisms in Children, Domestic Abuse and Finance
- Guaranteed free initial conversations setting out your options
- A range of price options including reduced fees

Choosing a solicitor or a mediator for first time can be a difficult decision. By using the OnlyMums and OnlyDads Family Law Panel you will be able to see photographs and comprehensive profile pages helping you to make a personal and informed decision.

It is stressed throughout this book just how important it is that you get on with and trust your chosen professional. We recommend that you take time and care making your choice. Using a Family Law Panel member means that you will also be choosing a professional that has committed to supporting our social enterprise.

All members of the panel are signed up to the Resolution Code of Practice that promotes a constructive approach to family issues.

Notes

What I learnt is it becomes normal. If it weren't for my parents divorce I'd never have met my amazing new step parents. Ben (16)

What is the role of friends in separation?

About the author

Charlotte Friedman

Charlotte is a psychotherapist. One of her specialities is divorce and she was previously a family law barrister. She has facilitated numerous divorce support groups, divorce and separation workshops and run many seminars on divorce. She is the author of *Breaking Upwards: How to Manage the Emotional Impact of Separation.*

One of the definitions of a friend is someone you can rely on.

Before you separate you believe that your friends will remain with you giving unconditional support. It probably never occurred to you that any of your friends would be a casualty of separation - understandably, it is something that you never gave any thought to.

Friendships during a long term relationship are complicated. Some of them might have grown out of the relationship i.e. friends you made together as a couple and other friends might be those that each of you brought with you.

Unfortunately there are so many other unforeseen losses involved in separation apart from the relationship and often one of them is that some friends fall by the wayside. Of course, that is particularly painful when, pre-separation, you had no reason to doubt them.

It is truly painful and shocking when you discover that good friends aren't as available to you as they have been or that they seem more interested in pursuing a friendship with your ex rather than you. It is difficult but not terminal if you can see it as part of the shake-up of separation.

Concentrate on those people who are loyal to you who deserve your appreciation and thought, not the ones who can't accommodate change. Those 'friends' who see their bread buttered by choosing your ex rather than you don't really understand the meaning of true friendship. It is important not to become preoccupied by it.

Some friends are simply too short sighted to maintain a friendship post-separation. When you come up for air you will see that the friends who have stayed are the important ones and there are many more waiting in the wings willing to share their experiences and their similar values with you and create with you new stories and memories.

Change

Change is extremely painful and frightening but out of it comes new choices and life. There is a choice to be made when you are

a bit further down the line from the shock or grief of new separation. That choice is how you wish to live your life which includes the type of people that you want to have in it. Those friends who have deserted you are probably not as good as you thought they were.

There are all sorts of friendships and some people are only in it for what you provide for them. Once that is turned around and you need something from them, you may not see them for dust. You don't need people like that in your life. It is a matter of adjusting to the new order of things.

Real friends stick around, can bear you telling the story of your pain over and over again and go

Support yourself. Confide in close friends and relatives while going through the process of separation. Don't be afraid of telling them what they can do to help you - they will want to help in any way they can. Factor in some 'me time' each day, even if it's just a few minutes to sit and read a book or go for a walk to clear your head.

Louise Buttery, Birketts Solicitors

out of their way to support you. Those friends need to be celebrated, a story of real connection and meaning. Real friends know how to give and take and can stay around when the chips are down. It doesn't matter if you are left with one or ten; the quality of your friendship is what is important.

What is important in a friend?

Make a list of what is important to you in a friend. Match that list against those you know and value the ones that meet your needs and wishes. Everyone else is unimportant. Sometimes people need you more than you need them but when you separate it is your turn to call in the help. If a really important friend of yours has fallen short and just can't be there for you, it is part of the loss of separation and something to be mourned. Inevitably, there are casualties but it is not just the end of something - it is truly the beginning of something new.

Your friend's job post-separation is to help you get back a sense of self-esteem and remind you that you matter to them and others. It is their role to listen to you and be there for you, whatever you need. If they can't do that, they are not worth it. They need to listen without pushing their own agenda. They may have all sorts of views about what you should feel about your ex, but it is more

THE ROLE OF FRIENDS - HELPFUL AND UNHELPFUL?

During separation and divorce it is extremely important to have support from friends. However there are a few things to consider:

- Sometimes it is wise to have just one or two close confidantes.

- Friends often give advice, remember you don't have to take it. Their advice will be coming from their own experience of similar situations either experienced as a child or an adult. It might not 'fit' your situation.

- If their advice sounds relevant, try not to act on it immediately. Take time to reflect before you proceed.

- Ask for what you need! Friends want to help and support you but they can only do this if they know what you need. E.g. "I really need to get this off my chest, can you please just listen to me and then give me a hug? I don't need you to offer suggestions on what I should do."

- Remember that your family and friends may 'close ranks' and become involved in your conversations with your ex to protect you. This may not always be helpful.

Adele Ballantyne

helpful to you if they can give you the space to express what you feel.

'Friendly' advice?

Friends, also without meaning to be hurtful, can try to get you to 'get over it' or 'move on'. Although they may have good intentions, it would help if you could tell them what you need from them and that you will be ready to get over it, but only

when you feel you are.

Sometimes even a good friend needs guidance on how to manage you in a crisis. A good friend will adapt to what you need.

If you have a friend who is dependable, non-judgemental and willing to listen, then you are going to be just fine.

I fell out with friends, they didn't understand. Anon (20)

My husband is having an affair and wants to divorce. What are my options?

About the author

Helen Pittard, 174 Law Solicitors

Helen is one of the founder members of 174 Law. Her approach is outcome focused allowing clients to look beyond the conflict to a more longer term future. She is a huge advocate for minimising harm caused to children arising out of parental conflict.

You first need to ask yourself whether you want a divorce and, if so, whether you want to petition him. There is only one ground on which a petition for divorce may be presented to the court by either party to the marriage which is that the marriage has broken down irretrievably. However, to establish this you must satisfy the court of one or more of five facts, three of which are to do with the passage of time with a minimum of two years or alternatively unreasonable behaviour or adultery. If the court is satisfied that a fact is proved, it must grant the decree nisi, which is a declaration that the marriage has irretrievably broken down.

Adultery

In the case of an extra-marital relationship, the most likely of the five facts you might wish to rely on is adultery which you find intolerable to live with. There are therefore two elements which must both be proved to the court; adultery and intolerability. However, section 1(6) of the Matrimonial Causes Act 1973 provides that only conduct between the respondent and a person of the opposite sex can constitute adultery. In the circumstances, you may prove or infer adultery in a number of ways.

The method most commonly used in undefended (i.e. the respondent agrees) divorce proceedings is a confession of adultery by the respondent. This can be by either a separate confession statement signed by the respondent, or by the respondent answering yes to the appropriate question in the Acknowledgment of Service (this is the form which is completed in response to the divorce petition).

In the absence of a confession, you need to produce evidence to prove or infer adultery which can include;

- the birth of a child on proof that the husband is the father;

- a conviction of the respondent in a criminal court of an offence entailing sexual intercourse; or

- a finding of adultery against the respondent in any earlier case.

In essence you have to establish to the court that your partner has had sexual relations with another person.

Intolerability

As well as the adultery, intolerability must also be proved. However, this element rarely causes any problem. You merely need to convince the court that you find it intolerable to live with the respondent. The intolerability can be proved by an assertion of intolerability in a statement sent to the court as part of the divorce proceedings. In practice, in undefended cases, courts do not even require the petitioner to state the reason why they find it intolerable to live with the respondent.

Once you've decided there is no going back, stop trying to score points over your ex and concentrate on the positives for the children.

Vicki, Mum

35

Co-respondents

There is the option for the person with whom your partner has committed adultery to be made a party to the divorce proceedings and they would therefore be the co-respondent. However, even if the co-respondent is made a party, it is not necessary to obtain an admission of adultery from them if the respondent admits the adultery. It is not necessary, however, to make the co-respondent a party to the proceedings and in fact it has become established good practice to refrain from naming them so as to reduce animosity between the parties and prevent the proceedings from becoming unnecessarily protracted in the absence of cooperation from that party. The Family Procedure Rules (Practice Direction 7A) go further and state that the co-respondent should not be named unless the petitioner believes that the respondent is likely to object to the divorce and there is a genuine risk that the proceedings will be defended.

Cohabitation

Cohabitation between you and your partner may affect your ability to rely on the adultery ground if you cohabited for a period, or periods together, exceeding 6 months after you discovered the adultery. This period runs from the time at which the petitioner discovers

the adultery and it is not relevant how long ago the adultery was actually committed. If the respondent has committed adultery on several occasions, time will not begin to run until after the petitioner learns of the last act of adultery. If the adultery is on-going then time is not an issue provided this can be proven or admitted to. Cohabitation for a period of less than 6 months must be disregarded by the court when determining whether the petitioner found it intolerable to live with the respondent.

Unreasonable behaviour

Perhaps the most useful alternative reason to rely on is your partner's unreasonable behaviour. This means that they have behaved in such a way that you cannot reasonably be expected to live with them. This is an objective test and your word alone is not enough. The court will have regard to the history of the marriage and your respective personalities. This is a question of fact in each case. It is important to note however, that this does not need to be grave or weighty behaviour and there is also no need to prove that the respondent intended to inflict misery upon you.

In a typical, undefended divorce, the court will look for 3 to 6 examples of the respondent's behaviour. The type of conduct that can be included will always depend on the particular

> Time is never on your side. Getting the right advice at an early stage is crucial to a separation.
>
> *Inayat Nadat, Nadat Solicitors*

circumstances of the case. Relevant matters may include, but are not limited to; physical or verbal abuse, intimate relationships with those of the same or opposite sex, cruelty and failure to provide money, food, affection or attention. The fact that the petitioner has simply become bored with the marriage, or fallen out of love with the respondent, will not be sufficient.

Separation

If you wish to pursue a divorce but don't wish to project blame then you may wish to rely on two years' separation and consent. This means that the parties to the marriage have lived apart for a continuous period of at least two years immediately preceding the presentation of the petition and that your partner agrees to the divorce. To prove this, you do not necessarily have to have lived in separate homes but you do have to have lived separate lives, for example, eating and doing domestic chores separately. This is notoriously difficult to prove and therefore, unless the parties

I found speaking to someone who didn't know me was better because then they couldn't judge me. Emily (16)

have been living physically separate lives for a period of two years, this fact is unlikely to be used. However, your partner will need to agree to this - if they don't the divorce petition will have to be dismissed and reissued using a different fact which can prove costly in time and money. This may even result in you having to wait until you have been separated for a period of five years.

Once you have filed for divorce, a copy of the documents will be sent to your partner. They will be asked to return an acknowledgement of service, confirming that the documents have been received and stating whether they intend to defend the divorce. Provided that the divorce is not being defended, you will then be able to apply for a decree nisi, which is a declaration by the court that your marriage has irretrievably broken down. Six weeks and one day after that, you can apply for the decree nisi to be made absolute. Once the decree absolute has been granted, you are divorced.

Costs

You can apply for costs against your partner within the divorce petition. If you are not exempt from the court fee, this is currently fixed at £550 disregarding any legal fees you may incur. On an application for costs, the decision is always in the discretion of the court, but the general principle is that an order for costs will be made in favour of the petitioner provided there has been compliance with the notice requirements concerning the amount of costs and there has not been any attempts by the respondent to

defend or file an answer. Often costs can be negotiated upon and agreed prior to the application for the decree nisi being made.

What if you are the respondent?

If you do not wish to pursue a divorce petition yourself then it will remain open for your partner to do so. Of course, they will need to establish a reason and you might believe they would not have any such reason. However, my experience in these circumstances shows that the other party could issue on the basis of unreasonable conduct leaving it open to you to have to defend such a petition if you don't want this to proceed. This can be a timely and costly exercise. It is recommended you try and agree how you wish to proceed so there are no hidden surprises or agendas and mediation can be recommended for this.

Notes

MAKING HASTY DECISIONS

It can be really easy to make a hasty decision, especially during an argument. When making decisions, remember that one of you is coping with a bombshell, even if you think it's been obvious for ages that things are not OK. Take time when making important decisions - there is no hurry to decide in the moment. Waiting a week or two and having conversations will really help in the long run. Often hasty decisions are made when feelings are running high. We often see things differently once we have calmed down.

Adele Ballantyne

WE ARE SEPARATING

What are your top tips when seeing a family solicitor for the first time?

About the author

Rachel Buckley

Rachel is a director and owner of The Family Law Company. She is head of the Divorce team. She is a specialist accredited by the Law Society and is on the Law Society's Family Law Panel. She has practiced as a solicitor since 2000.

ONLY
Mums & Dads

It takes a little effort to find the right lawyer to represent you and obtain a fair outcome for you.

Expertise

Firstly, it is important to use a lawyer with the right expertise. Experience and competence in this area are so important. Someone who understands the intricacies in family law will be invaluable to you in the long run; they will save you chasing issues that may not be advantageous to you, or even missing things that should be raised.

The best way to ascertain that your lawyer has the requisite

experience is to check whether they have any accreditations from the Law Society or other organisations. In family law there are specialist panels such as the Children Panel and the Family Law Panel. Resolution (formerly the Solicitors Family Law Association) also has specialist accreditation marks. You can check these by visiting the Law Society's website www. lawsociety.org.uk or Resolution's website www.resolution.org.uk/.

Reputation

The next step is to establish your lawyer's reputation. Ask friends or family who have used them in the past. It might also help to ask a trusted adviser such as an accountant or financial advisor who may be able to point you in the right direction.

Undertake some online research yourself; identify a short list of lawyers with the right level of experience and reputation. Many will have testimonials and case studies attached to their online profile, so have a look at these.

There are a variety of questions you should ask during your first meeting:

- Do you have any specialist accreditations?

- How many years have you been practising as a family lawyer?

- What is your approach to cases such as mine?

- Have you handled a case like

mine, and what was the outcome?

- What is your ethos towards family law?

- How will we communicate?

- How much is this likely to cost?

- Do you operate on a fixed fee basis or on an hourly rate basis - and what is your hourly rate?

- What other expenses, costs and payments should I anticipate?

- How will you bill me?

- What is your timescale for responding to calls, emails and letters?

- Will I be able to approve any letters and documents before they are sent out?

- What strategies do you recommend I follow for issues in respect of my children and my financial matters?

- Do you delegate some of the work to more junior members of staff or do you do everything yourself?

- If you do delegate to more junior members of staff, how are they supervised?

- Do you have a recommended reading list or any handouts or factsheets that I can look at?

It is advisable not to commit to a lawyer at the first meeting. Take notes and give yourself time to digest what you've been told. You could take a friend or relative with you as a second pair of ears (this mustn't be your opponent in the case or anyone who could be a witness). Your prospective lawyer may ask for information about your financial position and other personal questions, so you must feel comfortable with your friend or relative hearing your answers.

Pay particular attention to the philosophy and approach of the prospective lawyer and ensure that they are upfront in discussing likely costs with you.

What information should I take to the first meeting?

You will need to take information with you to that first meeting, such as:

- A photo identity document such as a driving licence or passport.

- Evidence of your address on a bank statement or utility bill dated within the last three months.

- A case summary noting the names of the people involved in your case, their addresses and dates of birth. You will need to give the lawyer the full names of any children, which schools they attend and whether they have any medical or educational issues.

I would have done things differently by accepting the family break-up sooner, de-attaching myself emotionally and not being too reactive.

Craig, Dad

- A chronology of events during your relationship which are relevant.

- A schedule of assets showing properties, your thoughts on their values, the likely amount outstanding on any mortgages, bank accounts with balances or at least an estimate of their balances, plus notes of any pension provision that you or your spouse may have.

- Any letters that you have had from your former partner's/spouse's solicitors, in chronological order. Take two copies with you, one for you to refer to and one for your lawyer to refer to.

Don't worry if you don't have time to put together all these documents. The main thing is to take your identification, evidence of your address and a list of what you are worried about. Ensure all the issues on your list have been addressed, before you leave the lawyer's office.

Anything else?

Other things to think about include what you want to achieve in relation to your children and/or your financial issues, and to consider what type of divorce you want. Be clear about what you can negotiate on and what is non-negotiable. And clearly tell the lawyer what your budget is for fees.

You may be tempted to talk about everything tiny detail in that first meeting, but it is advisable not to. This first meeting isn't the place to do all the talking but an opportunity to get the most out of the lawyer, make the best use of their time and ensure they're the right lawyer for you.

Notes

Parents: whenever possible, stick to the plans you make that involve your children. Bridie (22)

ONLY
Mums & Dads
parents meet professionals

Recognising and dealing with stress

About the author

Dylan Watkins, GP at Leatside Surgery, Totnes

Dylan has been a GP in Totnes for the last 20 years. As a Junior Doctor he undertook training in paediatrics and psychiatry as well as other specialities before deciding to be a family doctor.

What do they say the big life stresses are?

Moving house, having a child, divorce, bereavement, losing a job... People commonly quote them but it is hard to pin down actually which ones are worse - there seem so many.

The first for most I think is the life stress of having kids. Having a family can be unbelievably stressful. The kids are of course our greatest joy and delight too but the strain that parenting can put on a relationship is a great risk.

The second is then the separation. If you've got to the point where that is the best option then you have usually tried various means of compromise and getting along: perhaps been to Relate or a counsellor. By the time you get to separation this has been going on a while and you will invariably be suffering the strain of a stressful situation.

Third then is negotiating terms with your ex-partner: the house, finances and access rights.

Fourth is moving house. It happens so much in any separation and is hugely disruptive in your lives but stressful emotionally too.

How do you recognise that you are stressed though?

It isn't like being stressed for an exam - that, I think, you feel as a stressed brain.

In life-stresses the body often reveals the stress more than the mind. You can be so busy telling yourself you are OK in a situation that you don't recognise the tightness in the chest, the tremor and sweaty palms or the butterflies in the stomach for what they are. Disturbed sleep begins to kick in and tiredness with it. Fatigue just exacerbates the response to the stresses you are under.

Once stress begins to take hold, it can get out of control unless some kind of help is sought.

The pressures can tip over into depression, depression being more than just some sad, bleak thoughts, but something deeper and more pervasive.

The Royal College of Psychiatrists has made a list of typical symptoms someone with clinical depression might suffer. They might:

- feel unhappy most of the time (but may feel a little better in the evenings);

- lose interest in life and can't enjoy anything;

- find it harder to make decisions;

- not be able to cope with things that they used to;

- feel utterly tired;

- feel restless and agitated;

- lose appetite and weight (some people find they do the reverse and put on weight);

- take 1 to 2 hours to get off to sleep, and then wakes up earlier than usual;

- lose interest in sex;

- lose their self-confidence;

- feel useless, inadequate and hopeless;

- avoid other people;

- feel irritable;

- feel worse at a particular time each day, usually in the morning;

- think of suicide.

My mother told me, after I left my husband, that she was relieved but I shouldn't forget that, because we had a child together, I was with him for life!

Caitlin, Mum

I think it is a pretty good list. If you scan down the list going "Yes, yep, that one too..." then it really is time to consider getting some advice.

As a GP people come to discuss their problems with me at all sorts of points along this line.

I couldn't say if it is right or wrong to go to the GP earlier or later. We are all individuals with different backgrounds and we each, individually, seek help when we need to. A high proportion of GPs have been divorced or separated so they can usually empathise pretty well: and if they haven't themselves been through it they will likely have a colleague who has.

It doesn't have to be the GP that you talk to of course. Anyone who is a good listener can be great to offload on. There is something more though, I think, to be gained from talking with someone trained to listen and help you find your way forward. Whether that is a counsellor, doctor or priest... it doesn't matter.

I know what I do as a GP though. I will try to understand the problem and get its context. I will try to gauge where on the scale of anxiety or depression or stress scale my patient is at that point. I will then attempt to tailor my suggestions to the individual: in terms of helping them understand where they are at emotionally and understand how this might have come about. I'm

not trying to be a marriage guidance counsellor, but I might try to ascertain what my patient really wants as an outcome and to try to see if it feels achievable.

GPs can signpost patients on to support: counselling especially. If the stress symptoms are stronger, then most places now in the UK have easy access to psychological therapies; especially Cognitive Behavioural Therapy (CBT). This is often accessible by self-referral. Check your GP's website or search for "CBT self referral" in your local area.

Often I do prescribe some sort of medication.

Sleeping pills seem most helpful in the short term. Getting some sleep can be terribly regenerative.

SSRI antidepressant drugs are demonised in the press sometimes, but in my experience really can bolster your emotional state. I don't like to prescribe them long term, but find that using them for a spell when the stresses are most high can make a real difference. They counteract anxiety as well as lift mood a little. In my experience they can begin to work within just a day or two. They seem to have very few side effects, especially when used for shorter spells.

For severe anxiety there is diazepam. I don't tend to prescribe it a whole lot but it can be used for situational stress. (Mostly for fear of flying or going

in an MRI scanner). My worry with diazepam is that it may cloud the mind or judgement more than the SSRI pills so perhaps not best if you are stressed about attending court or similar.

I know GPs say they are busy, but you are the patient and if you recognise stress in yourself then starting to talk about it sooner rather than later with your GP is probably best.

We don't judge anyone, ever, for coming in feeling the effects of stress, so get talking sooner in the process.

If you can possibly afford counselling for yourself, do it. It really helped me see that my family of 4 was still a real family and not incomplete without 5 of us.

Vicky, Mum

Don't bottle it up, don't keep it to yourself - TELL SOMEONE! Tyla (15)

Samaritans

About Samaritans

Samaritans offer a safe place for you to talk any time you like, in your own way - about whatever's getting to you. You don't have to be suicidal.

Samaritans volunteers are available any time, from any phone. You can call the free helpline number, 116 123, and it will not appear on your phone bill. You can also contact Samaritans volunteers via email at jo@samaritans. org or go to www.samaritans. org/branches to find details of your nearest branch.

Reaching out for help when you are feeling low can be extremely hard. The feelings that can push you into (and keep you) in a low place - shame, loneliness, depression, low self-esteem, anger - can act as barriers to stop you opening up and getting the help you need.

Ironically, this is the time you particularly need support and someone to listen to you. It can be the first step on the path that leads to a better life. Suicide and suicidal feelings are very complex, and vary from individual to individual, but generally they grow in isolation and are fed by silence.

Volunteers

Samaritans has more than 20,000 volunteers who are available to help anytime, and can be contacted free from any phone. They know it is difficult to reach out, sometimes particularly for men, and they do their best to make it easier.

The charity, which was set up more than 60 years ago to prevent suicide, not only has a free-to-callers helpline, available night and day, but you can also contact the volunteers by email, or visit your nearest for branch for face-to-face help (see the side panel for contact details).

Samaritans' volunteers keep what you tell them confidential and they don't judge, and you can choose what you tell them and what you don't. They say that is one of the main reasons people get in touch, because they feel safer talking to

someone who does not know them and does not have the emotional expectations associated with family and friends.

Suicidal thoughts

Often there isn't one main reason why someone decides to take their own life, and suicidal thoughts are common - one in five people who responded to the NHS Mental health and Wellbeing (2014) said they had felt suicidal. It's how you manage feeling low that is a key thing.

Often feeling suicidal it is a result of problems building up to the point where you can't see past them, and you can think of no other way to cope with what you are experiencing. There is also a critical voice that can sit on your shoulder and compares your life to others, to your detriment.

A suicidal crisis will pass - feeling this way often only lasts for a short period of time. Talking can really help you to find a way through, and this is why Samaritans would encourage anyone who is feeling low to reach out for help.

Another issue that affects men is that they tend to compare themselves to a 'gold standard'

I'm still learning about the mistakes my parents made and I'm still learning how to better myself. Anonymous (20)

ONLY
Mums & Dads
parents meet professionals

Organisations

Org

ORGANISATIONS

of masculinity and when they don't achieve this, they can experience a sense of shame and defeat. There is also evidence that men find it more difficult to reflect on what's happening to them, which stops them reaching out for help.

Other factors, such as financial pressures, can also raise the risk of someone becoming suicidal. Deprivation, poor education, income, housing and unemployment can all contribute to suicide risk; men from lower socio-economic groups are at ten times greater risk of suicide.

Psychiatric illness such as depression can also increase suicide risk; but it is important to remember that the majority of those who suffer from depression will not take their own lives - suicide is not an inevitable outcome of mental illness.

Relationship difficulties

Relationships difficulties are in the top five most quoted reasons for contacting a Samaritans volunteer. Our close relationships are fundamental to our well-being - especially those with partners, spouses and children.

If relationships go wrong, you can be thrown into turmoil, and it can be difficult to function normally. Emotional pain is as real as physical pain and getting through the day can become a major undertaking if you are dealing with a breakup or separation.

Another consequence of relationship problems and separation is that you may not live with your children full time, so there is the emotional pain of missing them to deal with, plus the practical arrangements and the challenge of sustaining the relationship with them.

When you are in a difficult place emotionally it can be hard to see your life objectively and realise you need help. You don't need to feel lonely and isolated when there is help available, and the message to remember is that you might feel very alone, but you are not.

Once you have made the decision to leave, you may not understand that your partner is at a completely different point. They may think there's nothing wrong with the relationship or may believe that you are both still working on it. 'Theory of mind' refers to the ability to put yourself in someone else's shoes. That is, to see the world from their point of view. Use this innate ability to help you manage the conversation about leaving. Be clear, be concise, don't use clichés, don't be disingenuous. Explain what has been going through your mind preceding your decision, but try not to use blaming statements, shun responsibility or excuse. All of this will make your partner feel less attacked and therefore less defensive, and they will be more able to listen and process the information. It is so tempting to keep talking, but leave silences so that your partner can ask questions. You are also less likely to talk yourself into a difficult position. Finally, write down your main points so that you can refer to them should you start feeling fuzzy headed as the emotional heat goes up.

Adele Ballantyne

ONLY
Mums & Dads
parents meet professionals

How can technology help parents and children cope after separation?

About the authors

Melanie Bataillard-Samuel, Gregg Latchams Solicitors & Tom Brownrigg, Goodman Ray Solicitors

Melanie is a Senior Associate and trained collaborative lawyer. She is an active member of Resolution and co-chairs Resolution's Innovation Committee with Tom.

Tom is a Partner at Goodman Ray and a mediator. He also co-chairs Resolution's Innovation Committee. He is accredited by Resolution for private children issues, and medium to high net-worth financial matters. He is an FMC accredited mediator and trained in Child Inclusive Mediation.

Melanie and Tom have written this article on behalf of Resolution's Innovation Committee.

We live in an era where the way in which we live would be unrecognisable 20 years ago. Technology is intended to be there to make processes more efficient and to make your life easier. It goes to follow that it should make the separation process easier too. For every action there is an equal reaction though, and technology can be more trouble than it is worth.

Set out below are some examples of how innovations in family law can hopefully help people navigate through separation and keep up with their children's lives.

I've just separated - what happens next?

Get advice and learn about your options. The internet is a helpful tool, especially if you know what you are looking for but it is no substitute for understanding what your options are for your particular circumstances, or taking legal advice.

Finding a solicitor, mediator, therapist or barrister to speak to has never been easier - you do not have to just Google your local family solicitors. More detailed information is available online through:

- their professional bodies;

- organisations like Resolution whose members are committed to taking an amicable approach;

- legal directories such as Chambers & Partners and the Legal 500.

Some of the old ways are the often the best though, and it is always worth considering a personal recommendation.

Do your homework

Make sure that you don't just know your options, but that you understand them too. It can be helpful to read and learn about your options along side this, provided it is from a professional and reputable source. There are a number of good free, or cheap, resources. Resolution's website has guides and there are various other helpful videos, podcasts, interactive websites and online guides (such as Law for Life) which help talk you through the process.

There are other online resources which can help you and your children deal with the emotional strain of separation. Websites like the Parent Connection help parents with the separation process and Voices in the Middle can help children share their experiences with other children from separated families.

How are we going to work this out?

Over the last thirty years or so there has been a sea change in how family law issues are resolved. Alternative Dispute Resolution (ADR) is focused on adapting the family law process to discussions taking place in the right environment to ensure that parents can hopefully agree upon a solution amicably, instead of having to rely on a judge to make a decision.

Mediation is a voluntary way of enabling couples to have constructive confidential discussions with an impartial mediator. Mediators come from a variety of backgrounds, and can be therapists, solicitors, family consultants or barristers.

Solicitors have also adopted different approaches for advising their clients and working with other solicitors, with a greater use of face to face meetings. Collaborative law has developed where parents will commit not to go to court and to have a series of face-to-face meetings involving both parents and their solicitors.

Arbitration has been recognised to resolve most children and financial disputes. Unlike court, you can both choose an arbitrator with the skills to decide on your case, and it can be quicker than court.

How are the children going to cope?

In the 2011 census, one third of children in England and Wales came from families with separated parents. There is more pastoral support in school now, and support through child

consultants or family therapists is far more integrated into the way lawyers work too. They can also work with the parents to aid communication with the children.

The child's voice is now far more audible in the decision-making process. The government published a paper outlining its commitment to this in 2015 called "The Voice of the Child". It is increasingly common for children to be consulted as part of mediation, and the training process for Child Inclusive Mediation was overhauled substantially in September 2018.

Handovers

Handovers can be difficult for one, or both parents, especially when there has been a difficult separation. Where parents are struggling to communicate helpful information, there are now better resources to enable parents to share this information positively. There are shared online diaries or books such as The Handover Book, which is a more creative way of sharing information.

Depending on what arrangements the parents make, they could be going a long time without seeing the children. Video calling using Facetime or Skype has made this easier.

It was hard enough keeping track of arrangements when we were in one house. How do we manage it now we are in separate homes?

Many children's diaries are more jam-packed than their parents'. Keeping diaries in sync used to be a very difficult process, with misunderstandings causing friction between parents. There are now specialist online calendars for separated families, as well as programs like iCal which have share functions so that both parents can put plans into calendars to be accepted by the other parent.

There is no right or wrong answer to how to manage a child's expenses post separation, especially if parents are sharing the cost of a school trip or extra-curricular activities. Apps such as Splitwise can help keep track of expenses and how these need to be shared.

Separation can be a moment of crisis, and whilst it is important to draw on friends and family for support at this difficult time, it is also crucial to get sound professional advice.

Rob Parker, Lamb Brooks

Divorce for any child is one of the most defining moment of their lives. Sure, it gets better with time, but it never ever leaves you. Jess (17)

WE ARE SEPARATING

The arguing is getting too much. Can I ask my partner to move out?

About the authors

Fiona Yellowlees, Partner and Head of Family & Joanne Aggett, Associate, WBW Solicitors

Fiona has undertaken most areas of family law work both for married and unmarried couples but with particular emphasis upon the financial aspects associated with relationship breakdown and her interest in alternative methods of dispute resolution.

Joanne has particularly specialised in matters relating to breakdown of marriage and cohabitee relationships including children and financial aspects during her time at WBW.

Where a relationship has broken down, who can stay in the property will depend upon how the property is owned or if it is rented, the names included on the tenancy.

If you are married

If you are married, you both have a right of occupation if the property was the family home. The same applies if both are named on a tenancy but it is a little less certain if only one is the tenant.

If your living arrangements are getting too much, you can ask your partner to move out. However, you cannot make them do so without a court order. If the other person agrees to move out and they are a joint owner, they will not lose their interest in the property; this is a common concern.

Occupation Orders

If your partner will not move out, and there are continuing and significant difficulties in sharing your home, it is possible to apply to the court in certain circumstances for what is known as an Occupation Order under the Family Law Act. An Occupation Order is an order regulating who lives in the property - it may prohibit one party from remaining in the home and can extend to the surrounding area.

When considering whether to make an Occupation Order the Court must consider a number of factors:

- the housing needs/resources of each of the parties and of any relevant child;

- the financial resources of each of the parties;

- the likely effect of any order, or of any decision by the court not to exercise its powers, on the health, safety or well-being of the parties and of any relevant child; and

- the conduct of the parties in relation to each other and otherwise.

As this is an order which effectively forces the other person from their home, the court will not make it without good reason.

Most applications are made with notice being given to the other person, to make sure that they have an opportunity to give their views and for the court to make an informed decision.

The best response to unreasonable behaviour is to be unerringly reasonable.

Matthew Richardson, Coram Chambers

Non-molestation Orders

If there has been a history of domestic abuse, you could also consider an application for a Non-molestation Order alongside the Occupation Order, to prevent your partner from being physically or verbally abusive.

If the difficulties are less serious, but still really hard to live with, trying to arrange or negotiate changes and considering the needs of you both is sometimes possible and usually less stressful than court proceedings. Mediation is available to try and resolve issues through negotiation and except in cases of emergency, should be tried before a court application.

It is always best that you seek your own independent legal advice as the circumstances of your case are specific to you.

The amygdala is a little almond shaped structure in your brain which responds to threat. It fires off within milliseconds of a stressful situation and triggers the release of cortisol, the stress hormone. When your brain is flooded with stress hormones, it is harder to use all the logical parts of your brain to make decisions. Instead, decisions tend to be based on feelings - especially unpleasant feelings such as fear, anxiety, panic, which you want to escape or avoid. Emotional decisions are useful in some aspects of life and at certain times in life e.g. falling in love. But when it comes to making logic based decisions around finance, legality, and especially child care and contact arrangements, emotions need to be second to clear thinking, logic and understanding of your children's needs.

Angharad Rudkin

TELLING THE CHILDREN

Separation and divorce is a difficult time for all those involved. There are so many decisions that have to be agreed, including telling the children.

Children have told us what they need during this difficult time and following these simple steps will help to reduce anxiety and upset for your children:

- Be as prepared as you can before you talk to your children.

- Tell them what's happening in a simple language without all the 'intimate' details.

- Children often worry about the practical things, so make sure you have agreed who they will live with, including contact arrangements, before you tell them.

- Reassure them that it's not their fault and that you will continue to be their parents and be involved in their lives.

- Most importantly, LISTEN to your children and reassure them that you are still 'Mum and Dad' and will continue to be a part of their lives.

- Reassure them that you love them.

Adele Ballantyne

ONLY
Mums & Dads
parents meet professionals

MUST READ

Grounds for divorce - an explanation

About the author

Nigel Shepherd, Mills & Reeve

Nigel is a specialist family lawyer, collaborative practitioner and family arbitrator with almost 40 years' experience dealing mainly with the more complex financial issues (e.g. businesses, trusts and pensions) that need to be negotiated when a marriage or other personal relationship sadly comes to an end.

It's a sad fact that currently around four in every ten marriages end in divorce. If you are facing the breakdown of your marriage, this article will explain the basic legal principles and process for a divorce in England & Wales (the position is different in Scotland and Northern Ireland). It will provide some practical guidance to help you as parents navigate the divorce process in a way that reduces conflict for the benefit of your children. Finally it will highlight why the current law needs to be changed to support this. Although throughout the references are to divorce, the legal position in relation to the dissolution of civil partnerships is almost completely the same.

The "grounds" for divorce

There is in fact only one ground for divorce, which is that the marriage has "broken down irretrievably". However, this has to be established by proving one or more of five specific "facts". The person asking for the divorce is called the petitioner and the other spouse is the respondent. The five facts are:

- the respondent has committed adultery and the petitioner finds it intolerable to live with the respondent (adultery). This is not available for civil partnerships.

- the respondent has behaved in such a way that the petitioner cannot reasonably be expected to live with the respondent (behaviour).

- desertion for two years (very rarely used).

- separation for two years with the respondent consenting to the divorce (two years separation).

- separation for five years. No consent is needed (five years separation).

The court has to have jurisdiction to deal with the divorce based on your connection to this country. For most people born or living here for any period of time this is not a problem, but it's possible for more than one country to be involved and the rules are complex. Procedure and financial outcomes can vary significantly between countries and specialist advice is highly advisable if you have any international aspects in your case.

The process

The petitioner starts the process by sending a divorce application form to one of the regional divorce centres. If you are not using a solicitor the application can now be made online and in due course the plan is to extend this to all cases. You will need the original marriage certificate or a certified copy (which you can get online) and there is a fee of £550. If you are on certain benefits or a low income you may be able to get money off the fee.

When the papers arrive from the divorce centre, the respondent completes an acknowledgment of service. The questions on this form depend on which "fact" is being used. Unless the respondent wishes to defend the divorce (and for reasons explained below the vast majority are undefended) the petitioner then sends in a statement confirming the truth of the petition and if the court is satisfied that everything is in order a decree nisi will be pronounced. This confirms the entitlement to a divorce and six weeks later the petitioner can apply for the final decree absolute, which formally brings the marriage to an end. Divorce is an important change of status and there may be reasons for holding back on the decree absolute, for example to get certain financial arrangements in place first.

The "Blame Game"

Most divorces are based on one of the two "fault" facts of adultery or behaviour. This is not necessarily because couples want to blame each other. Often they don't. It's because in order to deal with things on a truly no fault basis you have to wait at least two years and most people don't want or can't afford to put their lives on hold for that long. The court's ability to make certain financial orders (even by agreement) depends on there being a divorce. For example, there has to be a divorce and a formal court order to achieve pension-sharing. This means that if you want to get everything sorted out sooner rather than later, you are pushed into alleging adultery or behaviour even if you agree that neither of you is more responsible than the other for the marriage breaking down and you want to keep things as amicable as possible so you can concentrate on making the best arrangements you can for your children and deal fairly with the financial consequences. It's important to note that the reason for the divorce itself almost never affects what happens in relation to these arrangements.

In practice there is a very low threshold to get an undefended behaviour divorce through. If you are using a family lawyer who is a member of Resolution you will be encouraged to keep the behaviour allegations in the divorce application as mild as possible to avoid causing unnecessary distress and conflict. If you're not legally represented you should still do the same. This is particularly important if you're looking to deal with the things through mediation or collaboratively. If you're the respondent you can agree to the divorce even if you don't accept everything that's said about your behaviour or that it's the actual reason for the marriage breaking down. This is why the current legal process is often referred to as the "blame game". The key is to do everything you can to focus on the future not what's gone wrong in the past. It can be really hard to do when emotions are running high and you're feeling hurt, but seeing the divorce process itself as a means to an end will help you move forward more positively. Crucially, the more you can avoid conflict the better it will be for your children and they will thank you for it.

This is why as a solicitor with over 35 years' experience in family law work and through my involvement with Resolution I've been campaigning for so long to reform our divorce laws. To end this blame game. Everyone who is committed to helping those whose relationships have unfortunately broken down agrees the law needs changing. I hope it will happen soon.

Notes

My dad's new relationship caused a lot of problems between my mum and him, which put me in a difficult position as a young child — I felt like I was torn in the middle as I didn't want to take one parent's side over another. Sophie (16)

How can conversations be transformed into a problem-solving approach?

About the author

Norman Hartnell, Managing Director, The Family Law Company by Hartnell Chanot

Norman is a solicitor, mediator, collaborative family lawyer and arbitrator and is experienced in all forms of family mediation. He has represented parents, guardians and children in private and public law cases and has considerable experience in complex divorce and related financial issues.

Words can wound or words can heal. In the context of a relationship breakdown it is often the case that the expression of unresolved hurt arising from the breakdown is reflected verbally, in letters either direct or with the added volume of solicitors letters, emails and text messages.

Any attack, whether verbal or in writing naturally evokes a flight or fight response; the first could result in either disengagement and capitulation to the person who is seen as the more powerful, or the second might trigger a response which may be of equal or even greater hostility, leading to an escalation of conflict.

Either way it results in one or both feeling angry, trying to re-exert the control over their lives they feel they are at risk of losing. Response leads to further response. The whole basis of litigation encourages a point-scoring, blame-attributing approach to justify one's own actions and undermine that of the other person. Yet Judges almost always express dismay at the inability of parents to understand that their conflict is harming their children, apparently oblivious of the fact that the very system of which they are a part encourages this adversarial approach.

So how on earth can this vicious cycle be broken?

How can conversations, whether direct or though legal channels, be transformed into a problem-solving approach?

I may not have all the answers but have found the following to be effective in many situations.

Receipt of aggressive communication

When receiving an aggressive or angry communication in any form, first listen to your natural internal response. It is likely to be one of protest, anger, a desire to respond and justify your own stance. It is the equivalent of being slapped across the face. Put into words how it makes you feel. I find it helpful to highlight or underline the provocative words which evoke your strongest response. They may be overtly rude or manipulative.

Give vent to your feelings

Put into words how you would have instinctively wanted to respond - in other words give vent to your feelings in a private note, **which will not be sent**. It is good to get the instant feelings out and acknowledged. Until that first step is done, it will prevent any further progress.

Review

Having paused and had a cup of tea, then review the communication again from a different perspective. This time you will be searching to ascertain whether the other person is being purely controlling or manipulative or whether, despite the words used, part of what they say is indicative of a valid point of view, worry or grievance which is being expressed poorly, in a childish way.

Considering your response

This is the time to separate the wheat from the chaff. Your challenge is to determine which parts of the communication you wish to respond to and which you do not. You do not have to answer everything.

Which parts require a response?

So, some parts of the communication will be gratuitously rude or hurtful. They are designed to get you hooked into an argument on their terms which they enjoy, their territory. The more insecure someone is the more they will seek to control their world, by pulling the strings or pushing the buttons they have learned are likely to get a response. Don't respond to these parts of the communication - you **can** choose not to.

Other parties may be motivated by something different. They may be simply angry about something - perhaps the other person is fearful and is trying to exert control themselves in a situation where they are fearful of loss and trying inappropriately to secure their position by threats.

You now have a choice as to how to respond to the different elements

In relation to the provocative hurtful gratuitous comments, the basic law you need to understand is you get what you reward. If you respond to those words, then you are likely to achieve nothing apart from to add fuel to the fire. Even a put-down of the other person by shaming them or remonstrating with them for their use of language will be seen as a response which will justify a further response from them - and so it goes on.

Therefore, the right response is to ignore such comments. Should you wish, you can record them to demonstrate later to a Judge or other person what language has been used on you to demonstrate their coercive approach. This

provides you with the best possible evidence of the approach adopted by the other person, as it comes from their own hand. If you read such words in that way, their power to hurt can be transformed into the satisfaction that they themselves have provided the best possible evidence should you need it later. Keep it.

Re-writing the communication

If there are concerns which are genuine to them but badly expressed and, which if expressed differently would have evoked an adult response from you addressing any concerns, then do the following:

- Re-write their communication in the way they should have expressed it. It should have started politely with "Dear ..." using your first name; and it should have been worded to express the following:

- What they are worried about;

- What they are asking you to do about it;

- Asking for a response within a reasonable timescale.

- Now draft your response to your reworked communication. You will also start with "Dear...." and you will end with "Regards" because you will be writing to them to model what good communication looks like politely as parent to parent.

You will acknowledge their worry and not dismiss it and you will put it into the words they should have used. You'll then go on to respond in the way you can to address any concerns. If there is a matter on which you are not going to agree, you should take this opportunity to explain why in non-emotive language,

One thing is certain, from a relationship perspective - unless there is coercive control, we cannot make anyone do anything that they don't want to.

It is extremely difficult when couples continue to have heated, unresolved arguments, especially in front of the children.

It might be more empowering to take control of 'your end' of the conversation.

Arguments can only happen if you both engage. I don't mean one of you should storm off - in fact the opposite. Rather than getting caught up in the argument, call a 'time out'.

Calmly say "I understand that this conversation is important but I'm feeling stressed/upset/angry at the moment so I'm going to make a cup of tea so I can calm down. Can we talk when the children aren't around?"

Adele Ballantyne

showing that your approach is one which meets the needs of all concerned children and adults alike. If you can provide some alternative choices and explain the pros and cons and why you recommend your preferred suggestion, then that will provide them with the opportunity to respond in kind. Your communication should model a good boundary-setting structure as follows by;

- setting out clearly factually what happened;

- explaining what its effect on you and/or the children was (factual);

- saying what now needs to happen;

- explaining when it needs to happen by (setting a reasonable deadline and agreeing to any justified request for an extension);

- explaining the consequence of it not happening by that deadline. The consequence will not be worded as a threat - it will be an expression that you are left with no alternative, in the absence of a positive response, to any other course of action to resolve the situation.

As this will be a new form of communication between you it may well take some time to take effect and bring about a change

in response. The exercise may have to be repeated many times; but sooner or later the difference between your communication and theirs should dawn on them, showing them to be unreasonable. They will come to realise that anyone seeing such communications (such as a Judge) will quickly come to the conclusion which parent is reasonable. That accountability will in most cases be the conversation. Your role is to set a good example of what communication between parents should look like and not respond to provocation.

Your children need you to be the one to take responsibility for being the adult. Hopefully using the above method, you will have educated the other parent to follow your lead for the benefit of the children.

By engaging in the mediation process parties can create building blocks on how to communicate in the future to ensure that any animosity is limited and that both parents remain focused on the child or children's needs rather than their own agenda.

Sarah Manning, Consilia Legal

Notes

I felt like I was torn in the middle as I didn't want to take one's side over another. Sophie (16)

Children

S eparation and divorce are difficult processes in themselves, but when you add children to the mix, the process enters a whole new level of complexity. This chapter covers important legal and emotional aspects of separating as parents such as arranging contact and visits, contact centres and liaising with schools. Communication between parents is key to an impact-minimising separation, as is an awareness of legal requirements. Relationships are the scaffolding of our lives. Knowing what support and guidance is out there will help parents maintain a positive, healthy relationship with their children.

We have children and we are separating. Do I need legal advice?

About the author

Michelle Saxton, Edward Hands & Lewis Solicitors

Michelle is a Fellow of the Chartered Institute of Legal Executives, specialising in all areas of family law including divorce, separation, civil partnerships, ancillary relief, Children Act matters and domestic violence. She is also a Resolution member.

A re you an unmarried father? Have you separated from the mother of your children and wonder where you stand legally with regard to them?

The first thing we need to ascertain is whether you have parental responsibility (PR) in respect of the child.

What is parental responsibility?

PR is the legal rights and responsibilities you have for your children as a parent.

A mother automatically has PR. A father has PR if he is married to the children's mother or is named on the child's birth certificate (see Questions 6 and 13 and the Must read article on Page 324 for more information).

Your legal rights and duties as a parent with PR are, but are not limited to:

- providing a home for the children;

- protecting and maintaining the children;

- disciplining the children;

- choosing and providing for the children's education;

- agreeing to the children's medical treatment;

- naming the children and agreeing to any change of name;

- looking after the children's property.

Obtaining PR

If you do not have PR, you can obtain this by:

- entering into a Parental Responsibility Agreement with the mother;

- applying to the court for a Parental Responsibility Order;

- jointly registering the child's birth.

We would always advise you to try and reach agreement with the mother of your child. This can be done by way of us writing to the mother or through mediation. However, we appreciate that this is not always possible.

Court proceedings

Court proceedings should be used as a last resort, not only because it is costly but also because it can be quite stressful to all parties.

If an application to the court is made, CAFCASS (Children and Family Court Advisory and Support Service) will carry out safeguarding checks on both you and your former partner. This will be for things like any past or current involvement with social services or the police. If no

None of my friends knew my situation at home. I just didn't want to speak about that with anyone. Evis

safeguarding concerns are raised, CAFCASS should have no further involvement other than to inform the court what they consider is in the child's best interests.

A CAFCASS Officer will act in the best interests of the child and work with the child and both parents. If there are safeguarding issues, CAFCASS are likely to suggest they carry out further investigations in your case and provide a report to the court on their recommendations. CAFCASS Officers are not the enemy. You should fully cooperate with them in order for them to complete their report.

FHDRA

The first hearing dispute resolution appointment (FHDRA) will be heard before a District Judge, legal advisor or Magistrates. It will be heard in private with no other parties allowed in the courtroom other than you, your former partner and your legal advisors. Prior to going into court, negotiations will take place between solicitors acting on your behalf. If an agreement can be reached, an order will be drafted by either solicitor, be agreed with the other party and handed in to court. This will be approved by the court.

If there are no other issues to deal with, this will be a final order and there will be no need to go back to court. If, however, agreement cannot be reached, directions would need to be agreed as to the next steps. This could be giving dates for a CAFCASS report to be filed, dates for statements to be filed by you, your former partner and any witnesses with a return date to court. It may be that the matter is set down for a final contested hearing for the District Judge/Magistrates to make a decision. The matter could still be agreed by consent at any time.

Once an order is made in respect of PR, it does not mean that you can interfere in the day-to-day upbringing of the child even though the order gives you the same legal rights as the child's mother.

Taking the child out of the UK

If you or your ex-partner wishes to take the child out of the country on holiday, where there is a Child Arrangements Order in force saying where the child should live, you may do so for up to 4 weeks at a time without the other parties' consent. However, if there is no Child Arrangements Order in place the mother will need to seek the consent of all the parties with PR before she can take the child out of the country.

If the mother requires your consent a simple letter should suffice. It is unlikely that a court would deny the chance of a child going on holiday unless there are real concerns for the child's well-being.

If you or your ex-partner wish to take the child on holiday and consent is not given, the party who wishes to take the child on holiday can apply to the court for a Specific Issue Order for the court to grant permission.

I always tell my clients that they must never regret the relationship that has ended as it has produced fantastic children. Therefore they have to find a way to communicate as there are going to be sports days, birthdays, school plays, graduations etc where they will need to be in a room together and their children won't thank them if they have to have two top tables at their wedding because mum and dad still can't be near each other. It's hard, and there will be bumps in the road but it can be done, and it's great for everyone when it happens.

Julie Hobson, Gullands Solicitors

Should we ask the children where they want to live, or is that unfair?

About the author

Emma Taylor, Chartered Legal Executive at Goodlaw Solicitors

Emma specialises in children and financial issues following separation, divorce or civil partnership dissolution. She advises on matters such as pre-nuptial agreements and parenting plans and has a particular interest in cases involving international/jurisdictional aspects and child welfare issues.

Wen parents separate, children are inevitably affected. What is important to remember is that they should not be drawn into any adult conflict. However, this needs to be balanced with ensuring that they are listened to and kept informed to some degree about the plans which are going to be put in place for their care so that they do not feel too anxious about their own future.

Far too frequently, children can feel stuck in the middle of their parents as if they have to choose one or the other. Whilst it is important to engage with the children and listen to what they want, it is also vital to reassure them and ensure that they do not assume the weight of responsibility for decisions regarding their care.

Child's voice

A child's ability to express their wishes and feelings accurately, with an understanding as to the implications of those wishes and feelings, depends on how old they are. Indeed, a court, when making a decision for a child, will apply the 'welfare checklist' found in Section 1(3) of the Children Act 1989, which states that wishes and feelings should be considered in light of the child's age and understanding (see Question 55 for more help on the welfare checklist). What this means is that, for example, an older child within any court proceedings may be given more of an opportunity to write a letter to the Judge or to express their views than that afforded to a younger child because they are more able to understand the consequences of what they are communicating.

Practical steps you can take when deciding on where the child lives

By directly asking a child where they want to live, it is possible that this will put them in an unfair situation where they feel

---

REFLECTIONS ON THE FIRST TWO WEEKS

The first two weeks can often be the hardest; getting used to a massive change in your relationship and your life, working out how to organise seeing the children, thinking about the practicalities of where you're going to live, financial and legal issues and employment. These are just some of the thoughts that will dominate this time.

Feelings of abandonment, rejection and humiliation are very real for most mums and dads and reeling from the shock of it all can leave you feeling emotionally and physically bruised. Don't be surprised if eating and sleeping are affected and that you feel exhausted.

Self care at this time is really important. Ensure you have support.

Adele Ballantyne

they have to choose. It may be more appropriate, depending on their age, to have an open discussion with them as a family to invite and listen to their wishes and feelings rather than asking direct questions.

CAFCASS, (Children and Family Court Advice and Support Service) provide guidance on their website about how to listen to the child's voice after separation. CAFCASS also provide a template parenting plan document, which may help separating parents to consider how best to approach discussions concerning the arrangements for the children.

Some parents also like to consider whether some form of family therapy is suitable to help guide parents and children through the emotional impact of a separation with practical plans also being established during the course of that therapy. Family mediation is another service that may assist parents. Within mediation you can discuss the arrangements for the children but also agree how best to talk to the children and listen to what they want.

Communication between parents

Ultimately, the majority of child arrangements cases that end up in court arise because there is a lack of communication between the parents. It is undoubtedly a difficult and stressful time for parents when separating but it is important to remember that the children must be protected; they love both as their parent and, whilst the parents are ultimately responsible for the decision as to where they live, they must feel listened to without being forced to choose.

Further information can be found on our family law website at www.familylawbrighton.com/children.

The pain you feel is about what someone has done to you. The sooner you can let go and focus on the future the better.

Dom, Dad

Notes

To parents: never make your child choose. El (17)

We're not married. Does this mean mum gets the children?

About the author

James Maguire, Maguire Family Law

James is the Managing Director & family law solicitor at Maguire Family Law and has an excellent reputation in the areas of international divorce law and child abduction. He also sits on the Law Society's child abduction panel.

There is no automatic presumption that the children would stay with their mother if an unmarried couple separate. The focus should be on looking at the arrangements which best suit the children and always taking decisions which are in the children's best interests.

The court has recently introduced a new provision which means that if they are asked to decide the arrangements for a child, the court shall presume, unless the contrary is shown, that involvement of that parent in the life of the child concerned will further the child's welfare.

What can sometimes complicate matters is if the mother and the father have a different legal status in relation to the children. A mother always has parental responsibility for her child or children. This is not automatic for a father. Whether a father does or does not have parental responsibility can impact on the practical arrangements for a child's care. This does not, however, mean that the father should be excluded from the child's life.

What is Parental Responsibility?

Parental responsibility (PR) is defined as all the rights, duties, powers, responsibilities and authority which by law a parent of a child has in relation to the child and their property.

This includes all fundamental decisions as to what the child does presently and in the future; for example, where the child goes to school, what medical treatment the child can or cannot receive and what religion the child should follow.

The more significant a decision regarding a child's welfare, the more cooperation and discussion there should be between the adults who have PR.

If a father does not have PR then this could make it more difficult for him to ensure the child or children attend medical appointments or are enrolled at school, and he may find that he has to obtain the mother's authority.

How do I know if I have PR?

All mothers have PR.

All fathers who are married to the mother have PR even if their name is not on the birth certificate.

Unmarried fathers with children whose birth was registered after 1 December 2003 and whose name appears on the birth certificate have PR.

Those unmarried fathers who are not on the birth certificate or whose children had their births registered before 1 December 2003, do **not** have PR.

The law is not about declaring winners and losers. If parents cannot agree appropriate arrangements for their children then the only winners will be the lawyers and the only losers will be their children.

Pete Littlewood, Chafes Hague Lambert

ONLY
Mums & Dads
parents meet professionals

How can I acquire PR?

All is not lost for a father who does not have the automatic right to PR. It can be obtained in one of the following ways:

- Entering into a Parental Responsibility Agreement with the mother. The agreement must be in a prescribed form, signed and witnessed by a court official. This is the most straightforward option, but it does require cooperation from the child's mother.

- Re-registering the child's birth and having the father's name added. Again, an element of cooperation from the child's mother would be required.

- Applying to the court for PR. This may be a standalone application or it may be made as part of an application for a child arrangements order (see Question 62 for more).

When making a Parental Responsibility Order the court will look at the father's degree of commitment to the child, the state of the father's current relationship with the child and his reasons for making the application.

- A Child Arrangements Order providing that a child lives with their father (for any amount of time) also confers PR. Any decision taken by the court about where a child lives has to have regard to the child's welfare.

- Being appointed as a guardian either by the mother or the court, although in these cases the father will only assume PR on the mother's death.

- By marrying the mother. This grants PR to the father, even if the child was born before they got married.

Summary

The issues relating to PR and the rights of a parent can be complex. The law and court practice procedure can be difficult and it would be advised that where a person is confused about the rights they have as a parent they should seek family law advice from a solicitor.

There are no fixed presumptions as to who will care for a child or children once a relationship breaks down. In many cases, it is about dealing with the practicalities first - for example, one parent may mainly stay at home to provide care whilst the other parent works long hours, possibly away from the family home.

TALKING AND LISTENING TO YOUR CHILD

Children are like sea shells. Once they clam up it is so very hard to prise them open and find out what is going on for them. There are some key points that can help you listen and talk to your child:

- Practice *really* listening. Use your non-verbal communication to show you're listening (e.g. nodding your head) but don't say anything. Even when they've just stopped talking, give it a moment before you speak. It's amazing how much information you can get out of someone when you don't fill up the spaces with your own words and thoughts.

- Children, even older ones, have shorter attention spans than adults. They can concentrate for perhaps 5 or 6 sentences before drifting back into a daydream. Don't talk to them with long monologues and don't pack lots of information into one speech.

- Children often open up at the least opportune moment. More often than not this is because they know you aren't over-prepared and that you won't 'make a big deal' at these times. Sometimes it could be because they just want to reach out to you and have some of your time and attention. Keep conversations low key. If you care less than they do about having the conversation then they are more likely to talk openly (even if you are just feigning this casual approach).

- Children find it easier to talk when you are not sitting face to face, perhaps when you're in the car, on a walk, while you're cooking. Being physically close, but not having to look at one another's faces, helps conserve brain capacity so that you can both process the conversation more easily.

I really don't think my ex is well enough mentally to look after the kids. What can I do about it?

About the author

Kate Barton, Partner at Boyce Hatton

Kate advises on and deals with all areas of family law including divorce, financial settlements, cohabitation, prenuptial agreements and children. She understands the need to resolve cases on an amicable basis and tries wherever possible to settle matters between the parties without going to court. Kate is a member of the Law Society's Children Panel and Resolution.

A fter a relationship breakdown, it can sometimes be difficult to let go and allow your former partner to look after the children you had together. This can be for several reasons, many of which are often unrelated to the children themselves. For example, you may have been emotionally hurt by your ex-partner, or you may be trying to agree what's going to happen

to the house, or what will happen with child support and maintenance. This is all part of the emotional and legal fall out when a relationship ends.

However, what happens if you have a genuine concern over your ex-partner's mental health?

Welfare of the children

The starting point must always be the welfare of your children. If contact or care cannot be agreed and it becomes necessary to ask the court to make a decision, this will be the court's paramount consideration. The court will also look at a range of other important factors, and it is helpful to start thinking about them at this stage.

The most relevant considerations in this situation would be:

- the emotional needs of the child;

- any risk of harm that the child has suffered or is at risk of suffering;

- how capable your ex is of meeting your child's needs.

Your child has an emotional need to have a relationship with their other parent, so they should be seeing them unless there is a reason *not* to. This reason could be any risk of harm they could suffer, or whether your ex is capable of meeting their needs.

For example, are they well

enough to prioritise the children, feed them, stimulate them and generally make sure that they are safe and secure during contact? If someone is mentally ill they may not be able to do so. If they are suffering from delusions, psychosis or depression then this could be frightening for children, and may cause emotional harm.

What should you do?

Firstly it is important to identify whether this is a *genuine* concern. It is natural to be nervous, or even unhappy about childcare arrangements after a relationship has broken down, but do you *really* feel that your ex is too ill to look after the children?

Psychiatric illness covers a whole range of conditions and severities, not all of which impact on someone's ability to care for their children.

Consider whether your ex has a history of mental illness. If they have, how has this been managed in the past? Were they

It does get better; the world is not ending so take care of your emotional well-being.

Vincent, Dad

taking medication or undergoing treatment? If so, are they continuing to do this? If properly managed, this should not prevent your ex from looking after the children.

Consider your ex's presentation and demeanour. What is it about them that makes you worried? Is it something that they may be able to manage while they are looking after the children, perhaps for a short period of time, if necessary?

Supporting your ex

Is there anyone who could support your ex during their time with the children? For example, a grandparent, a sibling or family friend who may be able to assist. Having someone else present may help to minimise any risk to the children without them even realising that such steps have been necessary. If you are able to share your concerns with your ex's parents or a trusted friend, then this could also help them to access further support. They may accept advice from other people in a way that they no longer feel able to do from you.

Whether or not your ex realises that they are unwell is also crucial. Do they recognise that they may be a risk to the children? If they understand this, and are willing to take steps to ensure that the children are safe in their care, the risk may reduce significantly.

Consideration should also be

given as to whether this is a short or long-term situation, even if that is not clear at the outset. If contact does not take place for some time, this in itself can present problems later down the line, even when the mental health issues have been resolved.

Stopping contact

If you have tried all of the above and your ex still wants to see the children, but you feel that they are not mentally well enough to do so, you may need to consider stopping contact. This is a big step and not one that should be taken lightly. However, if you have concerns that your children are at risk of harm if your ex was to look after them then you have no alternative.

Applications to the court

Do you think that if you stop contact your ex may try to see the children anyway, for example by trying to collect them from school without your knowledge or agreement? If this is the case then you should make an application to the Family Court for a Child Arrangements Order, and a Prohibited Steps Order.

A Child Arrangements Order confirms who a child should live with, when they should see the other parent and whether this contact should be supervised. A Prohibited Steps Order means that the person named in the order is forbidden from doing something. In this scenario, it could prevent a child being removed from your care by your ex-partner.

If the children are already in your ex-partner's care, you may need to collect them yourself if you genuinely feel that there is a risk of harm. If your ex will not allow them to come with you, you need to consider making an urgent application to court for a Child Arrangements Order stating that the children should live with you and outlining what contact they should have with their other parent. In that situation, the court may decide that it needs evidence of the risk of harm that you are alleging, for example by obtaining a report from your ex's GP or any treating psychiatrist.

Evidence

The court needs to be convinced that there is a risk of harm to the children before removing them from your ex's care or restricting contact, which takes us back to the questions raised earlier about how any mental health issues actually affect your ex's ability to care for the children.

The sad truth is that contact arrangements after the breakdown of a relationship are often highly charged and difficult for both parties to come to terms with. If your ex has mental health issues then this can make a difficult situation even more stressful and confusing, especially when you only want to do what is best for the children.

It is always helpful in these circumstances to see a solicitor to explain your concerns and obtain guidance on the best way forward for you and your family.

I now have no involvement in any argument between my divorced parents, and I feel a lot more comfortable to contact and see either of them without feeling like I'm betraying one. Sophie (16)

I'm really concerned that my ex does not look after the children properly. What can I do?

About the author

Sabrina Bailey, Family solicitor and director of Allard Bailey Family Law

Sabrina has a broad experience of all aspects of both public and private family law. She has a special interest in pre- and post-nuptial agreements as well as Children Act matters such as residence, contact and international relocation. Sabrina is also a member of Resolution.

When parents separate it is inevitable there will be occasions where mums and dads will disagree about parenting styles and the way in which each of them cares for the children. However, it is important to keep this in perspective and keep in mind that there will be diverse styles of parenting (unless you believe the children are at risk of harm). If there is an issue it should be approached in a non-confrontational way and not in the children's presence in order to have a minimal impact on them.

Communication

The first step you can take is to talk to the other parent, as communication is key in co-parenting when there are two different households. If you have concerns such your child's hygiene, dietary issues and/or lack of routine, these could be an indication that the other parent is not managing adequately, and they may need a wider support network around them or assistance and advice from professionals. It could be that, if they have never looked after the children by themselves prior to the separation, they may benefit from some third party support such as attending a parenting course.

If it is difficult to discuss such issues with your ex-partner, perhaps a neutral family member or a mutual friend could be there to support such a conversation, to ensure it remains focused on the children and isn't seen as a personal attack.

However, it can often be easier to have this conversation with a completely impartial person such as a mediator or a family therapist. They can act as an independent neutral third party who can help you talk through the issues and try to reach an agreement with the other parent.

Contact book and parenting plans

It may be wise to set up a contact book between you and the other parent so that you can continue to raise any concerns in a non-confrontational way. Producing a parenting plan can also ensure that your children's practical day-to-day needs are being met and not missed by either party. The plans can include who is responsible for taking them to the doctors, dentist and for vaccinations. It can even include expectations for meals and set bed times, so that the children can expect the same routines and rules in each household. There are several online tools available to help create a plan, including on the CAFCASS website. Having a parenting plan which can be referred to can avoid any future conflict over arrangements as it clearly sets out the agreement reached.

Safeguarding concerns

If your concerns are of a serious nature such as suspected abuse in any form, whether physical, emotional or neglect, it is essential that you act quickly in gaining help.

In an emergency, you should contact the police. You can approach your GP for any troubling concerns about a child, even if that concern is about the child's care with the other parent and they will be able to advise and refer to you other agencies such as social workers depending on the circumstances.

It would also be helpful to speak to the children's school or nursery to see if they have noticed any changes in behaviour and/or presentation. Each school will have a Designated Safeguarding Lead and will have received specialist training, so they can talk to you about your concerns. If they feel it is necessary, they have access to a number of services and can ensure the right help and support for your children.

If you believe your children have been, or are likely to be, at serious risk from their time with the other parent, it may be that contact with them should stop until any serious concerns have been properly investigated and advice from professionals received and followed. Depending on the situation it may be possible to arrange some supervised contact at a contact centre whilst matters are ongoing (see Question 20 for more).

Asking the court for help

If you are unable to resolve the issues with the other parent, you may wish to ask the court to look at the circumstances and make a decision in the best interests of your children. This could include who spends time with your child, where your child lives and the amount of time a child spends with each parent. Any decision a court makes will have to be applied to criteria known as the welfare checklist under s1(3) *Children Act 1989*. This will consider:

- the ascertainable wishes and feelings of the child concerned;

- the child's physical, emotional and educational needs;

- the likely effect on the child if circumstances change as a result of the court's decision;

- the child's age, sex, background and any other characteristics which will be relevant to the court's decision;

- any harm the child has suffered or may be at risk of suffering;

- capability of the child's parents (or any other person the courts find relevant) at

meeting the child's needs;

- the powers available to the court in the given proceedings.

The court may ask CAFCASS to meet you, the other parent and your children and produce a detailed report with recommendations to provide the court with a better understanding of the situation, whether the children's needs are being met and how they feel about contact.

Court orders

If there is a court order already in place setting out how both parents spend time with the children, and you have concerns about how they're being looked after, you will need to return the matter to court and ask for the order to be varied. In doing so, you can bring to the court's attention any concerns you have about the children.

If it is a serious concern and the child is in risk of immediate danger Children's Services or the NSPCC may do this themselves to protect the child. If you are concerned that a court order needs to be stopped or varied in any way you can seek some initial advice from a solicitor.

GENUINE CONCERNS ABOUT YOUR EX NOT LOOKING AFTER THE CHILDREN

Don't confuse a differing parenting style with neglect.

What is your evidence for thinking your ex is not looking after the children?

Are the children happy, clean, fed?

Are they worried or stressed? Are they worried because you're worried?

Remember: if you have been the main carer and the non-resident parent has been only semi hands-on during your relationship, there will be a certain amount of 'learning' taking place. That doesn't mean there is neglect.

Adele Ballantyne

Is four years old too young to stay with dad overnight?

About the author

Andrew Ormrod, Broudie Jackson Canter

Andrew's areas of expertise are children law cases between separated parents and cases involving Social Services including advising grandparents, family members and special guardians. He is an accredited specialist with Resolution.

The immediate and gut reaction to this question which has no doubt been posed by many separated dads is "No". However, as is often the case when dealing with family law and in particular child arrangements, there is no right or wrong answer. Every case is different, every child is different and what may be right for one child may not be so for another.

There is no rule or law that says age four is too young to stay overnight with dad, nor is there anything that says from age four children should be able to stay overnight with the non-resident parent, often still dad. There will

be a number of factors to consider, including for example the attachment the child already has to you and their other parent, the level and frequency of any previous contact, how secure the child feels in either parent's care, and any particular needs the child may have.

It is often suggested that with very young children, say babies and toddlers, frequent visits which are maybe of shorter duration are better for children of that age. This would enable them to better form an attachment to the non-resident parent through seeing and spending time with them more often, and, at the same time not spending too long a period away from their primary caregiver. That is not to say, however that overnight stays should not happen with very young children as clearly there will be many cases where upon separation dad has played a full and active 'hands on' role in meeting the child's needs up to that point, with a secure bond and attachment already formed. I come across many cases where

overnight stays have been happening long before the child's fourth birthday.

However, in any event by age three or four, a child's ability to communicate and therefore communicate their needs is much more developed. This means that they should be much better equipped for spending time away from their primary carer, and as such, spending time with dad on an overnight basis. Therefore, any argument against overnight stays at age four begins to fall away.

Whether your four year old is too young depends very much on the circumstances of your case. If, for example, there has been a significant break in contact emanating from the separation or the arrangements have broken down, then the starting point would be to deal with the resumption of contact with a view to progressing the arrangements to longer visits and then overnight stays.

In short therefore, the answer is clearly "No - age four is not too young for overnight stays with

Sharing the driving to and from handovers is the best thing to do. Many parents mention how that time in the car allows for one-to-one time with your children which can aid that (sometimes difficult) transition from one home to another. It also avoids unnecessary arguments about "one parents doing all the driving". It also demonstrates to your children that you are working together for their benefit.

dad" but the arrangements should be handled sensitively.

Tips to make it work

It will be vital that overnight stays start off as smoothly as possible to ensure contact progresses. As such, as is always the case, preparation is key. It is important to make sure your child is prepared for the first overnight stay, so for example make sure:

- they are familiar with where they are staying and with whoever else may be present;

- they are aware in advance of when they are coming to stay;

- they are aware in advance of when they are going home to see mum again;

- that there is communication, if possible, with the other parent about any little routines or habits; and

- that you have everything that they may need.

There are of course cases where any reluctance or anxiety is on the part of your ex-partner rather than the child and whilst you may be confident your child will be fine and you can make sure they are happy and well cared for whilst in your care, if your ex-partner is reluctantly agreeing or apprehensive then a little reassurance in that direction may help a lot in the longer term.

If your ex-partner is apprehensive

then often children will pick up on this and share in the anxiety. This can then lead to assertions that it is "too soon" or "they're not ready" and whilst this shouldn't happen, it does, and whatever can be done to avoid or minimise this will benefit in the longer term and avoid the risk of the arrangements breaking down. A lot of this is common sense stuff but can be easily overlooked in the eagerness to get overnight stays up and running or in the midst of fraught relations with your now ex-partner.

The key to positive contact that will progress and enhance the father-child relationship post separation and make it a success will also be in the quality, not just quantity of contact. In the event of litigation there may well be some CAFCASS (Children and Family Court Advisory and Support Service) intervention and this view is echoed by them.

If your case goes to court, CAFCASS may be asked to give advice to the court - CAFCASS themselves do not suggest that children as young as four or even three cannot have overnight stays, only that they may find it more difficult and that greater care should be taken with the arrangements.

Getting advice

If you are going to get legal advice or begin mediating then

Notes

again, go prepared. I'd suggest giving thought beforehand to your proposals, for example when visits should turn into overnight stays, length of stays, handover and sleeping arrangements etc. These will depend on when you last had contact or staying contact.

Essentially, you should have an idea in mind of what arrangements you want to put into place and put forward a well thought out plan. Try to pre-empt reasons your ex-partner may put forward opposing your proposals and come up with solutions.

Ensure your voice is heard, keep your head up and remember you'll get through it. El

What should I do about an unreliable ex?

About the author

Louisa Dickson, Southern Family Mediation

Southern Family Mediation was started by Louisa in 2014. Her wealth of knowledge, compassion and experience, combined with her work as a mediator, child consultant and family coach, helps her to support individuals and families going through the process of divorce and separation.

They don't show up, or show up late almost every time, leaving your child standing at the window, coat on, asking "how much longer?". They promise to call or Skype the children...and then don't. They frequently "forget" to share important information....your

daughter had a temperature of 102 degrees over the weekend, or your son scored the first goal of his life. Leaving you seething, and at the same time breaking each time you see them crushed and disappointed by the other parent.

Unreliable parents often don't seem to realise that their behaviour not only makes it almost impossible to co-parent with them, but also seem oblivious to the damage they are doing to their child.

A child's relationship with their parents

Children develop their sense of self-worth and their knowledge of the world through their relationship with their parents. A child's self-esteem is built on the unconscious thought, "I matter and am worthy to the extent to which my parents take an interest in me." Children operate in quite a binary way - it's fair/not fair, right/wrong, with the ability to understand the shades of grey that make up life not being developed until towards the end of their teens.

When a parent is unreliable or flits in and out of a child's life, the child may be emotionally wounded, feeling unworthy and

unloved. Their take-away from this experience is the belief that people can't be trusted, which will have profound effects on their emotional development and will make it hard for them to form secure attachments later on. They downgrade their expectation of love, questioning its value. They're filled with anxiety, guilt or shame, they struggle to trust.

Some may even demonstrate these feelings of unworthiness through disruptive and/or destructive behaviour. They turn inward with depression - or act out in anger, fear or despair. Long term this can result in the inability to form close relationships, dependence on alcohol or drugs, and depression.

But there **are** things you can do to ease the pain for your children, ameliorate the damage and actually use it as a positive learning experience for your children.

Communicating with your ex

- Tell the other parent that their relationship to the children is important. They may feel that you don't value their relationship with your children, and therefore not

If the child wants to see both parents, please don't make the child feel guilty about it
Meg (17)

see their behaviour as being that much of an issue.

- Remain calm. Do not reveal your anger or frustration to your children as this will only increase their bad feelings and guilt. However, do talk with your children about their feelings. Reassure them that you love them. It is OK to explain that their parent's actions are a reflection on difficulties they are having and not a reflection on the children. Do not disparage the other parent. When you bad-mouth the other parent, you bad-mouth your children because they know they are 50% of each of you.

- You may wonder why your child still loves or even idolises a parent who is unreliable, and this will in turn feel hurtful to you when you are the one that is always there. As I said above; your ex, no matter how terrible, is still "half" of your child. So to your child if that parent is "bad" then this means that they must be "bad" as well. In order for them to feel good about themselves, they may need to ignore their other parent's bad qualities and focus on the good ones. Be the adult and don't make them feel guilty for adoring your ex. Give them permission to love their other parent. As they get older, your child will acquire a more balanced view. Be the bigger parent. Remember that you love your children more than you may dislike (or even hate) your ex, and so you do it for **them**.

- Acknowledge how their other parent's behaviour makes them feel. Tell them "this has nothing to do with you, but I

know it hurts your feelings. I'm sorry." Use this as a great learning opportunity and talk to your children about what they can't control (other people) and what they can control (their own actions and thoughts).

- Always have a back-up plan. Make sure that your children are not left with nothing to do, allowing them to focus on their upset and get disruptive due to bad feelings. Direct their focus and energies into a positive activity that will make them feel good about themselves.

- Be an open door for their feelings. Let your child know that they can come to you with their feelings and questions. And let them know it's also OK not to talk, if they don't want to.

- Children have different ways of dealing with painful feelings; often coming out in bad behaviour or anger. It may be too overwhelming

right now for your child to speak about the other parent. Bring up the subject from time to time, but don't pressure your child to have a conversation if they don't want to talk. You just want them to get the message that you are always available to listen and that whatever feelings they have are OK and they are entitled to them.

Disappointment is a part of life, and we shouldn't insulate them from it. The key though is to keep them from seeing the disappointment as a reflection of their worth. Use this as a powerful learning experience. Help them understand the situation and make sure their time remains full. This will ease the impact of the situation and teach them the life skills of managing their emotions and how to deal with other disappointments that they will face in life; without going into the default thought of "it must be me".

If you agree to an arrangement with the children then stick to it - disappointment is hard for the children and for the parent having to try to comfort or explain the situation to them.

Natalie Wiles, Langleys

My child has been returned twice now with suspicious bruising. What action should I take?"

About the authors

Fiona Yellowlees, Partner and Head of Family & Joanne Aggett, Associate, both of WBW Solicitors

Fiona has undertaken most areas of family law work both for married and unmarried couples but with particular emphasis upon the financial aspects associated with relationship breakdown and her interest in alternative methods of dispute resolution.

Joanne has particularly specialised in matters relating to breakdown of marriage and cohabitee relationships including children and financial aspects during her time at WBW.

All parents have a duty to safeguard their children and must act in the children's best interests.

The first consideration is whether it is thought that this bruising is consistent with the child's age or whether it is likely to be caused by the other parent/family.

Much will depend upon the age of the child, the arrangement between the parents, how long the situation has been going on and the circumstances when it began. It may be that an older child will give an indication of how the bruising arose.

If it is considered that the bruising was caused by the other parent or someone associated with them, our advice would be to take the child to the GP; a GP would be able to give some indication of when the bruising may have occurred and possibly the circumstances. That may provide some reassurance but if it is of concern there would be an independent record. It may be that a report should be made to Social Services either by the parent or by the GP.

Social Services may make recommendations about the time which the child spends with the other party to ensure that they are safe. The time which children spend with the other parent does not necessarily have to be direct - it can be indirect i.e. letters/cards/email and telephone/video calls. In some circumstances it would be in the child's best interests to maintain the relationship whilst the concerns are being considered. A parent can still make the child available to spend time with the parent even if not face-to-face.

If the time which the child spends with the other party has to stop, or if arrangements break down, it is likely that court proceedings will need to be considered. The court, under The Children Act 1989, adopts a non-intervention principle which means that the court will only make an order if there is a dispute, and only then if it is in the child's best interests. Either party can make an application for a Child Arrangements Order but often it is the dissatisfied parent who would do so. A Child Arrangements Order is an order which can regulate who the child lives with and when the child should spend time with the other parent (see Question 62 for more information).

Making an application

The relevant application form is a C100 which would be sent to the court; a further form C1A can be lodged by either party if there is a concern about risk of harm, i.e. domestic abuse, exposure to drugs or abduction. Unless the matter is urgent, mediation should always be considered as a way to resolve disputes. A

referral to mediation must take place before a court application and if mediation has not been considered, the court can halt the court process whilst mediation is attempted.

When issuing an application, the court automatically passes a copy of the application to CAFCASS (Children and Family Court Advisory and Support Service), who undertake safeguarding checks of the Police and Social Services. CAFCASS will also contact both parties, before the first hearing, to ascertain their position and try and narrow the issues. CAFCASS will include that information in a letter to the court, making initial recommendations about how the case should proceed. If there are safeguarding issues, the court will want to address those issues before considering suitable orders for the child.

Section 7 report

A Section 7 (welfare) report is a more thorough report by CAFCASS within which they can assess the risk and make recommendations to the court.

The court will always do what is in the child's best interest, not what parents want. The court will always safeguard the child and try, whenever possible, to ensure that a child can spend time with both parents.

It is always best that you seek your own independent legal advice as the circumstances of your case are specific to you.

Voices in the Middle

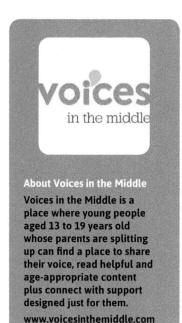

About Voices in the Middle

Voices in the Middle is a place where young people aged 13 to 19 years old whose parents are splitting up can find a place to share their voice, read helpful and age-appropriate content plus connect with support designed just for them.
www.voicesinthemiddle.com

E ven though everyone agrees that, when parents split up, it is important to think about the young people in the middle, their voices are not being heard. The association of family lawyers and mediators, Resolution, interviewed over 500 children and young people in 2016. Only 19% of them said they have a voice.

There can be lots of reasons for this, including:

- Young people do not know whom to talk to, when or how;

- Listening to young people

takes resources that professionals sometimes don't have;

- If parents don't agree with each other, they may want to keep children completely away from being involved;

- Emotional and mental health challenges for young people may be put as a reason for excluding them (for example, 'they are anxious because of exams').

Who are we?

Voices in the Middle is a collaboration between young people, the family law & mediation sector and The Family Initiative charity. Together they provide a dedicated place for young people to find help and support when in the middle of divorce and separation.

Over 50 family law and mediation firms support Voices in the Middle.

The service has four components: (1) a voice for young people, (2) help for young people, (3) advice for parents, and (4) campaigning for change.

Share stories

"Have you experienced your parents splitting up? Do you have something to say about it? What is your advice for

It takes both parents to be mature enough to be aware of their children, and how their decisions are going to impact their lives. Ellie (16)

parents or other young people going through the same?"

The feedback we receive from young people is the foundation for our advice to other young people and to parents.

Get help

"Here you will find content on what happens when parents split up, who is involved and who you can talk to. You can also read about feelings you may be going through and how to have your voice heard."

Content pieces are presented in four groups:

- Parents splitting up
- Talk to someone
- Your feelings
- Your voice

In addition to this content, young people can talk to someone personally on-line through a partnership with the on-line youth support service, The Mix.

Help for parents

"Here, in our area for parents, you can read about how to talk to and support your teenager in the middle of divorce and separation, including their rights, well-being and protecting their family relationships."

This help is based largely on material provided by young people when sharing their stories.

Content pieces for parents are in three groups:

- How to help your teenager
- How to talk about splitting up
- Troubleshooting

Campaign

1 in 3 children in UK will see their parents split up before they reach their 16th birthday.

Every child should be able to express their view in all things that affect them (United Nations Convention on the Rights of the Child), including:

- Be able to freely share their views
- Be listened to, as appropriate to their age and maturity

We are raising awareness of the impact of divorce and separation on young people in the UK. This includes providing a place to go for all young people, to find help.

Working with young people, we are also learning the best ways for young people to share their voice, without being put in the middle of any arguments. We are sharing this with parents, professionals and Government.

I've looked everywhere for support, even at school, but I haven't really found anything helpful.
Imogen (11)

My children have come home reporting inappropriate sexual behaviour. What should I do?

About the author

Emma Benyon-Tinker, Everys Solicitors

Emma is a specialist family solicitor dealing with all aspects of family disputes including divorce, civil partnership dissolution, financial issues, cohabitation disputes, pre-nuptial agreements, domestic abuse and children issues. She is a collaboratively trained lawyer, mediator and Resolution Accredited Specialist.

Your children have come home from spending time with their other parent, and they make a comment that leads you to believe that there has been some sort of inappropriate sexual behaviour.

What steps do you need to take?

It will depend on the precise nature of the allegation but as a parent you have a duty to safeguard your children, even from their other parent, if there has been any sort of inappropriate sexual behaviour. This could be the children being exposed to adult sexual behaviour that they are too young to understand or witness; or it could be that something inappropriate has happened to your child.

If there is a Child Arrangements Order in force determining what time your children should spend with each parent, then this is potentially a conflict with your duty to safeguard the children. In that case you need to inform the other parent that you are going to stop complying with the order due to your concerns, and you must then immediately seek an urgent order from the court. This might be a Prohibited Steps Order which is an order which would prevent your children from coming into contact with the person against whom the allegation is being made.

The court will then review the allegations and consider what level of contact may be appropriate between the parent and the child, not only if the allegation is proved but whilst the court is investigating the allegation itself.

Fact finding

The court may undertake a finding of fact hearing. This is a hearing where the court hears the relevant evidence and, using the civil test for the burden of proof, determines whether or not the allegations are proved.

It is important to note that the test for burden of proof in civil courts is whether the allegation is proved on the balance of probabilities. This is very different from the criminal burden of proof where the court and jury must be satisfied beyond all reasonable doubt. That is why you can have the same case and the same evidence with the criminal courts saying the allegation is not proved and the civil courts saying it is proved!

Will the court allow contact?

Depending on the seriousness of the allegation, the court may still order that there should be some contact between the parent and the child. The court is under a duty to consider the welfare of the child and contact will only be ordered if it is safe. This might mean there is supervised contact. It might mean that there is indirect contact only, for example the parent is allowed to send cards and gifts to their child. If the allegation is extremely serious then it is unlikely that any contact would be ordered.

What if there is no court order in place?

If there is a court order in force, you cannot simply decide to ignore the order and not return the matter to court. You must comply with the court order which is why an urgent application to the court is required.

What should you do however if there is no court order in force? You still have a duty to safeguard your children from harm.

You may still need to suspend any informal arrangement that you have with the other parent whilst the matter is being investigated. You would need to report the matter to your local social services and your GP. They will initially undertake what is known as a section 47 investigation. The local authority has a duty to investigate where they believe a child has suffered or is likely to suffer harm in their area. They can also involve the police if they deem it necessary. Social services may ask that the parents make the necessary application to the court and the court would then decide the issues as set out above.

In some cases social services may decide that they need to take court proceedings themselves to protect the children from harm if the allegations are extremely serious.

What if a criminal offence is suspected?

What should you do however if the allegation is so serious that a criminal offence potentially has taken place? In those circumstances, you will also need to make a report to the police. The police will want to interview your children and this will take the form of what is known as an achieving best evidence ('ABE') interview. The police will then decide whether or not a criminal offence might have been committed, and the CPS will decide whether or not there should be a prosecution. If the police are investigating an allegation, it does not stop the family courts being involved and determining the arrangements for your children. Often criminal proceedings and family proceedings are happening at the same time on the same facts.

It is important that you seek urgent legal assistance if you believe your children have suffered from some sort of inappropriate sexual behaviour.

Notes

I am happy that I never chose a side, because I knew my parents could teach me valuable lessons and morals in life. Isaac (15)

What do schools need to know?

About the author

Roy Souter, Headteacher, Stoke Hill Junior School

Roy is the headteacher of Stoke Hill Junior School in Exeter. He also works in collaboration with other headteachers to develop positive, inclusive and innovative approaches to teaching and learning.

One of my early memories is of being extremely upset at school because I had to take a letter home addressed to my mum and dad. I was upset because a few weeks previously my parents had separated and my dad had left home. None of the teachers knew and they didn't know what to say when I explained it to them. This was horrible for everyone, and would have been unnecessary if there had been better communication.

I also remember hating the fact that my mum had told my teachers about my dad leaving. This made the whole situation feel real and permanent. I felt like my life would never be the same again, and that by knowing what had happened the teachers were now part of my new reality.

I've shared these memories because I see children going through this situation all the time and can see how the parents' behaviour impacts on their children when their relationship breaks down. How parents handle a separation makes a big difference to the long-term effect it has on their children. We see a huge range of approaches taken, none ever with the intention of making children's lives more difficult or causing them to be more upset than necessary. There are, however, some key things that we have found over the years that make life as easy as possible for children at a potentially traumatic time of their lives.

Communication with school

The first action to take is to let the school know that the separation has happened. Children need to know that this conversation is going to happen, and to know exactly what will be said and who will be told. They will often seek out a trusted adult to share their feelings with and need to know who already is party to the facts.

It's really important that schools hold contact details for both parents, and the order in which parents should be contacted if there's an emergency. Schools also need to know contact plans (days of the week that the child is with each parent) which allows them to identify any patterns and changes in behaviour, and also ensures they hand the children over to the correct person at the

> When I look back I cringe at how I got everything off my chest to anyone who would listen. I was hurting so much. It may have helped me deal with it, but I would aim to be more measured with my emotion if I went through it again.
>
> *Dom, Dad*

end of the day. It also helps schools to know which parent to contact if a child is late for school or does not arrive. It wastes time and causes unnecessary stress if they inadvertently contact the wrong parent.

Correspondence

Schools should provide copies of all correspondence to both parents, including copies of school reports and details about parents' evenings, concerts etc. The school will need to be given both sets of contact details and will need to be asked to send additional copies of information. This is easier if the school uses an email system (such as Parent Mail) to share information, but still manageable if they don't. Parents need to be proactive and let schools know if they are not receiving information. Mistakes are easily rectified if schools know they have happened.

It's important that parents present a united front and show that they both value and care about their child's education. This can include attendance at school events and parents' evenings. Where possible parents putting their differences aside to attend together gives children a really positive message about how important school is, as well as how important they are to their parents.

A shared response to any problems in school is also really helpful - children are extremely good at playing one parent off against another. We work on the basis that all behaviour is a form of communication, and that if a child is unsettled or behaving differently to their usual pattern then they are telling us something that they may be finding difficult to explain in words. Working with school to help get to the root of problems, and parents talking honestly to each other, makes a massive difference to their child.

Contact

It's really important that parents don't use contact as a weapon or a punishment. Withdrawing contact as a consequence for bad behaviour is unfair on the child, and damages ongoing relationships with both parents

(as well as between parents). We find that children can become extremely distressed if they are expecting to spend time with one parent and this is denied. This can then express itself in worse behaviour at home or at school, clearly the opposite of the intended outcome.

We also find that variable contact arrangements can be really difficult for children to cope with. Certainty is really important for children at any time, but especially when they are going through an unsettling

time. Parents can set these arrangements up with the best of intentions, but it can be really hard for some children to cope with if they are unsure about where they are staying and who they are staying with.

Finally, I'd like to re-emphasise the importance of communicating with school, and for both parents to remain fully involved in their child's education. It's worth the effort involved.

Notes

You automatically think it's your fault or you had part in it, but it's not, it's between your mum and your dad. People fall out of love, people have arguments. It's how things go.
Sammie (17)

Can you answer some of my concerns about child contact centres?

About the author

Phil Coleman, Service Development Manager at NACCC

Before Phil's appointment at NACCC, this, he was directly involved setting up and managing Child Contact Centres and has been working with NACCC undertaking enhanced and supported accreditation inspections. Phil has experience of working in Residential Parenting Assessment Centres, Contact Centres, Children's Homes, Children's Nurseries, Anger Management, Life Story, Parenting Assessments of people with Learning Difficulties and supporting families in their own homes.

A question we hear a lot is: *"I can't imagine seeing my kids in a strange place and being watched - won't it be awkward?"*

It is quite normal to feel this way - spending time with your children in an environment which you are not used to can seem very daunting and intimidating. Many parents have not come across child contact centres before and so can feel apprehensive. If you are going to be using a supported centre the volunteers and staff are generally in the background and do not sit with you watching or listening to what you are saying. They want you and your children to have a positive experience and spend good quality time together. The volunteers and staff will go out of their way to make you as comfortable as possible.

An environment to help you have quality time with your children

We aim to create a warm, sociable atmosphere where you and your children can relax and enjoy yourselves. Contact centres have toys, games and books for children of all ages. Tea, coffee and other refreshments are provided.

Research your local centre!

Find out as much as you can about the centre so that it is more familiar when you go for your pre-visit. There may be photos on your local centre's website showing what the various rooms look like and you should also be sent a leaflet from the centre explaining what it is like and how they run.

Pre-visits

If your local contact centre is accredited by NACCC you will have already been invited to the centre for what we call a 'pre-visit'. This gives you the opportunity to discuss your worries with the person who runs the centre before the first session when you'll be seeing your kids.

During the pre-visit you'll get a chance to look round and the co-ordinator will go through some paperwork which helps them to double check that the service their centre offers is going to be appropriate for your situation.

Your ex-partner and children will also be invited for a pre-visit on a different occasion to you. In this respect it can be compared to the preparation visits when a child is first starting school or nursery.

Again, part of their visit will include a look round the centre so that the environment can become more familiar and your kids can see the types of toys and games that the centre has.

For more information about accredited contact centres please check the NACCC website.

My children don't like going to the contact centre

It is important to find out why your children are not enjoying coming to the contact centre. It might be a good idea to speak to the coordinator, volunteers or team leader at the centre to see if we can make things more comfortable for your children. We may be able to help by providing toys that your children particularly like.

Parents can also support their children with the emotions related to contact centres by making it 'OK' to talk about contact in a positive and exciting way. Children are very perceptive and will feed off the emotions and anxieties of the resident parent.

Helping your children express their feelings

Your centre may have a way of your children giving feedback if they find it hard to put into words how they are feeling. For example, centres in Yorkshire have developed some 'Buzz my feeling' sensory boxes (in consultation with the Family Justice Young People's Board) which support children particularly if they lack the confidence to verbalise their emotions and feelings. It is hoped that this tool can help volunteers, staff and parents to pick up on issues sooner, so that appropriate encouragement, reassurance or other relevant follow-up can take place.

Reviews

You will not be using the contact centre forever. Ideally, contact centres provide a stepping stone to having contact in a more natural environment. In due course you should move on to perhaps just using the centre as a place to pick up/drop off (known as a 'handover') and then to make your own independent arrangements for your children

without needing the centre at all. The centre co-ordinator will organise a review to help you prepare for this. If this seems too daunting there are some great free online resources to help you make this next step.

CAFCASS produce a range of information that will support you when experiencing separation and/or accessing a contact service. We particularly like the Parenting Plans that support separated parents to consider how they might be able to co-parent in a way that puts the needs of children first.

I haven't seen my kids for ages and am going to see them for the first time in our local contact centre. I am very nervous!

It's normal to feel nervous and many parents think that their kids will have forgotten them but when they see their kids they realise they haven't. It's a special time for you and your kids so take deep breaths and enjoy it.

One dad shared his experience with us:

"I was shown in the hall... suddenly the boys came in running to me, their arms open, both shouting 'Daddy, daddy, daddy!' Big hugs for each one. It was like a rugby scrum only for once I was crying. They had not forgotten me."

Will my kids be safe in the contact centre?

All centres on the NACCC website are accredited and inspected by NACCC to ensure they provide a safe and neutral environment. This endorsed accreditation process demonstrates that the centre is working to agreed and approved national standards, ensuring the safety of you and your children. The national standards are updated by NACCC in line with legislation and good practice.

Which contact service is best for your kids?

There are a range of contact services which can be used depending on your situation and the level of risk.

Supervised contact

Is there a potential risk of harm? Supervised contact ensures the physical safety and emotional well-being of children in a one-to-one observed setting.

Supported contact

Supported contact keeps children in touch with parents if trust has broken down or communication is difficult. Parents or family members do not have to meet and several families use the facilities at the same time.

Handover service

This is when the centre is used for a short period as a drop off/

My parents' divorce has been a positive change, and although it may initially seem hard, once you get into that routine, everything will start feeling homely and normal again. Stephanie (17)

pick up point. Again, family members do not have to meet.

Ways to help your contact run smoothly

The centre has strict rules which are there to make the contact run as smoothly and safely as possible for your children. Typical rules at a supported contact centre would normally include the following:

- Parents are responsible for the safety and supervision of their children at all times while at the centre. No child may be left without a parent in attendance.

- The resident parent must leave a contact number when leaving children at the centre.

- A child can only be taken from a centre during a visit if this is

stated on the referral form, or with written consent of both parents.

- Relatives or friends can only attend if they are named on the referral form.

- There must be no arguing in front of any of the children. Abusive or aggressive behaviour and racist or other offensive remarks will not be tolerated. Any visitor acting in such a way will be asked to leave.

- No mobile phones, photographs (unless agreed with the coordinator) portable computers or pets are allowed.

- Alcohol, drugs or anyone under the influence of these will not be allowed on the premises.

Always be there and be honest to your children. Never put down the other parent and teach your kids it's wrong to say bad things about people.

Philip, Dad

Notes

How can I help my children cope with stress and recognise when professional help is needed?

About the author

Dr Sabina Dosani, MBBS MSc MRCPsych

Sabina is a consultant child and adolescent psychiatrist with many years of experience in helping children, teenagers and their families with psychological and psychopathological conditions. She regularly acts as an expert witness for the Family Court. Her clinical interests are in childhood behavioural disorders and autism spectrum disorders. She also has an academic career in the medical humanities.

S tressed people are often the last to recognise what is happening. Our children are no exception.

Could my child be stressed?

Just because your daughter isn't complaining about finding your divorce stressful, it doesn't mean she's not suffering. If your toddler seems to be behaving differently: irritable, crying more than usual, having nightmares and regressing, chances are she's stressed. Likewise, if younger children are permanently tired, not sleeping, whinging and doing badly at school, they too may be stressed. Teenagers, on the other hand, may surprise you with outbursts of anger, missing school and generally feeling bad and miserable about themselves and the rest of the world.

Children who have ongoing stress are more likely to develop colds, digestive problems, anxiety disorders, headaches and obesity. Unless they learn to cope with stress, they're more likely to misuse drugs and alcohol in their teens and adult life and become depressed and even suicidal.

What kicks off stress?

It could be almost anything. Common sources of stress include the death of a pet, arrival of a new brother or sister, dad being made redundant, parental separation, moving home, changing school, exams, university applications, being bullied, the death of a grandparent or an unresolved family argument.

What helps?

Sound, confiding relationships with adults are enormously helpful. It doesn't matter who they are: parents, grandparents, aunts, uncles, godparents, family friends or teachers. Stressed children may not know what is causing them to feel awful and behave differently to usual. The trigger may be divorce, but ongoing stress in children often overwhelms them when there is more than one difficulty. What helps is being an active listener and being prepared to ask open questions to tease out what is wrong.

Being heard and taken seriously by a parent helps children of all ages cope better with stress.

What else helps?

- Breathing slowly and deeply
- Having a long warm bath and listening to favourite music
- Exercise
- Hobbies to retreat into
- Relaxation exercises

Even very young children can learn a relaxation exercise called progressive muscle relaxation.

When to seek professional help

All children and adults feel stressed from time to time. Experiencing some anxiety in childhood and beyond is normal. As parents know, most toddlers are afraid of monsters and many children show some signs of anxiety on their first day at school.

Anxiety becomes a problem when it interferes with a child's life. For instance, fear of contamination can lead to avoidance that gets in the way of friendships, fear of being away from home often affects a child's ability to go to school and fear of the dark stops a child going to sleep. Children and young people with anxiety disorders experience extreme fears, worries or a sense of dread that is out of proportion with a real or imagined threat, and impacts on many aspects of life.

Anxiety disorders change how children and young people think, often affecting their ability to make logical decisions. Although historically thought to be harmless, these disorders can interfere with academic, social and family life.

Although anxiety disorders are so common in children and teenagers, they are also one of the least well understood conditions in this age group. Most anxiety disorders begin between the ages of 12 and 21, although they are often first diagnosed later in life. Anxiety disorders affect between one in five and one in ten children and teenagers at some stage of their lives. There is good evidence for early intervention and self-management for children and young people with anxiety disorders. Delays in diagnosis, failure to involve patients in

treatment and poor follow up can lead to further deterioration.

When to see a specialist?

1. Does your child worry or ask for reassurance almost every day?

2. Does your child consistently avoid certain age-appropriate situations or activities, or avoid doing them without a parent?

3. Does your child frequently have tummy ache, headaches, or episodes of hyperventilation?

4. Does your child have daily repetitive rituals?

Ask for specialist assessment and therapy if:

1. Your child or teenager has persistent worries or intrusive thoughts, extreme clinging, avoidance, or repetitive behaviours that interfere with school performance, friendships or family life.

2. Your child has palpitations, chest pain, abdominal pain, vomiting, shortness of breath or sleeping problems for which no physical cause can be found.

Notes

I blamed myself and I let my anger take control and I did cut myself. That is the one action that I deeply, deeply regret because I now have scratches on my body that can never be removed. Kay (16)

Relaxation exercises

Progressive Muscle Relaxation relaxes the body progressively as children focus on different muscle groups. There are 3 basic steps:

1. Isolate a muscle, inhale, and tense it.

2. Hold the muscle tense for 5-10 seconds.

3. Exhale, and slowly relax the tense muscle. The relaxation phase needs to be at least as long as the tensing phase, possibly longer.

The progressive tense-hold-relax sequence moves up or down through the body. Some children prefer to move from toes and feet up towards their face. Others prefer to move down from their head, beginning with scrunching their eyes up and working down the body.

- Ask your child to lie down.

- Get your child to bend her legs at the knees so her feet are flat on the ground.

- Say, "close your eyes and pretend you are at the beach, lying on the sand."

- Ask your child to pretend she hears the water lapping against the shore.

- Ask your child to imagine that it's a beautiful, sunny day. The sun feels warm against her skin. The sand is warm underneath her body.

- Have your child take a few deep breaths as she "watches the waves go in and out".

- Now ask your child to squeeze the sand between her toes. Inhale, hold, exhale, relax.

- Now squeeze both feet. Inhale, hold, exhale, relax.

- Say, "Do you feel the difference when you are relaxed?"

- Now ask her to tighten her legs. Inhale, hold, exhale and relax.

- Now her bottom, tummy, and chest. Inhale, hold, exhale and relax.

- Now her hands and arms.

- Then her shoulders and neck. Inhale, hold, exhale, relax.

- And then her face. Sometimes children don't know how to tense up their face. You may need to say something like: "Screw your eyes shut tight" Inhale, hold, exhale, relax.

- Finally, have her squeeze her whole body. Inhale, hold, exhale, relax.

- Ask her to take a few more deep breaths.

- Remind her to feel the warm sun and sand. Hear the water lap against the shore.

- Ask her to open their eyes.

Although this is a great exercise to do at home, it's worth learning a more portable relaxation technique as well. Tensing and relaxing muscles is not exactly what most children are going to feel comfortable doing on the school bus before a Geography GCSE mock. For those out-and-about times, there is another relaxation technique that children like because they can do it anywhere and nobody else can see what they're up to. I call it 'the calming place'.

MUST READ

The calming place

Find a quiet place where you won't be disturbed for a few minutes, and close your eyes. Cast your mind back to the time in your life you felt most deeply relaxed. Some people like to think of a holiday, but feel free to choose anywhere. Imagine yourself in that calming place now. Try to bring it to life vividly, using all your senses. What can you see, hear, taste, smell and feel? Stay in the place for as long as it takes to feel calm. One of the great things about very young children is that they are better at imagining than adults. When you teach them to imagine their calming place, they have an individualised, portable stress-management tool, for life.

Older children may struggle to visualise at first. One trick is to practice when they are not feeling particularly tense, so that they can use it easily when they need to.

ONLY
Mums & Dads
parents meet professionals

Organisations

Org

ORGANISATIONS

Child and Adolescent Mental Health Services (CAMHS)

CAMHS

About CAMHS

Child and Adolescent Mental Health Services (CAMHS for short) are specialist multidisciplinary services, funded by the NHS, to assess and treat children with mental illnesses, and emotional and behavioural disorders.

You will need a referral from a GP to be seen by CAMHS, who will work with the whole family to support a young person's mental health.

This could, for example, include both parents coming along to assessment and treatment appointments depending on the child's age and what level of involvement they want.

CAMHS usually see children up to the age of 18, but in some areas, they are only funded to see young people up to the age of 16.

Can CAMHS help all families during parental separation?

No. CAMHS are there for those with mental illnesses. In an average class of 15 year old pupils, 3 are statistically likely to have had a mental illness, but 10 are likely to have experienced their parents separating.

What sorts of conditions can CAMHS help with?

1. Anxious away from care givers (separation anxiety).

2. Anxious in social situations (social anxiety/phobia).

3. General anxiety (generalised anxiety).

4. Compelled to do or think things (OCD).

5. Panics (panic disorder)

6. Avoids going out (agoraphobia).

7. Avoids specific things (specific phobia).

8. Repetitive problematic behaviours (habit problems).

9. Depression/low mood.

10. Self-harm.

11. Extremes of mood (bipolar disorder).

12. Delusional beliefs and hallucinations (psychosis).

13. Drug and alcohol difficulties (substance abuse).

14. Difficulties sitting still, listening or concentrating (possible ADHD/ hyperactivity).

15. Behavioural difficulties.

16. Poses risks to others.

17. Doesn't get to the toilet in time, or wets at night (elimination problems).

18. Experienced abuse from caregiver.

19. Disturbed by traumatic event (PTSD).

20. Eating issues (anorexia/ bulimia).

21. Problems in attachment to parent/carer (attachment problems).

22. Peer relationship difficulties.

23. Persistent difficulties managing relationships with others (includes emerging personality disorder).

24. Does not speak (selective mutism).

25. Gender identity disorder.

26. Unexplained physical symptoms.

27. Unexplained developmental difficulties.

28. Self-care issues (including neglecting to take insulin for diabetes).

29. Adjustment to health issues.

Who works at CAMHS?

Child and adolescent psychiatrists

Psychiatry is the specialty of medicine dealing with mental illnesses. A child and adolescent psychiatrist is a doctor, with a degree in medicine and several years of postgraduate training in diagnosing and treating mental, emotional and behavioural disorders.

Psychiatrists carry out assessments, take a clinical history, conduct semi structured

interviews, undertake physical examinations and blood tests and may request brain imaging.

Treatments include drug therapies and psychotherapies, individual, family or group. They work as part of multidisciplinary teams in CAMHS.

Letters to look for:

MBBS (medical degree)
MD (medical degree in some countries, confusingly it's a postgraduate research degree in others).

MRCPsych, FRCPsych (member or fellow of the Royal College of Psychiatrists).

MMed Psych FF Psych FC Psych (alternatives to MRCPsych in some countries).

FRANZCP (Fellow of the Royal Australian and New Zealand College of Psychiatrists).

Psychiatric nurses

These are qualified nurses with specialist training, skills and knowledge in treating mental, emotional and behavioural disorders. As well as prescribing medication for some conditions including ADHD, many nurses are trained in one or more talking treatments.

Letters to look for:

RMN (registered mental nurse).

Psychotherapist

Psychotherapists use playing, art and talking to assess symptoms, explore feelings and understand relationships. By helping children and young people understand the roots of their distress, they guide them towards recovery.

Meetings are usually weekly. Unfortunately, anyone can call themselves a psychotherapist, but good ones are members of overseeing bodies like the United Kingdom Council for Psychotherapy (UKCP) and the British Association of Counselling and Psychotherapy (BACP).

Clinical psychologist

Clinical psychologists have an honours degree in psychology and further clinical doctorate. Their role includes therapy for young people, such as cognitive behaviour therapy or Acceptance Commitment Therapy, and therapeutic support for families. They can also carry out cognitive assessments.

Psychologists cannot prescribe drugs.

Letters to look for:

BSc/BA.

Dr at the front of their name.

Registered Psychological Practitioner (HCPC).

Social worker

Many social workers working in CAMHS are trained therapists, often in family therapy, where multiple members of a family are seen together. Social workers

can also help with issues arising from coping with mental illness or hospitalisation.

Letters to look for:

DipSW (Diploma in Social Work).

CQSW (Certificate of Qualification in Social Work).

NQSW (National Qualification in Social Work).

BSW (Bachelor of Social Work).

Occupational therapist

These trained professionals use work and leisure activities to develop or regain physical and life skills. Many have training in talking therapies as well.

Other therapists include Art therapists, Drama therapists, Education therapists and Music therapists.

What happens at CAMHS?

Your first session should be an assessment, often with two or more people from the CAMHS team working together. Children and young people have an opportunity to speak without their parents present, and parents similarly are offered an opportunity to do this.

At the end of your assessment, you can expect answers to these questions:

- Is there something the matter?

- Is there a name for that, or a formal diagnosis?

You are not alone, don't you worry my dear,
remember, your family love you so don't shed a tear.

A quote from a poem by Kat (15)

- How many times do you think we will need to see you?

- How long will appointments be?

- What type of treatment do you offer?

- How long does treatment take?

- Are we able to contact you between appointments and how can we get in touch?

- What do we do in an emergency?

Notes

Although there have been recent announcements about increased funding of mental health, child and adolescent mental health services have had severe funding cuts in the past decade. During this time, there has also been a steep increase in the numbers of young people with serious mental illnesses and a national shortage of CAMHS psychiatrists.

These combined pressures have led to much higher thresholds of severity before a young person is seen in many parts of the country. There are simply not enough resources to meet need.

More families are using health insurance or savings to seek private assessments, which can be a faster way to get a diagnosis and treatment plan. There are other private services who can help children after divorce, who do not meet thresholds for CAMHS. For example, the Institute of Family Therapy offer family therapy to separating couples and their children. If CAMHS are not able to accept a referral, ask for a list of who provides relevant services locally.

I am sure my ex is drinking too much when looking after the kids. What should I do?

About the author

Heather Broadfield, Hill and Company

Heather is a Partner and Family Law Solicitor at Hill & Company and is a Member of the Law Society Family Panel.

This is a difficult issue to address without knowing the reasons behind the concerns and how the suspicion has arisen. If there is evidence in support of the suspicion, or the children are already being affected by a parent's alcohol consumption, the issue needs to be addressed at the earliest opportunity.

It is OK for a parent to enjoy a couple drinks with their meal or at a family party for example. Parents need to remember, however, that alcohol affects different people in different ways and need to have an awareness as to how alcohol affects them personally. For example, one person may have a couple of alcoholic drinks at a family BBQ and it does not affect their behaviour or awareness in anyway. Another person may consume the same amount of alcohol and become sleepy which could pose a risk to younger children if left unsupervised, or become louder, agitated or start to use bad language, all of which would be upsetting for children.

How much is too much?

There are no specific laws or guidelines as to how much is too much and common sense must prevail. Moderation is the key and ensuring that as a parent, you are in control and able to care for children without putting their safety at risk. A parent should always be alert to any potential risks to children and ensure that in the event any child was about to, or had hurt themselves, they can act as quickly and appropriately as possible. Consuming alcohol to excess can delay reaction times, can make people drowsy or sleep deeper which can put children's safety at risk. Excessive alcohol consumption is also often linked to violence and domestic abuse which are dangerous and damaging for children to become caught up in.

If you have a relatively amicable relationship with your ex-partner, it could be a good idea to broach this subject in a sensitive way, when the children are not present of course. This would enable you to ascertain further information, voice your concerns and potentially put your mind at ease. This does of course require the other parent to be open and honest about their alcohol consumption. If there is an acceptance on their part that they do consume alcohol, a short-term solution could be that the children no longer stay overnight until the issues have been addressed. There could be an agreement that alcohol will not be consumed prior to or during contact and contact could take place at a children's play area or swimming pool for example, where the temptation of alcohol is not there.

Safeguarding your children

In situations where it isn't possible to have these frank discussions with the other parent or there is an obvious denial, you must ensure that you safeguard your children if you believe they are at risk of harm. This does not necessarily mean to prevent the children from seeing the other parent as this can also be emotionally damaging for them, but to have appropriate safeguarding in place. This could be, for example, having another family member to supervise to ensure that the other party has not consumed alcohol prior to

ONLY
Mums & Dads
parents meet professionals

Organisations

Org

ORGANISATIONS

contact and does not do so during contact.

If the children are overnight with the other parent and you are led to believe that the other parent is intoxicated and placing the children at risk of harm, for example one of the children contacts you by telephone upset, you should make arrangements to collect the children. If this is not welcomed by the other parent and they become abusive or refuse you entry, the police can be contacted to carry out a welfare check. It is extremely important to note however that this is only in emergency situations and is not to be used

as a means of 'checking up' on parents without good grounds to do so.

If the other parent does not accept the concerns raised and therefore does not agree to any reduction in contact with the children, an application to the court may be necessary to ensure that the concerns are fully investigated and the appropriate level of contact is taking place.

If drinking alcohol to excess is raised during the course of court proceedings, the court can order that testing is carried out which will be followed with a report setting out whether the results

are consistent with excessive alcohol consumption. In the event that tests show excessive/chronic alcohol consumption, the court may wish to see further testing in say 3 months time as evidence that the issue is being addressed. In the meantime, contact may be restricted to visiting contact as opposed to overnight and possibly supervised, depending on the seriousness of the concerns.

If you do have concerns and are unsure as to the best way to deal with the issue, you should seek advice from a family solicitor to discuss your options.

Adfam

About Adfam

Adfam is the national charity working to improve support for families affected by drug or alcohol use.

Adfam's mission

"Drug and alcohol use can threaten and ultimately destroy family relationships and wellbeing. We empower family members and carers, support frontline workers and influence decision-makers to stop this happening."

What do we do?

Improve life for families affected by drugs and alcohol.

We produce resources and signpost people to support, we empower family members through community projects, we support front-line workers, and we influence decision-makers.

When should people get in touch?

If you are affected by a family member or a friend's drug or alcohol use you will find lots of resources on our website including a map of local family support groups.

How best to get in touch

Visit our website www.adfam.org.uk. Follow us on Twitter, Facebook and LinkedIn and sign up to our mailing list to keep up-to-date with our work.

I am sure my ex is taking drugs when looking after the kids. What should I do?

About the author

Carol-Anne Baker, Consultant Family Solicitor, Bridge Law Solicitors Ltd

Carol-Anne qualified as a solicitor in 1991, specialising in Family Law throughout her career. She is an accredited member of The Law Society Advanced Family Law Panel and a member of Resolution, abiding by their Code of Practice.

This is a statement heard commonly in children cases and can be a real issue, but further consideration needs to be given before the court or Children's Services will become involved. Whilst not condoning drug use, a parent may take certain drugs in a way that may not impact upon their parenting. The "looking after the kids" part of the statement is important as the issue is whether it is impacting on the welfare of the children. Be wary of comments from third parties who may have their own agenda.

When are drugs being taken?

Are the drugs being taken around the time spent with the children, being left around the house or causing serious lifestyle concerns?

The other parent may admit that they take certain drugs (commonly cannabis) but deny taking it when the children are in their care or say that they are getting help from substance misuse services. Other parents will deny any drug use. In more obvious examples, parents can appear to be under the influence of drugs to others regularly and may be involved in chaotic lifestyles linked with this usage, such as being homeless, constantly changing address, having damage to their home, having other adults spending extended periods at their home or being involved in crime.

If you are on speaking terms with your ex, you may wish to raise your concern with them initially. Try to do so in as non-confrontational way as possible. Explain why you have a concern and see what the response is. It may be that you feel reassured that either it is not happening or that it is not going to affect the well-being of the children.

Reporting substance abuse

If you are not reassured and are worried you could report this to Children's Services if you believe there is a risk of harm to the children. You could also decide to protect the children by stopping the other parent spending time with the children, limiting the time or insisting that the time is supervised perhaps by a family member you trust to ensure your ex is not under the influence of drugs around the children. Often it is difficult to communicate directly and be reassured or take protective steps without support. You may wish to see a solicitor for advice or you could make an application to court yourself for a Child Arrangements Order, mentioning that you do have concerns around drug abuse in the application.

Court involvement

The court will have to decide if drugs are being taken that impact upon the care of the children and if so what to do about it. Sometimes, if a parent agrees for example to smoking cannabis, they could be asked to give an undertaking or promise to the court that they will not do so within a certain time before, or during time spent with the children.

The court may order drug testing to be carried out. This is expensive and with no legal aid generally, both parents will be expected to pay for it. This is usually carried out by way of hair strand testing, which can show a pattern of use over several months for most drugs rather than just at a single point in time, which is easier to manipulate. If

the results are positive, a decision will be made as to whether this usage is likely to impact upon the parent's care of the children and if so steps will be taken to protect the children from harm. This could include the time spent with the children being stopped, reduced or supervised whilst the parent attends substance misuse services and further testing being carried out to review whether the issue is being addressed and if it is safe to change the arrangements.

In some circumstances, it may be the main carer for the children or both parents that are heavily involved with drugs. In those circumstances, Children's Services may become involved to determine whether it is safe for the children to be cared for by that parent or either parent. In some circumstances there could be a decision made that the children have been harmed or are at risk of harm from the drug related issues to the extent that it is felt necessary to seek a care order and remove the children from the care of the parent(s). The UK introduced a drug and alcohol court in 2008 and there are a number across the country as a way to try to help parents with such problems rather than remove children. They involve agencies such as the court, housing, social workers, psychiatrists and drugs workers working together to support families.

Notes

My ex has changed the kids' school and doctor without telling me anything. What should I do?

About the author

Rachel Duke, Aletta Shaw Solicitors

Rachel is a solicitor specialising in all aspects of family law with a particular emphasis on complex financial cases involving substantial assets; private children matters; divorce proceedings; civil partnership disputes; pre & post nuptial agreements; domestic violence issues and financial provision for children for unmarried parents. She is a member of the Advanced Family Law Panel.

The first key question here is whether you share something called 'parental responsibility' (PR) (see Questions 6, 11 and 13 and the Must read article on Page 324 for more information). Sharing parental responsibility means that both parents have to consult each other about important decisions relating to bringing up their children. That doesn't mean that you have to do this in relation to routine, everyday decisions, but it does include changing a child's school or doctor's surgery. So, if you share parental responsibility then in theory you should never be in this situation.

But sometimes it happens and if so, what should you do?

Act quickly

The first thing to do is to make sure that you act quickly. The law sets out certain factors that are relevant to deciding these kinds of issues. One of those factors is to consider the effect upon a child of a change in their circumstances. If you leave it too long to object after the change has been made, then you could find yourself in a situation where it won't be in your child's best interests for the change to be reversed because a new 'status quo' has been established. There could also be an issue with losing the place at the previous school or surgery.

Communicate with the other parent

You should immediately notify the other parent that you don't agree to the change. You should also notify both schools or the GP practices and the relevant education/health authority.

It is generally worth trying to sort these issues out by agreement if possible. You should try to find out why your ex has done this. Is the GP surgery more convenient? Does it have a wider range of services? Does it have better reviews? Although you should have been consulted, it may be that it is in fact better for your child. That is the question that you should ask yourself. If you still don't agree then you should explain your reasons and request that the change is immediately reversed.

Getting the court involved

If the other parent is not willing to cooperate, then you can apply to court for a specific issues order. This type of order does

Instead of hiding from my feelings I started helping my friends by telling them how I coped, and this really helped. Cerys (15)

what it says on the tin. In this case the issue is the proposed change of school or doctor. The court will have to decide if the change is in your child's best interests. The court will want to see a good reason for it.

You should research and compare both schools including reading the latest Ofsted inspection reports. If you don't already have them, you should get copies of your child's recent school reports to see how they were doing at the previous school. You should speak to the teachers also. Is the new school more difficult for you to get to, so that you won't be able to pick up your child, or drop them off anymore? Is the new school fee-paying and if so, who is going to pay the fees? You will need to be able to explain all the reasons why you don't believe that the proposed change is better for your child.

If you don't have PR then the other parent does not have to consult you before changing your child's school or doctors. This is one of the reasons why PR is very important for both parents. But you can still apply to the court for a specific issues order if you don't think that the change is in your child's best interests.

If you get wind that a change of school or doctors is proposed but hasn't yet happened, then you should immediately get legal advice. It may be that you want to apply to court for something called a prohibited steps order to stop the change happening in the first place.

Ultimately it is far better to avoid these situations happening if possible. It may be worth considering why your ex didn't consult you. Mediation might help the two of you improve your communication, trust and joint parenting.

Take personal responsibility for improving your parenting skills and learn how to co-parent without criticising your ex.

Andy, Dad

Notes

What is a School Support Worker?

About the author

Jo McCarthy, Federation Education Support Worker, Stoke Hill Nursery, Infant and Junior School

Jo's job is to help our children get the best from their learning environment, and supporting parents and teachers in helping to make that happen.

Jo works closely with Educational Psychologists, Mental Health and Medical professionals, Social Workers and Emotional Health Practitioners, for adults as well as children.

One of the hardest life changing events children may have to face is hearing the news that mummy and daddy are not going to be living together anymore. Taking away routine, familiarity, loved ones and prized possessions from a child is a bereavement, a loss.

In the schools where I work, we do all we can to ensure both parents take an extra interest in their child's education, of course alongside Parents Evening and Parent/Teacher discussions. It's not unusual for us to arrange for mum or dad to come into school for lunch with their child, a tour of the school, some special non-rushed private time for the child to show their work to their parent. This is so effective if a contact plan is not as reliable as it should be, or possibly not as consistent. Or just even that your child is having a blip about missing mum or dad because they haven't seen them in a few weeks. This happens. Some of the most enlightening and emotional moments I have experienced in my role, is hearing a child thank their parent for taking some time out from life or work, sharing school lunch, often just a plain old cheese jacket potato with beans........"I never realised how much you cared about my school work because you are not at home to ask about it anymore'.

We are very quick to identify and step in when a contact weekend hasn't gone well or had to be cancelled at the last minute due to an unforeseen circumstance. School staff know your children very well, and the likelihood is they will see and sense if something isn't quite right after a weekend. Talk to school staff. Let them know if your child has said something about a contact time. A worry, a fear or an anxiety can lead to a child not wanting to come to school......but only because they need their safety needs topped up so want to stay home with a parent. That is very common, and the most successes we have had in helping children feel good about themselves, to improve their feelings of self-worth, is when parents communicate to us when things aren't quite right or appear to be going wrong.

I always regard our children in school as being like little bowls of ready-made pastry with the ingredients prepared at home. Sometimes, the ingredients are a little unbalanced, for a variety of reasons. No matter what we do to try to fill those pastry cases, we are never going to end up with a perfect pie. As parents, you provide the foundations (the ingredients) to your child's learning and to their future. Without that vital groundwork preparation done by you, everything we as a school do to build on those foundations could cause an overload and your child could topple under the added education and social skills teaching that we in school put on your child every day. Home and school, when they work together and communicate with each other, can form and produce the perfect ingredients and filling, the end result being a pie we can all be proud of.

8 pieces of advice we give parents who are going through separation

1. When announcing your separation, be as open and honest as you can. There is no need to share the intimate details, especially if other people are involved in a parental separation. Your children don't need to know that.

2. If you haven't got as far as arranging a contact plan, then tell them that. Ask them what they would like, how they would like it to work. Your child is putting their

faith in you and your ability to manage their safety and happiness. Giving them an aspect of control in their parent's separation will help enormously and will allow them to voice their own needs, if old enough to identify them.

3. If you have discussed contact arrangements, be very clear with when and how your children will see each of you. Discuss this together prior to talking to your children. They will need to know they will see you, and you must stick to what has been agreed. Never use contact time as a punishment or a flexible arrangement to meet your own needs and social lifestyle. It has to be set in stone, at least until your children are confident and satisfied that you are prioritizing spending time with them. You have told your children that you will always love them and you will always be there for them. Now it's up to you as parents to prove that to them

4. Think quality, not quantity. Make contact time special, but don't make allowances for what you know is not normally acceptable when your child is with the other parent. A one off late night is fine. But school nights are early to bed, homework is a must with whichever parent

they are seeing, untidy rooms are still not ok and treating others as we want to be treated ourselves is still a family expectation. Right? Parenting is a partnership, regardless of living arrangements. That has to be in your mindset from the start.

5. When children suffer a trauma, their primary need is to feel safe. Boundaries are more important than ever and relaxing those boundaries will allow your child to step out and over into the 'unknown' - this will no doubt make your child feel insecure and vulnerable.

6. Be nice about your ex-partner when discussing them with your child. Many of the parents I have worked with find that hard. No matter how much heartache you are going through, or have gone through during your separation, you must not allow that sense of betrayal to be passed to your children, no matter how subtly you try and make those under the breath comments. Your child will love his/her other parent, may even be worried about them and will most definitely miss them. They don't want to hear bad things said about them - that will only lead to resentment and anger directed at you, if not now, when they are old enough to

remember and understand.

7. Support each other as parents. You may not like each other as lovers, but when you created a child together, you gave yourselves a life-long job commitment - you became parents. Whatever it takes, grit your teeth, clench your fists, bite your tongue. When you are a parent, you are part of a duo. Be united in your expectations of behaviour - by creating a divide between you and your expectations will allow your child to escape right down the middle of you both, again, into unknown and unsafe territory.

8. Try and be as strong as you can, even though you may be breaking inside. If they see you frequently crumbling, falling apart and losing control, the chances are they will too.

Final thought

Separating parents doesn't have to mean the end of a family as many first fear. Just a changed one. With both parents pulling together, working together, communicating with each other, (or engaging with alternative communication methods), there is absolutely no reason why your children can't develop and mature into the grounded and confident young people you want them to be.

There are people and support lines you can contact, ordinary teens just like me that will always be a shoulder to cry on. Jade (17)

Co-parenting: alternative but effective?

About the author

Andrew Spearman, A City Law Firm

Andrew is a founder of A City Law Firm and is distinguished for his work in helping couples complete their journey through surrogacy. He is a firm advocate of LGBT rights in this field (as is the firm as a whole) and engages government bodies and fertility organisations to advance their understanding of surrogacy procedure and practice.

Every family is different; every child's upbringing unique. However, having more than two adults in a child's life is not particularly uncommon in a modern family, as couples separate and new partners arrive on the scene. Step-parents have been an accepted form of parenting for a significant period of time.

In contrast to step-parents however, laws on co-parenting, which have radically changed this year, specifically affect individuals who wish to conceive a child together but are neither in a relationship or ever intend to

be. A prime example of this would be when a gay man wishes to have a child with a lesbian. Unlike with surrogacy arrangements, there is no immediate intention of removing the rights of the biological parent from the arrangement but often a common wish to jointly raise the child.

The respective biological parents may also have a long term partner or Civil Partner of their own and wish this person to have a role in the child's life. As there can only ever be two legal parents, it is important at the outset that people understand how the law addresses who can be on the birth certificate and retain this legal right. However, there is also the option to grant 'Parental Rights' which governs who can make decisions about fundamental aspects of the child's life, such as medical procedures, education or religion and this can be granted to a third or fourth party.

The law can be complicated so we have set out a number of scenarios to demonstrate how it might work for you. In each scenario Sarah is the birth mother and Mark donates his sperm via artificial insemination

Scenario 1

Mark and Tony are in a Civil Partnership and Sarah, a single woman, conceives at home using Mark's sperm. Mark and Sarah will be the legal parents as far as the law is concerned, can be named on the birth certificate immediately and will be considered financially liable for

the child. It is interesting to note that, as with heterosexual couples, Sarah will have to give consent for Mark to be on the birth certificate otherwise an application to court is needed. Once Mark is on the birth certificate he will have Parental Responsibility for the child and can make decisions in relation to education, health and religion.

Tony, in contrast, has no automatic rights or obligations towards the child. In comparison to surrogacy where you would want to remove the birth mother entirely, co-parenting is structured towards keeping the mother involved. Therefore, the best option available to Tony is to sign a Parental Responsibility Agreement with Mark and Sarah. He will then acquire the power to make decisions regarding the child while Sarah and Mark's rights are left intact.

Scenario 2

The facts are the same as above, but this time Sarah conceives the child through a licensed UK fertility clinic. As Sarah is not married or in a Civil Partnership (but she does have a partner Jane), she will have the choice to nominate who the second legal parent is. This person would have to sign a number of forms at the clinic consenting before conception, but they then will become the legal parent and have the right to have their name added to the birth certificate upon application. It is important to note that the birth mother can choose who the second parent is and this can be Mark, Tony or

Jane. They will then be the legal parent with financial liability. It is important to note that if no second parent is nominated Mark will automatically become the legal parent and acquire financial responsibility, but will not gain parental responsibility or appear on the birth certificate.

If Mark has signed the forms, he will be the legal father and so will be financially liable for the child, but he will still have to apply for parental responsibility either by having his name put on the birth certificate or ask the court to grant a Shared Child Arrangements Order (either with consent of the birth mother or not).

Scenario 3

The facts are the same as above but this time Sarah is in a Civil Partnership with Jane. Whether the child was conceived at home or at a clinic, as the birth mother is in a Civil Partnership, Jane will appear on the birth certificate (there are only a few exceptions). Mark will not be the legal parent of the child and if he or Tony wishes to gain Parental Responsibility for the child, they will need to apply for a Shared Child Arrangements Order from the court. Provided that all the parties consent to this, this can be a relatively straightforward process. However, it is important to note that such an order will still not place either Mark or Tony on the birth certificate.

Co-parenting agreements

The above is a simple overview of the law and may not specifically apply to your circumstances. However, whichever scenario applies to your own a Co-Parenting Agreement is strongly recommended between all the parties before conception. While this document is not strictly legally binding, it is incredibly persuasive if the court becomes involved at a later date and it can help to understand how the child will be raised and what each party's roles and responsibilities will be. It can include issues ranging from who the children live with, contact, education and any religious influences. This will hopefully avoid any disputes at a later date and give important structure and stability in a growing child's life.

In conclusion...

The law in this area is intended to be flexible in order to adapt to each family's unique circumstances. Regrettably as a direct result, the law is also fairly complex and so for each family the best course of action will have to be assessed on a case-by-case basis.

If you are looking to enter into a co-parenting arrangement, then seeking independent and professional legal advice before you embark on the process is essential. While fertility clinics are incredibly helpful, do not assume that they will know all the answers or understand the legal complexities of the situation.

I was never going to be able to control what my parents did, I could never have changed it because they're their own person just as I am mine. Kay (16)

Housing & finance

We need the security of knowing we are safe, have a roof over our head, and enough food and resources for the future. When we know this we can then channel all of our energies into feeling healthy and happy. This chapter explores the essential elements of security and safety - money, homes, pensions. Though these may be the last things you feel able to think about in the whirlwind of separation, discussing and planning housing and finance from the very start will smooth the transition into life post-divorce.

My soon to be ex-husband has money all over the place. Where do I start?

About the author

Rachael Oakes, Freeths

Rachael is a specialist divorce lawyer, accredited mediator and collaborative professional dealing with all areas of family work including divorce, civil partnership proceedings, all issues relating to cohabiting couples and children. She also specialises in the preparation of pre- and post-nuptial agreements.

It isn't unusual for one person within a marriage, let us say the husband, to be in control of the parties' finances. This does, however, mean that the other party has little or sometimes no knowledge of their financial circumstances.

Duty of full & frank disclosure

If the financial matters that need to be resolved when going through a divorce are, or become, bitterly contested, there can be all sorts of allegations of non-disclosure or even fraud against an ex who does not disclose details of their financial circumstances or discloses income and assets that may be a lot less than what the other party expected.

There have even been cases where one party, again let us say the husband and in anticipation of getting divorced, may try and divest himself of assets so as to produce a more modest balance sheet, but a party who does this has to be very careful. A party going through a divorce cannot take any action that would deliberately minimise the other party's claim. To do so could, potentially, even amount to fraud. This could mean that any financial settlement reached during a divorce could be set aside and potentially, in the case of fraud, the guilty party might even be prosecuted for perjury.

To offer some sort of reassurance, each party going through a divorce has an ongoing duty to provide full and frank disclosure about their finances until a financial consent order is made. It is only on the making of such an order that the financial settlement the couple reach is legally binding on them both.

It is also important to remember that your instructing solicitor, if you use one, are officers of the court. This means that they cannot mislead the court; neither can they present a financial picture that does not represent the truth. Furthermore, solicitors cannot continue to act for a client who refuses to tell the

The last mile in a settlement can be hardest. All anger/distress/sorrow is still there, but rather than resting upon a wide ranging dispute, it weighs HEAVILY on the issues which remain. The argument about the teapot is not about a chattel, but the last totemic lash of the tail.

Rhys Taylor, The 36 Group

truth.

Judges do not like a party who doesn't comply with the duty of full and frank disclosure. If one party refuses to disclose financial information or deliberately delays the court process it can lead to a Judge drawing an adverse inference from their behaviour, to their detriment.

Freezing assets

Depending on your concerns about the finances, it is possible to freeze the other party's assets if you are certain that the other party, again let us say the husband, is shortly about to sell or get rid of assets with the intention of preventing you from receiving some of that financial benefit. This is not just limited to assets in the UK - it can relate to assets worldwide.

So, on a practical level what can you do then if your ex has money all over the place?

Don't pry!

First, it is important to remember that you must not open your ex's post or log in to their email or accounts. Up until 2010, it was possible to do this and make copies of information found, a useful tool if one party thought their ex was trying to hide assets. However, a case now known as *Imerman* swept away those rules meaning you can no longer use information obtained in that manner. So, do not be tempted to do this but do make a note of any information about assets (e.g. a statement that is left, say, on the kitchen table or in a room that you both normally use, i.e. a joint study). This can then be cross-checked against the information your ex does provide when you exchange financial information

in due course.

Secondly, make a list of what you do know the two of you have together as this will be a useful checklist. Your lawyer may also want to know about certain aspects of your relationship that might be indicative of your lifestyle during the marriage. With this in mind, also make a note of what holidays you took, where you travelled, how much they cost and how the trips were paid for. How often would you eat out?

Also, remember there are different ways that couples can reach a financial agreement and most processes will require exchange of financial information. Once that exchange has taken place, there is then the opportunity to ask questions on the other party's disclosure. It's at that stage that, if you think information is missing or has not been fully disclosed, questions

Maintain your network of friends. Don't hide away into a new boyfriend/girlfriend.

Lucilee, Mum

can be raised in the hope that the other party will then provide full and frank disclosure.

Furthermore, whilst it is always a very last resort, there is always the ability to ask the court to deal with the financial matters. In that scenario and once the court timetable has been issued, if one party still does not comply then it is possible to take enforcement action at that stage.

Finally, whatever your circumstances, we would always recommend you obtain legal advice early on so that you fully understand your options.

Knowing where you stand from a legal perspective offers individuals peace of mind so they know the next steps involved and how they can best move things forward.

POST-SEPARATION SUPPORT

Once you have separated the need for support can be vital. You can find support in many places and from different people. Below are some options:

- Family

- Trusted friends

- Relationship counsellors

- GPs

- Family solicitors

- Support groups - Only mums, Only dads, Voices in the Middle, Gingerbread to name but a few

- Samaritans

- Citizens Advice

Adele Ballantyne

My parents paid the deposit on our house. Does my ex have a claim on this money?

About the author

Jennifer Curtis, Maguire Family Law

Jennifer specialises in issues relating to relationship breakdown, including divorce, financial matters, children and domestic abuse.

The family home is, in almost all cases, the central consideration for a separating couple.

There are different scenarios where this question may arise and the outcome will depend on:

- whether the separating couple are married/civil partners or not; and

- whether the deposit was paid as a gift or a loan, and whether there are any documents confirming this.

Unmarried couples

For unmarried couples, the starting point is quite crude and the way in which the house is dealt with starts with the records held at the Land Registry. If the money paid by the parents is to be returned to them, then this may be recorded at the Land Registry as a loan or 'charge'.

If one of the parties, or indeed the parents, wish to argue that the Land Registry record does not properly reflect what they intended, then this can potentially be challenged through the courts. There would need to be clear evidence of the contributions and everyone's intentions (i.e. was it a gift or a loan?) if the claim is to succeed.

Married couples/civil partners

For a married couple, the court is less concerned about following the specific records and the Land Registry and more focussed on dealing fairly with the parties' assets.

Two of the key principles that the court takes into account are:

- the parties' needs; and

- the family home usually has a central place in any marriage.

For these reasons, the court may not be readily open to arguments about a payment from one party's parents towards the home. The court may have no choice but to look at the money in the house (the equity) and to simply question how this money can best be used to meet the parties' needs.

However, there are some circumstances where the court may find it is able to consider taking into account the source of the deposit:

- If there is a formal loan agreement detailing how much has to be repaid and when, then the court may well take that into account when considering how much equity there is in the property. However, even if a loan

I just wanted to please my dad, because if I told them I wanted to go home he would be upset. Jade (17)

agreement is taken into account, the court may find that if the parents were prepared to loan this money for the purchase of this house, they may be prepared to loan these sums again to their child once it has been repaid.

- If the money can be shown as being gifted to one party, the court may be prepared to entertain the idea that this is an unmatched contribution from that party and may take this into account if there are sufficient assets available to meet the other party's needs.

One complicating factor could be if it is disputed as to whether or not the money given by the parents was intended to give them an interest in the property or not. There may be circumstances where the parents need to become involved in the dispute between the parties so as to protect their position. This is known as 'intervening' in a case. This can, unfortunately, make the legal process longer to resolve and can potentially increase the legal costs of the parties (as well as any legal fees the parents incur).

How to avoid this problem

No couple likes to think about what would happen if they separate and often a gift from parents is a welcome boost at the beginning of a relationship. However, a reasonable and clear conversation at the outset may help to avoid problems later on.

The key things to consider are:

- If the parents expect to be paid back, then this should be recorded in a legal document which makes clear the terms of repayment and what would happen if the parties

separated before the money was repaid.

- If the money is a gift but to only one party, then the couple should record this. If the agreement is that one party should receive the gift back first, before any other proceeds of sale are divided, then this can be recorded in a deed and the Land Registry informed; and if the couple are married or intend to marry, then this agreement can be carried through to a pre-nuptial or post-nuptial agreement.

Summary ·

Resolving a couple's finances on divorce/separation can be complicated, and the contributions from one party (or their parents) are only one potentially relevant factor. Early legal advice should be sought to ensure that the most appropriate legal arguments are pursued in the strongest possible way; and always bearing in mind the question of proportionality. The approach to be adopted for a £2,000 gift towards a million pound property may be very different to the approach for a £30,000 gift towards a £150,000 property.

There are no fixed answers when it comes to finances on divorce, with the court considering what is fair and considering whether or not an equal division of assets is fair or not. For a non-married/non-civil partnership case, the initial answer may be more straightforward i.e. what the records at the Land Registry show; but that in turn makes the legal arguments more complicated when one party seeks to challenge this.

Notes

Remember that whatever happens, the two parents will be that child's two parents forever. One day that child may graduate from university or get married, and those two parents will have to face one another at those special events.

Laura Martin-Read, Family Law Group

Pre- & post-nuptial agreements: when would you use one?

About the author

Samantha Jago, Solicitor & Mediator at RHW Solicitors

Samantha has a wide range of experience in all family matters including prenuptial agreements, cohabitation agreements, divorce, disputes over jurisdiction, cohabitation disputes, civil partnerships, children matters, injunctions and resolving financial matters arising from the breakdown of a relationship.

Pre- and post-nuptial agreements (together called 'nuptial agreements') are agreements made either before or after marriage, setting out how the parties to a marriage will deal with some or all of their matrimonial assets. They are particularly useful for preserving assets that were acquired before marriage (for example, shareholdings in family companies, or particular family assets and heirlooms), and also for regulating what may occur in the future if one or both parties inherit assets and heirlooms from their own side of the family.

Is the law catching up?

Nuptial agreements are a rapidly developing area of family law. It is a useful example of how society eventually forces the law to adapt and change.

The past: The background

Over 20 years or so ago nuptial agreements were not generally enforceable in English law. There were two fundamental problems. Firstly, Judges were not allowed to give effect to agreements that contemplated the possibility of a future divorce, and were therefore void because they might encourage the breakdown of marriage. Secondly, Judges were not allowed to give effect to agreements that might interfere with the courts' own powers and way of doing things at a later date.

The present

Gradually, however, there have been various landmark legal cases which have opened up the ability of the courts to deal with nuptial agreements, and in 2010 in a ground-breaking case (*Radmacher v Granatino*) the Supreme Court said that, amongst other things, provided each person has a full appreciation of the implications of the agreement, then the court should give effect to those agreements unless it would be unfair. These principles are more or less identical to the principles applied in most divorce financial settlements.

Current practice

Accordingly, it is possible to make nuptial agreements either before or after the marriage, and provided that they are fair and that they also meet various other conditions and guidelines, they are likely to be enforced by the court. One difficulty remains, though, and that is when the parties have children.

Clearly, if the parties make a nuptial agreement and then go on to have children together, but the nuptial agreement does not make proper financial provision for those children, then the courts will override the agreement in order to provide for the children. That is, and always has been, the courts' priority. In a sense there is nothing new or unusual about the courts taking such a view (it is probably what we would want the courts to do!).

Think about what you want your life to be like post-separation and work out what is important to you and relay this to your lawyer. Try to focus on the bigger picture.

Fiona Turner, Weightmans

Current & future guidelines

Combining the current practice and future guidelines, it is recommended that the following are observed:

- Ensure that any agreement that you draw up is contractually valid and enforceable (there are certain legal rules to be followed before a contract becomes legally valid).

- Ensure that the agreement is also drawn up in the format of a deed, and is executed as a deed.

- Ensure that the agreement contains a statement signed by each party that he or she understands that the agreement will restrict the courts' discretion to make financial orders.

- Ensure that the agreement is not made during a period of 28 days ending on the day in which the marriage (or civil partnership) is formed.

- At the time the agreement is formed each party must have made full written disclosure of all information about their finances to the other.

- Ensure that there is an option to review the nuptial agreement at specific "trigger events" such as the birth of a child, purchase of a replacement property or, for example, every 5 to 10 years to ensure it remains relevant.

- At the time the agreement is formed both parties must have received independent legal advice, and a compelling statement to that effect

should be contained on the face of the agreement.

The future of nuptial agreements

It is interesting that lawyers have moved to catch up with society's needs, but what is now needed is for the politicians to move too and to bring a draft bill relating to nuptial agreements into effect. There have been moves towards this but a significant change in legislation is still yet to occur.

However, even before the draft bill comes into effect, do please remember that agreements which follow the guidelines set out above are still likely to be viable and accepted by the courts today, provided that they also meet the overall objective of being fair.

In the middle of a difficult divorce/separation pensions are probably the last thing on the mind. Children, housing, and immediate financial concerns of course take precedence. It is worth taking note of the advice in this section though and raising pensions with your solicitor/mediator if you have appointed one.

What is child maintenance?

About Gingerbread

Gingerbread is a national charity that provides expert advice, practical support and campaigns for single mums and dads.

Child maintenance is when a parent who does not live with their children pays money towards their upkeep, including food, clothes, and other essentials. It helps to provide a stable home and is a way of making sure that children are brought up in the best circumstances possible.

Child maintenance usually works by the parent who does not live with the children most of the time paying money to the parent who does. It can also involve that parent spending money directly on their children as part of a family-based child maintenance arrangement.

Child maintenance has nothing to do with contact between parent and child. Legally a parent must pay maintenance even if they do not see their child. Equally a parent cannot be denied contact for not paying child maintenance.

Who has to pay child maintenance?

Child maintenance is a legal requirement, as all parents have a responsibility to look after their children financially. Any parent who has their child living with them for less than half of the time is expected to pay child maintenance. The amount of child maintenance that has to be paid will depend on how much time each parent has the children staying with them.

Child maintenance has to be paid for:

- all children under 16;
- children under 20 who are in full-time non-advanced education (A-levels or equivalent);
- children aged 16 or 17 who are not in full-time education but are registered to work or train with a careers service.

If you are not sure if your situation requires child maintenance you can always contact Gingerbread or Child Maintenance Options for advice (see below).

How to arrange child maintenance

There are three main ways of organising child maintenance:

- Family-based arrangement;
- Consent order;
- Child Maintenance Service.

If you and the other parent can reach an agreement then you can make either a family-based arrangement or a consent order. If you can't agree with the other parent then you can pay child maintenance through the Child Maintenance Service (CMS).

Making a family-based arrangement

A family-based arrangement is simply when parents agree among themselves how child maintenance is going to be paid. You can make any arrangement you like for child maintenance, as long as both parents agree. This could be regular payments of money, lump sums for certain items, or payments in kind such as buying school uniforms or nappies. It could be a combination of these things.

The Child Maintenance Options service can provide a form for you to write down what you agree. You can download it at www.cmoptions.org.

Family-based arrangements are the simplest option for child maintenance, as you can agree on whatever amount of child maintenance you want, in whatever form you want. Unlike other options they are free. It also helps to have an agreement in place to avoid potential arguments later on.

However, these arrangements are not legally binding - they're simply an agreement between both parents. If one parent changes their mind or stops paying there is no way to legally enforce it. If the arrangement does break down, you can still use the Child Maintenance Service.

Consent orders

If you reach an agreement with your child's other parent another option is to apply to the court to make the agreement legally binding. This is called a consent order. Both parents must agree to the terms of the order. A consent order is usually used when parents are divorcing and sorting out their finances, so it might include other agreements, such as who is going to pay the mortgage.

Consent orders have the advantage that they can be enforced through the court if the child maintenance isn't paid. However, this option is more costly as there are court fees for making and enforcing the order. You should also get independent legal advice which you would have to pay for. You can't apply to the Child Maintenance Service for one year after a consent order is made, so you should be confident that it is going to last for the foreseeable future.

Using the Child Maintenance Service (CMS)

If you can't reach an agreement with your child's other parent you can use the CMS to arrange child maintenance for you. You can also do this if you don't have contact with them.

Before you can apply to the CMS you must call Child Maintenance Options to discuss if you could make a family-based arrangement instead. If you have tried this and failed, or if such an arrangement wouldn't be possible, then Child Maintenance Options will give you a reference number that you can use to make your CMS application. There is a £20 application fee.

The CMS will work out the

amount of child maintenance which they believe should be paid and notify both parents. They can take action against the paying parent if they don't pay the required amount. However, you can't control when and how the CMS takes enforcement action if the other parent doesn't pay.

Using the CMS is the best option to use if you have experienced domestic abuse. Gingerbread provides information about how to apply to the CMS if you have experienced domestic abuse.

How much should child maintenance be?

There is no definite answer to this. If you are using the CMS the amount is worked out using a standard formula that takes into account the paying parent's income and any other children that they are responsible for.

If you are making an arrangement with the other parent you can arrange any amount of child maintenance you like, as long as you both agree. Knowing how much to agree on can be difficult. The Child Maintenance Options leaflet 'Talking about Money' can help you look at your budget and what may be needed for children at different ages. The leaflet is available on their website and an online maintenance calculator can be found at www.gov.uk/calculate-your-child-maintenance.

What if the other parent lives abroad?

If your child's other parent lives outside the UK you won't be able to arrange child maintenance through the CMS. If you can't reach a family-based

arrangement then you could apply for a court order that can be enforced in the country where the other parent lives. This is called a Reciprocal Enforcement of Maintenance Order (REMO). You can call Gingerbread for more information about this.

Where to find help

Gingerbread: www.gingerbread.org.uk

The single parent charity Gingerbread provides lots of information about child maintenance and other issues affecting single parents on their website. If you are the parent who would be receiving child maintenance you can also call the Gingerbread helpline on 0808 802 0925.

Child Maintenance Options: www.cmoptions.org

Child Maintenance Options provide free information and support on child maintenance. They are also the organisation you will have to contact before you can use the CMS. You can call them on 0800 988 0988.

Family Mediation Council: www.familymediationcouncil.org.uk

Mediation is where an independent professional mediator helps you come to an agreement with your child's other parent. The Family Mediation Council can put in you in touch with a local mediation service.

My ex just refuses to pay any maintenance. What are my options?

About the author

Lisa Burton-Durham, Family Law Partners

Lisa is a Director and Resolution trained Collaborative Lawyer with Family Law Partners. She has over 25 years' experience in family law. Lisa specialises in finances and children issues following separation, divorce or civil partnership dissolution.

The answer to this question is that it all depends on what type of arrangement is in place for receiving child support from the other parent in the first place. Unfortunately, there's no single answer or solution that will suit every case.

The different types of arrangements you can put in place are expanded upon below.

Family Based Arrangements

Parents don't have to use the Child Support Agency (CSA) or Child Maintenance Service (CMS) to arrange child maintenance.

Over half a million families choose to make arrangements between themselves. This is known as a 'family based arrangement'.

You should be aware that family based arrangements are not generally legally enforceable.

What should you do if child support is not paid in accordance with your agreement?

If it is safe to do so, speak to the other parent. Try and find out why they have stopped paying. If it is shown that circumstances have changed, try and agree a voluntary change to your agreement between you.

If that doesn't work you will need to contact the government's statutory service, the CMS. The CMS will work out the amount of child maintenance due using a standard formula. They can collect payments on your behalf and can also take enforcement action if the other parent stops paying through this arrangement. But please note, there are fees associated to using the service depending on whether you use the full collect and pay service (currently the paying party pays a fee of 20% of the payment and the receiving party pays 4%) or just the assessment service.

Statutory child maintenance arrangements

The CMS opened in 2012 and manages all new applications for a statutory arrangement. The CSA is now closed for new applications but it does still manage many arrangements that were set up before December 2013.

An arrangement through the CSA or the CMS is legally binding. This means that action can be taken by either service if the payments stop.

The CSA and CMS have significant powers which include the following:

- Taking money directly from the non-payer's earnings (a **deduction from earnings order**).

- Taking money from the non payer's bank or building society account (a **deduction order**).

- Applying to the court for a **liability order**. Once a liability order is obtained it can be referred to the bailiffs who can take property away from the non payer to be sold to cover arrears and costs.

- Applying to the court for a **charging order**. Once obtained the non payer can be forced to sell property and use the money to pay off child maintenance arrears.

- **Taking money from the non payer's benefits** if your arrangement is under the CSA scheme.

- **Applying to the court for the non payer to be disqualified from driving or sent to prison** if all other enforcement methods have failed.

- Recently new powers exist to **disqualify a non-resident parent with child maintenance arrears from holding or obtaining a United Kingdom passport**

The CSA or CMS also have the power to apply to the High Court to prevent the non payer from getting rid of property or transferring property if they believe he/she is doing this to avoid paying child maintenance or if already disposed by applying to the court for an order to cancel the sale or transfer of property.

There is usually no time limit within which the CSA or CMS can collect child maintenance arrears including the discretionary power to recover from a deceased's estate.

Consent Orders

This is a type of court order which makes the agreement legally binding. These types of agreements are often made with the benefit of legal advice, usually within divorce/dissolution/separation proceedings. They can be enforced through the courts if either parent is in breach. So, what should you do if payments stop?

1. If payments under the consent order are not made you should apply back to the court to enforce the payment of arrears.

2. The court's permission is needed to recover arrears of longer than 12 months.

3. If, and only if, the order is more than 12 months old you can approach the CMS so that they can carry out a fresh assessment. However, the CMS can't recover arrears under the court order.

4. On an assessment, payments may change - up or down.

You should also note that if you apply to the court to enforce the arrears, the other parent may well make their own application to the CMS so that they take over the responsibility of the child maintenance arrangements as opposed to the family court.

It's important to get any application to the court to enforce arrears as quickly as possible.

Like the CSA and CMS, the court can take a number of enforcement measures which include:

- A deduction from earnings order;

- Taking property away from the non-payer to be sold to cover arrears and costs;

- Taking money directly from the non-payer's bank account;

- Forcing the non-payer to sell property and use the money to pay off child maintenance arrears;

- A judgment summons which means the non payer could be sent to prison.

Please note there are fees in applying to the court and if you use solicitors you will need to assess the cost/benefit of paying for advice and/or representation.

Enforcing child maintenance if a parent lives abroad

Parents can still make family based arrangements even if they live in different countries.

In some circumstances parents are also able to use the CMS if the paying parent lives abroad and they are a civil servant; works in Her Majesty's Diplomatic Service; is a member of the Armed Forces; works for a company that is based and registered in the UK or is working on secondment for a prescribed body like a local authority.

Countries in the EU - at least for the moment - must enforce court orders for child maintenance and decisions made by the CSA or CMS.

If the paying parent lives in Australia the Australian CSA may be able to assist.

If the paying parent lives outside the EU and Australia and you have a court order in respect of child maintenance you may be able to get the court order enforced in a foreign country. The UK has a number of reciprocal arrangements with foreign countries (which is updated regularly). Where reciprocal arrangements exist and a maintenance order needs to be enforced abroad the first port of call is the Reciprocal Enforcement of Maintenance Orders (REMO) Unit.

The impact of Brexit is likely to involve significant changes to some of the reciprocal enforcement arrangements.

Top tip - get some early advice before arrears get too large and look at the most cost-effective way to deal with matters based on your personal circumstances.

My partner owns the house but I have done all the improvements and upkeep. Where do I stand?

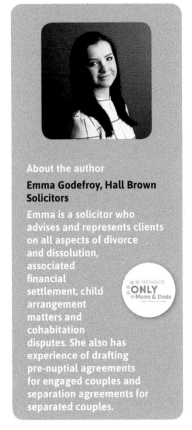

About the author

Emma Godefroy, Hall Brown Solicitors

Emma is a solicitor who advises and represents clients on all aspects of divorce and dissolution, associated financial settlement, child arrangement matters and cohabitation disputes. She also has experience of drafting pre-nuptial agreements for engaged couples and separation agreements for separated couples.

It is increasingly common for couples nowadays to put the idea of marriage on the backburner, instead prioritising setting up a home together. Some may not want to marry, being content to live together. Often one of the couple will move into a property already owned by the other, or they may buy a home in one of their names.

They may open a joint bank account, combine their finances, purchase furniture and undertake renovations to the property, often blissfully unaware that there is no such thing as a 'common law marriage,' or rights for cohabitees (see Question 6 and the Must read article on Page 30 for more information).

This means that if the property is owned in the sole name of one party, the other has no legal entitlement to a share of the property, even if they have spent considerable sums on improvements and upkeep.

This article will briefly explain the legal position arising out of this scenario, and then detail the practical measures you can take if you find yourself in this difficult situation.

The law

The law that applies in this scenario is general property law. There is no specific law which governs couples who live together.

It is set out in the Trusts of Land and Appointment of Trustees Act 1996 ('TOLATA') which creates legal principles based on the law of trusts. The question is who owns the beneficial interest in the property, and therefore an interest in the equity in the property?

The starting point is that the beneficial interest will follow the property title. Therefore, if a party is named on the title (they are named as the registered owner with the Land Registry), this constitutes an express trust and they will have the legal and beneficial interest.

The problem above arises when the property's title is held in one party's ('A') sole name, but another person ('B') has invested their own time and money into the property and view it as their home. The other party, B, will then have to establish a beneficial interest by way of a constructive trust, in order to establish an interest in the equity in the property.

To establish a constructive trust, B needs to show **all** of the following:

1. A common intention between the couple that B was to have an interest in the property, and not just that they would live there;

2. B acted to their detriment or altered their position in reliance on the common intention; and

3. It would be unconscionable for A to deny B's interest.

'Common intention' is usually expressed during conversation and it does not need to be a formal offer and acceptance. For example, if A says to B "what is mine is yours", or "you will always have an interest in this house", that would constitute an express intention. Sometimes behaviour in itself, such as opening a joint account and combining finances, may not in itself constitute common intention although it is still useful to refer to as it shows a pattern of behaviour.

'Detriment' is a concept subject to the discretion of the Judge if the dispute were to proceed to court. Improvements and upkeep to the property are likely to qualify, depending on the level of detriment incurred. Re-decoration or low cost general maintenance is less likely to qualify; however, financing a new kitchen or replacing a roof, for example, is more likely to be considered as detriment.

It must then be decided, taking into account all of the above, whether it would be unconscionable (i.e. unjust or unfair) to deny B's interest.

I often tell the financially stronger party: "there is no weakness in generosity". So often people are told by friends not to be taken advantage of when in fact they want to provide for their family, but just don't want to be seen to be being rolled over.

Barbara Corbett, Corbett Le Quesne

Practical steps

If you find yourself in this situation, how, you may wonder, do you go about meeting the three-stage test in practical terms?

Litigation in this area can be very expensive, especially because these claims are dealt with by the civil courts, rather than family courts. Claims are potentially 'high stakes' due to the risk of paying your ex's legal costs as well as your own because, in civil cases, the general rule is that the loser pays the winner's costs.

Unlike family courts, civil courts are less interested in the concept of 'fairness.' Their role is not to adjust interests in a property, but rather to determine and declare interests. The status of your relationship bears no weight however long you have been living together (unless you are engaged, which means you may benefit from protection under the Married Women's Property Act 1870).

TOLATA litigation is front-loaded, and as a claimant you would be required to set out your case fully at the outset, with as much supporting evidence as possible. Often these cases can seem like 'one word against the other,' so a paper trail or other corroboration is key.

To evidence common intention, any written correspondence such as text messages should be produced. Was there a conversation before any improvement work took place on the property? Was there an understanding that if you paid for the improvements, that was your 'contribution' to the property? What discussions took place when the house was purchased

or when you moved in? Were promises made in the presence of, or were they repeated to, third parties? Consider the reasons why you were not on the legal title if there was a common intention you would have a share. Was it intended that you would be added to the legal title at some point in the future, but you simply never got round to it?

To evidence that you have incurred detriment by paying for improvements and upkeep for example, you should produce the relevant bank statements and invoices.

An alternative

As people are becoming more conscious of the expense and risks of starting formal court proceedings, they are increasingly open to attempting mediation as a much cheaper and more conciliatory option. Indeed, the courts will expect you to have tried mediation before starting proceedings. Rather than being subject to the decision of a Judge, bound by the strict statutory framework and inability to adjust interests, it is often preferable to discuss matters directly with your former partner with the assistance of an independent third party. This can be beneficial, especially where there are children of the relationship.

I'm separated and need to prepare a new will - 10 things to think about

About the author

Julie McDonald, Julie McDonald Family Law

Julie is a solicitor and the Principal of Julie McDonald Family Law. Her team of lawyers specialise in all aspects of family law including divorce, dissolution and separation, the associated financial settlements and issues relating to children, plus relationship agreements including prenuptial agreements and cohabitation agreements.

Everyone should make a Will and, if you already have one, review it regularly to ensure it reflects your wishes and the current law. Executors and Beneficiaries may die before you, children and grandchildren are born and may not be provided for and the law changes on a daily basis.

Many matters need to be considered when making a Will and if you are separated, it is even more important, particularly if you have children.

So, what are the 10 main things to think about?

1. **Executors** - you need to appoint someone to take care of your affairs when you die. Executors find out what you have got by way of assets, etc and then follow the terms of your Will. If you appoint just one Executor it is advisable to also appoint a reserve, just in case your chosen Executor dies before you, or is otherwise unable or unwilling to act. If any of your Beneficiaries are children or will not receive their share of your estate straight away, two Executors are required as they will become Trustees to look after the money for the Beneficiaries until they inherit.

2. **Guardians** - you need to decide who will look after your children if you die before they reach the age of 18. If you are separated, there may be reasons why it would not be in the best interests of the children for the other parent to look after them. Or, if the other parent dies before you, you need to consider who will look after the children. Your appointed Guardian would obtain Parental Responsibility, so would be legally allowed to make decisions about the upbringing of the children, e.g. medical decisions and choices regarding schooling (with anyone else who also has Parental Responsibility).

3. **The family home** - if you still own the family home with your ex, you need to take advice from a family solicitor to protect your interest/share. Also, in your Will, you need to decide how your share is dealt with. Are you happy for your ex to live in the property with your children until they reach the age at which they would inherit their share? Or should the property be sold and your share held in trust for the children?

4. **At what age should the children inherit** - this is always a difficult decision. Should the children receive their share of your estate at age 18, or should you stipulate age 21 or older? You will need to consider what the children will need and when, and also any potential tax implications, particularly when children are to inherit in their 20's or older.

5. **Pets** - deciding who has the family pets upon separation can be as difficult and emotional as who takes care of the children. However, only a small percentage of Wills have a provision for pets. You need to decide who will take care of your pets when you die and also whether you should leave a sum of money for their care.

6. **Excluding your ex** - if you are separated but still married, you need to include a clause in your Will to specifically exclude your ex (unless of course you do want to leave

them a share of your estate). Unless you are divorced and have a financial clean break (a Consent Order) sealed by the Court, excluding your ex in your Will is not enough to stop any claims. It is essential therefore to take advice from a family Solicitor at the point of separation or even if you are considering separation.

7. **Pensions** - although pensions are dealt with separately, you do need to consider who will receive your pension benefits when you die. You would need to contact your pension provider(s) and complete a nomination form or letter of wishes to deal with this.

8. **Life assurances and death in service policies** - as with pensions, you can nominate who is to receive your life assurance and death in service benefits when you die. You would need to contact the provider(s) and complete the necessary paperwork.

9. **Lasting Powers of Attorney** - making a Will deals with matters when you die. However, if you lose the capacity to deal with your financial affairs, it is immensely helpful and much cheaper if you have already made a Lasting Power of Attorney to appoint someone to deal with matters for you.

10. **Other considerations** - if you own a business with your ex, you need to consider how to deal with separating your business interests as well as your personal affairs.

There may be other issues to consider in addition to those outlined above. It is essential, therefore, to take advice from both a family Solicitor and a private client (Wills) Solicitor as soon as possible either after separation or when you are considering it.

Notes

The worst thing I remember was being sat on the floor between my mum and dad and being told to choose who I wanted to live with. Kaitlyn

What if we are separating but have a joint business?

About the author

Andrew Spearman, A City Law Firm

Andrew is a founder of A City Law Firm and is distinguished for his work in helping couples complete their journey through surrogacy. He is a firm advocate of LGBT rights in this field (as is the firm as a whole) and engages government bodies and fertility organisations to advance their understanding of surrogacy procedure and practice.

If you're shrewd then you may already have a Shareholders Agreement in place with deemed notice transfers and plans for this eventuality; your ownership and contributions to the business will be clearly documented and you will have service level agreements with restrictive covenants for all high level directors or managers.

Unfortunately, life is rarely found in such neat, square boxes that we lawyers dream about and, when pressing business owners, I often hear the words, "Isn't that all a bit unromantic?"

English matrimonial law

In summary, if you have no documentation that suggests otherwise, then all your assets (including the business value) go into a single 'matrimonial pot' and the court will consider a fair division of those assets between you. An equal division of the matrimonial pot is frequently the starting point for family proceedings and, unless you can show why that is unfair, it may also be the finishing point too.

If you own a business together, you will also have to decide the practicalities of how that falls to be divided. On this I always remind couples that the financial separation is exactly that: a *separation*. The aim is to divide assets between you and achieve a clean break as far as possible, not create new ties or obligations. If one spouse is the actual business worker and the other a more symbolic appointment (usually for tax reasons), then a court is unlikely to allow the symbolic director/shareholder to retain their shares and position as a part of the divorce. That doesn't mean they relinquish them for free either though.

In contrast, where the parties have set up the business together and work together at it, the outcome is less clear. Can you work together with your spouse for the business good? Can the business be divided without significant impact? How can one spouse justify keeping the asset to the exclusion of the other?

Business continuity and transparency

Before the above formal division of the matrimonial assets, you will still both remain joint owners of the business. If you do not have day-to-day involvement in the business, you may query if your spouse is being entirely truthful or transparent with the business accounts. If you are a director, then you are entitled to see those accounts and you can expect to be involved in any decisions. If you are a shareholder, then the rights are

I really want them to get back together and it work out, but it is not that simple. Emily (9)

different but can be exercised to gain information and hold directors to account.

A company's liquidity may also prevent a truly clean break from occurring. Be mindful of changes in business assets decreasing this liquidity, assets being sold at an undervalue or company goodwill being more conservatively valued. The family court has far reaching powers to reverse transactions or 'count in' assets at the actual value instead so that no loss is suffered, but it may become necessary to have an independent accountant to obtain the real business value.

Amicable resolution

Not everything has to end in an argument or a court battle. The reality for most couples is that the business is an asset which will be traded against other assets for either capital or income potential which is being gained or lost respectively.

If you wish to have a more amicable divorce when you own a business together, then here are some simple tips:

- Keep clear and distinct financial records; record monies paid in and withdrawn, clearly record any loans to the company and the intention for the repayment of that loan.

- Understand the value of the intellectual property (IP) and the goodwill of a business.

- If you are not actually working in the business, avoid making verbose claims of keeping shares or remaining a director. Remember, you are trying to separate assets, not simply wind up your spouse, and fairness will ensure the company value is accounted

for regardless.

- Instruct lawyers and good accountants known to resolve issues rather than litigate. Members of Resolution are committed to a non-confrontational approach and you should find a lawyer who has this membership.

- Mediation and/or arbitration is always available to discuss and agree matters amicably. They are forums designed to help challenge you both into finding a realistic solution, but they are not advisors.

Wider impact

Separating business assets is a difficult process, but acrimonious actions aimed at crippling the business or stopping it from working effectively will have longer lasting impacts not just for you both, but income available for your children and employment of your staff.

You should be realistic about how the business would continue and look to how both of you could go on to make your own money independently. Ultimately, the concept of 'fairness' will rule the day.

> More often that not, once a couple have reached an agreement over the financial division of assets, their relationship improves and they can parent more collaboratively. Uncertainty fosters mistrust and unpleasantness and once their financial future is more certain, they can concentrate on working together for the sake of their children.
>
> *Tessa Bray, Simons Muirhead & Burton*

What happens to my will on divorce?

About the author

Matthew Sterling, Arnold Greenwood Solicitors

Matthew is experienced in dealing with cases following the breakdown of relationships between co-habiting couples, pre- and post-nuptial agreements and disputes relating to children, including removal cases with an international element. He is a specialist divorce solicitor accredited by Resolution.

If you are separated from your spouse or going through a divorce you may not want them to receive anything from your estate in the event of your death and therefore it is important to think about your will. Even if you are separated, until decree absolute has been granted (which is the court order finalising your divorce), your spouse will benefit if they are named as a beneficiary in your will or, if you don't have a will, under the rules of intestacy. In these circumstances, it is best to seek advice about making a new will.

Once decree absolute has been

granted, your whole will is not automatically revoked. When you are divorced your will takes effect as though your former spouse has died before you. The effect of this is that any provisions contained in your will benefiting your former spouse will automatically be revoked upon the making of decree absolute. For all purposes, your former spouse will be treated as though they have died and will not inherit under your estate.

If your will specifies beneficiaries other than your former spouse, then your estate will pass to those beneficiaries in accordance with the terms contained in your will. If, however, your former spouse is the only beneficiary named in your will, then your estate will be distributed in accordance with the rules of intestacy, which may not be in accordance with your wishes. Consequently, if your former spouse is the only beneficiary, or the main beneficiary under your will, it is advisable to prepare a new will once decree absolute has been granted. These rules apply not only where your

former spouse is a beneficiary, but also to any provision appointing them as an executor or trustee; such provisions will also be automatically revoked upon decree absolute.

In circumstances where you still wish to provide for your former spouse, you are able to do so in your will but this intention would need to be expressly stated. You could, for example, create a codicil to your original will which provides that, although you are no longer married, your former spouse should still receive the benefit of any provisions you have made for them in your will.

Another important point to note is that a former spouse may still make a claim from your estate under the Inheritance (Provision for Family and Dependants) Act 1975. To avoid this, it is important to consider seeking a financial consent order as part of your divorce proceedings which can provide for a clean break preventing your former spouse from being able to make such a claim.

When dealing with assets like houses and work / private pensions we always recommend that parents take the best possible advice. Check the OnlyMums/Dads Panel www.thefamilylawpanel.co.uk (see Page 32) to find family law and mediation specialists who specialise in finance and pension law.

Will my husband's private pensions form part of the divorce settlement?

About the author

Pete Littlewood, Chafes Hague Lambert Solicitors

Pete is a Partner and Head of Family Law at Chafes Hague Lambert. He is collaboratively trained and always tries to help clients resolve issues in a collaborative and constructive way, guiding them towards civil resolution of their issues with former partners. He is also a Resolution Accredited Specialist.

There are usually a number of financial issues to be resolved following the breakdown of a marriage. These often include dividing capital assets and pensions and the provision of maintenance for either party of the marriage or any children of the family.

The court has the power to make orders including maintenance for one of the parties (and in certain circumstances for any children of the family), property adjustment orders, lump sum orders and pension sharing or attachment orders.

The court has very wide discretion and takes various factors into account when considering what orders should be made. The court will consider all the circumstances and will give first consideration to the welfare of any children of the family. The court will then have regard to the following factors:

- The income, earning capacity, property and other financial resources which each of the parties to the marriage has or is likely to have in the foreseeable future.

- The financial needs, obligations and responsibilities which each of the parties to the marriage has or is likely to have in the foreseeable future.

- The standard of living enjoyed by the family during the marriage.

- The age of the parties and the duration of the marriage.

- Any physical or mental disability of either of the parties to the marriage.

- The contributions which each of the parties has made or is likely in the foreseeable future to make for the welfare of the family.

- The conduct of the parties.

Full & frank disclosure

The starting point in any financial settlement is to establish the nature and extent of each party's income, assets and liabilities. Both parties will be expected to provide full and frank financial disclosure of their respective financial positions whether you reach a voluntary agreement or not. The Form E Financial Statement is a good template to use to ensure that all the relevant information is provided.

It is important that pensions are not overlooked when considering a financial settlement on divorce as consideration will need to be given to how both parties' needs can be met on retirement. If either party has any pension funds then they should be considered.

Details of the pension fund including the cash equivalent

Message to parents: support whatever the child wants to do, and don't influence their thinking. Jade (17)

value should be obtained from the pension provider along with information about any other benefits. The cash equivalent value reflects the capital value of the pension benefits which have been accrued to date or which are already in payment. With some schemes the transfer value may be different to the actual fund value and advice will need to be sought from a pension expert.

How to deal with pensions on divorce

When considering if a private pension will form part of the divorce settlement there are three main ways of dealing with pensions on divorce:

Pension sharing - this allows a percentage share of a member's pension to be transferred into the ex-spouse's pension scheme.

Pension offsetting - this involves balancing the value of a pension against another asset. For example, if one party retains their pension fund the other party retains a bigger share of the other assets.

Pension attachment - this is where a percentage of a member's pension is set aside for the ex-spouse to claim on retirement.

There are situations where a private pension would be more likely to form part of a divorce settlement. For example, one party may have taken time out of work to care for children and not had the opportunity to build up their own pension where the other party may have built up a significant fund.

In some cases, the pension may be the only significant asset. In other cases the pension fund

may be even more valuable than the family home.

In some circumstances it may be appropriate for there to be an unequal division of the pension capital, for example if one party has a greater income need in retirement due to a health problem or disability.

There are situations where a private pension would be less likely to form part of a divorce settlement, for example where there is a short childless marriage or where the parties divorcing are still both young and retirement is some time in the future.

A pension might not be considered as part of a divorce settlement where one party has other non-pension income available to them in retirement which is sufficient to meet their needs.

Pensions are complicated and expert assistance will often be required from an actuary and an independent financial advisor.

Top tips

It is important that you try and resolve financial issues amicably without court proceedings. There are a number of options available from direct negotiations, lawyer led negotiations, mediation and collaborative law.

If you can reach an agreement then a consent order should be prepared to outline the agreement reached to ensure that it is legally binding.

Not all cases are settled by voluntary agreement and if an agreement cannot be reached within a reasonable period of time, or if one party will not co-operate or provide financial

disclosure, then it may be necessary to commence court proceedings.

The Family Justice Council has prepared a useful guide called Sorting out Finances on Divorce which is designed to help litigants in person. The guide provides a general overview of the law and some explanation of issues that may arise including pensions.

Going to court is rarely the answer when sorting out the financial issues that need to be addressed as part of a divorce or separation. Most cases settle before any final hearing because Judges encourage and support discussions and negotiations but by then a lot of money will have been spent on the litigation process. Where possible you can avoid costly litigation by negotiating and preparing at the outset a list of what you really want and what you would be prepared to negotiate on. You will then have a very clear focus and an idea of what your negotiation parameters are.

Rachael Oakes, Freeths

Can you advise me on pension sharing?

About the author

Mary Shaw, David Gray Solicitors

Mary is a solicitor and mediator who advises on pensions as part of divorce and works with couples in mediation and collaborative practice who are sharing their pensions.

KISS - the phrase 'Keep It Simple Stupid'- whilst rather forthright, can be a reminder not to over-think some things when getting divorced: for example, painstakingly trying to value all of your house contents is probably a waste of time.

But not so for pensions - because pensions are complex and can be a much more valuable asset than you may realise. Only married people and civil partners can share their pensions on dissolution of their relationship. The court is tasked with considering whether the pension in those circumstances should be shared.

If you are divorcing or contemplating divorce then this is what you need to know:

Two of the most important decisions that you will make about your divorce will be about timing and process: pushing on with a divorce when your spouse is reeling from the news could backfire very badly; and deciding how to sort your separation/divorce business out can be a critical decision determining what state your relationship with your ex will be in at the end. This is key if you have children or if you have warm relationships with your in-laws. Talking-round-a-table processes such as mediation and collaborative practice lend themselves very well to discussing how to sort out pensions

Your spouse or civil partner's pension is likely to be a matrimonial asset which can be shared. Clients will often say 'He (or she) worked for it and earned it and I don't want any of it'. The court looks at contributions and whilst your partner was earning their pension you were quite possibly bringing income into the relationship or staying at home keeping house and raising children: in other words your marriage was a joint effort.

Before you make any decisions about whether you want to share or have a share of a pension it is important to get its 'cash equivalent value' (CEV). This is easily obtained and you are entitled to a minimum of one a year at no cost to you (Providing the pension is not in payment; if it is in payment you may pay a fee for the CEV).

The cash equivalent value of a pension is not a pound for pound accurate measure of the pension's value - this is where things get complex and 'apples and pears' becomes a good way of explaining why: a personal pension could be considered an 'apple' whilst many occupational pensions (in particular public sector and 'uniformed' pensions) are 'pears'. This is because £10,000 of capital value of a police pension will buy you a whole lot more than £10,000 of a personal pension with, say, Scottish Widows or Standard Life. If there is a choice of pensions to share, and you share the wrong one, both parties may end up worse off than if the right pension were shared.

If you and your partner want to come to an arrangement where one of you keeps their entire pension and the other one gets more of the savings or the house, a pound of pension cannot be treated like a pound of savings or a pound of equity in your home so understanding the 'offset' value of your pension will be important. This is a highly technical area.

The particular rules of different schemes can inform how you should share pensions to *both* get maximum income from them.

So doing a quick calculation on the back of an envelope risks you losing out on income for the rest of your life at a time in your life when you could need it most - unless you can successfully sue your solicitor for negligence because they did the calculation on the back of the envelope.

How can people deal with debts when they divorce or separate?

About the author

**Hasan Hadi,
Southgate
Solicitors**

Hasan specialises in all areas of divorce and family law but focuses mainly on representing medium to high net worth people going through a separation. Hasan is a Resolution member and an Accredited Member of the Law Society's Family Law Advanced Panel.

When married couples divorce or cohabiting partners separate their first concerns will probably be about child arrangements or how to divide their assets.

Before long, however, they may have to tackle an equally difficult issue: how to settle their debts, some of which might be in joint names. Who is liable to pay? Could you end up being held responsible for your partner's debts, even if you knew nothing about them?

The law can be complex and to make things even more difficult, different rules may apply for married and cohabiting couples.

Debts in one person's name

As you might expect, you will be liable for debts that are in your name only, but not for those in your partner's name only. However, for married couples, debts in one person's name that were used for the benefit of the family may be subject to division or sharing between the spouses or civil partners.

It is generally more difficult for cohabiting couples to seek the other partner to share debts in sole names, unless there is a legal agreement between them.

Debts in joint names

Things get a little more complicated for debts in both your names. You will be held jointly responsible and separately liable for these debts - this means that the creditor can either seek for both to settle the debt, or pursue only one of you to settle it.

What can the court do?

It is not unusual for couples to disagree about responsibility for debts and they may have to take legal action to determine liability. In these circumstances, the court will look at the debt and consider how it arose, whether the partners benefited jointly or individually and then decide who should bear the burden of repayment.

For example, if the debt was used to pay for school fees or a family holiday then it's likely that the court would rule that both partners are jointly liable.

However, if one partner incurred the debt largely for his or her individual benefit then the court may decide that they should bear most or all of the liability. This could apply in cases where one partner has spent lavishly on a hobby, bought an expensive car for their own use or run up gambling debts.

The courts are more likely to order that liability should be shared for debts incurred during the marriage than before the relationship began, although this might not apply in exceptional circumstances, such as in a very long marriage.

Deciding responsibility for debts can be complex whether you are married or cohabiting and it is always advisable to seek advice from your solicitor before incurring any debts.

Gingerbread

Gingerbread
Single parents, equal families

About Gingerbread

Gingerbread is a national charity that provides expert advice, practical support and campaigns for single mums and dads.

A single parent is typically defined as any parent with the majority care of their children. It doesn't matter how old or young you are or the circumstances under which you became a single parent - Gingerbread can help.

We know that circumstances are not always black and white, and parents may well consider themselves single parents when they do not have majority care of their kids (often known as a 'non-resident parent') - we welcome you to use our online services if you see yourself as a single parent. You are likely to find, however, that our helpline and training courses are less suited to your needs. Our policy and campaigning work also tend to focus on single parents with majority care.

Support from Gingerbread

We know that single parenthood can be tough. But bringing up children as a single parent is also commonly the proudest achievement of many of the parents that we hear from at Gingerbread. We're here to support every single parent - whatever you're facing - and to champion your voice, needs and concerns so that your family can thrive.

Depending on your needs, the charity has a range of free, impartial services that can help.

Looking for information?

Finding accurate, trusted information when you need it can be difficult. Gingerbread has a website full of information tailored to single parents - covering everything from housing and benefits, to going on holiday, arranging child maintenance payments or getting support with childcare.

Need more in depth advice?

Most parents find that they get the answers they need from Gingerbread's website. But sometimes there's a complicated problem that can't be resolved without expert advice. That's where Gingerbread's free,

The grass always seems greener, but it isn't. You can soak in long hot baths, watch whatever you want on the telly, get a cat and wear orange.

Patricia, Mum

confidential helpline comes in. Our advisors are all trained to speak about any issues which may impact a single parent, so there's no single topic we cover. However, some common examples of topics people call us about are child maintenance, contact, employment, education, welfare benefits and tax credits, housing, and debt.

Hoping to speak to other people in your situation?

There can be highs and lows to being a single parent, and sometimes only others going through the same thing can really understand. So, at Gingerbread, we offer ways for single parents to connect with each other. Run by single parent volunteers across England and Wales, Gingerbread friendship groups provide a space for single parents to support each other, or just have a cuppa and chat while the kids play. Alternatively, if you'd prefer to hear from others from the comfort of your sofa, the Gingerbread forum (only for single parents) is a great way to ask questions, chat and receive support.

Want to get back into work?

Some single parents can find it hard to find suitable work that fits around caring for their children. In London and the North West, in partnership with Marks & Spencer and others, we support single parents who are out of work through training and work placements.

Org

Changing the system

Our work doesn't end there though. Our services can help with some of the challenges you might face now, but we also want to make sure that single parents face fewer hurdles in future.

Our campaigns, research, and policy work share the concerns of single parent families with a wider audience and make sure that your experiences are listened to.

We research how single parent families are impacted by government policy and influence the government and the public to ensure that families, whatever their shape and size, are valued and treated fairly.

Working alongside single parents, Gingerbread has secured changes that make the Child Maintenance Service fairer, encouraged companies to create single parent-friendly holiday deals, encouraged mayors to offer more childcare support for single parents, and more.

We're here for you

There are nearly 2 million single parents in the UK - and everyone can benefit from Gingerbread's support and be part of shaping the work that we do.

Join Gingerbread as a member (it's entirely free!) to receive regular information and updates that affect you and your family, and be part of a community that is making the world a better place for single parent families.

Notes

CHILDREN SAYING ONE THING TO ONE PARENT AND ANOTHER THING TO THE OTHER

Children do this in families where parents are still together. They are even more likely to do this when parents are living apart.

When parents don't 'get on' or have poor communication, this can cause many problems.

Some tips for when this happens:

- If your child comes home following a contact and says, for example "Mum says I can have that new bike", before you react with fury, upset, and anxiety, check it out.

- Calmly and without emotion ask your child if that statement is correct.

- Mention that you're probably going to check with mum that she has indeed said that.

- Often if the child is playing one parent against the other they may confess at this point.

- At a convenient time contact mum and explain the situation in an enquiring and non accusing way, for example: "Matt came home today and said that you had agreed that he can have a new bike. I am just calling to ask what, if anything had been discussed?"

- If you can agree in the early days of separation how to handle this kind of situation then calls like this will become familiar.

Adele Ballantyne

How can I move from a 2-income to a 1-income household?

About the author

Tom Farrell, Tom Farrell Financial & Mediation

Tom is an experienced Family Mediator and Independent Financial Planner. He runs a specialist practice, exclusively working with people who are going through separation or divorce.

Divorce or separation can mean radical financial change. You may not have much experience of dealing with certain aspects of your finances and that can cause anxiety.

Add the stresses of change and the emotional context of your situation to the mix and you have the perfect excuse to put things off. Although this might be a natural response, it's not a sensible one.

If you get yourself organised and work in a methodical way, you will be able to get to grips with everything and I promise you that you will feel better once you've done it. Taking control and having a sense of future is worth the effort.

Cash flow

Cash flow is money in, versus money out. Without an understanding of this, you won't be able to plan, identify problems or make sensible changes.

Money In

This could be from:

- earned income or pension, after tax;
- maintenance that is paid (maintenance is tax free);
- benefits received (some are taxable, some are not);
- interest or income from savings and investments (again, some are taxable, some are not).

Money out

Have your bank statements to hand, or access your accounts online, and make a note of everything you spend your money on, like:

- rent or mortgage payments;
- credit cards and loans;
- household bills;
- weekly shopping;
- insurance costs;
- car and transport costs;
- children's clubs and activities;
- school costs;
- nights out and entertainment;

- cash withdrawals (try to think about what these are usually for).

If more is coming in than going out, then great. That means you have scope to save and to plan for other things, like holidays and bigger expenses.

If it's the other way around, then don't panic. With a little analysis, you can work out the shortfall and try to do something about it. Look again at your expenditure and find ways to economise.

Tips

- Try to put your cashflow into a format that you can keep track of and update over time. You could put it into a spreadsheet or write it out. Doing this will cement the information in your mind and help you understand it. Alternatively, use one of the online tools provided by charities and other organisations.

- Don't be afraid to ask for help. If you can afford to pay for advice, then find a good independent financial planner. If not, then talk to trusted family and friends who may be able to help you. You could also book an appointment with Citizen's Advice, or access some of the free online resources available.

- Don't ignore things on your statements that you can't identify. You may be paying for something that you don't need!

- Try to categorise your expenditure, between the essentials and the things that you could do without if you had to.

Debt

Mortgages

You may have an existing mortgage. If so, take the time to understand it:

- how long is it for?
- how much do you still owe?
- is it a repayment mortgage, or interest only?
- if it's interest only, how are you planning to repay it?
- are there penalties if you change your mortgage or repay early?
- do you have Life Insurance to cover your mortgage?

If your financial circumstances have changed, your ability to borrow money will have changed too. Mortgage lenders are far stricter than they used to be about lending. They will want a detailed assessment of your income and expenditure, to asses 'affordability', before making a decision.

If you receive maintenance, it can count towards income for some lenders, but usually only once it has been in payment for six months or a year and only if it is subject to a court order.

There are new mortgage products coming to the market all the time and some of them will allow your family to offer security or to borrow on your behalf.

If your mortgage deal has come

to an end, you could see your payments go up, or down. It might be a good time to look at a new deal with your existing lender or move to a new one.

Credit cards, store cards, overdrafts and loans

It is frightening how easily people can access borrowing and how quickly it can get out of control. You need to know:

- what is the balance owing?
- what interest rate you are paying?
- are your payments just covering the interest or paying the debt off too?
- are you near your borrowing limit?

Tips

- Consolidating debts can save money, or reduce monthly payments, but be careful about the overall costs and how long you will be paying things off.
- Seek proper independent advice before making mortgage decisions, it could make the difference between getting a mortgage or not and could save you a lot of money.
- If you are struggling to make your mortgage or debt repayments, don't ignore it. Seek debt counselling advice and open up a dialogue with the people you owe money to.

Benefits

You may be entitled to benefits now that you didn't qualify for before. Child benefit, free childcare, Universal Credit; the list is long and the rules can be very complicated. Taking the time to find out what you are entitled to could be life-changing

though, so put in the work.

Tips

- Access the many free online resources provided by government and charities, they will give you the best start in identifying what you might be able to claim.
- Make an appointment with Citizen's Advice or a charity that offers advice.

Resources

Money Advice Service: https://www.moneyadviceservice.org.uk

A huge resource for all aspects of managing your finances. Register on their site and you can save your work as you go. Excellent budget planner and good signposting to all manner of advice.

Citizens Advice: https://www.citizensadvice.org.uk

An excellent website with lots of information and good advice. You can make an appointment for face to face advice and telephone them too.

Expect a big change in your lifestyle. Your life is going to change dramatically - it is the surprise of this that can often lead to resentment and breed conflict. Your partner's life will be changing too and they will be having the same problems, adjusting as you are. Yes, really.

Peter Martin, OGR Stock Denton

What is a Form E?

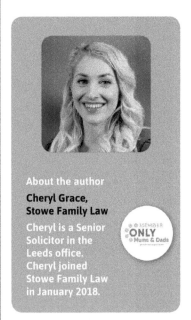

About the author

**Cheryl Grace,
Stowe Family Law**

Cheryl is a Senior
Solicitor in the
Leeds office.
Cheryl joined
Stowe Family Law
in January 2018.

The Form E is a court document otherwise known as a Financial Statement. It is used within financial remedy court proceedings to enable both parties to provide their financial disclosure. The document, which runs even as a blank form to some 27 pages, requests comprehensive information and documentation to confirm your financial position.

However, the Form E is often also used when separated spouses are trying to resolve financial matters outside of the court process. It is a standard format for providing disclosure which lawyers are familiar with and, because of its comprehensive nature, should ensure that all key information is provided. As both spouses have to complete their own document, it should also ensure that each spouse provides the same information and

documentation if applicable to them. As a result, each spouse should be aware of the true financial position of the other. It is like putting both pieces of a two-piece jigsaw together to get a full picture.

What's in the form?

At the back of the document, there is a list of the documents to be attached (if applicable), including mortgage information, statements for bank accounts, investments and life insurance policies, business accounts, pension valuations and income details through pay slips and/or tax returns.

A Form E must be completed as accurately as possible with up to date information. There are serious penalties for inaccuracies or excluding assets if the form is used in court proceedings. Further, if it transpires that the Form E was not accurately completed and a settlement is reached without court proceedings having commenced, it is then possible to get that agreement set aside.

The Form E contains 5 sections. The opening section of the form gathers general information about you, your children and your living arrangements so is usually fairly straightforward to complete.

Section 2 is the most time consuming as it asks for financial information concerning property and personal assets. It is divided into 10 parts which are discussed in more detail below.

Part 1 requests:

- The valuation of the family home and any other land and buildings you own along with details of the outstanding balance of any mortgage and estimated costs of sale. You do not have to provide a valuation of any of the properties or land from an expert when you complete your Form E but you should provide your best estimate of the current market value;

- Details of any bank accounts, savings and investments which are in your sole name or in joint names (whether with your spouse or someone else) with details of all bank accounts and investments. For each, you must confirm the value of your interest;

- Details of any life insurance policies you have either in your sole name or in joint names;

- Information about monies owed to you, cash sums and personal belongings worth more than £500.

Part 2 requires:

- Details of any liabilities of any kind which you have and are not mentioned elsewhere in the Form E (for example, a mortgage would not be included in Part 2 as it is included in Part 1);

- Information about whether any capital gains tax is due upon the disposal of any of your assets

Part 3 requests:

- Details of any business interests you have along with copies of your business accounts for the last 2 years;

- Confirmation of any directorships you hold.

Part 4 asks for:

- Details of any pensions you hold other than the basic state pension. The most critical piece of information in this section is the cash equivalent transfer value of your pension. Additional important information is required to complete this section and the best way to obtain everything is to write to each of your pension providers, with a pension enquiry form (known as Form P) to complete at an early stage as it can take a while for the provider to respond. If your lawyer makes the request on your behalf, you will need to provide your authority to the pension provider releasing information to them. Your lawyer will be able to help you with this.

Part 5 concerns:

- Any other assets not captured elsewhere such as share option schemes, trust interests, and assets held on your behalf by a third party. Your lawyer can give you further guidance on whether assets should be included in this part or elsewhere.

Parts 6 to 10 request:

- Details of your income from employment, self-employment or partnership, investments, state benefits, or any other income such as pension income. It is important that you provide accurate details

of your income and that it is inserted in the appropriate section included in these parts. Your lawyer will be able to give advice on this.

Section 3 requests:

- Details about the income needs of you and any children living with you. Essentially this asks what your outgoings are on a weekly, monthly, or annual basis, whichever timeframe you prefer to use. I always use monthly. You should complete sections 3.1.1 and 3.1.2 (if applicable) fully so that they are accurate as this could affect any financial settlement or order made. Your lawyer will probably have a precedent schedule which sets out the usual items of expenditure people have to pay and using this will help to ensure that you do not miss any items from your schedules at sections 3.1.1 and 3.1.2 (if applicable).

- Information about the capital needs of yourself and your children. You can include items such as the cost of a new house (if you know at this stage what that cost will be), a car or replacement furniture. Your lawyer will be able to give you advice about the items you can include and the amounts you can include as your estimated cost, if indeed it is appropriate to include an amount.

Section 4 asks:

- For details about changes in your assets and income;

- For information about the standard of living you and your spouse enjoyed whilst you were married;

- Whether you made any

particular contributions to the family;

- For details of any bad behaviour by your spouse;

- If there are any other circumstances which are relevant to the distribution of assets, income and liabilities such as your earning capacity and inheritance prospects; and

- For financial details about any new cohabitee you have.

The sub-sections in section 4 are an opportunity to provide information which is relevant to the financial agreement or order made. Your lawyer will be able to advise you on what matters may be relevant in your particular circumstances, and to draft the wording in the sub-sections in a way which assists the case you wish to put forward.

When completing the financial disclosure forms, print off the form and have a pad and pencil with you. Cross out the pages that are not applicable to you and make a list of information that you need to obtain - breaking the task down helps to make it feel more achievable.

Cressida Burnet, Cressida Burnet Mediation

Section 5 requests:

- Details of the order you seek. Your lawyer can give you advice on what is appropriate in your case taking into account your particular circumstances.

The section, once completed, will explain to your spouse and the court (if applicable) what you are asking for by way of a financial remedy.

Exchange of Form E

The Form E is often exchanged early in court proceedings or in out of court negotiations as, without financial disclosure, a solicitor cannot advise on settlement and the court cannot make a final order in contested proceedings. This disclosure is really a type of due diligence to ensure that both spouses and their lawyers are fully informed of each other's financial positions. Whilst you may think you understand your financial position completely, do not assume that your lawyer does. It can be difficult to deal with assets that have been overlooked after the court has approved a settlement so it is essential to complete the Form E properly.

Following exchange of Forms E, sometimes there are questions to be raised asking for further information and documentation. For example, a spouse may have disclosed a life insurance policy on their Form E but they may not have provided a copy of the policy document. Without the

policy document, there is no documentary evidence that the policy exists and that the surrender value is as stated on Form E. Such questions may either ask for missing information or evidence, or they may ask questions arising from information that has been provided e.g. a question may arise about transactions in the bank statements provided. Wherever possible try to anticipate these questions by annotating your documents or including further information in the Form E.

Once any questions have been answered fully, the spouses should have a full picture of one another's financial positions and this is a solid foundation on which to start settlement negotiations.

What do I include in the Form E?

Most of the questions the Form E asks are factual in nature, so you should include information taken from the supporting documents you enclose. Make sure that you use the correct information, as otherwise you will not be setting out your true financial position.

Preparing the Form E

Given the importance of the Form E, it is always advisable to get legal advice even on a draft that you have prepared. However, if you are unable or do not wish to obtain legal advice, my top tips are:

- Carefully read through the document to see what information and documentation it requests. The list in the previous section of this chapter will help you but it is critical to read through the whole document carefully;

- Start preparing your Form E and, in particular, collate supporting documents at an early stage as it will probably take longer than you think to obtain everything;

- When you have a date for exchanging Forms E, if you have a pension (whether in payment or not) and your annual statement is more than a few months old, contact your pension provider to request documentary evidence of the cash equivalent transfer value;

- Gather all the documents you need to enclose; separate them into the sections they appear in the Form E; label and order them accordingly. For example, copies of your bank statements should be labelled section 2.3 and appear before copies of ISA statements which should be enclosed at section 2.4;

- Prepare an index for the documents you plan to enclose;

- Organise your bank statements in chronological order;

- Make sure the content of your

Message to parents - Don't guilt trip us! Meg (17)

Form E is accurate and as up to date as possible according to the documents enclosed. For example, if you have a bank statement which says that the balance of your bank account was £500 on 7 September 2018, make sure that you write this information at section 2.3. If the balance is different because you do not have the most up to date statement then add a note in the Form E to confirm this and the date of the balance you are quoting;

- Be entirely honest and truthful. Ensure you disclose all your assets, income and liabilities. There are consequences for failing to do this when in court proceedings as it constitutes contempt of court. It is also very easy to be tainted as a non-discloser and everything you subsequently disclose will be treated with greater suspicion which will not assist either in settlement negotiations or court proceedings.

Following these tips will hopefully help to ensure that your Form E is well organised and therefore easier for all to work with. It is always recommended, however, to get professional legal advice from a family lawyer to make sure the content is accurate and aligned with your case.

Notes on completing Form E

Are assets split equally on divorce?

About the author

Andrew Meehan, MD Harrogate Family Law

Andrew is experienced at: dealing with difficult spouses; finding hidden assets and income; solving complex divorce cases; divorces involving businesses, pensions, properties, trusts and/or high incomes; getting a fair split for his clients.

It is not uncommon for one party to have left dealing with money during the marriage to their other half. One party may have been the breadwinner and the other the homemaker. English and Welsh law recognises that the contribution made by the person who has not been the breadwinner can be equally as valuable as one made by the person whose job it was to provide financially for the family. Neither party is supposed to be discriminated against because of the roles they adopted in the marriage.

This means that, when a marriage comes to an end, you are entitled to ask for a share of the assets built up during it. This is the case even if the assets are not held in your name. They will form part of the financial resources that will be divided between you.

Each of you can claim for financial provision to be made for you from the property and assets. For example, the law gives the court the power to order that property should be transferred to one of you, or that it should be sold and the proceeds paid out in whatever way is fair. It also has the power to split pensions and to require one party to pay maintenance to the other, amongst other powers.

However, every marriage is different. This means that there is no fixed formula for deciding who gets what on divorce. It is normally a question of negotiation. A financial settlement on a divorce must be "fair" in the eyes of the court. To decide what is fair, various factors must be weighed into the balance, such as:

• the welfare of any children under 18;

• what assets you each have, can access or may have in the foreseeable future (whether they are in sole or joint names);

• what you both earn and could earn;

• what your expenditure is;

• how old you both are;

• your state of health;

• how long you have been married;

• what you each need to house yourself and pay for everything you need to;

• whether you had a pre-nup and, if so, what it said and whether it was fair.

The starting point is that the assets you have built up during the marriage, as well as the house you occupied as the family home, should be shared equally. This starting point is, however, often departed from and an unequal share of the assets happens. This is because simply dividing the assets built up in the marriage might produce an unfair outcome to one party. The priority tends to be to ensure that the parties and their children have a roof over their head and enough money to live on, as far

My parents' separation changed my whole world, not necessarily for the better, but I had no option but to go along with it. Cerys (15)

as is possible.

Assets that are not built up during your marriage might be treated differently. This is because they have come from an external source, not by your joint efforts. For example, an inheritance, or a gift, or some other asset that a party owned before the marriage might not be shared.

The starting point for these types of assets is that they should be put to one side and not taken account of in the split of assets. However, very often these assets do need to be looked at to ensure that the settlement is fair. If they have increased in value during the marriage, this increase in value can be shared even if the underlying assets aren't.

The source of these assets and how they have been used might be very relevant to how they are treated. If they have been paid into a joint account and used in some way for example, then this might also affect the starting point.

Deciding what is a fair outcome is an art not a science because of the lack of a fixed formula. Divorce tends to be a once in a lifetime event, so people tend to have little to no experience of what a fair outcome is likely to be. For this reason, it is vital that you get legal advice from a specialist solicitor. They can check that your spouse's financial resources are fully investigated.

One party might also try to hide assets or use them so that there are fewer assets to divide between you. In addition, there can be different ways to value assets which can produce markedly different results. A specialist solicitor can check that

the assets have been valued fairly and that your position is protected against them being hidden or used.

Most importantly, an expert solicitor will have far more experience than you of divorce cases. They will be able to advise you what they think a fair outcome is likely to be. This will ensure that you do not make any mistakes which could otherwise cost you a lot of stress and money.

Notes

I always remind parents who are arguing on silly things that their job is to make this process as easy as possible for their children; that they ultimately win if in 20 years time their children have no negative effects from the divorce or separation and are able to form happy healthy relationships for themselves. That is the true win - not managing to keep a bit of furniture etc.

Charlotte Harper, HF Legal

Mediation

Before separating, you may never have heard of Mediation. This important process is demystified and explored in this chapter with articles clarifying what Mediation is, what happens in a Mediation Information and Assessment Meeting (MIAM) and how to write Parenting Plans. Mediation supports the key challenge in separation and divorce - communication, with one author describing mediation as putting "a break in the spiral of conflict". Having a third person can help couples to discuss difficult topics, to behave non-defensively and to think about the long-term.

Top tips which may help you before your first joint mediation meeting

About the author

Sheena Adam, Children First Family Mediation

Sheena is a mediator with and Director of Children First Family Mediation based in Manchester. Sheena has worked extensively with separating families in the voluntary and statutory sector for over 30 years.

These are my 5 top tips:

1. Try to focus on the future and solutions rather than the past and recriminations - consider what you want to achieve from mediation for yourself and your family. Blame is very tempting but does not usually help change anything and uses up a lot of your precious emotional energy. If there is a lot to sort out then it can also help to ask yourself

   "What is the one most important thing I wants to come away from today having achieved?"

2. Think "problem solving". Try to imagine this might be someone else's problem and what would you suggest. This is not to deny your strong feelings but to apply some of your positive rational side and to avoid the emotional aspects overwhelming you.

3. Mediation often talks about "Win/Win" outcomes. This means that we are aiming for outcomes which benefit everyone especially any children involved rather than one person feeling they have gained a lot and the other very little. That means thinking of compromises which you can both live with. If both of you approach mediation in terms of there being only your own preferred outcome, then you are locked in conflict "My way versus yours". However, if you can look wider at alternative solutions which might not be perfect but can work for both of you then these are more likely to be achievable. For example, if both of you really want the children to live with you, which is understandable as you both love them, then a shared care arrangement can work really well and help the children avoid the loss of either parent.

4. During the joint mediation session, you will be keen to say all that is important to you. The mediator should help ensure this happens for both of you, but it will also help if you can try to slow down and listen to your ex-partner rather than assume that he or she has nothing useful to say. You might be surprised and avoid missing perhaps a positive offer or willingness to meet you half way.

5. Towards the end of your joint mediation session make sure that you understand and are on board with what has been agreed. Again, the mediator should help clarify and summarise what you have agreed but it is really important that you do not:

   - agree to something which you know will not work

   - feel awkward about asking questions to make sure you understand the outcome

   You should then both receive identical written summaries of the outcome which reflect what you have agreed.

Can I refuse to go to mediation?

About the author

Deborah Butterworth, Mediation Dispute Solutions

Deborah helps separating and divorcing couples to find fast, practical ways to end their relationship amicably and with less stress. She has had a broad experience in conflict resolution and encourages creative thinking. In parenting plans she helps parents to successfully move forward as separated co-parents.

People only ask the above question when they are convinced they should be going to court. They feel that a Mediation Information and Assessment Meeting (MIAM) is just another thing preventing them from getting what they want or they are the respondent who is being led unwittingly towards the court.

The answer of course, is yes - you can refuse. Mediation in the UK is still voluntary. A mediator cannot work with reluctant participants who are unwilling or unable to listen and engage with the other partner. However, the real question is:

'Should you refuse and what are the consequences if you do?'

Role of the mediator

Family mediators have two very different roles in the family law process. Their main function as a mediator is facilitating and working with separating couples to help them find a way to agree how to co-parent, separate their finances and assets and make sure they both have somewhere to live and the money to make those proposals work. People who engage in this process will work hard with a mediator to sort out their difficulties.

The other role for an Authorised Family Mediator is to see the prospective applicant (and invite and encourage the respondent) so they can hear more about their dispute resolution options before they make the court application. This can and, in my view should, be seen as an opportunity to put a break in the spiral of conflict which so often surrounds and takes over when couples separate. The mediator sits down separately with each client and tells them about all the different methods people use to decide what will happen to their assets and children. A mediator cannot force someone to mediate or sit in the same room with the other person and talk. The mediator informs each person about the process of mediation and where it fits in family law.

So often the history of conflict and the reasons why the relationship broke down makes everything too raw and too personal. The couple have seen each other as vulnerable, hurt, angry and scared. They also know about each other and will often accuse each other of lying, being vindictive or just out to hurt the other person. With that back-drop what is the point? Most people have probably never been in such a toxic relationship breakdown before. By trying mediation, a couple has nothing to lose and everything to gain, starting with their self-respect. If a couple can separate with dignity they give their children a good future and save money.

Remember it is easy to make a mistake when dividing assets if you don't fully understand the process or long term implications of your choices (legally and personally). A good mediation service will step you both through the process and help you both consider options and outcomes that are safe for each of you.

Sarah England, Green Light Mediation

Mediation v court

To put the family court process and the requirement for a MIAM into perspective, only a very small number of family disputes end in a contested court hearing. How many of the potential cases are diverted from the court after the MIAM process is hard to tell because the best result is a consent order. The National Audit Office reported in 2014 that the average cost and time of mediated outcomes was significantly less than using other methods - money and time which could be better spent re-building lives and moving forward.

If a court application is made without attending a MIAM a person may find their case is adjourned, pending a MIAM, causing a delay they did not want. Under section 10(1) of the Children and Families Act 2014, it is now a requirement for a person to attend a MIAM before making certain kinds of applications to obtain a court order. (A list of these applications is set out in Rule 3.6 and in paragraphs 12 and 13 [of the Act].) The person who would be the respondent to the application is also expected to attend the MIAM. The court has a general power to adjourn proceedings in order for non-court dispute resolution to be attempted, including attendance at a MIAM to consider family mediation and other options.

If the parties do not attend they are losing the opportunity to stay in control. Most family mediators can give couples a real insight in to what the court process is like. As soon as the application is received, the court takes over the case management and the couple's control over the outcome diminishes.

Going for a MIAM works because it gives the couple an opportunity to realise that they need to resolve the problem.

They can do it with a mediator and they can get what they want: an end to the conflict, a fair financial settlement and a happy life for their children.

Notes

HOW DO I GET ACROSS HOW MUCH I LOVE MY CHILDREN?

This can be an issue for the resident parent but often the non-resident parent worries about this too.

Some top tips for showing children that you love them:

- Tell them, whenever you can.

- Be interested in their lives, listen to them and validate their experiences.

- Keep in touch. We live in an age where we have never been more connected so text, email, skype, send letters and cards.

- Try to negotiate with your ex about attending important events such as sports, parents evening and performances.

- Try to share taking children to any clubs they attend regularly (it's great if you can as everyone benefits).

Adele Ballantyne

I have an abusive ex. Is mediation right for me?

About the author

Anna Vollans, Vollans Mediation

Anna has extensive experience in the resolution of interpersonal disputes, often in high-conflict situations. She is an accredited family mediator with the Family Mediation Council and a member of the Family Mediators Association. She is qualified to undertake Child Inclusive Mediation.

I f you want to take your case to court, in most cases (unless you have made an allegation of domestic abuse and have specific evidence in support of the allegation) you will be expected to attend a Mediation Information and Assessment Meeting (MIAM). For anyone wanting to explore whether mediation is right for them, attending a MIAM is a really good place to start.

What is a MIAM?

The MIAM is an individual face-to-face meeting that will take place between you and the mediator. Your ex-partner will not be present at the first meeting. Sometimes people bring a friend or family member to the first meeting for support.

The mediator will not expect you to attend a joint mediation session. At the first meeting, the mediator will help you to consider whether mediation is right and safe for you and will identify when mediation will or will not be suitable. Where mediation is unsuitable the mediator will make sure you know the alternatives and will signpost you to appropriate sources of advice and support.

At the MIAM, the mediator will hear about your situation which will include asking about whether domestic abuse has occurred in the relationship. Domestic abuse is 'any incident or pattern of incidents, of controlling, coercive or threatening behaviour, violence or abuse (whether psychological, physical, sexual, financial or emotional) between individuals who have been intimate partners or family members regardless of gender or sexuality'.

What if you're at risk of harm?

Abuse covers a wide spectrum of behaviour including isolated incidents, on-going patterns of behaviour, threats of and actual physical violence. The mediator will discuss with you how the abusive behaviour and its impact might influence what happens in any joint mediation session.

If it emerges that you or your children are at immediate risk of harm, the mediator will help you to consider what action to take. Sometimes it might be necessary for the mediator to break their usual duty of confidentiality to ensure the safety of a child or an adult. In these circumstances, mediation would not be appropriate.

It is important that in the mediation setting, you not only feel safe but also comfortable and free to speak openly and honestly so that any discussions are balanced. If you would feel unsafe, fearful or intimidated by coming to a joint mediation session then it might not be suitable for you.

However, even where there has been domestic abuse, some people feel strongly that they want to mediate because of the possible benefits it offers. Mediation can still take place as long as all those involved are willing to participate, and appropriate safety measures can be put in place.

Shuttle mediation

For example, mediation can take place on a 'shuttle' basis meaning that you and your ex-partner sit in separate rooms and the mediator moves

between you. If you are fearful about coming into contact with the other person outside the joint session, you can arrive and leave at separate times and wait separately. In any mediation, the mediator will ensure that there are 'ground rules' to ensure that mediation is undertaken in a respectful and cooperative manner. If the ground rules are broken and the levels of conflict are excessive or harmful, the mediator will intervene and, if necessary, stop the session.

The key message for anyone who has experienced domestic abuse is that family mediation is a voluntary process and a joint session will only take place if you decide, with a mediator, that mediation is right and safe for you and where appropriate, the right safeguards are in place.

Mediators are trained, skilled and experienced in working with families where there has been domestic abuse. Your safety, and the safety of your children will be any mediator's main concern.

National Family Mediation (NFM)

About the author

Jane Robey, CEO National Family Mediation

Jane became CEO of National Family Mediation (NFM) in 2004, having previously practiced as an accredited family mediator, Professional Practice Consultant and service manager. She is a published author on family mediation and a contributor to Government policy-making forums.

Family mediation was founded in 1982 by NFM.

NFM provides family mediation services direct from the national office and through a network of member services. NFM is a founding member of The Family Mediation Council, the regulator of family mediation.

Our unique and defining characteristics are:

- A focus on children;
- A not-for-profit system of providing services;
- Mediation that seeks to improve communication as well as achieving settlement;
- Specialised experience in the field.

NFM and its member services differ from other family mediation providers because:

- Services are distinct and separate from legal practices;
- In addition to providing family mediation that covers all issues including children,

finance and property they also provide adult and child counselling and support services;

- The fee structure is affordable;
- It is a network of services linked by affiliation criteria that supports professional and business practice;
- Our network provides national coverage and is responsive to local need.

Mediation is not an easy process. It takes guts and commitment to see it through. But the benefits can be life changing.

What is 'controlling behaviour' and how should I deal with it?

About the author

Norman Hartnell, Managing Director, The Family Law Company by Hartnell Chanot

Norman is a solicitor, mediator, collaborative family lawyer and arbitrator and is experienced in all forms of family mediation. He has represented parents, guardians and children in private and public law cases and has considerable experience in complex divorce and related financial issues.

So many relationship problems seem to relate to the issue of 'controlling behaviour' or the feeling of 'being controlled' within those relationships. Possibly its presence or absence is an indicator of the sustainability of relationships, highlighting the difference between those relationships that will last and those which are doomed to either ultimately fail or lead to a position in which at least one person is trapped into staying in a destructive relationship through the inability to leave.

A mediator's experience

A mediator like myself is given the privilege of hearing and understanding the perspective of each of the couple in a dispute.

I frequently hear each of the couple say: "I feel controlled by the other person", yet they will also say: "I deny controlling the other person".

How can that be? Can both honestly feel controlled whilst being unaware that their own behaviour is perceived by the other to be controlling?

I think that the answer is yes, but it does call for an explanation.

The impact of fear

When in conflict it is easy for fear to dominate thinking. Fear is a very powerful emotion that taps into our most basic need to survive, and when we feel threatened the flight, freeze or fight response is triggered. In an attempt to address fear, we naturally try to control our environment to make it feel a safer place to be. We then exercise any power we have to provide a feeling of being safe and in control in those circumstances where we feel out of control. This is often instinctive, out of a sense of self preservation, not consciously out of a need to diminish anyone else.

How do individuals use power in relationships?

So, what power is available to each in the context of a separating couple?

- Power from *financial knowledge and control* of the money.

- Power in the *ability to exercise influence over children* by both the person with whom the children live and on whom the children are dependent, to whom they instinctively show the greater loyalty and the other parent who may see themselves in a battle.

- *Relationship power*, to give or withhold cooperation, politeness, clarity and information that is held by only one of the couple, the ability to push buttons, to manipulate the other, to keep the other person off balance and in a state of uncertainty.

What are the fears that stimulate the instinctive exercise of power?

Fear comes in a number of guises, often unspoken. The person is sometimes unaware of them as they have not been put into words as we are in the territory of instinct.

Generally, fear relates to a perceived threat to a basic need or right (such as the need for basic provision, home, clothes, food, money or the need to maintain a relationship with children which is under threat)

being limited or even extinguished in some way.

Fear is a powerful motivating force and needs to be identified to be addressed and understood by the other.

The instinct of self-preservation takes over once separation is seen as likely and often the previous focus on mutual interests disappears.

Fear is fed by not only our own nightmares but by those around us - family and friends who encourage us to see ourselves as the victim in any situation and the other person as the aggressor. Self-interest is dominant, often even above parental protective notions.

We try to meet any fears by exercising any power available to us, in the hope that the leverage it gives us will give security. However, being on the receiving end of the exercise of such power generates ever greater fears in the other person, a spiral is created and the sense of being controlled follows.

Some practical examples

A couple of practical examples from my own experiences will help to explain better. I have used stereotypical gender, but these apply equally to both genders.

Let's take a mum who has never had to budget because her husband has always paid the bills. Her greatest fear may be that the mortgage isn't paid, the electricity is cut off, she won't be able to feed the children, or she could lose her home. These are fears that basic needs might not be met. The husband can choose to:

• feed and increase those fears

by not paying bills, leaving her in a position of not knowing and allowing those fears to grow by doing and saying nothing; or

• exercise a conscious choice to recognise that fear and take steps to put her mind at rest.

The first would undoubtedly call for an instinctive response in which mum protests - maybe through lawyers - or exercises what power is available to her, and the circle of conflict will either grow or diminish depending on the course chosen.

The second example is a dad whose greatest fear is that he, having left home, will lose his relationship with his children.

Mum's choices include the following:

• to feed that fear by discouraging or impeding contact or undermining the dad by criticizing him or perhaps his new partner; or

• to choose against her instincts and put her own sadness or anger aside to foster a good relationship between the children and their dad by encouraging contact, overcoming obstacles and giving the children permission to love both parents, whatever she thinks of him as a partner.

The better way

The better choice in each case is counter intuitive - by doing something positive for the other parent when we are hurting, we deny our instinct to hurt another whom we feel has hurt us. However, one small positive action, one acknowledgement, one thank you, one kind word or action has the power to break that vicious cycle.

Every separating couple is faced with such choices at the time of separation.

Family lawyers are well placed to help clients who may understandably be in distress and fearful of the future as they address such issues. They should first take time to understand and acknowledge the fears of their own clients (rather than ignoring them or pretending they don't exist). Their aim should then be to help the client to find a way of addressing the fears and needs of all concerned, using as the benchmark the overriding needs of their children, rather than focusing on the problem being the 'other person'.

The choice for every family lawyer is whether to feed the fear that generates conflict and cost, or help take the heat out of the situation by following the Resolution code, wherever it's both possible and safe to, in the following ways:

• Focus on identifying not only the client's interests but also the mutual interests of the separated couple/family.

• Aim to find solutions to all issues which work for all, minimise conflict and costs, and treat the other person and their representatives with respect.

• Keep the improvement in the lives of any children involved as their guiding principle.

You may rightly ask: "What if one parent or lawyer gets it, but the other doesn't? Doesn't that expose my client to be disadvantaged?" See the Must read article on Page 50 on transforming conversations for a discussion on that issue.

Do I have to go to mediation?

About the author

Louisa Dickson, Southern Family Mediation

An accredited family mediator with the Family Mediation Council, Louisa is passionate about helping couples to move forward, make the necessary decisions and create a new co-parenting relationship. Her wealth of knowledge, compassion and experience, combined with her work as a mediator, child consultant and family coach, helps her to support individuals and families going through the process of divorce and separation.

An often asked question to which the simple answer is No.

The law changed in April 2014 which means that, if you have a problem with your ex about the arrangements for your children or finances and you feel that

court may be the only option for you, then before making an application to the family court a person must attend a Family Mediation Information and Assessment Meeting (MIAM) (see Question 40 for more information). This is to see if mediation could be used to resolve the issues rather than going to court. At the end of this meeting, the mediator will tell you if they think mediation is suitable for you and advise you of the next steps, but it should be remembered that further mediation is entirely voluntary. If the mediator feels that mediation is not suitable, they will sign a form to say you have attended, at which point you can decide if an application to court is necessary. Going to court should be a last resort.

I'm afraid of my ex. Do I still need to follow the MIAMs procedure?

Your ex will be expected to attend a MIAM but they won't be at the same meeting as you. In some cases, you don't need to attend a MIAM, for example in cases of domestic violence which has been reported and prosecuted; involvement of social services regarding the welfare of a child; urgency and threats of the removal of a child from the country. Other exemptions may apply.

Choosing the right mediator for you can be a difficult process. The OnlyMums/Dads Panel www.thefamilylawpanel. co.uk (see Page 32) contains details of leading family mediators with their specialisms and profiles set out clearly for you to browse through.

So then why should I go to mediation?

In a nutshell - your **children** need you to.

I could give you many reasons why separating couples want to go to court, such as "going to court is expensive but we love our children so much we would ultimately spend whatever it took for whatever was best for them".

No, this is about your children. Going to court inevitably pits parents against each other in the battle to have their view of what is best validated and be proved 'right'. In reality that rarely happens.

Often parents will genuinely believe their children are coping amazingly well with their

I blamed myself and I let my anger take control. Kay (16)

separation and that the change from one to two households is working well. "We don't argue in front of the kids". "They never see me upset". "I'm always civil on handovers".

Some parents are at the other end of the scale and find the other parent unbearable, they cannot even speak to them and the children are well aware of their feelings.

Wherever you may fall within this range your children will definitely be hiding their true feelings from you - even if asked what they think and feel about the situation a child will almost certainly not be able to express their true feelings because they do not wish to upset you, and want to protect you and your emotions.

Separation is hard, on everyone. Shame, guilt, low self-esteem and a poor self-image are common among children where a divorce or separation has been bitter and drawn out. Our children need us

to be bigger, calmer, wiser and stronger than they are. When we are not, they feel stressed, unsafe and destabilised. When a child grows up afraid or under constant or extreme stress, their brain and nervous systems may not develop normally.

Children learn their self-worth from the reactions of others, particularly those closest to them. Parents have the greatest influence on a child's self-esteem and value. The message that children take from seeing their parents caught up in a 'war' with

each other is that the fight is more important than they are. The constant stress will make a child feel worthless and despondent, and they often blame themselves.

Mediation can help you both to make decisions and protect your children from all this. Your children don't need to know about your relationship - they just want their parents, and to feel safe and untroubled.

I look back and wish that
I had spent more time
enjoying what I did have, not
preoccupying myself with
what I didn't.

Anna, Mum

Notes

How should I prepare for a MIAM?

About the authors

Sarah England & Karen Shirn, Directors of Green Light Mediation

Sarah trained as a family mediator in 2011. She brings a down to earth approach with a particular empathy for children's issues, with strong problem solving skills.

Karen trained in 2011 as a family mediator. She brings a wealth of experience of relationship breakdown and dispute resolution.

A MIAM is the first step whether you think you need to make an application to court, wish to mediate or even a combination of the two. You cannot make an application to court without attending a MIAM unless you are exempt (see Question 39 for more information on exemptions).

What should I take to the MIAM?

If there are any relevant court orders make sure you take them with you. Otherwise, all you will need is a notepad to jot down any useful information you may hear.

There is absolutely nothing to be nervous about. The mediators are there to help you resolve matters so they will explain the process and principles of mediation. They will then ask you to sign an agreement to mediate. Don't worry - this does not commit you to anything other than to abide by the principles of mediation *if* you attend mediation. It ensures you both keep matters discussed confidential.

How to choose a mediator

If you are looking for a mediation service to provide a MIAM for you, top tips would be:

- Have a look at their website - is it helpful?

- Look at the costs of both the MIAM and the mediation session - if it goes well you will be paying for both.

- Check whether the mediator is accredited for children and family cases (this tells you your mediator has both experience and some successful outcomes).

- Ask whether the service is run on a sole mediator basis or co-mediation basis and, if the latter, whether they charge extra for this.

Co-mediation simply means you have the benefit of two mediators working for you to resolve the issue and, therefore, hopefully able to offer a higher success rate.

Most people choose to have their MIAM alone and that can be useful for both clients and mediators as it is a chance to calmly express your perspective regarding the dispute and understand how the process can help you.

A MIAM is an opportunity to meet and build rapport with your mediator and to ask any questions you might have so if you have a burning question write it down on your pad ahead so that you don't forget to ask.

Any order made by a court is a blunt instrument - you are far more likely to have something that works for you if you can negotiate a settlement which can be as detailed as you want it to be, yet still endorsed by the court if necessary.

Keri Tayler, 42 Bedford Row

How do I go about choosing a mediator?

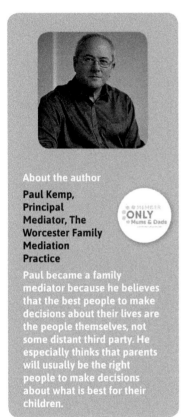

About the author

**Paul Kemp,
Principal
Mediator, The
Worcester Family
Mediation
Practice**

Paul became a family
mediator because he believes
that the best people to make
decisions about their lives are
the people themselves, not
some distant third party. He
especially thinks that parents
will usually be the right
people to make decisions
about what is best for their
children.

The most important question to ask when considering a mediator is: 'Are they registered with the Family Mediation Council?' If not, then avoid them like the plague - they may not be properly trained, supervised or subject to basic professional standards.

Accreditation

A registered family mediator may be either accredited or working towards accreditation under supervision. All registered mediators, whether accredited or

not, will have had previous experience in a relevant professional role - some will have been lawyers, others social workers or therapists.

Having been selected for training, a would-be mediator will undertake 'Foundation Training' approved by the Family Mediation Standards Board. This involves attendance at teaching sessions as well as reading and other assignments and is but the start of the mediator's preparation to practice.

The next step is to gain some practical experience with an experienced mediator. This will be done under the supervision of a 'Professional Practice Consultant' who will decide when the mediator is ready to take on the responsibility of mediating alone.

To become accredited, a family mediator must submit a portfolio of evidence of their competence. The standards required for this are high and many do not pass at the first attempt. It may take up to three years or sometimes longer.

Registered mediators

Every registered mediator must continue to have a Professional Practice Consultant who will provide continuing supervision and will check that they are continuing to study and develop.

If a mediator is registered, then perhaps look at their website to find out about their background

and other interests. Check out a few and allow your feelings to guide you - but remember that the mediator will be working with both of you, and must be a fit for your ex as well as for you. If you have a solicitor, they may know about a particular mediator's strengths and weaknesses and may be able to recommend a mediator to suit your situation.

Before family mediation starts, there is always a preliminary meeting (known as a Mediation Information and Assessment Meeting or 'MIAM') (see Question 40 for more information). During this meeting, you will be able to form a clearer impression of the mediator and their approach to the process. If you don't feel comfortable with the mediator, you are at liberty to look for another one. Do check whether the mediator you see for the preliminary meeting will also be undertaking the mediation itself.

Everyone enters mediation with doubts and worries and concerns. The important thing is to tell the mediator what these are. No point keeping them to yourself.

Things to note:

- It is important that you are confident that a mediator will keep you safe and comfortable in the mediation meetings - the mediator should screen carefully for issues of abuse or other factors that might cause you difficulty and should be prepared to adapt the mediation model to keep you safe.

- Mediation is always voluntary - you cannot be forced to mediate, nor will you be punished by a court if you decide, after the MIAM, that mediation is not for you.

- Not all people holding themselves out as family mediators are properly trained or supervised. Mediators who are part of The OnlyMums & OnlyDads Panel will always be registered.

- Mediators are not permitted to give legal advice, though they may provide neutral legal and financial information. Mediators are working with both of you to help you make good choices, but they will never make choices for you or tell you what you should do.

- Only accredited mediators are able to sign the MIAM certificate required before you can start court proceedings, so if a mediator is not yet accredited, and you think you may need a certificate, check whether their Professional Practice Consultant will sign the certificate for them.

Notes

How can I get the most out of mediation?

About the author

Jane Robey, CEO National Family Mediation

Jane became CEO of National Family Mediation (NFM) in 2004, having previously practiced as an accredited family mediator, Professional Practice Consultant and service manager. She is a published author on family mediation and a contributor to Government policy-making forums.

O nce you've decided that family mediation is the right service for you, you have a number of practical things to consider. But first and foremost, what you need most of all to underpin a successful mediation is the right attitude and an open frame of mind.

If you're completely consumed by anger and resentment towards your ex, the prospect of discussing and negotiating an agreement over vital day-to-day parenting, money and property arrangements will be nearly impossible.

But if your mindset is focused on moving things forward - not just

for your own benefit but more importantly for children that are involved too - then mediation can work and be a great success.

So, assuming that as you've read this far you're interested in progressing with mediation, here are a few top tips to help ensure you get the most from the process.

Choose the right mediator

There are a number of factors you'll take into account in your choice, but number one must be quality assurance.

Get a mediator who's properly qualified. If you need a roofer or plumber you'll look for trade quality marks. The Family Mediation Council (FMC), the professional regulator, has an accreditation scheme: FMCA. Mediators holding this status have undergone relevant training and continuing professional development, working to high standards, and they follow the FMC Code of Practice. No FMCA? Rule them out of the equation.

Costs are always right there when choosing any professional. So look carefully at the fees you'll be charged for mediation - not just the initial Mediation Information and Assessment Meeting (MIAM) but for work that follows too. This will largely be shaped by the range of issues you want to mediate: this determines the number of sessions you will need and, therefore, the final cost. But do bear in mind that family

When a close relationship ends, you have seen the best and worst of each other. You know what buttons to press! The analogy I use is you are co-workers/co-parents speaking to each other to get the best out of each other, like you would in the work place, to avoid a confrontation.

Tracy Allison, Allison Family Mediation Services

mediation is almost certain to be considerably less expensive than pursuing matters through an acrimonious solicitor/family court route.

Your choice of mediator might also need to take account of child-inclusive mediation. If you feel your child would benefit from being included in the discussions (and it's not for everyone), do ensure from the start that the mediator is qualified to include children in the discussions.

Like any business relationship, personal qualities will play a part too. Does it feel like you can get on with the mediator, do business with them? What can you find out about their track record and their success rate in negotiating agreements?

ONLY
Mums & Dads
parents meet professionals

What issues?

Consider all the areas of your future that you'll want to mediate over. Separation is going to affect just about everything in your lives. Some things will be easier to settle than others, but be clear about where potential disagreements may lie.

- Where will each of you live? Is that temporary, or for the foreseeable future?

- Where will the kids live, and how will both of you continue your parenting responsibilities?

- What about money issues, including too often overlooked debt and pension issues?

- What support payments will need to be made, when and by whom, in respect of the children?

- Who'll have the car?

- What happens to the dog?

Be as clear as you can at the outset which of these things you'll need to include in your discussions.

Prepare for compromise

Understand you're not paying for an expensive lawyer to 'hold your hand' and charge you lots of money every step of the way. Your mediator is shared with your ex. They aren't there to battle solely for you and win you a 'victory'.

Family mediation is not about telling your story to someone, outlining where things went wrong, how you hate him or her for it and your determination to settle those old scores.

Mediation is about the thoughtful construction of a future that works for everyone involved. Both people need to be ready to accept they won't get everything they want. It's that

'attitude' thing again. Put any remaining anger and hostility in a box and leave it behind. Shift your focus to the present and, more importantly, to the future - for your kids' sake, and for your own.

Think about the needs of everybody in the family. It's hard when your ex is one of them and you're feeling hurt and wounded.

But mediation is about compromise and negotiation, because at the end of the day those are things that will help you reach agreements that let you get on with your lives.

Notes

My parents' separation changed my whole world, not necessarily for the better, but I had no option but to go along with it. Cerys (15)

Is it possible to mediate with an 'implacably hostile' parent?

About the author

**John Hind,
Director and
Founder, Compass
Resolution Ltd**

John is a mediator
and lawyer
and focuses
exclusively on the most
effective ways of helping
and supporting people in
conflict, to work together to
solve a wide range of disputes
including family, inheritance,
workplace, contractual and
business partnership disputes.

In this article, I share my
experience of doing just that, in
the hope of encouraging more
family mediators to take on
similar, seemingly intractable
situations, and encouraging
parents, in similar situations, to
grab the opportunity that
mediation offers.

With a very hostile parent, the
key challenge and skill is how to
support them to positively
engage with the other parent in a
mediation process which needs
them to take some responsibility
for working with the other parent
to improve the co-parent
relationship and where

necessary, make the necessary
changes to their behaviour.

Case study

A few months ago, I met Sheila
for a MIAM. She had apparently
been told by her solicitor to see
me to "get her MIAM certificate",
so she could go to court.

Having listened intently to Sheila
for about 30 minutes, I knew it
was going to be a difficult
mediation when, having
established some rapport, I
carefully and sensitively got
round to asking Sheila:

> *"Can you think of anything **you**
> might be able to do to
> improve the parenting
> relationship with Bill?"*

Although her reply was very
hostile, the intensity of her
response and what she
complained about also told me
much about what she valued and
needed for herself and from Bill.
This gave me hope and
something to focus on. So, I
decided to meet with her former
partner, Bill, before deciding
whether to offer to mediate.

From the hostile parent's
perspective, the question I asked
Sheila can feel incredibly tough
to answer openly and honestly,
when the truth they hold about
the other parent is locked away
in a heavily rehearsed, reinforced
and guarded negative narrative,
rooted in blame and self-
justification, serving to protect a
fragile self-esteem and avoid
taking responsibility for the

situation and outcome.

This certainly seemed true of
Sheila.

As a mediator, I knew I was going
to have to tread the fine line of
helping Sheila to positively
engage in mediation whilst
enabling her to retain and
protect her sense of self-worth,
self-image and integrity, to say
nothing of ensuring that Bill did
not feel neglected along the way.

Herein lies the main challenge
and risk for me of mediating
cases of seemingly implacably
hostile parents, where one
parent absorbs so much of the
energy and time in mediation,
leaving everyone exhausted and
the mediator feeling 'de-skilled',
wondering what else could have
been done.

During the pre-mediation
meeting I decided that if, among
other things, I could help Sheila
in mediation to work towards
acknowledging that Bill's
perspective was valid, without
seeing him as right and her as
wrong, I might be able to make
some headway with helping her
take some responsibility for
improving the situation with Bill.
The same, of course, went for Bill.

When I met Sheila, she described
how she was feeling extremely
vulnerable, anxious and angry, as
she told me all about Bill and
how, about 2 years ago, he
seemed to suddenly change. To
her, he had become a 'different
person'. Indeed, he seemed to be
suffering from 'some kind of

personality disorder'. She described how, having 'abandoned his family', he had become more distant, more interested in his new family, more angry, volatile and controlling.

In my experience, it is quite common for two parents to believe each other to be controlling. This is what they may truly feel, as they each seek to 'win back' some control over what they perceive as control being exerted by the other. This is especially so when the past pattern has involved one parent 'being controlled' and who is now, through support, able to assert themselves.

For Sheila, it was clear that the more abandoned, rejected and angry she felt, the more she felt the need to attack and punish Bill as the person she blamed for her predicament and for making her feel the way she did. She was punishing him in the only way she knew how; through the children.

According to Bill, Sheila constantly change her mind about when he could see Tommy, aged 5 and Chrissie, aged 7, to the point that Bill had turned up for one visit to be told that the children were not there and he had got the wrong day. He later discovered that they had been told that he had not bothered to turn up. He was completely frustrated and had, quite simply, had enough.

Sheila demonstrated very little insight into how her conflict with Bill might be affecting the children. When I sensitively asked her about this, she neatly and expertly re-framed the situation, laying the blame clearly at Bill's door.

I had to decide, in the pre-mediation meeting, whether I was going to be able to do any useful work with her and Bill in mediation. On the other hand, what option did this couple have? Were they to be added to the growing heap of cases passing through the over-crowded court system?

I have always felt it very important to remain hopeful and optimistic for my clients and ensure that they feel this optimism from me, beginning with my welcoming them into mediation and commending them on their decision to work together, with me, to reach their own decisions.

I strongly believe that so many parents who sadly end up in court in fact have the capacity and, with the right patient support, are able to find the motivation when it comes to their children to develop a better parent relationship, and they deserve the opportunity to be able to do so.

Let's face it, our brains are hard-wired for the self and external awareness, rational reflection, and self-restraint necessary to succeed in mediation. The equipment exists. It is the guidance and practice that is so often lacking, and this often starts in mediation, continuing outside mediation, with the support of coaches, therapists and a range of court based and private organisations.

Sheila had spent the last few years filling a warehouse of resentment about Bill which had clearly been influencing her behaviour. Although I am not a therapist, I was convinced that much of Sheila's worse behaviour towards Bill, often in front of the

children, had been in a high state of alert, effectively shutting down other parts of the brain responsible for reflection, rational response and decision making. This behaviour would have the effect of labelling her to many as 'implacably hostile'.

In mediation, there seemed an almost visible tussle going on in Sheila's mind between her reflective self as she listened to Bill, with the occasional positive response, and her reptilian self (the bit that influences fundamental needs), ordering her reflective self to shut down as she sporadically erupted over Bill when she felt challenged or threatened by something he said or did.

Bill for his part seemed to be well practiced in saying very little on these occasions to antagonise Sheila, although he readily admitted that he had 'lost it' on a few occasions in the past and now finds it hard to be civil to Sheila, 'after everything she has put him through'. He was pushing back.

It was about 1 hour into a hard mediation as I was attempting once again to calm the process down when a small breakthrough came as Sheila listened to the following interaction between me and Bill. Mediators sometimes call these 'light bulb moments'.

'What does Sheila say you do which justifies in her mind you not seeing the children'.

I repeated this question, more slowly for a second time, turning briefly to Sheila, encouraging her to listen and reassuring her that I will return to her in a moment to balance the dialogue. Bill replied:

'Well, she could say that I am sometimes a bit volatile and loud'.

I went on:

'What does she say you do to make her think you are loud'

Bill responded:

'Well, I guess, that sometimes I can lose it, but it is not surprising in the circumstances'.

Ignoring the 'but...' part of Bill's answer and intuitively sensing Bill's willingness to take some responsibility, I asked him:

'What does Sheila think your opinion is of her'.

I flicked my head to catch Sheila's eyes. She was listening for Bill's reply. I sensed the importance of the moment.

'I think she would say I hate her'.

I repeat his words very slowly back to Bill:

'You believe that she thinks you hate her'.

'So, what do you think you might be able to do to help her decide that the kids should see you'.

In essence, I was asking Bill what he thought he could do to ensure that Sheila hates him less or, put in non-violent communication terms, having identified his perception of Sheila's feelings of hatred towards him, I was asking Bill to consider what Sheila

might need from him for her to feel differently and therefore, perhaps, begin to behave differently towards him.

Sheila quickly replied:

'I don't hate you, I just find you.......'

At which point she listed what she finds most frustrating about Bill. This gave us all an insight into what Sheila was needing from Bill and some things for us to work with.

The dialogue with Bill concluded with Bill offering to do a number of things and make a number of changes for Sheila.

Attention then turned to Sheila and, although there was some resistance, the powerful instinct of reciprocity momentarily won over the self-justification blame narrative resulting in a subtle shift of attitude, approach and a willingness to listen to what Bill was feeling and needed in this situation.

Slowly but surely, momentum took over and the dialogue became one of what Bill and Sheila could each do to build confidence in each other to work together as parents for their children.

Bill agreed not to ring Sheila all the time. Detailed drop off and collection arrangements were agreed. Sheila agreed to produce the children on time and prepare them for their visit. In all this, I emphasised to Sheila and Bill

that they were now treading a new path and had an opportunity to create something special for their children, a good parenting relationship they and their children could look back on in years to come with pride. Something that was really worth working for.

Mediation had given Bill and Sheila an opportunity to live up to their parenting responsibilities which, I am very pleased to say, they were able to do.

I cannot tell you that Sheila and Bill left their first mediation session with a skip in their step but they readily booked another session and another. Against the odds and with some support, they grabbed the mediation opportunity, took responsibility and their story ended well.

As they left their first mediation session I explained that, in my mind, they had chosen to move on from their 'old relationship'. It was no longer fit for their purpose. It needed redesigning and constantly working at to be fit for the most important purpose in their lives, that of jointly raising Tommy and Chrissie to be well balanced, healthy individuals.

Things calmed down when we moved out. The time we spend with dad is healthy, quality time. Stephanie (17)

How does child mediation work?

About the author

Angela Lake-Carroll

Angela has over 30 years' experience of working with separated families and she has written a range of short guides for separating families. Angela works across the broad range of family law and family dispute resolution as a practitioner and adviser. She has also worked with and contributed to government policy for families, children and young people.

When you separate there may be so many things to think about that it can feel very overwhelming. As a parent, it is not unusual to be worried or concerned about how your children may be coping. Parents never want to cause their children hurt or upset and you may be concerned about how best to help them. Your family life will go on, but it will be arranged differently - sorting out how it is going to work best for you all is something that you can discuss together and arrange in mediation.

Mediators are trained and qualified to help you focus on how to help your children through the changes that are happening and to plan for the future. Your mediator will be concerned to get a sense of each of your children, what you think is important in any decisions you will make for them and to talk with you about what you think is important for each of the children. Depending on their age and understanding, each of your children will have different needs and your mediator will help you to think through what those needs and priorities might be. Mediators understand that it can often be difficult for you to be sure of your children's views or perspectives and that you may be worried about what you should say to them, how you can best talk with them and what they need to know about what has been happening and will happen in the future, especially before you have had the chance to think through the practical things to be sorted out.

Your mediator can help you to talk together about what is helpful for children, go through some of the things that can be damaging for children and discuss how best to start laying foundations to ensure your children's future security and well-being. Children often have questions to ask but can feel uncomfortable or be concerned about asking you, especially if they are aware that you are upset. So planning together how best to talk with them, to provide simple explanations and to encourage your children to ask any questions can be a very good way to help your children.

If you are concerned that your child or children may need additional help or support, your mediator can also help you think about who may be best to contact.

An increasing number of mediators are trained and qualified to talk directly with children and young people whose parents have chosen to mediate. Sometimes this can be a helpful way for parents to get a sense of how their children view things and what is important to them for their parents to know. It is important to say that trained and qualified mediators are not yet available in every locality but if a mediator is qualified to see children, that is included in the information available on the FMC Register (www.familymediationcouncil.org.uk/find-local-mediator).

If you think this might be helpful for your children, there are some things that are important to know and understand. First of all, both parents (and anyone who has parental responsibility for each child) must agree that their

Stay out of the arguments, don't take sides and just explain how you are feeling. Jade (17)

child or children can be offered an opportunity to meet with a mediator. Usually, mediators invite children who are 10 or over and it is the child's choice as to whether they decide to come and talk with them. Some mediators prefer to arrange for a colleague co-mediator to invite and to talk with children. Where this is the case, your mediator will explain how they arrange this, including a meeting with you and their colleague to discuss and agree arrangements.

As their parents, you will be asked to sign an agreement about the arrangements for your child to be invited and to talk with a mediator. The agreement will ask you to consent to the practical arrangements and understand that in the same way as your meetings with your mediator are confidential, so would any meeting a mediator has with your child. Children can choose what, if any, information or messages they would like you to receive.

It is important that you also agree together that you won't try to influence what your child says or try to find out from them what they have said to the mediator in their meeting, and very importantly that you accept that any view the child agrees to share is their view and is respected. Any mediator who talks with children will explain all of these arrangements carefully to them in a way that they can understand and will check that they have fully understood things. Mediators also have a responsibility to ensure that a child knows that if they tell the mediator about any harm that has happened to them or the mediator has a concern about harm being caused to

them that they would need to speak to a professional whose role it is to protect children and families from harm.

They will also explain that their parents are talking together with the help of their mediator to try and decide what is going to work best for everyone in the future and have agreed together that it would be helpful for them to know what is important for their children, whether there are things that their children would really like them to know and understand and what the children think might be working well, or is or would be difficult for them in their everyday life.

Your mediator will also talk with you at some length so that you can consider all of the things that are important about hearing what your child might choose to share, the effect that might have on you and how best to talk with your children afterwards, especially once you have reached some decisions together about the future.

It is unlikely to be helpful for your children to be offered the opportunity to talk with a mediator if there is a lot of conflict between you, especially if you have very fixed ideas about who your children should live with. A child is not coming to talk with a mediator to be asked who they want to live with, to give an opinion on either of their parents or to feel that they are being asked to make decisions. If your child is already being helped or supported by another professional, or if they already have been seen by a CAFCASS officer, your mediator will want to discuss whether it is appropriate for them to be invited to talk to a mediator.

Your mediator will want to make sure that if your child is going to talk with a mediator, it will be helpful and reassuring for them and not make things worse or cause confusion or inappropriate upset for your children or for you. It may also be the case that having talked with you about your child or children and the situation for you all, there may be other reasons why your mediator might feel mediation is inappropriate. If this is the case, the mediator will discuss with you the range of ways in which you might get a sense of what is important for your child/ren.

It is also important to know that mediators are not child counsellors or therapists and they do not and cannot provide any kind of report about their meeting with a child - just as in any mediation with parents, discussions are confidential. Their role in talking with children is to provide the child with a private space to talk about what is important to them, what they would like their parents to know and understand and to answer any general questions they may have about what is happening for their family.

Mums and Dads: make sure your kids are happy with the contact arrangements. So often in Child Inclusive Mediation, in conversation with the kids, they say they are not at all happy. Involve them in the arrangements. It'll pay off.

Bayla Klyne, Mediation Solutions North West

ONLY
Mums & Dads
parents meet professionals

Are arrangements made in mediation legally binding?

About the author

Rebekah Gershuny, Evolve Family Mediation

Rebekah is an accredited family mediator, and founder of Evolve Family Mediation. She also practices as a family lawyer at Freemans Solicitors. Rebekah has extensive experience helping separating and divorcing couples make arrangements in respect to their finances, and parenting plans for their children. As a Child Inclusive Mediator, Rebekah helps parents to focus on their children's wishes and feelings, and to take their views on board.

In most cases, working out your own arrangements in mediation following separation or divorce is the best way forward. This is because it is quicker, less expensive, and less stressful than court proceedings. Together with the mediator, you set the agenda, and you retain control of the outcome. To find a local mediator see familymediationcouncil.org.uk, nfm.org.uk or thefma.co.uk

Following separation, it can be difficult to make arrangements because there has been a breakdown in trust and communication. A family mediator, who acts as an entirely neutral impartial third party, can help to facilitate difficult conversations and assist you to structure arrangements that are unique to your own particular circumstances, whether these relate to financial matters, children or the future of your relationship. A family mediator will manage the process so that it is less overwhelming, and will help to reduce conflict and improve communication.

Where do mediations take place?

Most mediations take place with you and your ex in a room together with the mediator. However, if you have concerns about sitting in a room with your ex, you can discuss these in detail with the mediator in your initial meeting, and where appropriate, the mediator can arrange 'shuttle mediation'. This means that you and your ex will be in separate rooms, and the 'mediator' will shuttle between you. (For further information about domestic abuse see the National Domestic Violence Helpline website). The initial meetings that you and your ex have with the mediator are held with each of you separately, and are confidential. This gives you the opportunity to explain your circumstances, discuss your concerns and find

out in detail about the mediation process.

Without prejudice discussions

The discussions that take place in mediation are 'without prejudice'. This means that they cannot be referred to in court, and the arrangements that you reach are not binding. At the end of the mediation process, your mediator will provide you with a document that will set out the proposals that you have reached. This is called a 'Memorandum of Understanding'. The mediator will also set out details of your financial information in a document called an 'Open Financial Statement'. Unlike the Memorandum of Understanding, the Open Financial Statement can be referred to in future court proceedings if these become necessary because mediation breaks down.

> Mediation cannot change what has happened in the past but it can help shape the future for you as individuals and your future co-parenting relationship.
>
> *Cressida Burnet, Cressida Burnet Mediation*

How are mediation decisions made legally binding?

If you are getting divorced, the proposals that are recorded in the Memorandum of Understanding in respect of financial arrangements can be made legally binding by incorporating them into a 'consent order' which is submitted to the court for a Judge's approval.

If you have not been married, you can formalise the arrangements that you have reached in mediation in a 'separation agreement'.

It is a good idea for a specialist family solicitor to draw up the consent order or separation agreement to ensure that your proposals are properly implemented, and that if necessary you can enforce them in the future if your ex doesn't stick to what has been agreed.

Parenting plans

One of the major advantages of mediation is that you and your ex can draw up comprehensive arrangements for the future co-parenting of your children. These can be incorporated into a parenting plan which, in addition to covering the day-to-day living arrangements for your children, can also deal with broader issues relating to your children's health, religion and education.

Whilst it is not usually necessary, a court can make an order in respect of the arrangements if you do not think that your ex will stand by the child arrangements that you have reached in mediation. A family solicitor can advise you if this is necessary, and can draw up the court order for you.

OUR CHILDREN WANT TO LIVE IN DIFFERENT PLACES

As parents we want our children to be happy. This is never more important than when you separate. Obviously when children get older, they might want some input into decisions, but certainly for younger children it is imperative that the decision about where they are going to live lies with you, their mum and dad.

Asking a child who they want to live with puts them firmly in the middle of you both - how can they possibly choose when they love you both?

So, decide together and present it to them stating that the non-resident parent will see them regularly.

Sometimes teens pose a challenge when they are pushing against rules or boundaries. Try not to get into parent 'ping pong'. Be strong and back each other up. Emotionally it's much better for the child not to keep chopping and changing where they live.

Adele Ballantyne

Children suffer when their confidence in their parents is fractured. Mary

What happens after mediation?

About the author

Peter Burgess, partner and mediator, Burgess Mee Family Law

Peter is an FMC accredited mediator with Resolution and family law solicitor. He advises and mediates on all aspects of family law including finances and children for high net worth individuals and their partners.

So, you and your partner have spent hours with a mediator painstakingly looking at different outcomes and options and come up with an outcome which you can both live with. What happens next? This article aims to answer that question.

How does a mediated agreement become binding?

It should have been explained by your mediator that reaching an outcome in mediation does not mean you have a binding agreement. There are established rules and procedures in place which deal with how the outcome you have negotiated is turned into an agreement.

The first thing that you and your partner will need to do is be given the option of taking legal advice on the outcome. Ideally, the parties should be represented throughout the mediation process so that the views elicited and put forward by them during the mediation can be with the benefit of legal advice. If they've not been able to take advice or haven't done so for some other reason, probably the next step would be for them to have a meeting with a solicitor so that they can receive advice.

The mediator is not able to *advise* the parties during the process. They are only able to provide *information*. The difference between advice and information is a subtle one - broadly as I explain it to my clients in mediation, information is anything which, if you knew where to look, you could find on Google. Advice is the application of information to your particular circumstances.

The mediator is able to say whether an outcome reached between the parties is outside of the bracket. The job of the lawyer, though, is to weigh up all the circumstances of the case and to consider whether or not the outcome is an outcome that is fair to the client and that the client is willing to accept in exchange for a compromise of any claim arising.

Hopefully, with a mediator's help, the parties will already have considered the aspects of the case which might give cause for concern to a solicitor giving advice afterwards. If they have done so, the process of obtaining advice and converting the outcome into a legally binding agreement should be straightforward.

Documents

At the end of the mediation process, the mediator will produce two documents. One is called an Open Financial Statement. This is a narrative summary, usually accompanied by a schedule setting out the parties' finances. If the case is child related only, there will be no Open Financial Statement.

The second document is a 'without prejudice' document called a Memorandum of Understanding. The Memorandum of Understanding sets out a narrative summary of the proposals made by the parties to each other and the outcome that has been reached. It will probably provide some explanation to the solicitor looking at this deal afterwards about why the parties arrived at the outcome that they did.

The Memorandum of Understanding and Open Financial Statement should be provided to your solicitor. This will be the cornerstone of the advice that will be given. There is no obligation on the parties to take advice but if they have both had the opportunity to do so they can proceed to the conversion of the Open Financial Statement and Memorandum of Understanding into the documents which will make a legally binding agreement.

In the case of finances, the

documents are as follows:

- **a Minute of Agreement and consent order** - this is a document which will be lodged at court after the decree nisi stage of the divorce process (conditional decree for a civil partnership dissolution). It is written in plain English and there is a standard form of such document. The consent order will have in it a number of recitals and agreements, detailing the background for the agreement, possibly some undertakings (promises to the court to do or to refrain from doing certain things) and specific court orders which deal with, for example, the payment of a lump sum, sale of a property, transfer of a property via a Property Adjustments Order, pension sharing and the payment of maintenance. At the end of the document there will be some dismissal clauses. These are the clauses that effectively end the claims on which the agreement is based.

- **a D81 Form** - this is a form which sets out, in summary form, the details of the parties' assets and liabilities and their incomes and the basic information that the court will then need to approve the consent order. Both parties need to have seen the other's D81 or the parties have the option of doing a joint D81. These need to be counter-

signed by a Statement of Truth at the conclusion of the document.

- **forms A for Dismissal Purposes** - these are the documents which 'open' the parties' claims against each other so that they may be dismissed in the consent order. Again, they are in standard form.

Children cases

In relation to children matters, the parties have number of options. Under the Children Act, the court does not make an order unless the parties ask it to. Therefore, usually, there is no court order for child arrangements following divorce.

Sometimes, if proceedings have already been started or if there is a particular reason why the parties need a court order (for example international relocation), the parties can collaborate to make an application for an order under the Children Act and then lodge a consent order to be approved by the court at a later date.

More often than not, after mediation, the child arrangements can be set out in either a session note produced by the mediator or a parenting plan. The parenting plan gives the parties an opportunity to set out not only the actual arrangements reached but also some more broad-brush elements of their agreement which perhaps would not be put

into a court order. These might include, for example, some statements about the ethos they are going to follow as co-parents. It is likely to include the minutiae of everyday life as well.

Parenting plans are not binding. They are a written record of what the parties have agreed. Even a Child Arrangements Order itself is subject to variation depending on what is in the child's best interests.

Once the documents have been perfected, (and in the case of the Finance Order on divorce or dissolution and the Children Act Order, have been approved by the court), the parties can proceed to implement the terms of their agreement. The final step would be to apply for the decree absolute/final decree on divorce.

Other aspects that need to be considered

The parties may also need to consider, when taking advice on any outcome reached in mediation, whether they require either financial advice or accountancy advice (for example in relation to tax and structuring) and also whether they ought to be making a new will (see Question 31 and the Must read article on Page 111).

Often any agreement reached in mediation will encompass the arrangements if one of the parties dies. On decree absolute or a final order on a dissolution of a civil partnership, any existing

You do have a voice, speak up before no more can be said. Ellie (16)

ONLY
Mums & Dads
parents meet professionals

will takes effect as though the other spouse died on the date of the decree absolute or final decree as the case may be. Therefore, there is usually a good opportunity at this stage for updating any will or entering into a codicil. If the parties have discussed and agreed child arrangements, they may also like to agree any guardianship provisions in respect of wills going forward.

Sometimes it may be necessary to come back to mediation later on. Mediation is a versatile option in any number of situations and I have myself mediated a number of implementation issues. These have included things like house prices changing from what has been agreed, variations of maintenance and changes to the child arrangements regime.

If it's not binding, could it all fall apart?

In my experience it is quite unusual for parties to move away from an outcome agreed in mediation even if they have taken advice. The process can be emotionally draining and difficult but generally speaking has a good track record of producing outcomes that parties do not move away from. Because the mediator themselves has not been involved in advising or directing the parties towards a particular outcome, they often feel that they can take ownership of the decision-making process in a way in which is more difficult if they have pursued a more adversarial route such as solicitor led negotiations or court proceedings.

Being able to resolve any disagreement between yourselves rather than requiring

a third party to make a decision on your behalf means that parties find it easier to accept responsibility and have some closure on a process which is emotionally bruising.

The most successful mediations often result in a consensus being reached that neither party anticipated at the beginning. For example, I mediated a case about an internal relocation where one party wanted to remain in London and the other wanted to move to Sussex. By looking at the proposal side by side and discussing them in an adult and calm way, the parties were able to agree which option was the best for them as a family going forward. They took ownership over the planning process and I am pleased to report they left the mediation process together happy with the decision that they had reached and with the guidance and structure provided to them by me as a mediator.

Of course, not all outcomes are as successful or happy. Often parties will feel perhaps that they did not get the best deal they could, and it is a trite saying among family lawyers and mediators that if both parties feel that the deal was not quite what they were looking for, it is probably within the bounds of a fair outcome. There is certainly some truth in that and often advising after mediation as a solicitor you can tell by their reluctance to re-engage or open up negotiations again that actually there is an acceptance that that is the case.

In an ideal world, a comprehensive mediation process should cover all eventualities but sometimes it is necessary to return to deal with

unexpected circumstances. Maintaining a good relationship with a mediator so that they can provide clarification or offer further sessions of mediation if needs be, is important for the participants. At the end of every mediation I always offer to host further sessions if the parties would like me to.

When talking to parents who ended up going through the court process they will tell you that they gave up on mediation too quickly. 'Stick at it' is our advice to parents.

What are the benefits of a mediated settlement?

About the author

Jo Edwards, partner, mediator and head of family at Forsters LLP; past chair of Resolution

Jo specialises in dealing with issues which arise on relationship breakdown and resolving arrangements for children, including cases involving relocation with children. She also has expertise in advising on pre-nuptial agreements and acting in cases involving unmarried couples.

I feel privileged when parents approach me about mediation and entrust me with helping them work through the children aspects of their separation. From run of the mill child arrangements cases with mild-mannered parents who have sadly fallen out of love, to highly conflicted parents arguing over whether one of them should be able to move abroad with the children, I have seen it all.

When speaking to parents in mediation, I tell them about the devastating impact of litigation. In certain cases, for example where there are parental alienation or domestic abuse issues, child welfare concerns or where one parent has an unrealistic view about what's in the children's best interests, court is inevitable and not to be demonised. But for the vast majority of separating parents, it is better for their children for them to make their own arrangements.

So, the question may be asked:

"What are the benefits of a mediated settlement?"

I highlight seven main themes:

Tailored outcomes

I have done many mediations where parents have wanted to think 'outside the box' and come up with creative solutions that a Judge may not. In one case the dad's holiday entitlement was so limited that he was prepared to let mum have the child for most of the holidays in return for having a more even sharing of term time than may otherwise have been the case (because he worked longer hours than she did).

I went to the mediation thinking that mum wouldn't agree, but eventually she did.

In another, dad wanted to move overseas with the two daughters, both of whom wanted to go, but mum was resisting in court. After three mediations, it became apparent that she did not oppose the move but wanted to defer it for a few months until she had found a job in the overseas country, so that she could move there also. Litigation is something of a blunt tool, with outcomes quite formulaic; who better than parents to come up with the best solutions for their kids?

Maintaining relationships

I say to parents in mediation:

"You may have fallen out of love with each other, but you have a lifelong relationship as parents".

There is nothing that ruins a parental relationship, sometimes irreparably, more than hard-fought litigation in which allegation after allegation has been made. I have parents I acted for in litigation 10+ years ago who contact me because they still cannot agree on anything, battle-wounded from the court experience. It is difficult to get parents back on the same page in parenting terms after litigation, even with family therapy.

In mediation, whilst parents may not always see eye to eye, I encourage them not to dwell on difficult memories from their relationship, but to look positively to the future - what can they each offer the children and how can the children benefit from all that they have to offer? That positive focus can reap rewards for future parenting.

Keeping control of the process

The most difficult cases I do, in litigation or mediation, are where parents are at different stages in the grief cycle. Where there are court proceedings, my experience of working with the left behind parent is that they are, at different points, in states of shock, denial, anger, bargaining, depression and (finally) acceptance.

How long each of those phases lasts will vary from person to person. The court timetable will not wait for them; their instructions can (understandably) be erratic and the process upsetting.

When working with a couple in mediation, it is easier to identify where they are in the grief cycle. Often I will encourage the person who is further on emotionally to

give things time; to agree what the child arrangements are going to be for the next few weeks or months but not to push discussions around the longer-term arrangements until the other parent is ready.

I often also involve a therapist to help a parent who is struggling. By being able to control the pace, the parents are more likely to reach an agreement in the longer term interests of the children.

Longer lasting outcomes

The child arrangements which are most likely to stick are those agreed by the parents, rather than those imposed by the court.

I have had several instances of court-ordered arrangements breaking down. In some cases, one parent is unhappy with the outcome and will do everything they can to unsettle the

arrangements or come back quickly for a second bite of the cherry.

In other cases, both parents are unhappy with the outcome and limp along with the arrangements before one of them applies back to court. Conversely, the whole point of a mediated settlement is that it has the parents' buy-in.

There is also an opportunity with a mediated arrangement to 'road test' any proposed child arrangements; I encourage couples to trial the agreed arrangements for a month or two and then come back to iron out any wrinkles (sometimes things as simple as, 'we had forgotten that Jamie's football lesson is at 4pm on a Thursday so handover at 4.30pm isn't practical'). All of this makes the arrangements much more likely to stick, and to evolve naturally as the children get older.

Hearing the voice of the child

Whilst there has been much discussion about bringing in greater opportunity for the voice of the child to be heard in the family courts, in practice this is still inconsistent across the country and often unsatisfactory.

In mediation, assuming that they are 10 or older, I will always discuss with the parents whether it would be appropriate to speak to the children. There is much more scope for planning this in mediation - the parents will agree the terms of a letter I may write to the children, the practicalities and agreed messages. For children, it must feel like a less intimidating/ stressful prospect to know that their views are being expressed

Mediation can be a positive reassuring process that can help you both reach decisions about the practicalities of separation and more importantly decisions concerning your children.

However it is important that you are both in a position to agree in order for it to be successful.

Attending mediation when your partner is still at the 'car crash' stage of loss or has reached the angry stage will not always promote a conciliatory atmosphere. Counselling might help at this point.

Before you go to mediation ensure that you have thought about what you would like, especially where children matters are concerned.

Completing a Parenting Plan is a really good place to start.

Adele Ballantyne

to help mum and dad reach an agreement, rather than to inform an outcome imposed by a Judge.

Safe brainstorming space

Another benefit of the journey of arriving at a mediated settlement about child arrangements is that it affords a safe space to discuss ancillary issues. Many of the parents I see have solicitor negotiations or court proceedings on other issues in tandem. Sometimes one or both of them will turn up to mediation with reams of correspondence, complaining that it has cost them x thousand pounds to try to resolve, for example, an issue around the children's passports or the interim finances/living arrangements.

I tell parents that no topic is off bounds, provided they both agree it should be covered. Often with open, facilitated dialogue, an issue which may have become polarised is resolved.

Cost

A huge benefit of a mediated settlement is the saving in costs that will be made.

I saw a couple in mediation last year who had spent thousands and thousands of pounds trying unsuccessfully to reach an agreement. Over a series of sessions I helped them work towards an agreement. I couldn't help but think: imagine if they had come to see me two years earlier, they could have saved all that money.

Ultimately, it is far better for parents to preserve as much of their hard-earned money as possible by avoiding litigation and attending mediation. Parents will feel happier that money remains for the children, rather

than a significant chunk having gone to lawyers.

The benefits of a mediated settlement, for parents and children, are hopefully clear. Whilst 90% of separating parents reach their own agreement over child arrangements, 10% don't. It has got to be our aim to reduce that 10% further, hopefully through mediation or other alternatives to court.

In child arrangements/contact cases I suggest the "wallpaper test". People don't like to be told what to do by their ex, so if you give them 3 different options as to times/dates etc which are acceptable to the resident parent and let the other one choose the option they want, that often results in agreement. I used to do this with wallpaper with my husband. He wanted to choose it. So I would bring back 3 samples of wallpaper that I liked and he chose the one he wanted. He chose the wallpaper but I was happy with it!

Barbara Corbett, Corbett Le Quesne

Notes

Arbitration

ike Mediation, people are often unaware of Arbitration before they separate. But, like many other concepts, it soon becomes part of the new language of divorce. As with Mediation, the process relies on communication and compromise. But, unlike Mediation the outcomes of Arbitration are legally binding. Talking about challenging issues in a meeting room rather than a court can help couples feel less panicky and less criticised, and can lead to more reasoned decisions.

What is arbitration?

About the author

**Claire Webb,
Mediation Now**

Claire is a qualified family mediator, a specialist in child consultation and a collaborative lawyer (all with Resolution), and is also a qualified civil mediator and arbitrator. Claire also has special accreditation through Resolution as a specialist family lawyer in cohabitation and children law.

Arbitration is the latest process available to couples who want to end their marriage or civil partnership. It combines the emphasis on communication and benefits from avoiding court found through mediation with the legally binding ruling associated with court as arbitrator.

What is involved in arbitration?

Both parties are invited to attend a voluntary meeting with an arbitrator to discuss finances, assets and provision for any children the couple share. The arbitrator will listen to each party, examine all the written evidence brought by the couple, lead discussions to explore all possible solutions and ask any questions before making decisions.

Arbitration works best if a couple are in the same room. There is no need for lawyers but many people do bring their lawyers with them. Arbitration can be accessed at any point - as the first course of action, after/during mediation or as an alternative to waiting for court.

What is an arbitrator?

An arbitrator is a legally trained professional with a minimum of 10 years' post-qualification experience in family law. Candidates must be nominated and approved for training and, if successful, go on to attend intensive courses which consist of lectures, audiences with top Judges and role playing scenarios. There are only around 100 arbitrators currently in the UK.

What is the difference between arbitration and mediation?

The outcome. What an arbitrator decides for a couple is final and legally binding. For individuals who fear that any agreement made in mediation won't be stuck to in the real world, arbitration offers the same assurance and guarantee as an order from the court.

Arbitration is an evolution of mediation. If mediation fails, couples are usually sent to arbitration or court. In Canada, the authorities have created 'Med-Arb' which, as the name suggests, combines the two processes, so if a couple cannot come to an agreement in six sessions, the mediator becomes an arbitrator and makes decisions.

Are children involved?

In accordance with the government's 'Voice of the Child' initiative, children can have their wishes and feelings expressed through an interview with and report from an independent social worker. This would incur a small cost for parents wanting their children's input.

when my parents split up it broke me, but now I'm independent and I look back on it as a lesson in life. Ivy (19)

Can an arbitrator's decision be appealed?

Only if there has been an error in law, not for any personal reason.

What are the advantages of arbitration?

Couples can wait months for a case to be heard in court, but arbitration can take place as soon as the couple are able to arrange the meeting and be resolved that same day.

The courtroom can be an intimidating and hostile place for many people. The relative informality of three people having a discussion is often much more appealing and a couple can find more creative solutions outside the constraints of the law.

Unlike mediation, the arbitrator has the power to step in and make decisions that are legally binding and final.

Arbitration will cost the couple £750 each. Whilst it is true that a court appearance to resolve matters relating to children costs £215, that is without any legal representation (never the best idea) or expenses which can mount up considerably.

Being able to be in the same room, enter into discussion and resolve issues makes for a positive future, especially for parents who will be co-parenting children. Just because a relationship is finished does not mean a family is.

Notes

Is arbitration right for me?

About the author

Julian Ribet, Levison Meltzer Pigott

Julian is a specialist family lawyer who has an impressive track record in dealing with complicated financial and children related disputes arising on relationship breakdown/ divorce. He is a qualified specialist family arbitrator and is a member of the Chartered Institute of Arbitrators.

Arbitration is a means of resolving disputes which takes place outside a formal court room. Because it is a move away from the traditional structure of court room litigation, it is classed as Alternative Dispute Resolution ('ADR'). As well as arbitration, ADR typically includes early neutral evaluation, negotiation, conciliation and mediation.

In arbitration, the parties appoint an arbitrator, usually a lawyer, who has the appropriate qualifications and experience to adjudicate a dispute concerning finances or children. The parties agree to be bound by the reasoned and written decision of the arbitrator. This decision is called an 'award' when it relates to finances and it is known as a 'determination' when it concerns children.

Is arbitration right for me?

The first question you must ask yourself is not just whether arbitration might be right for you but also how likely it is that the other party will agree to arbitrate; without this consensus of approach, arbitration is not an option.

If it is a viable route, there are some significant benefits to the parties:

Time management: with the increasing burden on the family court and the resultant delays, there is more control of your time and that of your advisors in arbitration. You may have to wait six months or more for a final court hearing; an arbitration could be heard next week. The hearing is at a time and date of the parties' choosing and it can even be at evenings and weekends. It can be set up quickly and there is little risk of it being moved or postponed. Also, you may need to attend only one hearing and the case may also be able to be decided on upon documents alone.

Choice: you get to choose the arbitrator, although you may wish to refer to your legal advisor for advice on this point as they will have a view on who may be best for your case. You and your advisor can also choose the venue, provided it is agreed by the arbitrator and the other party, so travel time and related costs are minimised. Also, very importantly, you get to choose the remit of the arbitrator and the issues to be arbitrated. It is a Judge's obligation to look at the whole case; if you wish, an arbitrator can decide only certain issues on which you are not agreed.

Communication: the same arbitrator will be used throughout the process and your legal advisor will be able to communicate and liaise with them directly, both sides being copied in.

Privacy and confidentiality: the whole process and the determination are confidential. The media are not entitled to be admitted at any stage.

However, there is a downside. If you don't agree with the arbitrator and their decision, you then have to resort to the courts to appeal against the decision.

Nonetheless, if you are someone who values this degree of involvement, choice, confidentiality and control, then arbitration may be the more cost effective, quicker and less stressful solution for you.

What preparation should I do?

Parties can refer a matter to arbitration themselves or through legal advisors although most arbitrators only accept instructions from solicitors. This can be at the beginning of the dispute or part of the way

through. Either way, the first step is to complete a form and send it to the IFLA. The forms are Form ARB1FS (in the case of financial disputes) or Form ARB1CS (in the case of children disputes). The form essentially confirms the terms and conditions. Depending on the stage of the dispute there may be additional checks such Disclosure and Barring Service (DBS). The arbitrator is then appointed and a planning meeting arranged, although this can be by phone.

You will be expected to work with your legal advisor to identify and clarify the key issues relating to the case. Expert reports may be considered if required to support your case. You will be helping your legal advisors to produce the necessary supporting background information or evidence. These papers, referred to as a 'bundle' will be sent to the arbitrator in advance of the actual arbitration.

Typically the bundle will include:

- a case summary;

- a schedule of issues to be considered;

- a timeline;

- any application documents filed in any court proceedings;

- statements of the parties with supporting evidence; and

- any expert reports and relevant financial documents if appropriate.

How to find a family arbitrator

Because it is relatively new, there are comparatively few trained family arbitrators but that number is increasing. Your legal advisor is there to help but if you want to research yourself, the

Institute of Family Law Arbitrators (IFLA), and its website which lists all qualified specialist arbitrators is a good place to start.

Conclusion

Arbitration is an alternative form of dispute resolution which is also growing in popularity for those who recognise the benefits in relation to their specific case and circumstances.

Notes

Court & 'fighting' for the children

Welfare Checklist, SPIP, C100, CAO. These terms serve as a reminder of how the previously emotional based commitment of marriage/partnership is now moving into the realms of law. Just as the language changes to reflect this move, the way you think needs to change too. Dealing with the legal aspects of a divorce requires reason, logic and cool-headed thinking. These processes use different parts of the brain, moving from the emotional decision-making of most days (e.g. "I feel furious, I'm going to text them right now") to rational-decision making (e.g. "I feel furious, but I will write down my thoughts on a piece of paper and wait until tomorrow to decide whether to send it or not). When our brains are flooded with stress hormones and fizzing with anxiety, our decision making processes change. This chapter points you in the direction of all the support and guidance available out there to help you make clear decisions which have your child's best interests at heart.

How should I prepare for court?

About the author

James Belderbos, Director, Bird Belderbos & Mee Solicitors

James is a Family Law Specialist advising individuals on divorce, matrimonial finance, children and cohabitation disputes. He is a member of Resolution and qualified collaborative lawyer.

The thought of attending court for those who haven't been before can be harrowing but being properly prepared and informed will reduce a lot of that stress. The more you put in, the less stressful you will find the process.

Whilst this short article is prepared to assist you in preparing for court it is worth repeating here that applications to the court should be considered as a last resort.

Reasons why you should avoid seeking answers and solutions through the court process include other people making decisions about your family, you not being in control of the process, greater costs and the inadequacies of the court system with overburdened staff, lack of accommodation and delay. A court order is a blunt instrument for resolving unique issues for you and your children.

You may have no choice but to attend court if other solutions including mediation and the collaborative process have failed or you are responding to an application made by a former partner.

Whatever type of hearing you are facing, it is vital that you are prepared for what may happen at court and at home whilst you are there.

Representation

To be fully informed and prepared, representation by a solicitor or a barrister is best. They will lift a considerable burden from you. Some solicitors will offer fixed fees or you could instruct a barrister on a direct access basis (see Question 50). Most solicitors offer a reduced fixed fee for an initial consultation during which you can make an informed decision over what is right for you. If you can't afford legal fees, publicly funded representation or legal aid may be available if you can fulfil strict criteria. Always consider who the right representative is for you. You need an expert, preferably accredited by Resolution and someone you feel comfortable with.

If you are represented, simply ask the solicitor or barrister what will happen at court and what you will need to do. That overview should give you the peace of mind that you require to approach the case constructively.

As a solicitor I always discuss with my client, as soon as I have a hearing date, what will happen on the day so that I can address any fears and dispel any myths that may be clouding my client's view on what they can achieve for their family.

You may be surprised to hear that your first attendance may be the first of three or four hearings, possibly more. In the majority of cases there is the opportunity to settle a case so always ask your solicitor what can be done to avoid further hearings and costs.

Take along a friend or relative

Whilst they won't be allowed into the court room you will find it beneficial to have them with you. Think about the right friend or relative. If you have a new partner they are unlikely to be the right person to take along. Always consider what your former partner will feel if they see you accompanied by someone. Will the person you choose to support you assist or aggravate an already difficult situation?

Keep the day free for you

You must ensure that you have the date marked clearly in your diary and, as far as is possible, booked off from work and other responsibilities. This means ensuring that someone is available not only to look after the children in the event of illness but there to pick them up from school and give them their tea.

Whilst a hearing may be listed for 9am with a time estimate of one hour it is best to set aside the whole day. Courts will often list many cases at one time and it is rare for hearings to start at the published times or time estimates adhered to. The last thing you want is to be concerned that you are not going to be at work for the afternoon if you've just taken the morning off.

If a hearing finishes early, you deserve a rest or the opportunity to catch up with all the other things that you haven't been able to do. Frequently negotiations take a considerable amount of time and can cause delay. This can, however, be advantageous if they result in a settlement, especially where this was never considered a possibility.

Make sure you know where the court is

On the day itself you will find your mind preoccupied with what is going to happen at court. If your solicitor has not told you where the court is, ask them and find out where the best place to park is. Find out the cost of parking and have the right change with you. If taking a friend then make sure they know when to nip out and top up the meter. Better still, choose a car park with payment on exit or one which offers internet payment.

Documents

If you haven't done so already, ensure that your lever arch file with your papers is in good order. If represented, your solicitor should have prepared a bundle of core documents for the hearing. Ask for a copy of that

from your solicitor. Try to avoid bringing large amounts of documents to court but if you do bring new ones ensure that you have sufficient copies for your representative and your former partner or representative.

On starting your case, open an email folder in your inbox specifically for letters and correspondence relating to the matter and a separate folder to include your own documents and those received.

You may prefer to have hard copies of all the documents and so it is always worthwhile having a lever arch file or box file in which to hold all your documents. It is vital that if you wish to hold hard copies of documents that you are sent that this file is as organised as possible so that you can easily find what you are looking for.

Whilst technology at courts is improving, keeping everything on your laptop isn't always helpful - wifi at courts isn't as good as you might expect.

Make sure your laptop and/or phone are charged and both turned to silent.

Bring your diary and dates that you need to avoid, like holidays, medical appointments or other events, for the next hearing. Dates can be changed but doing so isn't easy and may necessitate another hearing and further costs.

Security

A trip to court is no holiday but the security is similar to that experienced boarding a flight. Umbrellas are best avoided and if you bring one it will be left at security along with drinks and a whole host of other items. Drinks

even in sealed containers will be checked by court staff. Avoid bringing anything you don't need that will set off metal detectors as you are scanned on arrival. Security officers are told to confiscate anything that could be used as a weapon, even stiletto heels!

Court hearings are not enjoyable for parties and you will undoubtedly find them difficult, but being nervous is normal. The more you can do to prepare and the more open minded you are the more likely that you will get what you want from the day. You will be tense but you must remember that each court hearing can be another hurdle conquered bringing you closer to what you want to achieve. This moment like all will pass.

ONLY
Mums & Dads
parents meet professionals

Should I appoint a barrister?

About the author

Lucy Reed, barrister at St John's Chambers

Lucy's practice spans all areas of family law with a particular emphasis on children work. She often acts in complex, multi-party or high conflict intractable private law disputes. In public law children cases she acts for parents, children, local authorities and the extended family. Lucy has written *The Family Court without a Lawyer*, now into its 3rd edition.

Not a lot of people know this, but since 2010 it's been possible to instruct a barrister to advise or represent you without going through a solicitor (this is called 'public access'). To understand whether or not that's something you need to know or care about, you need to understand what the difference is between a barrister and a solicitor.

They are all lawyers. Barristers are not senior to solicitors, and you do not graduate from solicitor to barrister. But the two types of lawyers do perform different roles. In a nutshell the difference is this:

A barrister is a specialist advocate - they will also be a specialist in their field. Their work will be exclusively in-court advocacy and negotiation and advising their clients. Barristers are self-employed and out and about. This means their infrastructure and administrative support is slender, but their overheads are lower, making them cost effective in the right circumstances.

A solicitor will handle the paperwork - they will issue the applications, deal with the correspondence and send documents to the right person. They too will advise their clients. They may also do some or all of their own advocacy but, because of their additional responsibilities and the different business set up, few solicitors will be in court as frequently as barristers, or will deal with as many complex trials as barristers.

A solicitor will usually instruct a barrister to represent their client in court for two reasons:

- their commitments to their other clients mean they can't attend court on that day; or

- they feel that the case requires a specialist advocate or expert guidance.

Having said that, the legal sector is in the process of deregulation and the ways that lawyers organise themselves are changing and are likely to change even more. Public access instruction of a barrister is just one example of those changes.

Google research is not equal to expert legal advice.

Hasan Hadi, Southgate Solicitors

When should I consider instructing a barrister directly?

You might particularly consider instructing a barrister directly in the following circumstances:

- You are not involved in a court case but think that you might be, or that you might need to start a court case. A barrister could give you some advice so that you can understand where you stand and what application you should make.

- You are unlikely to be able to afford to pay lawyers to represent you continuously through a court case but need some one-off advice.

- You would like some advice before you decide whether to pay for representation at a hearing.

When direct access might not be appropriate

If you need urgent advice, if you need to issue an application very quickly, or if you want to be represented at a hearing in the immediate future you should seek advice from a solicitor. This is because a barrister is likely to

COURT & 'FIGHTING' FOR THE CHILDREN

be in court much of the working week and may be unable to respond to urgent enquiries in the same way that a solicitor's office can. A solicitor will be part of a larger firm and will be able to rely on administrative staff and other solicitors to deal with urgent matters, but a barrister's business model cannot allow this. They can instruct a barrister to represent you if needs be - and if necessary should be able to locate one who is available at short notice on your behalf.

If your case is likely to require significant amounts of correspondence, the gathering of lots of evidence (for example obtaining police records) and preparation of witness statements, or the instruction of experts your case might be better dealt with by a solicitor.

Assessment for public access

Before a barrister can agree to advise you or represent you they have to assess whether or not it would be better for you to be represented through a solicitor. If you are struggling to manage your paperwork or to organise your thoughts, or if you are going to have real difficulty in managing the administrative part of your case a barrister will probably have to refuse your case as a public access case and suggest that you contact a

solicitor (you could still instruct a solicitor and ask them to instruct a particular barrister for you).

If you would like to get some advice directly from a barrister the best way to ensure that your case is suitable for public access is to follow the guidance below:

Leave plenty of time: The commonest reason that barristers decline public access instructions is that things have been left too late. Remember that a barrister's diary will be full up in advance with court bookings. You need to leave enough time for them to consider the papers and to advise you. If everything is up to the wire you will probably be better off going to a solicitor first - they can access a pool of barristers and will usually be able to find someone who can make the date of your hearing. If you want to instruct a particular barrister you are entitled to ask them to do this for you.

Organise your paperwork: Before a barrister can take a case on they have to be confident you can manage the administrative side of the case that a solicitor might otherwise handle. Keep your papers in order: file orders and applications, statements, correspondence and other material separately and in chronological order. Generally a barrister will need to see all the papers in the court bundle even

if you think they are not relevant. If you are asked for a particular document send that document - let the barrister decide what is and is not relevant.

Formulate your questions: Know what you want the barrister to do. Do you want general advice about how strong your case is? Do you want a specific technical question answered? Do you want practical advice about what application to make or what to do next? Or do you want advice about how to maximise your chances of getting the best possible outcome?

Be frank and balanced: Your barrister will need to know not just how you see the case but also how the other party sees the case. It is pointless asking for advice about the case when you have only given half the story. Explain the issues being raised by the other party even if you don't agree with them. Be honest with yourself and your barrister about the weaknesses in your case.

Legal aid is not available to pay for the costs of instructing a barrister through public access, so if you are likely to be eligible for free legal advice/ representation it is likely you will be advised to instruct a solicitor in order to benefit.

Heartbreak - yes there's nothing worse, it haunts you, like an evil curse.
A quote from a poem by Kat (15)

What does it mean to 'instruct' a solicitor?

About the author

Melanie Bataillard-Samuel, Gregg Latchams Solicitors

Melanie is a solicitor and co-chairs Resolution's Innovation Committee with Tom. She is also a trained collaborative law solicitor.

Separating from your partner will inevitably mean going through some changes in your life which will often become more complicated when children are involved. Where will you both live? Who will the children live with? What about money? The list can feel endless - where do you start?

Do you need a solicitor - first steps?

A good first step is to consider whether you can discuss things with your ex. Being clear about what you each want and are expecting the other to do will go a long way to making moving on easier. If you feel you need a little support at this stage, then consider mediation. You and your ex would still be in charge of the negotiations, but with the added help of a neutral third party who would facilitate these negotiations.

It is highly recommended that you take steps to understand your specific legal position before entering into discussions. This will help you to be clear on your issues regarding children (if you have them), finances and other matters. It will also help with reaching an agreement you and your ex are both happy with. Speaking to a solicitor and obtaining legal advice when you first start considering a separation can often provide reassurance which in turn may help to smooth out the stress of the situation. It's never too early to seek legal advice. And, of course, if discussions or mediation are simply not a possibility then a solicitor will help with the court process should you need it.

> Success is all about how far you are willing to travel in terms of fairness and compromise.
>
> *Nav Mirza, Dads Unlimited*

First meeting?

The first meeting with your solicitor is important - you should leave their office with enough options and information to allow you to make decisions. The more prepared you are for the first meeting the more you will get out of it. It is therefore not a bad idea to turn up with the following:-

- An idea of what is it you want out of the situation - financial settlement, care of the children, etc. If your solicitor has an idea of what you are considering they can advise on that or propose other options for you.

- A short summary of your situation to include some details about you and your family with dates. This will provide your solicitor with a

He walked out of the door and it felt like my life had been demolished before my eyes. Mia (12)

quick overview of the situation and allow more time in the meeting to discuss your legal position and options.

- Any previous letters/emails/texts exchanged with your ex/their solicitors or any documents you might want your solicitor to look over (such as an offer or an application made to the court). Although your solicitor may not have sufficient time or the information necessary during that meeting to fully advise you on these documents, they can consider everything in outline and give you an idea of what to look out for or what now needs to be done.

- Make a list of questions you want to ask - it'll help to keep the meeting focused on what you want to know and will help the solicitor tailor their advice to you. Of course, your solicitor will probably think of a few extra things to discuss that are not on your list!

- A friend/family member to accompany you. This is a stressful time and you will have a lot to think about - someone taking notes of the discussion for you to consider later on may remove the pressure of remembering everything your solicitor says. Some solicitors do provide a written note of the meeting so you may want to ask about that when you book the meeting.

- ID - both photographic and a proof of your address.

Going through a separation is a stressful situation where emotions can run high. Listen to what your solicitor is saying - they will let you know if you're

being unrealistic and propose other options they think will benefit you. Use this meeting to identify the important issues that need to be addressed first.

Don't be afraid to ask questions if you don't understand or if you're worried - there are no silly questions.

To instruct or not to instruct

Once you've had that first meeting you should be in a position to decide whether you want to 'instruct' (or hire) your solicitor to act for you. This may not always be the case - perhaps you only wanted to understand your legal position before discussing things with your ex, or you've decided to represent yourself and just wanted to know where you stand.

If you want to hire a solicitor to act for you pick one you trust and feel comfortable with - personalities play an important part in choosing a solicitor and don't be afraid to specify if you would rather instruct a male or female solicitor. If the first solicitor you meet does not suit you, you should look for another one. Shop around!

This can be a nerve racking experience for mums and dads.

It is never too late to settle any disputes prior to hearings and decisions made together are always preferable to ones made on your behalf.

Try to keep calm. It's an unfamiliar environment so nerves are inevitable.

Keep to the point, so only talk about the presenting issues.

Try to keep emotions at bay, not easy but they can overwhelm and cloud your thinking.

Listen to your legal team, they know what they're doing.

If you get angry try to negotiate a 'time out' so that you can calm down.

Listen fully and if there is something you do not understand, ask.

Adele Ballantyne

Court waiting rooms are dreadful places. Your ex may well be there. If you don't have a professional advisor with you it is perfectly in order to take a friend along to sit with you. You are also free to ask the court usher if you might be able to sit alone in one of the ante-rooms. These are often occupied however.

Can I get the Judge to speak directly with my children?

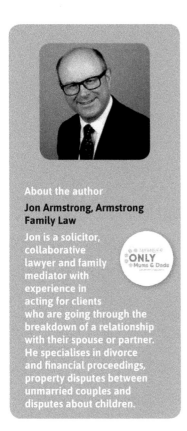

About the author

Jon Armstrong, Armstrong Family Law

Jon is a solicitor, collaborative lawyer and family mediator with experience in acting for clients who are going through the breakdown of a relationship with their spouse or partner. He specialises in divorce and financial proceedings, property disputes between unmarried couples and disputes about children.

Parents in cases involving disputes about children will often feel that it is important that the children's views are taken into account, rather than have their views ignored by the grown-ups. The law recognises this. It says that children's views will be taken into account in light of their age and understanding. Therefore, a child aged, say, 5 years old, is not likely to have any weight attached to his or her views, whereas a child of, say 13, will find that the court will take into account their views, albeit that these views will not be the only factor that the court will take into account.

Older children may find that their views are the determining factor. It is relatively rare to see disputes about children aged between 14 and 16 being dealt with at court, as the court will often take the view that it cannot make a child of that age do something which they do not wish to do. (The court cannot usually make orders about children aged 16 or above).

Will the Judge speak to the child?

Judges will often be very reluctant to speak directly to a child. They generally prefer to leave that to people who are better trained to do so - the CAFCASS Officers.

At an early stage in any application to the court (usually at the First Hearing Dispute Resolution Appointment or FHDRA), the court will consider whether or not it should order a section 7 report to be prepared to provide the court with independent recommendations about what it might be ordered. These reports (which grizzled older solicitors and barristers sometimes still refer to as Court Welfare Reports) are usually prepared by the CAFCASS Officer.

Sometimes the only thing that the CAFCASS Officer has to address in their report is the child's wishes and feelings. The CAFCASS Officer will not simply parrot what the child says. The Officer will speak to the children about what they want and will also bear in mind that it is common for children who are at the centre of disputes to be telling each parent what they want to hear, rather than what the child actually wants. Experienced CAFCASS Officers can be very good at getting to what the child actually wants.

In a small number of cases a Judge has talked directly to the child in a case. One Judge, Mr Justice Peter Jackson was praised in 2017 by family lawyers for the sensitive and intelligent way in which he wrote a letter to a child in order to explain his decision to the child.

Mr Justice Jackson has even used emojis in such letters to help communicate with children about their case. However, he is somewhat unusual in his approach. Most Judges prefer not to speak to the children directly and instead rely on parents to explain the court's decisions to their children.

What is collaborative law?

About the author

Peter Martin, Head of Family at OGR Stock Denton

Peter is a mediator, collaborative lawyer, and arbitrator and has particular expertise in high-net-worth financial matters, issues relating to who a child should live with and how often they should see the other parent.

Collaborative law is a non-confrontational way of helping divorcing/separating parties to resolve matters in an alternative manner to traditional proceedings involving the court and adversarial litigation.

This process is most suited to separating/divorcing couples who are going to be open about their financial positions, comfortable in discussing everything with the other person present, who believe the other person has a similar wish and who want the outcome of financial settlement to be fair to both.

It generates a dignified and co-operative attitude to negotiation. The commitment of the separating couple and their lawyers is to achieve a settlement which will be as suitable as possible for the family as a whole - not just their client - without the threat of court proceedings.

How does collaborative law work?

You and your former partner meet together with your own collaboratively trained lawyers, openly communicate about what issues each of you would like to resolve and aim to work through these whilst all together in the same room. The process uses similar documentation (the Form E) to other processes to ensure there is full disclosure of financial information. Lawyers will often be advising their own client in front of the other person and their lawyer, so there can be no false claiming of

"Well, my lawyer says I am entitled to this"

from the client; and no

"Well, my client insists..."

from the lawyer.

You can move at your own pace and voice all the things that are important to you without any behind the scenes negotiations or lengthy and aggressive correspondence between your lawyers. You will both be able to ask questions and see and hear how they are answered directly, which often helps to build a rapport with all participants who become engaged in the problem-solving process of finding the best (or least worst) outcome for all of you, especially any children. Sometimes it even enables you to see things from your partner's point of view, which can help you to work together to resolve your issues.

It is also possible to bring in support from other independent advisors such as family consultants, independent financial advisors, child specialists etc who are familiar with the collaborative process to act as a neutral specialist should you require it.

What makes collaborative law successful is the control over the content and pace of the meetings

It was strange to begin with living with my dad, I'd never had that much to do with him before. But we both knew that if we were going to get through this, we had to do it together. Sally (16)

and continuing contact with your former partner in a structured way. This enables you to have a better chance of resolving issues amicably and most importantly helps maintain a relationship as parents are able to cooperate with each other for the benefit of the children.

Can my lawyer represent me in court if the process breaks down?

No. Your collaborative lawyer will be absolutely committed to helping you find the best solutions by mutual agreement rather than through conflict, because they will not be permitted to represent you in court if, for any reason, the collaborative process breaks down.

Top tips and FAQs

Who is this approach suitable for?

Couples who want to resolve matters amicably and who can talk to each other, particularly with the help of other people.

Are all family lawyers collaborative lawyers?

No. A collaborative family lawyer needs to have special additional training. You should ask before instructing the lawyer if they do collaborative law. If the answer you are given is "no, but I try to settle cases without going to court anyway", then the person is not a collaborative lawyer.

What happens if I get upset?

The training that collaborative lawyers receive enables them to deal with emotional issues and it is understood that people will get upset, angry and tearful at times. Many collaborative lawyers are also trained

mediators who are well used to dealing with these issues. It is always possible to have breaks from the meeting if it begins to get too much.

How long will it take?

This will be up to you and your lawyers. There are no court delays and it is often a question of how quickly both parties want to proceed and how quickly all the information is available.

How much will it cost and is it more expensive?

The cost will depend on the hourly rates of your solicitors. It can often seem more time intensive as most of the work is done in meetings. However, in the long run, the cost is very similar to solicitor-led negotiation through correspondence. It is cheaper in most cases than using the court process, even if you settle at an early stage. It is a huge amount cheaper than going to court for a Final Hearing which can easily cost tens of thousands of pounds.

What happens if we don't reach agreement?

The process is relatively new and statistics are still being collated. However, in my experience, 90% of the cases I have dealt with collaboratively reach settlement. If you do not, then it is still possible to go to court. The financial information obtained is able to be used in court, but not the negotiations. However, you will need to instruct new lawyers in view of the lawyers' commitment to the process referred to above .

> Make sure that you spend time at the outset asking about the different options to reach a resolution; you don't have to go to court. Consider mediation or working collaboratively with your partner and their lawyer.
>
> *Bernadette Hoy, Garside & Hoy*

Advocate

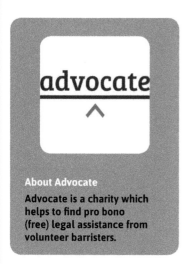

About Advocate

Advocate is a charity which helps to find pro bono (free) legal assistance from volunteer barristers.

Who are we?

Many people struggling with family legal issues are unable to afford legal representation and do not qualify for legal aid. We are a free service that matches those in need of legal help who can't afford representation or get legal aid with volunteer barristers who kindly donate their time and expertise.

Since we were founded by Lord Goldsmith as the Bar Pro Bono Unit in 1996, we have helped thousands of individuals and small organisations to get expert free legal help. We became Advocate in October 2018, with a renewed focus on modernising our service so that we can help provide the right legal help to as many people as possible across England and Wales.

Our vision

Our vision is to be able to match everyone needing legal help quickly and easily to the right expert barrister.

We can assist with:

- Specialist legal advice, drafting and representation;
- Cases in all areas of law;
- Cases in all tribunals and courts in England and Wales.

On average, we hear from 50 new people every week facing a legal problem alone. Each year, we receive more family cases than cases in any other area of law. Our applicants might be struggling to see their children, attempting to gain a custody order or going through a difficult separation.

Barristers can:

- Give legal advice in a meeting or in writing;
- Draft documents such as skeleton arguments;
- Represent in any court or tribunal.

Barristers cannot:

- Prepare a case and paperwork for the court or tribunal;
- Lodge papers at the court or tribunal on your behalf;
- Provide administrative support;
- Write letters on another's behalf.

Advocate ensures that in each case the barrister providing assistance has the same expertise and experience as would be expected in a paying case. We may be able to help if:

- An individual or organization cannot get legal aid, pay

privately, or get legal help elsewhere;
- The matter involves the law of England and Wales;
- The case is appropriate for assistance on a pro bono basis;
- The help needed will take 3 days or less (exceptions may apply);
- The case needs a barrister who can act if necessary without a solicitor.

How to apply to Advocate for help:

- All applications must be made through a referring agency such as a solicitor or advice agency (e.g. a Citizens Advice Bureau, a Legal Advice Clinic or Law Centre).
- An application may also be referred by your MP.
- The application form is available on our website or we can send out hard copies on request.
- Once completed, the application form needs to be returned to us in hard copy along with copies of any case documents.

The referrer:

- helps make the initial application to Advocate and can identify the supporting documents required.
- can, if they wish, act as a point of contact throughout the process.

ONLY
Mums & Dads
parents meet professionals

Eligibility

- If you can pay privately or are eligible for public funding (legal aid) for your case, we will not be able to help.

- We cannot help in cases unless we receive the completed application and all the relevant documents at least three weeks before the hearing or deadline, unless there are exceptional circumstances; i.e. your child would be taken into care.

Assistance

Assistance cannot be guaranteed as we rely on the services of volunteer barristers.

We are not a frontline agency and do not have barristers in our office to give legal advice directly. We are an application-based service that focuses the Bar's pro bono resources where they are most needed.

Case study

Daniel is the father of three young children. He applied to Advocate for legal assistance in seeking a residence order against his children's unstable mother. Advocate was able to match Daniel with a volunteer barrister who represented him in court. The case was successful and the residence order was granted, offering Daniel and his children more stability and hope for the future. Daniel spoke about his experience with the Advocate:

"I cannot thank the Advocate enough for the incredible help and support you provided for a desperate father. The barrister you supplied came into my world yesterday and completely changed the landscape of myself and my children's future. Without her work and the work of yourselves, my life would be in a terrible state; instead I look forward to a future with my children."

To find out more about us and the work that we do to help people like Daniel, please visit our website: https://weareadvocate.org.uk.

> When your children are upset (as they will often be during the period after parents separate) it is better to respond to their feelings and not their behaviour - you can best help by showing understanding and respect for your child's feelings.
>
> *Paul Kemp, The Worcester Family Mediation Practice*

Notes

COURT & 'FIGHTING' FOR THE CHILDREN

Can I change my CAFCASS Officer?

About the author

Mark Leeson, partner and co-team leader at Brachers Solicitors

Mark trained as a family mediator in 1995 and was accredited by the Family Mediators Association. He has been an Accredited Resolution Specialist since 2002 and a collaborative lawyer since 2007. He specialises in family, wills and inheritance disputes.

I n a word: no.

Who are CAFCASS?

CAFCASS stands for Children and Family Court Advisory and Support Service. CAFCASS is separate from the court service itself but provides expertise to the court when required. When a children application is made to the court CAFCASS will initially undertake a safeguarding check on the parents which includes a criminal records check. They will usually try and speak to both parents and then provide a short report to the court on any issues which arise.

At the First Hearing a CAFCASS Officer (who will have a social work background) will meet with both parents and make recommendations to the court as to next steps. If no issues emerge which create a concern about the children's welfare then it is likely that CAFCASS will have no ongoing involvement in the proceedings before the court.

Section 7 report

If however issues do arise which affect the welfare of the children then the court can order that CAFCASS prepare a report (called a 'section 7' report) on the issues and make recommendations to the court about the most appropriate arrangements for the children. These recommendations will have a significant influence on the eventual outcome of the application.

CAFCASS Officer

The CAFCASS Officer is appointed by the court. It is not possible to change the CAFCASS Officer because you do not agree with the conclusions they have reached. If you do not agree with the recommendations that the CAFCASS Officer has made it is possible to challenge their conclusions in the court.

If you have a concern about a CAFCASS Officer's performance or conduct whilst undertaking their duties CAFCASS have a complaints procedure and there is a useful fact sheet on their website at cafcass.co.uk. However, it will still be the decision of CAFCASS or of the

court as to whether a CAFCASS Officer's performance or conduct is such that they should be removed from the case.

In some cases where the issues are complicated and the CAFCASS Officer has been unhelpful it may be possible to ask the court to make the children a party to the proceedings. If that order is made the court will appoint a guardian who also comes from CAFCASS. However, the guardian's role is to represent the children's position and can therefore provide an alternative view to that of the CAFCASS Officer.

If you go to court you will be asking the judge who doesn't know you, doesn't know or love your child or probably ever meet your child to tell you what your future arrangements are going to be for your child. Is this what you want?

Helen Pittard, 174 Law

What is the Welfare Checklist and do I need to know about it?

About the author

David Starkey, solicitor at John Hodge Solicitors

David specialises in family law and deals with divorce, financial arrangements, cohabitation disputes and children matters. He is a member of Resolution and is also on the Law Society Family Panel.

I f you are contemplating divorce or separation from your partner, your first concern will probably be about where your children will live and how they will spend time with both parents. As parents, you know your children best, so you will be best able to consider the effects of your break-up on them and, hopefully, together devise the most suitable living arrangements for your children.

Family mediation services, together with Resolution mediators and solicitors, can help you to achieve this outcome.

If you can't agree upon the arrangements, you can ask the courts to decide the matter by making an application for a Child Arrangements Order. Prior to making any application to the court, it is necessary for the parties to attempt mediation.

Welfare checklist

The Children Act 1989 is the main piece of legislation dealing with family disputes about children. The Children Act states that the child's welfare is the paramount consideration when the court considers any question in relation to the upbringing of a child. Therefore, the court will apply what is known as the 'welfare checklist' to help it make its decision.

The welfare checklist looks at:

The wishes and feelings of the child (considered in the light of their age and level of understanding)

This will normally be determined by CAFCASS or Social Services, and reported to the court. The

I always tell separating couples to remember that they are parents and regardless of their relationship having failed, they must not fail their children. I stress that there will be many occasions where their children will want them both there, their children must not be forced to choose or be in an awkward position but rather see their parents putting on a united front for THEM.

Amanda Adeola, BHP Law

court will take into consideration whether or not a child's wishes and feelings are their own, or whether outside factors may have influenced their decision. The court will balance the views of the parties concerned, including the views of a child who is of an understanding age (normally 9 years of age) and mature enough to form their own opinions.

Parents, don't bad mouth the other parent to your child. Josie (15)

Their physical, emotional and educational needs

A child's emotional needs can be quite difficult to deal with, and the court will consider who is best able to provide for the emotional needs of the child, both short term and long term.

The likely effect of any change in their circumstances

The potential impact of changes to the child's life will be considered. The courts will aim to make an order that causes the least disruption to a child's life - however, this will be balanced against the other factors to be considered.

Their age, sex, background and any characteristics which the court considers relevant

The court will consider specific issues such as race, religion and culture when making a decision about a child. They may also take into consideration the parents' hobbies and lifestyle choices if they feel it will impact on the child's life, either now or in the future.

Any harm which they have suffered or are at risk of suffering

The courts will look at the risk of harm to the child. This will be immediate risk of harm as well as the risk of harm in the future. 'Harm' includes physical, emotional and mental harm. The courts will decide upon the potential risk of harm to the child in the future and make an order as they feel is appropriate. An order may include safety measures to protect the child.

How capable each parent is of meeting their needs

The courts will consider how able each parent is to care for the child and to meet their particular needs. This will be subjective and depend upon the facts and circumstances of each case, the needs of the child and the abilities of the parents concerned.

The range of powers available to the court

The court must weigh up all of the factors under the welfare checklist, and consider all available orders within their discretion. It will then make the best order available that is in the best interests of the child.

The welfare checklist is therefore extremely important when considering where a child should live and how much time they should spend with each parent. It is the framework by which the courts use in order to reach their decision. As a result, it is important to know and understand the welfare checklist prior to making any application to the court regarding your child.

Notes

Have you any tips for dealing with an abusive partner at a court hearing?

About the authors

Claire Fitzgerald, Partner and Sue Scott, senior solicitor, Barrett & Thomson

Claire is a member of Law Society Children Panel and is authorized to act for children and parents. She is a Resolution accredited specialist in Domestic Abuse and Private Child Law.

Sue is a senior solicitor and has many years experience in all aspects of family law including divorce, change of name, separation agreements, pre-nups, financial provision, contact/residence disputes, domestic abuse and child abduction.

If you can afford legal representation (i.e. have someone speak on your behalf) it is likely to be easier for you to face your ex-partner. Unfortunately solicitors and barristers can be expensive and not everyone can afford to pay their fees. However, many solicitor's firms are very understanding and may be able to help you in a number of different ways such as:

- Offering a discounted rate if you are on low income;

- Acting on a fixed fee basis (this will need to be agreed in advance);

- Helping you with a specific piece of work, such as preparing a statement or completing an application form (this option is known as "unbundled services" - see Question 100 for more information).

Instructing a solicitor

It's wise to shop around before instructing any solicitor. You need to find one who not only specialises in family law but more especially in domestic abuse cases.

Accredited Resolution specialists in domestic abuse can be found on the Resolution website http://www.resolution.org.uk/domesticabuse. The "Find a solicitor" section of the Law Society website http://solicitors.lawsociety.org.uk is also useful to help you find a solicitor in your

area, and it will give details of whether they undertake Legal Aid work plus their specialisms registered with the Law Society e.g. family panel or child panel.

Instructing a barrister

Some barristers will accept direct instructions from a client (this is called Direct Access) rather than the usual method of through a solicitor. So if you just want representation at a hearing this is something to consider but remember that barristers will not help you prepare any paperwork needed beforehand. Make sure you find a set of barristers' chambers that specialises in family law.

You may qualify for Legal Aid if you are the victim of domestic abuse. If you do qualify, you will be able to get representation at a hearing. You can check your eligibility on the LAA website https://www.gov.uk/legal-aid .

Don't believe everything your partner tells you about your rights or lack of them.

Carol-Anne Baker, Bridge Law Solicitors Limited

COURT & 'FIGHTING' FOR THE CHILDREN

McKenzie Friends

If you cannot afford a solicitor or barrister then you may consider a McKenzie Friend to offer support and assistance in court. There are different types of McKenzie Friends, including:

- family members, or friends;

- voluntary helpers attached to institutions or charities especially domestic abuse agencies, who generally do not charge for their help;

- fee-charging McKenzie Friends. Their charges can sometimes be quite high and you may be better off instructing a solicitor. So please do your research beforehand and if possible use someone who has been recommended.

McKenzie Friends can help by, providing moral support, taking notes in court, helping with paperwork but they are not allowed to speak in court unless the Judge gives permission.

Who is representing the perpetrator?

If the perpetrator has a solicitor or a barrister then they should be easier to deal with - they may try and negotiate with you before you go into court to narrow down the issues. They may question you in court but they have to follow certain rules.

If both parties have legal representation the court hearing will be easier to handle as any discussion will take place between the representatives.

If neither of you have representation the Judge will lead the conduct of the case.

> ### WILL MY FORMER PARTNER BE IN COURT?
>
> It would be best if you prepare as though they will be. Sometimes partners say they're going to attend and don't, just to wind the other up, but if you prepare calming strategies (e.g. mindfulness exercises) and ask for a recess if you feel too upset then you will be managing your feelings. If you are represented then make sure your rep knows how you feel, as they can petition the court for some protection from the ex, e.g. not allowing them to intimidate.
>
> *Mike Flinn*

Making applications

Things to consider when making an application to the court are:

- **Confidentiality**. If your address is confidential and is not known to the perpetrator you can request the court's permission not to disclose it to them on any documents. This is done on a C8 form which is available on the court website https://assets.publishing. service.gov.uk/government/ uploads/system/uploads/ attachment_data/file/687801/ c8-eng.pdf . Once granted permission by the court you can leave your address off any documents that they will be sent.

- **Finances**. If dealing with finances then ensure you blank out any details which may reveal your whereabouts before they are disclosed to the court, for example cash withdrawals or debit or credit card expenditure in your local area.

- **Children**. If dealing with Children Act matters you should complete a form C1A (see https://www.familylaw. co.uk/system/uploads/

attachments/0006/9033/C1A. pdf). On this form you will give the court details of the abuse you and/or the children have suffered and it will ask if you need any "special measures" (see below).

Waiting at court

Before going to court you need to let the court know in advance that you will need what is known as "special measures" to be put in place for you to attend safely. This can include separate entrances from the perpetrator, separate waiting rooms or a screen in court so you don't have to face them. You should contact the court manager in plenty of time before the hearing to discuss the special measures you require. Be aware that every court has different facilities available and some have none at all! Get them to confirm in writing if possible.

On arrival at court make yourself known to the security staff and if necessary show them any written confirmation you have that special measures are to be put in place. It is usually a good idea to call the court a day or two before the hearing to check that they

have made the necessary arrangements.

Security at court is very similar to that at airports so don't worry about the perpetrator bringing in any weapons.

In addition to any legal representation or McKenzie Friend, always take someone with you (a good friend or family member) to support you while you wait to go into court. Be warned: you may have to wait a long time before you go into the courtroom. It's therefore useful to have someone there to talk to and take your mind off things as well as run errands, for example getting a drink or speaking to the usher to find out what is happening. They will not be able to come into court with you, so they may want to take a magazine or newspaper to read while they wait.

Refreshment facilities differ from court to court. Some have a café and some vending machines, all of which vary in quality. So go prepared. Security will ask you to sample any drinks on the way in.

In court

If no screen is given then **do not look at the perpetrator,** just look at the Judge. The perpetrator or their representative may ask you questions in court but the Judge is the person who needs to hear the answer.

Be prepared for the perpetrator to make false allegations against you, particularly if they are acting in person. They may

accuse you of being a drug addict, violent or seen as an unfit parent, etc. Remember that just because they are making accusations it doesn't mean that they will be believed. Judges are used to hearing false allegations so bear that in mind when you go in.

Answering questions

Look at the Judge. If you are not sure how to answer the question you can ask for it to be repeated - this will give you more time to think.

The perpetrator may try and intimidate you in court, often by staring. They may know how to wind you up or to make you more nervous so just try and ignore that. The Judge is likely to notice their attempts to intimidate you and intervene. The Judge will also stop any questioning that is irrelevant, argumentative or abusive.

If you are representing yourself you may like to provide a Position Statement setting out your position prior to the hearing which can be given to the Judge. It is not a statement of your evidence but is, as its name suggests, your position on the matters the court is being asked to deal with at this hearing. Use bullet points or numbered paragraphs to help keep your position statement succinct. You could instruct a solicitor (on an unbundled services basis) to help you prepare this, if necessary.

A lot of people worry that their

ex-partner will not agree to a fair settlement, particularly in financial proceedings. You need to be aware that the Judge can impose an order on the other party and therefore you don't have to back down or to be bullied into agreeing to something that you are unhappy with or you think is unfair.

CAFCASS

If the court proceedings relate to children, CAFCASS (https://www.cafcass.gov.uk) are likely to be involved at some point in the proceedings. They usually have to do a "safeguarding check" before the hearing and will send a letter confirming the outcome to the Judge. You will usually have the opportunity to speak to CAFCASS before the hearing. Make sure that you list the allegations, or make CAFCASS aware of the allegations, that you are making against your former partner. CAFCASS should check police records and check with social services to see if there have been any incidents in the past. Details of any incidents will be included in the letter to the court.

Stuck in the middle. Not a good place to be. El (13)

What is a McKenzie Friend and how might they help in a family law case?

About the author

Ann-marie Gallagher

Ann-marie is a former solicitor with over 14 years experience in the family law field and was accredited to represent children in family cases. She has also lectured in family law and undertakes occasional McKenzie Friend work.

Everyone has the right, should they so wish, to represent themselves in court.

What is a McKenzie Friend?

Anyone who does represent themselves 'in person' as it's known, is able to receive assistance from another 'lay' person - that is someone who is not legally qualified. In the family courts such people became known as McKenzie Friends (MF's).

Originally a Mckenzie Friend was envisaged as someone who would provide moral support, so a friend, family member or member of an advice group, on an unpaid basis. Their role was quite limited, usually simply accompanying and sitting next to someone acting in person. In

recent years, no doubt as a result of the cuts to legal aid there has been an increase in the use of McKenzie Friends, many of whom now offer their services on a paid basis. There are a wide variety of MF's currently operating in the family law field. At one end of the spectrum are former or semi-retired solicitors who may well have extensive experience in family law. At the other end of the spectrum are friends or relatives who can offer support, if not legal advice.

What sorts of things are McKenzie Friends able to do?

The courts have issued guidance detailing certain aspects of their role, such as;

- Taking notes in a court hearing;
- Helping with case papers;
- Providing moral and practical assistance;
- Quietly giving advice on any aspect of the conduct of the case during the court hearing.

This is not an exhaustive list and the guidance is at pains to note that the activities of an MF are not limited to the above. However, when it comes to advocacy, (addressing the court in the hearing) the courts have been reluctant to allow MF's the right to speak on someone's behalf. The guidance states that only in 'exceptional cases' will this be permitted.

Looking at the role of the McKenzie Friend in more detail

Undoubtedly representing yourself in court can be a daunting experience. Even in the low(er)-key atmosphere of the family court, certain formalities are adhered to and rules of evidence and procedure need to be complied with. Family cases are also often more emotionally charged than other kinds of cases. So many people may find the experience of representing themselves quite overwhelming, but also find the cost of using a solicitor simply out of their reach.

The courts are also becoming more open and in some cases looking with favour at the use of MF's in the family court. There have been concerns in the past over MF's who wished to hijack the proceedings to promote their own agenda, or who were simply unaware of the law in the family context and who were therefore at risk of giving bad advice.

However if an MF is chosen with care and used in the right circumstances, they can be a valuable ally.

Practical ways in which they can help

Family law cases can broadly be divided between those concerning finances and those concerning children. It's very often in the latter case that MF's are used. In these cases, known as 'private-law' children cases,

there will be initial court hearings where the court will make decisions about how the case is to be managed, for example; how it is to be timetabled; what the issues in the case are; and any expert/welfare reports which might be needed.

MF's who are legally qualified, can help with preparing applications and position statements, which are updated as the case progresses. If agreement is not reached during the proceedings and a final full hearing takes place, then matters of evidence need to be considered, court bundles need to be prepared, witness statements collated and again an MF can assist with this, as well as help you dealing with correspondence with the other solicitors who are being instructed.

Some Do's and Don'ts when using a McKenzie Friend

Do's

- Do ensure a short summary giving basic details of your MF and any relevant experience they have is filed at the court.

- If your MF is charging for their services, then do:

  - Check what their relevant experience and qualifications are and consider exactly what kind of help you might need from the MF - will you, for example, need help in preparing statements and writing letters as well as support at the court hearings.

  - Have something in writing detailing exactly what will be charged for different

aspects of the case. Solicitors generally have an hourly charge-out rate and even a legally qualified MF should be substantially lower. Or, they may charge fixed amounts for attending hearings, helping to prepare applications / statements/letters. Check what is included and check what any travel charges will be.

- Whether or not your MF charges, confidentiality is important so do check how they will keep the details of your case confidential, so you may wish to check how they store any information - digitally or otherwise and how they ensure that no-one else has access to that information.

- Do realise that an MF may well not be allowed to speak on your behalf in court - to do so the court will need to grant permission. If your MF is legally qualified then it's more likely that will be granted but there's no guarantee.

Don'ts

- Don't use an MF who has an agenda. This may be the case if they are affiliated to a protest group, or it may be as a result of a legal case that they have been involved in. If an MF's knowledge is based on their own individual experience this is going to be very limited. Every family case is different; whether it is a case involving children or involving money, be wary of anyone who tells you that such and such always or usually happens in these kinds of cases, or tries to guarantee you a particular outcome.

- Don't use an MF who is

confrontational in their approach, or who does not realise that the courts main concern will be the childrens' welfare.

- Whilst it is of course good to feel you have an ally, it's also far better to have someone who is objective about the proceedings, so don't use an MF who has any kind of personal involvement in the case.

A good MF can provide moral support at court, help you to present your case in the most effective way, provide legal advice if they are qualified and save you money, but it is important to note that you are still representing yourself. As such it's also important not to under estimate how much time and energy can be involved in doing so!

Representing yourself in court

About the author

Olivia Piercy, Bindmans LLP

Olivia Piercy is an Associate solicitor at Bindmans LLP. She advises on all aspects of family law, with particular expertise in cases with a cross border or international element. She is a domestic violence activist and a campaigner for access to justice for all.

N avigating the Family Court without representation can feel daunting. This article aims to demystify the process and give you some useful pointers to help you to represent yourself at court.

Who's who?

If you are representing yourself in court proceedings you are called a 'litigant in person'. The litigants in a case are known as 'the parties'.

The party who made the application to court is called 'the applicant' and the other party is called 'the respondent'.

Sometimes there is more than one respondent and it can get confusing when more than one

person makes an application. You might find it easier to refer to yourself and the other party as 'the father' or 'the mother' or just by your actual names.

Your case may be heard by magistrates or by a judge.

The court may appoint a CAFCASS officer to investigate your case and report back to the court.

What to call the judge

If your case is heard by a district judge or by magistrates, call them 'Sir' or 'Madam'.

If your case is heard by a judge with the title 'His/Her Honour Judge X', call them 'Your Honour'.

If your case is heard by a judge with the title 'Lord/Lady Justice X', call them 'Your Lordship/ Ladyship'.

Making an application

If you want to make an application to court, you need to

use the correct court form for the application that you are making. You can ask your local family court which is the correct form to use. The most common forms are:

- Form C100 - to make applications in relation to your children.

- Form DIV1 - to apply for a divorce.

- Form A - to start financial remedy proceedings in relation to divorce.

- Form FL401 - to apply for protection from domestic abuse.

You can make your application by posting it or handing it in to the court. You may need to pay a fee so check with the court how much that will be. If you cannot afford to pay the court fee, you may be eligible for a fee remission, if you complete Form EX160. The court will 'issue' your application and will send a copy to you and a copy to the other

> **DO I HAVE TO TELL THE COURT EVERYTHING - I FIND IT HARD TO TALK ABOUT THINGS**
>
> I assume you've made a full statement, which will be a court document. Your ex's representative will probably ask you about it, and it would be a good idea if you prepared calming strategies (e.g. mindfulness exercises), ask for time to answer, do it at your pace, and point out to your rep and the judge if you feel upset with the questions, or how they're being asked.
>
> *Mike Flinn*

party. If appropriate the court will arrange a court hearing.

TIPS

- It is a good idea to read the guidance on the back of court forms, which sets out how to complete the form.

- You can find all of the court forms on the Form Finder page of the HMCTS website.

- If you do not hear back from the court, telephone them to make sure they have received your application, as paperwork does sometimes go astray.

- Provide the court with three copies of your application form and three copies of any other documents you file - one for you, one for the other party and one for the court file.

- Read any paperwork you receive from the court very carefully.

- Any documentation that you provide to the court will be sent to the other party. If you don't want the other party to know your address, do not put it on the application form. Instead, include your address on a Form C8 and do not put it on any other documentation. The court will keep the Form C8 with your confidential address on the court file.

How to prepare for a court hearing

Letters from the court: carefully read all of the documents from the court and the other party as soon as you receive them. They may include important information such as the date and the venue for the next court hearing. They may also set out

important directions including documents you need to provide by certain dates.

The bundle: at a court hearing, the judge and parties will usually have a file of the relevant documents, called the 'bundle'. If the other party is represented, their solicitor will prepare a court bundle. They should agree the contents of the bundle with you in advance and they should also provide you with a copy of the bundle. If both parties are unrepresented, the court will prepare the bundle, but you should still bring all relevant documents to court with you.

CAFCASS: a CAFCASS officer may telephone you before the first court hearing to ask you if you have any safeguarding concerns about your child or the other parent. Try to be as helpful and honest as possible with the CAFCASS officer.

Position statements: before each hearing, you should also prepare a position statement. This is different from a statement of evidence. A position statement includes a summary of what has happened so far and sets out your position for the hearing, including what you would like the court to order. Your position statement should be typed if possible. It should not be more than four A4 sides long. You should email it to the court and to the other party the day before the hearing. You should bring a few copies to court.

Special assistance at court: if you will need arrangements to be made due to a disability, or the assistance of an interpreter, make sure you contact the court well in advance to put in a request. If you are afraid of the other party, you can ask the court

> Don't expect the other parent to behave how you behave. Understand that it's difficult and different from both sides.
>
> *Mandy, Mum*

to find a separate waiting room for you and a separate entrance to the court. You may even be able to have a screen in the court room so you can't see the other party, or to join the hearing via a video link. Ask the court how they can assist you. You should chase this up with them more than once to make sure they have put the special measures in place.

Representing yourself at the court hearing

There are different kinds of hearings depending on what application has been made and the stage of the proceedings. Usually the first court hearing is used to see whether the parties can agree. If they can't agree, the court will direct what evidence each party needs to provide so that the court has all the information it needs in order to make a decision. The following tips may be helpful whatever kind of court hearing it is:

- You should get to court an hour before the hearing if possible.

- If you are representing yourself you can bring a friend or family member with you. They are called a 'McKenzie Friend'. Tell the court and the other party that you have brought a McKenzie Friend.

MR

Your McKenzie Friend can sit next to you, take a note and help you to organise your papers. They cannot speak on your behalf unless the court gives them permission.

- When you arrive at court, check the notice board to see which court you are in. Find the court room and hand your position statement to the court clerk. Explain who you are and ask them to hand it to the judge or the magistrates so that they can read it before he court hearing.

- Sign in at the front desk. You may see that the other party has already signed in. They may wish to negotiate with you before the hearing. You can try to agree matters if you wish, but you don't need to. It may be that some issues are agreed and others are not. Remember to give them a copy of your position statement as well.

- When you are in the court room you should take a note of everything that the judge says. Check that the judge has had a chance to read your position statement. If not, give them another copy.

- You may feel angry or upset in the court room. It's OK to cry, but it's important not to lose your temper with the judge or with the other party. If you do not feel you have had an opportunity to express

yourself clearly, make sure the judge is aware that you still have more to say. It's important to put all of your most important points in your position statement in case you get nervous in court and forget to say them.

- After each hearing a court order will be drafted. If the other party is represented, their lawyer will prepare the order. If not, the court will prepare the order. Make sure that you have exchanged email addresses with the other party's lawyer and with the judge's clerk, so that you can check the order and so that you are copied into any correspondence with the court.

- Make sure you know and that you write down (1) when the next hearing is, (2) whether you have to file any documents and if so, by what dates, and (3) whether the other party has to file any documents and if so, by what dates.

Representing yourself in the Family Court can feel overwhelming, especially when the case is about your children and it matters so much to you. Court proceedings follow a process and are usually broken up into stages. So long as you have read everything from the court very carefully and you have followed the directions that the court has given you, you can't go

too far wrong.

The most helpful thing you can do to make sure you are really prepared is to draft a position statement in advance of every hearing and bring along a lot of copies. Don't be shy to ask your friends and family for support. It can be really hard to take in and remember everything that was said during a court hearing or during a negotiation with another party, so it can be a great help to have someone else there to take a note. If you don't feel you have anyone to ask, you can contact the Personal Support Unit ('PSU'). The PSU is a charity which operate in many family courts around the country. They can often make someone available to support you at court and even during your court hearing.

Above all, remember that the CAFCASS officers and the judges are all very overworked and busy. However, their main priority is to make decisions in the best interests of your children. Try to present your case clearly so that the right decisions are easier to make.

Advice: Find comfort and support everywhere, don't feel that at school you can't speak to anyone. Cerys-Sophie (16)

What is a C100?

About the author

**Rajan Thandi,
Associate Family
Law Solicitor
at Southgate
Solicitors**

Rajan specialises
in all areas
of divorce and family law
and focuses primarily on
family law matters involving
children. He represents his
clients every step of the way
and provides advocacy at
court to ensure their views are
properly put forward.

The C100 is the title of the application form many people will need when applying to the court for a Specific Issue Order, Prohibited Steps Order or a Child Arrangements Order. When seeking any of these types of orders you may be told by people or even solicitors that you need to apply or put in an application. The C100 is that form.

Although it sounds very technical, the form is fairly straightforward. However, if you are completing or preparing an application yourself make sure that you double check that everything which is relevant to your case is completed,

otherwise the court may send the application back which will only cause delays.

Most solicitors (if you have one) will have access to the forms through various software packages. If you are completing it yourself then the Gov.uk website is the main source for court forms and should be used over any other website. You can find the C100 form on the Gov.uk website under the Parenting, childcare and children's services section.

Types of orders

Specific Issue Order: Where there is a dispute between (usually) parents about a specific issue such as schooling or perhaps medical treatment, then a Specific Issue Order is the order you will be asking the court to make.

Prohibited Steps Order: If you want to stop the other parent doing something or from taking a course of action you will be seeking a Prohibited Steps Order, for example if one parent is

talking about going abroad and you are worried they may not return with the child.

Child Arrangements Order: Finally, if you cannot agree on arrangements between yourselves as to who your child lives with or spends time with then you will be seeking a Child Arrangements Order.

Completing the C100

On the front page of the form where it asks if there are concerns about risk of harm, you need to tick the relevant boxes and then provide further information on Form C1A. Again, the Gov.uk website is best for this - just type in C1A into the search box on the main website to access the form.

When completing the form, it is important to put in as much information as you can, especially when it comes to details of the other party - the court will need this to be able to send a copy of the application to them so that they are aware of the proceedings.

At the start of a separation, think of a statement which sets out your hopes and aspirations for your children after the process has ended. If negotiations or discussions become difficult, you can go back to your statement and remind yourself of what is most important. This may help you to unblock an impasse.

Rachel Duke, Aletta Shaw

There is a requirement to provide your address details as well. However, if you do not wish to disclose these because you are worried about the other party having your address then a C8 form (again, search for this on the Gov.uk website) will need to be filled out - this is a very simple form which asks you to list any details that the court is to keep confidential.

When completing the form, it is helpful to put as much detail as you can about the orders you are seeking. You do not need to put the history of the case in lots of detail as that can be explored later but the court needs to know what you are seeking and why.

If you are seeking a Specific Issue Order or a Prohibited Steps Order then try to be as specific as possible since these are usually for singular issues and the court needs to know why there is a dispute.

For a Child Arrangements Order it is helpful to have an idea of the type of contact you are seeking or if you want your child to live with you - the more detail you can give the better.

When filling out a C100 you will see that the front page and pages 4 to 9 talk about a Mediation Information and Assessment Meeting (MIAM). It is now a legal requirement that, before applying to the court for an order, the applicant (i.e. the person seeking the order) has to have attended a MIAM unless an exemption applies. The idea is to encourage people to resolve issues outside of court between themselves.

Sometimes this is not possible or appropriate, for example in cases of domestic abuse or child abuse - in these sorts of cases you do

not have to attend a MIAM. The C100 lists the evidence that the court will accept as proof of domestic abuse or child abuse and you will need to attach that to your form. There are other exceptions such as urgency; insufficient contact details for the respondent or that you have previously attended a MIAM.

If your case does not fit into any of these exceptions then you will need to attend a MIAM and you can use Resolution's handy search tool to find a trained and accredited mediator in your area (see resolution.org.uk).

Urgent applications

An important point to note when completing a C100 is that the usual time frame for the court to deal with these applications is 4 to 6 weeks. There are times, however, where you cannot afford to wait that long and need an urgent order. In that case you can tick the box on page 1 of the C100 setting out that an urgent order is needed. You will then need to complete pages 11 and

12 setting out why the application is considered urgent and whether:

- you are asking for a 'without notice' hearing i.e. you need a hearing immediately and the other person isn't told about the first hearing, being only asked to attend a later return hearing; or

- 'abridged notice' is required i.e. there is a deadline (e.g. with a school application) and an issue needs resolving quickly but doesn't need a without notice hearing.

In those circumstances you need as much detail as possible to show the court why no or shortened notice is needed.

The C100 looks much more complicated than it is. Take your time filling it out, be specific and make sure that any other forms such as the C1A, C8 or domestic abuse/child abuse evidence/ MIAM form are attached.

Notes

![ONLY Mums & Dads - parents meet professionals]

What is a C1A?

About the authors

Joe Colley & Kathryn Ainsworth, Machins Solicitors LLP

Joe commenced his contract as a trainee solicitor with the firm in July 2018 and is currently studying his Legal Practice Course and Masters in Law at the University of Law in London.

Kathryn is the Head of the Private Family Law Department for both Berkhamsted and Luton. She is a Member of Resolution, a qualified Resolution Collaborative Lawyer and a Member of the Law Society's Family Law Advanced Panel with specialist accreditations in Financial Remedies in Divorce and Complex Asset cases.

The C1A form is a supplementary form filed with a C100 which is an application for a Child Arrangements Order. It can accompany any type of application for a Child Arrangements Order be it in relation to the time a child or children spend with each parent, a specific issue of health or religion or an application for a Prohibited Steps Order to prevent the temporary or permanent removal of a child or children from England & Wales for example. The C1A is designed to set out safeguarding concerns or issues, both in relation to you and/or the children, and which the court needs to be aware of when considering what orders to make.

What are safeguarding concerns?

Safeguarding concerns can be in relation to domestic violence or abuse, of any form, whether physical, mental, sexual, emotional or financial. This can be in relation to you and/or the child or children. It may relate to a third party who the child or children have regular contact with. The form allows you to set out all the relevant incidents, the duration, when they occurred and the help you have sought or trying to seek. The content of the form can include events in which a child may have heard or witnessed you or another relevant child being subjected to any form of domestic violence or abuse.

It must be remembered that the form takes into account any risk of harm. Therefore it covers emotional harm as well as physical harm. If you feel you or the children are at a possible risk of either emotional or physical harm state this and the reasons why you think this to be true.

How does the C1A assist the court?

Before considering this please remember that when considering any type of application for a Child Arrangements Order, the court must always have regard to "The Welfare Checklist". The checklist deals with:

- The wishes and feelings of the relevant children;

- Physical, emotional and educational needs;

- Age, sex, background and/or any characteristics the court feel relevant;

- Any harm suffered or risk of harm to the child;

- The capability of each parent or other relevant person of meeting the needs of the child;

- The range of powers available to the court in such proceedings.

Your C1A should therefore be cross referenced to the Welfare Checklist. The C1A then assists the court with an overview of all and any safeguarding concerns. In turn, this enables the court to make the appropriate orders for case management and ensures the case is allocated to the appropriate level of Judge. The

ONLY
Mums & Dads
parents meet professionals

C1A will also provide the court with the information they need to consider when determining the child arrangements order.

The Do's when completing a C1A form

- Read the guidance at the back of the form.

- Answer all relevant questions

- Provide all details of the children including dates of birth.

- Give a brief description of the incidents including when they occurred, the duration and any help sought.

- Try to be as exact with the dates as possible.

- Read the different elements of the form carefully and ensure you are answering the question being asked as clear and as simple as you can.

- Ensure all claims are true.

- Provide any relevant case numbers of other proceedings you may have, for example an application for a non-molestation order.

- If you are not represented by a solicitor, make this clear.

- Think about what you are asking the court to do and what you would like them to do to safeguard your or the children.

- Link what you say to the Welfare Checklist.

- Attach any relevant orders.

- Proof read your form before filing it with the court.

- If you are a litigant in person send 3 copies to the court for them to be served upon all parties.

- Sign and date the form.

- Make you pay the correct court fees and if eligible apply for the appropriate refunds.

- Keep a copy of the form for your records.

- If you are responding to the form, it is advised to go through each allegation and state whether these are denied or accepted.

The Don'ts when completing a C1A Form

- Do not exaggerate the claims being made by you.

- Ensure you do not defame the other party in the proceedings.

- Do not make false allegations of domestic violence.

- Do not give full detailed accounts of the allegations being made as there will be an appropriate time for this when you file witness statements later in the proceedings.

- Do not tell anyone who is not a party to the proceedings what is said in the C1A. These documents are confidential.

A Statement of Truth

You must remember that when completing this form you are signing a Statement certifying that what you are saying is true. Therefore everything said in the form must be in its truest form. Remember it is possible to mislead by omission. If the court finds that what you have said on your form is false, proceedings for contempt of court can be brought against you.

If you think you will need someone to represent you at a court hearing, talk to one of the OnlyMums/Dads Panel Members (www.thefamilylawpanel.co.uk - see Page 32) They will talk you through your options and if they think you need a Barrister they will have all the local names and contact details. Professional diaries are busy though and the earlier you sort things out the more chance you have of being represented by the professional best placed to help on the day itself.

What are directions orders?

About the author

Norman Hartnell, Managing Director, The Family Law Company by Hartnell Chanot

Norman is a solicitor, mediator, collaborative family lawyer and arbitrator and is experienced in all forms of family mediation. He has represented parents, guardians and children in private and public law cases and has considerable experience in complex divorce and related financial issues.

Family law and family life is complicated, or at least it can be.

Courts are there to apply family law to help find solutions to problems which spouses, partners or parents (collectively called 'parties to the proceedings') can't find themselves by negotiation. Courts approach their problem-solving role in a clear and methodical way by making 'directions orders' to gather together all relevant information to equip the Judge to make the best decision possible. These directions orders specify what steps are to happen to gather all the evidence.

Whether a problem relates to children, money or the relationship itself every court application starts with a set application form giving all basic information, but that is far from a complete picture. There are always two perspectives (at least) and sometimes there are other people who know and can contribute information for the court. In financial cases, these may include property valuers, or pension experts; in children cases, CAFCASS Officers and sometimes experts such as psychologists.

Directions hearings

In some cases, as soon as court proceedings start, the court issues standard (the usual) directions. This happens, for example, in every financial case when a timetable is set, and those starting or on the receiving end of proceedings are told what documents they need to file (send to the court) or serve (send to their opponent) and by what timescale. In other cases, there may be one or more 'directions hearings'; that is a hearing when the Judge will make orders as to how and when missing information is to be gathered.

Courts have tried to standardise this process as much as possible, so that the norms of how problems are to be solved are known from the outset, and as much preparation as possible can be carried out in advance. Once the court has set a timetable, it will expect it to be followed to avoid unnecessary delay.

Enforcement

The court does not automatically keep an eye on the progress of the case so, if orders are not obeyed, the court will expect someone to alert them to what is happening. In those cases an enforcement order can be sought, in which case the person who has not complied with the previous directions order may be ordered to carry out a task by a certain date or face imprisonment. This is the court's main sanction, by means of what the court calls a 'penal notice' - a formal notice warning of the

For 15 years I've wanted a voice. At 18, I'm ready to talk about what my parents, and their divorce, have done to me. Kaitlyn (18)

COURT & 'FIGHTING' FOR THE CHILDREN

consequences of not obeying a court order.

Apart from the gathering of evidence, the court has to consider setting a hearing date which could be a date when the court will check on progress or a final hearing date when the decision will be made.

Tips

So, if you are attending a directions hearing:

1. Always think about what information the court will need to make its decision.

2. Go to court prepared with solutions, not problems, for the Judge.

3. If you think that you will need an expert of some description go on the internet and read FPR Practice Direction 25.

You'll see how much advance thought has to be given to such matters. If your case involves any allegation of harm in a children case, read Practice Direction 12J. In all children cases, it's Practice Direction 12B; in financial cases, 9A. There are practice directions covering every conceivable situation.

4. Get advice. These are complicated matters. The directions hearing sets the whole direction of the case. If you start off taking the wrong fork in the road it can take an enormous effort to get the case back on track. Sometimes that is not possible as once a track is set it is extremely hard to go back if a mistake is made.

Family law solicitors and barristers live and breathe these

matters day by day and are well placed to help, even if they are limited to giving you guidance to enable you to do as much of the work yourself to save legal costs.

Family Judges have been known to end their judgment by stating if both parties leave court today equally as unhappy with my decision then I've done my job. I will often use this phrase to focus clients on achieving resolutions and avoiding the court process.

Laura Clapton, Consilia Legal

Notes

What happens at a fact-finding hearing?

About the author

Fiona O'Sullivan, Weightmans LLP

Fiona specialises in the financial aspects of relationship breakdown, with particular expertise in pensions. She has a reputation for being an astute negotiator who concentrates on cutting to the core of the issues in a relationship breakdown resulting in prompt resolution whether by settlement or court decision.

In cases concerning arrangements for children, it is very common for factual disputes between the parties to arise. The court must be very careful to distinguish between allegations, which if true, would impact on the welfare of the child or children concerned.

The court exercise great caution and consider the relevance of allegations to the issue to be determined. If, for example, serious allegations are made against one of the parents, but the incidents occurred before the child was born, or when the child was much younger, then the court is unlikely to investigate those historical allegations, as they will not directly impact on the time that parent will spend with the child [see the case of *Re V (A child)* [2015] EWCA CIV 274].

Where the court is satisfied that the allegations, if true, will impact on the welfare of the child, then the court will order a separate hearing to consider the evidence about the allegations. Having considered the evidence the court will make findings in writing. The hearing is known as a fact-finding hearing.

A fact-finding hearing may be necessary if the following allegations have been made:

1. Alcohol or drug abuse;

2. Physical or sexual abuse;

3. Verbal or emotional abuse;

4. Repeated non-compliance with previous court orders.

The decision to direct a fact-finding hearing is a judicial decision, not one for the CAFCASS officer or for the parties. However, in considering whether to direct a fact-finding hearing, the court will consider the views of the parties and of CAFCASS, It will also consider whether the party facing the allegations has made admissions, which could provide a sufficient basis on which to proceed, or whether there is other available evidence which provides a sufficient basis on which to proceed.

Although a fact-finding hearing may delay the case and mean that additional time is spent at court (in some cases many additional days), the early resolution of whether relevant allegations are found to be true by the court enables the substantive hearing to proceed more quickly, and enables the court to focus on the child's welfare with greater clarity.

Having reached the conclusion that a fact-finding hearing is necessary, the court will then give detailed directions as to how the fact-finding hearing is to proceed. These directions will include specifying the written evidence from the parties and considering whether documents are required from third parties, such as the police or health services.

To assist the court and the parties, the court usually directs the party making the allegations to prepare a template (called a Scott Schedule) itemising the specific factual issues to be decided by the court. The template is set out in such a way that the responding party is able to comment briefly by stating whether the allegation is agreed or denied, and a separate column is included to record the findings of the court having considered all the evidence. This template enables the court, when subsequently adjudicating on the substantive issue, to have a clear summary of the findings of fact. The party making the allegations should draft them in such a way that the court can give a yes or no answer on the Scott Schedule.

The aim of the fact-finding hearing is to ensure that the allegations are put and responded to. Both parties have an opportunity to give oral evidence and to cross examine the other party. The burden of proof is on the person making the allegations. The court determines the matter on the balance of probabilities, not on the higher, criminal, standard of beyond reasonable doubt.

Having considered the evidence, the court will make findings of fact. The court will then give directions as to the future conduct of the substantive hearing. This may include directing a report from CAFCASS.

Once a fact-finding hearing has taken place, the court must consider the child arrangements in light of their decision. If no findings are made, the court must proceed on the basis that the allegations did not happen. If some findings are made, then the court must consider the child arrangements in the light of those findings, and must consider how any risk to the child can be managed.

Fact finding hearings will not therefore be ordered in every case, but can be a very useful tool to provide a template for the court in taking into account proven serious allegations which are likely to impact on the welfare of the child.

Notes

What is a Child Arrangements Order?

About the authors

Shanika Varga-Haynes & Jennifer Hollyer, Stowe Family Law

Shanika has a particular interest in domestic abuse cases and children work, including reaching an agreement in relation to where children will live and how much time they will spend with the non-resident parent. She has also been involved in external and internal relocation cases and has experience in dealing with grandparents' rights.

Jennifer has experience in most areas of family law including divorce, financial remedies, domestic abuse, cohabitation and international family law disputes. She has a particular interest in complex children matters such as international children cases.

A Child Arrangements Order is a court order which regulates where a child lives and/or how much time a child spends with the other party. A Child Arrangements Order can also say that a child lives with both parties and it can provide for other types of contact such as through phone calls, video calls, cards and letters etc.

Unfortunately, these orders are not always complied with or situations change and they are no longer considered to be the best arrangements for the child. There can be a number of reasons for an order not working including (but not limited to):

- One party breaching the order by withholding time with the child from the other party;

- The party's circumstances change meaning they can no longer comply;

- The needs of the child have changed;

- There is a concern that the child is at risk of harm.

What can you do if your ex-partner breaches a Child Arrangements Order?

Unless an agreement has been reached between the parties to informally vary the order, one party will be in breach of the order if they do not comply with it.

If it is possible, the parties should try to discuss the breach of the order and resolve the matter between them. However, if this is not possible then an application will need to be made to the court to either enforce the order or vary it. The court charges a fee for this which is currently £215.

Since 2008, all orders dealing with arrangements for children have a warning notice attached to them which states that if you do not comply with the order, you may be sent to prison and/ or fined, made to do unpaid work (community service) or pay financial compensation. Orders that were made before 2008 do not contain these warnings and so before you can enforce them, you have to apply to the court to have the warning notice added to the order. Once it has been added, you can then apply to enforce the order.

What power do the courts have?

Failure to comply with the order can result in the defaulting party being found in contempt of court. This does not necessarily mean that it will lead to a term of imprisonment. The court will have a number of options which will depend on the nature and frequency of the breaches. The court could:

- Make a referral for the party in breach to attend a Separated Parents Information Programme - a course which helps parents understand separation from a child's point of view and learn the fundamental principles of how to manage and reduce the impact of conflict on their children.

- Vary the Child Arrangements Order - to make it clearer or

alternatively in serious cases, change who the child lives with to the other party.

- Make an Enforcement Order or Suspended Enforcement Order - An Enforcement Order imposes unpaid work up to a maximum of 200 hours.

- Make an order for financial loss - for example, for the cost of a holiday which may have been lost due to the breach.

- Committal to prison - generally the last resort and will usually be suspended (put on hold).

- A fine - again, this is generally a last resort.

If it becomes apparent that the party has a reasonable excuse for breaching the order, then the court will not enforce it. It may instead consider whether it is necessary to vary the order.

If a party finds that they are not able to comply with the order and an agreement cannot be reached to change it then they should make an application to vary the order before it is breached so that the court can consider why the order is not working and if necessary, change the arrangements so that they are considered in the best interests of the child.

If the party who is in breach of the order is the one who is supposed to be spending time with the child and they are not then it becomes more difficult to deal with. The court will have the power to enforce the order but it may not consider that it is in the best interests of the child to force someone to spend time with them when that person does not want to or make any effort to. It can be quite emotionally harmful to a child to be put in this situation as it may make the child feel more unwanted than if the contact just stopped. In such circumstances, the court could consider discharging the order if an application is made, meaning that the order would no longer exist.

What can you do if the order no longer works for you or your child?

It is quite common for parties to reach the stage where the Child Arrangements Order is no longer working for the child or for the parties themselves. Before an application is made to the court, all other methods of negotiating should be explored. Solicitors can be instructed to negotiate on a party's behalf or the parties can, for example, attend mediation. In some cases where there are older children involved, they too can engage in the mediation to tell the mediator what it is that they want. Arbitration is also another possibility in children matters.

At any point, until the child reaches the age of 16, either party can apply to the court for the Child Arrangements Order to be varied. Once a child is 16, it will only be in exceptional circumstances that the court will be able to deal with the case.

The primary concern for the parties and for any court is the welfare of the child. Where possible, trying to resolve any issues related to a Child Arrangements Order is a more preferable route to going back to Court. Clear legal advice is important in all cases to support and guide you through the process and get the best result for you and the child.

> The best thing about a break up can be the introduction of whole new extended families to their children's lives, because the more people that love their children and think they are amazing the better.
>
> *Julie Hobson, Gullands Solicitors*

ONLY
Mums & Dads
parents meet professionals

Do courts automatically think kids are better off with mum?

About the author

Gillian Bishop, Family Law in Partnership

Gillian is a trained mediator, arbitrator (children issues) and collaborative lawyer. She focuses on all aspects of divorce and family law, in particular in the financial repercussions of relationship breakdown and complex private law children matters.

My first reaction to being asked to write an article on this topic was that I had drawn the short straw. "Can I pick again?" I wondered.

The reason for my reaction I think is obvious to most family lawyers and those people who have had the misfortune to have to take disputes concerning their children to court. Ask this question to a group of them and 9 out of 10 would immediately answer "yes" and ask what the next question is.

I am acutely aware, too, of how emotive the whole issue of a separated father's role in a child's life has become. There are any number of dads out there who feel very badly let down by the system in the face of parental alienation and often with very good reason. There are other fathers who have become quite militant and, regrettably, given their cause a bad name.

What is undeniable is that the ideal situation for a child is for them to have a good relationship with both parents and for their parents to have a good enough working relationship as co-parents. And I believe that CAFCASS and Judges start from that view point.

We live in a society which still has the mum, dad and two kids ideal at heart (although more diverse family units are becoming increasingly common). And within that ideal mum, as the child bearer, is regarded as the primary carer if the idyll is broken and mum and dad separate. Since our Judges and CAFCASS are drawn from our society it is unsurprising that most of them will also start from that idealistic view point.

In any event, there is no getting away from the fact that in the majority of cases before the courts the mothers are the child bearers and as a result will have had a very different and, at least to start with, closer bond with their children. I know an eminent child psychiatrist who says that a child under 7 should not, in an ideal world, spend more than 7 to 10 days apart from their mother at a stretch.

So I decided that there was not much point talking in generalities when it came to trying to answer the question. Everyone knows the generalised answer. I decided to draw on my own experience and to ask my colleagues what their experience was.

Pro-father cases

Some of the instances that were described to me were:

- A District Judge telling a mother at the outset of a case that he expected her to agree to mid-week contact even though she had been opposing it;

- A Judge ordering shared

The splitting up taught me that happiness can be found with more than one person. Bryony (16)

residence notwithstanding the finding that the father was a bully to both the mother and the three children;

- A Judge finding against a mother who wished to return to her native European country because the father enjoyed an equal time split, even though when the child was at his father's house he actually spent more time with his paternal grandparents than with his father.

For each of these apparently 'pro-father' cases there were ones where it seemed societal norms prevailed.

Pro-mother cases

- An order for shared residence with a time split slightly in favour of the mother, despite CAFCASS reporting that the children had a closer bond with their father who had been their primary carer;

- No changed residence order despite the mother making dreadful and unfounded allegations of child abuse against the father. This in a case where the mother retracted the allegations and agreed to work with the relevant services to enable contact to re-establish;

- Any number of leave to remove cases where the mother has been able to return 'home'.

Parental alienation

When you get litigation over children you get stressed children who, mostly, will tell CAFCASS what the parent they feel most bonded to wants, as if that is their wish too. In a vastly overstretched and underfunded

service it is no surprise if CAFCASS take these 'ascertainable wishes and feelings' as gospel.

But there is no doubt that times are changing and changing quite fast. Leave to remove applications are not the 'shoo in' for mothers they once were. CAFCASS has launched a pilot scheme to crack down on parental alienation and there is significant interest in parenting coordination as a means of supporting families stuck in a high conflict situation.

There is a greater realisation among all involved in family justice, and some father's groups like Families Need Fathers, that the answer lies not in the amount of time a child spends with either parent but in the ability of the parents to work co-operatively together as separated parents.

This is borne out by the recent increase in workshops and courses being run for separated parents. There is the in-court Separated Parenting Information Programme (see Question 71)

and the Parenting After Parting workshops run by my firm to name but two. The requirement that all parents wishing to bring Children Act applications will have to be assessed for mediation is, at least in part, an indication that the bigger picture is understood by a wider spectrum of society.

Society is changing, and it needs to change more, but with that change will gradually come a different answer to the question. Eventually, it won't be necessary to ask the question any more.

Kids are not weapons or bargaining chips - they are innocent bystanders. The relationship didn't work, so try to make the separation work.

Kevin, Dad

Notes

My ex has told CAFCASS that I have abused her. How do I defend myself?

About the author

Simon Dakers, Partner and Head of Family & Matrimonial at Gordon Brown Law Firm LLP

Simon deals with complex children cases and represents parents, grandparents and children in private and public law proceedings. He is a member of the Law Society Children Panel (Children Representative), Family Law Panel and a Resolution Accredited Specialist in private children law, domestic abuse and advanced financial provision.

I t is not uncommon for allegations of domestic abuse to be made or feature in cases involving children. Domestic abuse is, of course, harmful to children and can put them at risk of harm, whether they are subjected to it or witness a parent being violent or abusive to the other.

The role of CAFCASS

The report will be to an officer of the Children and Families Court Advisory and Support Service (CAFCASS) known as a Family Court Advisor (FCA). They have a duty of care towards, and must safeguard and promote the welfare of, the child. Their role is to complete an analysis of the circumstances and make recommendations to the Family Court regarding the best course of action and the arrangements for the child.

It is not, however, for the FCA to decide who is telling the truth. That is the province of the Judge.

The FCA will be prevented from conducting a full case analysis and will be unable to make any final recommendations until presented with a firm factual foundation upon which to base their enquiries. The FCA cannot make recommendations in a vacuum without findings of fact being available to deliver the clarity required as to whether there has been verbal and/or physical abuse.

Fact finding hearing

If any allegation of domestic abuse is relevant to deciding the arrangements for the child, it will be necessary for the court to determine whether they are true or false. This is done by conducting a fact finding hearing.

The party making the allegations will be expected to set out in a Schedule of Findings sought (sometimes called a Scott Schedule) a list of the allegations, cross referenced, where possible, to any corroborating evidence. The Schedule should set out the date on which each incident is said to have occurred and include a brief description of what is said to have happened and where. A response to each allegation will then be inserted so that it is clear to the Judge whether there is any acceptance and what is in dispute.

Sometimes mums and dads can be accused of terrible things regarding their children. Some may be true, that occurred when they were still together. Others may be 'news to them'.

Sometimes accusations can be made as a form of 'punishment' to either partner. This can occur if either mum or dad are at the angry stage of loss. It is not unusual for past behaviour to be seen through a different lens when angry or upset.

Respond by being honest and try not to involve the children by asking them what they think.

Adele Ballantyne

This type of hearing involves the Judge considering written evidence, such as any information held by the police, medical records and witness statements, and hearing oral evidence, which will include the cross-examination of witnesses.

The contested facts will be aired, the credibility, reliability and demeanour of the witnesses assessed by the Judge and all the evidence considered.

The 'balance of probabilities' test

It is for the person making the allegations to prove, on the balance of probabilities, that the incident(s) did happen. The test - balance of probabilities - means that an allegation is only proved if the Judge is satisfied that each incident was more likely than not to have occurred. The burden of proof is, therefore, on the party making the allegation and not on the person who is said to have been the perpetrator.

Once the court has decided whether each allegation did or did not happen, this will form the factual foundation upon which

the case can proceed. This may include an assessment of the welfare needs of the child, which can now be completed by the FCA, and/or a risk assessment if any of the allegations are found to be proved.

Usually, the court will direct that a transcript of the Judgment at the end of the fact finding hearing be made available to assist the parties and any professionals involved in the arrangements for the children, including the FCA. This helpfully sets out the evidence considered by the Judge and explains what the Judge found, as well as the process of reasoning by which they arrived at any findings.

Terminology

In the Family Court arena, the reference to a person 'defending' themselves is not often heard. Typically, a party faced with allegations of domestic abuse,

which are denied, will seek to challenge them. The court is keen to encourage the use of appropriate terminology and the term "defending" is probably best left for use in the Criminal Courts.

> Be the bigger person. Even if your nearly ex is trying to play dirty, don't rise to the bait. It is easier said than done, but I often hear from people who years later regret that they allowed themselves to get lowered to that level.
>
> *Peter Martin, OGR Stock Denton*

> Being nervous in court is normal. Most parents are. If you are *really* struggling, tell the judge or one of the court staff. They are there to help and support.

Notes

Will the court agree with my ex that I can only have supervised contact?

About the author

Gail Cook, Chartered Legal Executive at Quality Solicitors/Yates & Co

Gail has over 30 years' experience in family law including divorce, relationship breakdown generally, financial disputes, property disputes between couples living together, disputes about children and grandchildren, domestic violence, living together agreements and pre-marital agreements.

O ne of the first factors a court will look at in determining or reviewing child arrangements is whether you have parental responsibility ('PR') for your children. This is defined in the Children Act 1989, which governs applications to court relating to children, as 'all the rights, duties, powers, responsibilities and authority which by law a parent of a child has in relation to the child and his property (see Questions 6, 11 and 13 and the Must read article on Page 324 for more).

All mothers and most fathers have PR for their child. A father has PR if he was married to the mother when the child was born (divorce does not end that relationship) or if he is registered on the child's birth certificate if the child was born on or after 1 December 2003.

Can a father without PR have contact?

Even if the father does not have PR, this does not mean he cannot have contact with his child. It is not for the mother to dictate the level of contact. It is for all those with PR to make suitable arrangements. In the event of a dispute, the court will be asked to decide. When the court is asked to decide, the child's welfare must be the court's paramount consideration.

The child can be living with either parent or share time between both under a shared care arrangement. There is a clear preference for parents to be able to make their own arrangements. If they cannot, then the court has a checklist of seven criteria they look at when making the decision for the parents (see Question 55 for more on the welfare checklist).

Court proceedings

When looking at whether contact should be supervised, the court will have to be satisfied that there is a risk to the child if contact is not supervised. This means a real risk of harm, such as physical abuse, neglect or being exposed to drug/alcohol issues. The court will not agree to supervised contact unless there is a good reason; that reason is not because your ex doesn't like you and wants to cause you a problem. It is all about what is best for your child and it is not usually best for their well-being and depth of relationship if there can only be supervised contact with you.

Involvement of CAFCASS

The court uses the services of CAFCASS (Children and Family Court Advisory and Support Service) to assist in their decision

Advice to young people: It's not your fault. It's a natural thing to occur and blaming yourself is a bad way to deal with the situation. Jack (17)

COURT & 'FIGHTING' FOR THE CHILDREN

making. Each family going through this process is assigned a CAFCASS Officer, who has a social work background and is there to gather more information about the child's experience. They do this by contacting schools and other relevant organisations, as well as through meeting with the children if they are old enough to express informed wishes and feelings. All of the information gathered is passed on to the court to help with an assessment of the above criteria.

It is often the case that one parent claims the other is abusive and it is always difficult to prove either way. If your ex is likely to do this, it is a good idea to make sure any conversations are in writing, text or email. Don't be goaded into responding to abuse from your ex as phone calls can be recorded and can come across as one-sided. The same applies to texting or emailing in response to a phone call as there will only be a record of what you have written.

The main advice we can give is - these are your children. You know them and you are responsible for their happiness. Don't do anything that will upset them, including arguing with your ex in front of them. Listen to what your ex says as they may actually have genuine concerns you need to address. If things get nasty, step back and seek legal advice.

Listen, check meaning then reply - you don't have to agree. If you get upset use a time out system. Do not use a blame, or a right/wrong system. Your children will copy your behaviours, so if you do the above, so, by and large, will they. Try to suggest not instruct.

Mike Finn, Counsellor

WHAT DO I SAY IN A LETTER TO MY CHILDREN?

It depends how frequent your letters are. Generally, at some point, ensure you tell them you love them, and miss them. Give them some info on your recent life and ask them about theirs. Mention something or someone in their lives, whether this is a sports match, their class teacher, or an event like Christmas if you don't have many details of their lives. Don't discuss parenting issues with them, or criticise the other parent, or family members. Put yourself in their shoes - you were a child once. Try to show empathy and understanding for their position, which they didn't choose. Remember you are a role model for them, so what you say and how you say it might come back to you in the same style.

Mike Flinn

Will the Judge take my criminal record into account in children cases?

About the author

Vanessa Gillbanks, Director at Gillbanks Family Law

Vanessa has 28 years experience of family law and is a divorce, family and domestic abuse specialist. She is a long-term member of Resolution and is an Advanced Family Law Panel member.

When an application relating to children is made with the court, safeguarding checks on the child and the parties are carried out. A safeguarding letter is filed with the court and this will detail any criminal convictions or cautions of the parties, so the court will be made aware of any criminal records or involvement with the police. That information is usually only one piece of evidence that is before the court, the relevance of which is likely to depend on the nature of the convictions and how long ago they were committed. The relevance of the information will also depend on the issues the court is trying to decide.

If it is felt that the information that the police have might be relevant to the issues, then there will be directions for further disclosure to be made by the police. This will not be necessary in every case.

The child's welfare is paramount

The overriding principle for the family court when considering issues for the child is that the child's welfare shall be the court's paramount consideration. A family court will make findings of fact by looking at the evidence before it and will place more importance and weight on different pieces of the evidence.

The court must decide what is true and what is not true. The existence of convictions needs to be weighed up with regards to the issues in that case and what the evidence of convictions is going to assist with. The court then applies all these facts to the welfare checklist including:

- The wishes and feelings of the child concerned considered in the light of their age and understanding.

- Their physical, emotional and educational needs.

- The likely effect on them of any change in the circumstances.

- Their age, sex, background and any characteristics of which the court considers relevant.

- Any harm which they have suffered or they are at risk of suffering.

- How capable each of their parents and any other person in relation to them the court considers are of meeting their needs.

- The range of orders available to the court under the Children Act.

The existence of criminal convictions could be quite relevant but in many cases it will not be the key or central piece of information.

If you think you will need someone to represent you at a court hearing, talk to one of the OnlyMums/Dads Panel Members (www.thefamilylawpanel.co.uk - see Page 32). They will talk you through your options and if they think you need a barrister they will have all the local names and contact details. Professional diaries are busy though and the earlier you sort things out the more chance you have of being represented by the professional best placed to help on the day itself.

Top tips and other issues around this question

- Be honest and upfront with those dealing with your case; the solicitors, mediators, the CAFCASS officers and the court. They will find out about any convictions, so it is better for them to know in advance.

- Be prepared to disclose what the convictions are, when they occurred, what sentence/ punishment was received and some information about the nature of the conviction (for example what happened to lead to that conviction) and highlight what steps have been taken since to change or avoid further charges.

- Remember that convictions are only part of the evidence that will be considered in the case.

- Establish what the issues in the case really are.

- Highlight any involvement there has already been with the child or children.

- Say whether the other party was aware of the convictions, and, if so, from when.

Questions and issues to raise if going to see a mediator or solicitor

- How relevant is this conviction to the issues that need to be resolved for the child?

- What are the issues or concerns for the child and how can these be addressed and dealt with to meet the child's welfare?

- What other information on this conviction might be needed?

- How long will it take to get information? Can there be contact in the interim or progress whilst waiting for information and documentation?

Notes

What should I do if the children's Social Worker does not believe my children are in danger living with mum?

About the author

Erin Clarke, Brearleys Solicitors

Erin is a trainee solicitor in Brearleys' family department based at their Batley office.

If you are the father or any other family member of children who live with their mother and are concerned they are in danger, it can be a worrying time.

The thought of Social Services being involved with your family can be very daunting; often families may not trust their Social Worker and can feel as if their concerns are not being dealt with.

Social Services will usually become involved with a family if they have concerns that the children are at risk of harm. The Children Act 1989 defines harm as ill-treatment, or impairment of health or development of the children:

- "development" means physical, intellectual, emotional, social or behavioural development;

- "health" means physical or mental health; and

- "ill-treatment" includes sexual abuse and forms of ill-treatment which are not physical.

Once Social Services have become involved with a family, the children will be assigned a Social Worker. The role of a Social Worker is to assess any risks that may put the children in danger of harm - they will carry out a series of planned and unplanned visits to the family home and will speak with both parents, and sometimes the children's teachers and doctors to obtain their views. Under the Children Act 1989, the welfare of the children must be their first consideration.

If you have concerns that your children are in danger living with their mother, then you should make your views known to the Social Worker. If you, or anyone else, make serious allegations relating to the welfare of a child, the Local Authority have a duty to investigate. In this situation, a Social Worker would undertake a strategy discussion within 5 days of the allegation, and if required would undertake a Section 47 investigation. While the timescale within which the

Please remember that this is not your child(ren)'s fault. These are confusing issues and emotions for an adult, never mind a child. So often forgotten but so important to remember.

Grainne Fahy, Hanne & Co

Section 47 enquiry should be completed is 45 working days, the outcome of the Local Authority's enquiries must be available in time for an Initial Child Protection Conference which, where necessary, must be held within 15 working days of the Strategy Discussion/Meeting where the enquiries were initiated.

The Local Authority will take your concerns into consideration when making their assessments. However, upon investigation of your concerns, the Social Worker may choose not to take any further action if they believe that the children are not in danger. As a trained professional, they are entitled to make this decision.

If you disagree with this decision you should speak with the Social Worker and stress your concerns and the reasons for them, and provide them with any evidence you may have to support your claims. If you feel that the Social Worker is failing to carry out their duties you are entitled to make a complaint. You should raise your initial concerns with your Social Worker's Team Manager. The Team Manager is a more senior member of staff who is responsible for supervising your Social Worker's files. They will be able to look over the work carried out by your Social Worker and decide if your concerns regarding your children's mother were properly assessed or if any further work

should be carried out.

If you wish to further your complaint, each Local Authority has a different complaint's procedure, you can get a copy of this by asking your Social Worker or Local Authority Complaints Manager. The website of your Local Authority or Local Safeguarding Children Board may also have details. The time limit for making a complaint is 12 months from the date of the incident, although this can be extended in certain circumstances.

Alternatively, you could make an application to the court for the children to live with yourself. This is a private law application and would be self-funded unless you are eligible for Legal Aid. During this process CAFCASS would carry out safeguarding checks and if welfare concerns are raised they may undertake a full risk assessment of both parents to help the court decide where the children should be placed and if they are in danger.

Build a strong support network of friends and family, for the times when parenting becomes difficult or loneliness is overwhelming.

Mandy, Mum

Notes

How will the court decide on where the children will live?

About the author

Ruth Hawkins, Boardman, Hawkins & Osborne LLP

Ruth is a founding partner of specialist family law firm Boardman Hawkins & Osborne LLP and is an experienced family solicitor, and member of the Law Society's Children Panel, meaning that she specialises in public law children cases, involving social services, and complex children litigation. Ruth became a Family Mediator in 2012.

When families split up, it is often extremely stressful and emotions can run high. When parents are separating and/or divorcing, and cannot agree on arrangements for their children, this adds to the pressure.

There are a number of ways to resolve issues such as where the children will live, and when and how they see their other parent.

If parents are able to reach their own agreement, then the courts do not need to intervene. This is

known as the 'no order principle', contained in the Children Act 1989, which states that where parents are able to reach their own arrangements the court will not become involved.

Parents can reach their own agreements directly with one another, or by using a family mediator. CAFCASS ("Children and Family Court Advisory and Support Service") have produced lots of helpful guides, including a Parenting Plan to assist with this.

A family mediator would meet with both parents, preferably in the same room (but it can be separate - called 'shuttle mediation'). The advantages to this way of resolving issues include an often speedier and more targeted or personal approach; the parents are in control of this process, whereas if they are using the court process, the court is in control; it can often be a cheaper process; and legally aided mediation is available for those who qualify (provided there is a legal aid provider in the area!). It is also possible to arrange for child inclusive mediation with a qualified mediator, which can be a really good way of exploring the child's wishes and feelings.

But not everyone is able to reach an agreement, and it takes both parents to agree. Sometimes only one person is willing to try mediation, sometimes neither are or there may be good reasons why it is simply not safe or appropriate.

In those instances, a parent may need to make an application for a Child Arrangements Order ("CAO") to the court.

The courts no longer deal with 'custody' or 'access', or 'residence' or 'contact' and instead deal with the child's arrangements. This change in terminology was brought in in 2014.

If the court is considering an application, it will usually be about where the child is going to live, or when they will spend time with the other parent, although other issues such as which school they attend, or medical treatment and other specific issues, can also be considered by the court, where appropriate.

Imagine you are listening to your child/children at 18 talking to their friends about how they experienced mum and dad separating; you would want to hear: "it was ok - I was fine - knew I was loved by both and free to love each of them", not: "it was a nightmare..."

Debbie Wahle, Norfolk Family Mediation

The court's main consideration when deciding such matters, is the child's welfare. This is set out in Section 1 of the Children Act 1989 which states that "...the child's welfare shall be the court's paramount consideration".

The court is required to go through a 'welfare checklist':

- The ascertainable wishes and feelings of the child concerned (considered in the light of their age and understanding);

- Their physical, emotional and educational needs;

- The likely effect on them of any change in their circumstances;

- Their age, sex, background and any characteristics of theirs which the court considers relevant;

- Any harm which they have suffered or are at risk of suffering;

- How capable each of their parents, and any other person in relation to whom the court considers the question to be relevant, is of meeting their needs;

- The range of powers available to the court under this Act in the proceedings in questionnaire.

This all looks straightforward, but *how* does the court ascertain all of this?

A short safeguarding report or letter will be filed with the court and served on the parents before the first hearing from CAFCASS, confirming whether there are any safeguarding concerns from the police or social services perspectives.

Where there are safeguarding issues raised, the court can order a report from CAFCASS, to look into these aspects. This report is often referred to as a 'section 7 report'.

In families where there has been social services involvement, the court will generally ask the social worker who has been dealing with the family to prepare the section 7 report, instead of CAFCASS.

The CAFCASS officer, or social worker, will speak to each parent, and will usually speak to the child, usually in their offices, or sometimes at school, or occasionally at home. Once they have done so, they will prepare their report, file it with the court, and also serve it with each parent and/or their solicitors if they have them.

The court will generally have timetabled a short DRA Hearing (Dispute Resolution Appointment) shortly after the report is due, to consider whether the parents can reach agreement or not. If they can't, then the court will generally order a contested hearing to be listed for maybe a day or so,

depending on how great the issues are, and potentially how many witnesses may need to give evidence. In most cases, the witnesses the court will want to hear from will be limited to each parent and the CAFCASS officer or social worker, but occasionally other witnesses, including a new partner or family member, may be allowed too.

During these final hearings, the court will hear the evidence and then hear 'submissions' from the parents or their lawyers, and then the Judge or Magistrates will make a decision.

The only thing I had to keep me calm was my sport. Bryony (16)

What is a Leave to Remove application?

About the authors

Fiona Turner, Partner & Lottie Tyler, Associate, Weightmans LLP

Fiona's main practice areas include pre- and post-marital agreements, cohabitation agreements, divorce (including international forum issues), financial settlements, child law and international relocation cases for married and unmarried clients.

Lottie has over 10 years' experience advising on all aspects of family law. She is a Resolution accredited specialist in European and International family law, children law and complex financial and property matters.

For separated parents, the possibility of a move abroad is fraught with complexity. If a child's parents end up living in two different countries, it is going to have a substantial impact on their upbringing. This article looks at the considerations for the international relocation of children.

If a parent is looking to move overseas and intending that the children move with them, they will need the other parent's agreement to make the move, or alternatively an order from the court. A court application is for what is termed 'leave to remove' i.e. permission to take a child out of the jurisdiction of England and Wales.

Trying to reach a collaborative or mediated agreement is preferable to court. Such an approach would give the other parent time to adjust to the idea and the opportunity to contribute to a plan. Through either of these processes it would properly be a joint decision and one therefore most likely to benefit the children moving forward.

The law and the guidance

A court approaching an application for international child relocation should note:

- The welfare of the child is the court's paramount concern.

- There is no presumption in favour of either parent.

- There is a distinction between 'principle' and 'guidance'. Regard can be given to guidance in previous cases, provided that overall that particular case is decided on what is in that child's best interests.

- The welfare principle is key; the court's enquiry is the same whether there is a primary carer and or if there is a shared care arrangement. It is not about the labels given to child arrangements.

- The court should reach its decision by undertaking a global, holistic evaluation of the options. This requires it to:

  - conduct a welfare analysis of each realistic option for the welfare of the child on its own merits and in the context of what the child has to say;

  - conduct a comparative evaluation of each party's plans; and

  - if appropriate, scrutinise and evaluate each parent's plan by reference to the proportionality of the same; (considering the proportionality of the parents' respective plans is necessary to ensure that the decision reached is not open to challenge under article 8 of the European Convention of Human Rights).

What this means when preparing a case

Within the context of the evaluative approach, it is clear that the success of an international relocation case is heavily dependent upon the facts of each case.

In preparing a case, the following (non-exhaustive) list of points should be considered in conjunction with the welfare checklist set out in s1 Children Act 1989. The list is in no particular order:

- the nationality, domicile and habitual residence of the parties;

- the child's cultural background and ties, including the history of where they have lived and the frequency and quality of time spent in other countries and the languages that they speak;

- the child's personality and interests;

- significant people in the child's life other than their parents;

- the connection of each member of the family to the place of the intended relocation;

- the reason for the application including an assessment, where appropriate, of whether there is a motivation behind the application that undermines the reason;

- the 'infrastructure' in place in the UK and in the proposed new country in terms of income, accommodation and practical support;

- the intentions and feasibility/ practicality of promotion of time spent with the other parent and how it will be facilitated;

- the other parent's ability to relocate and whether there is any question that the 'staying parent' may not remain in the UK in the foreseeable future;

- what the child wants;

- the impact on the child's education, whether this is the right time for the move and whether this is a good moment to transition between schools/educational systems;

- the impact on the child of a potential reduction in contact; and

- the impact on both parents, to the extent it could impact on the child.

Advice from abroad should be sought

Unless a family law practitioner is dual-qualified in both the UK and the country the parent wishes to relocate to, their advice alone will be insufficient. The parent should also consult a lawyer in the destination country for advice on immigration/visa requirements; the extent to which any English order will be recognised; and the merits of obtaining a 'mirror order' (this is an order made in one country which reflects the original order made in another country).

This advice is an important part of strengthening a case, enabling parents to understand as early as possible any potential difficulties in enforcement. An overall understanding of the legal position may also help to allay the fears of the other parent.

What should I do?

Advice to anyone contemplating such a move who anticipates resistance from the other parent should research the resources available for the children in the new location and start building up a picture of what their life would be like. In advance of any discussions with the other parent,

information should be gathered and detailed consideration given to how it is presented to the other parent. It will also provide the other parent with the opportunity to do their own research into schools, nurseries and neighbourhoods.

Conversely, a parent who thinks their former partner is making decisions about their children's future without seeking agreement, or without providing full information about the arrangements, can consider making an application to the court for a prohibited steps order to prevent the children being taken out of the country, either at all or just until proper arrangements have been put in place. These arrangements will include when that parent will see the children if they were to relocate, and, until they have had an opportunity to take advice, what steps can be taken in the courts of the other country to ensure that that court would enforce an order made in England or Wales. Alternatively they could consider whether a 'mirror' court order should be made in the country where it is proposed that the children are to live.

Expert advice from a family law solicitor should be sought at an early stage of the planning/ discussion.

The Children Act paradox

About the author

Kathryn McTaggart, family solicitor at Woolley & Co

Kathryn specialises in divorce and separation, as well as related financial matters, and has a particular interest in disputes around children. This includes specialist knowledge of applications by a parent to move with a child to another country.

Writing about whether Family Court decisions are always in the best interests of children requires a gargantuan effort to separate the objective from the subjective. There is a 'best interests' criteria courts must follow and, if they do not do so, then the decisions are plainly wrong and can and must be appealed. That, however, ignores the vast human evidence that evaluates Family Court decisions and finds them wanting, unsatisfactory and sometimes unfathomable.

From my perspective as a family solicitor I cannot really recall any real shockers of decisions that stand out for their sheer ignorance or neglect of the best interests of the children involved. Perhaps that is because most of the children cases I deal with settle after hard work and compromise, or I usually end up with a court decision that I consider to be in the children's 'best interests' myself. This is not to imply that I have an unusually successful children law practice but rather, that I take the slightly unfashionable view that our antiquated and imperfect system, bolstered by the under resourced but battling CAFCASS officers, mostly has Judges who are committed, intelligent and sensible human beings who are determined, despite the challenges of the system, to make sound decisions in the best interests of children.

The premise is really that in most cases 'a relationship' between children and both parents is in those children's best interests.

Delay, emergency applications and actual emergencies

Unfortunately the system sets itself up for a fall. The Children Act makes it clear that delay is likely to prejudice the interests of any child. But when is a groaning court system, relying on at least four busy legal professionals, the reports of overstretched CAFCASS and Social Services and, occasionally, at least one obstructive parent, going to be able to make speedy and lawful decisions in the best interests of children?

Some of the worst decisions I have seen have been made swiftly without notice to the other parent on an emergency basis. The Judge has one sided information from a parent who considers the stakes are so high that to present misleading or even fabricated evidence is a reasonable thing to do in the 'best interests' of his or her children. The damage done, even on a short-term basis, is often not at all in the best interests of the child as time progresses. Better to get things done right than done quickly.

And it is also a case of priorities. Objectively, the fact that your week's summer holiday with your children in Spain may be at stake because the ex isn't playing ball can't really compete for court time with an application to stop a child being abducted to Yemen. However, that is not going to be of much comfort to the parent who has to explain to some very disappointed children that there is no holiday this year.

> You set out to be a parent and that role hasn't changed through separating. Be the best you can, regardless of the circumstances.

Suzanna, Mum

Content

Multiple Judges, multiple breaches, no changes

The need to secure a court hearing in a not untimely fashion means that the same Judge will not always be available. This is extremely demoralising for those parents whose time with their children is constantly frustrated by the other parent when a different Judge treats each occasion as a 'one off' blip rather than a systematic denial of a relationship between parent and child.

Enforcement of existing child arrangements orders remains problematic. New legislation and various carrots and sticks arise to deal with failing to allow children to spend time with their other parent and Judges try hard not be so namby pamby, but really hands are tied. When is it ever going to be in the best interests of children to reduce a mother's (and in the vast majority of cases it is mothers) income with a fine or remove her from her children for a short sharp prison shock? But that is cold comfort for fathers proceeding on the principle that a relationship with both parents is in the best interests of a child.

Parents oppose children spending time with the other parent for lots of reasons. Sometimes they have convinced themselves that no parent is better than one who does not measure up (in their eyes). Sometimes, personal feelings of rejection and hurt make it impossible to see the value of a relationship between the child and the other parent and it is too painful to have even limited contact at handover. Sometimes withholding a child is the most effective punishment for wrongs inflicted and, in any case, bad partner = bad parent. On occasion it boils down to suspicion, dislike of a new partner or simply control. For some it is the loneliness and fear of not having a precious child with them at all times. Whatever the reason, these feelings are formidable and some parents will go to extreme lengths to protect their child or, in reality, themselves.

False allegations

Accusations of abuse, physical or sexual, are always horribly difficult to confront. The court has no choice but to suspend, curtail or supervise time with that parent (in the best interests of the child) until appropriate investigations have been made. As a result the child in question suffers months of messed about time with that parent in artificial environments, is questioned (however appropriately and skilfully) and, in some cases, subject to physical examination. In the child's best interests? I think not.

But the risk of harm cannot be ignored either. More parents than you would think consider that the end justifies the means. In some cases, parents' bad behaviour seems to actually be rewarded by the court who assess that to continue to enforce child arrangements will expose the children to emotional damage at the hands of the hostile primary carer and it is therefore in the best interests of the child to let the relationship with the other parent fall by the wayside.

When twice weekly arrangements become twice annually arrangements

Often the cases with the highest stakes are those in which one parent seeks to relocate to another country either with their new family or to return to their home country. These cases are enormously complex and hinge on a multitude of factors individual to each family but, in

Notes

very simplistic terms, the effect on the primary carer (and new family) of being forced to stay in a desperate practical, emotional or financial situation is balanced against the effect on the child of a reduction in time with the other parent.

When is reducing time with a much loved parent in the best interests of a child? But I suppose, neither is living with a carer who is in dire straits. The courts are less ready to give permission to go than previously but still these difficult decisions are made, apparently in the best interests of the children concerned.

Missing out

Sometimes the court is faced with two parents whose hostility is such that only the most detailed and rigid order will suffice. So, if a best friend's birthday party falls on dad's weekend, too bad - the child misses out. If dad's ski chalet is only available in mum's week, the child does not go. Flexibility is almost always in the best interests of children but sometimes it is impossible and the court must do its best to ensure relationships between parents and children survive animosity.

Making it all 'equal'

In the days of shared care and 'hands on' dads the shared care order is king. Equal time is the new holy grail and some people really do make it work for themselves and, most importantly, for their children.

I cannot help but sigh inwardly when I am presented with a schedule by parents who have divvied up their children's days between them so it is all 'equal' and 'fair' and have not noticed that their little ones will sleep in a different bed every night of the week. Does this sound like it is in a child's best interests? I am not convinced.

The court and CAFCASS continue to have concerns about this type of arrangement, particularly for school age children but many parents believe 'equal time' is in the best interests of their children.

The imperfect parent

We continue to expect perfect decisions in less than ideal situations in an imperfect world. Not many of us would choose to have our children in the care of a cannabis user or with someone who has beaten his wife or who will have the children in the same bed in the morning with each new boyfriend. But if that is who the child's parent is then

that is what the court has to work with.

A relationship with both parents will be in the best interests of the child unless there are serious and pressing concerns about the harm this would cause to the child. Sometimes that leads to what are considered surprisingly lax decisions in the eyes of the other parent.

Beating the paradox

So when are court decisions in the best interests of children? The answer is always and, sometimes, never. It is the paradox of the Children Act. The objective and the subjective. A Judge is not of your family although he or she may well do their level best to educate his or herself about what that means. A decision will be made in the best interests of the children as identified and assessed by an unknown third party.

If parents want a decision that is truly in the best interests of THEIR children, then they must make that decision themselves, jointly with their co parent. Anything else will undoubtedly be in the children's best interests but, at the same time, probably not so.

My parents might not be together but I have all the support I'll ever need from family and friends. Anonymous (16)

DNA, hair drug & alcohol tests in families - what do you need to be aware of?

About the author

Dr Salah Breidi, Head of Forensic Toxicology, DNA Legal

Salah is a forensic scientist who is responsible for the interpretation of forensic evidence including drugs and alcohol analysis in family cases. He acted as an expert witness at the United Kingdom Courts and reported thousands of forensic cases.

C an a test show if my ex is still on drugs?

The misuse of both legal and illegal drugs can cause varying risks to your health and the welfare and safety of others around you. Drug testing is used to detect the presence of drugs in a person's sample, such as their hair, and can show a history of drug use over a period of time covering up to 12 months or more. All participants have the right to decline a blood and alcohol test, although this may have a consequence in cases that are ordered by the court.

When is a drug and alcohol test required?

A drug test might be required for several reasons, for example if an individual:

- is required to undergo pre-employment screening;
- is required to take part in a workplace testing programme Is on probation for drug-related crimes;
- has been driving under the influence of drugs;
- has health problems that may be drug related;
- is pregnant and thought to be at risk for drug abuse;
- needs to rule out drug use for child custody cases.

What is hair alcohol testing?

A hair alcohol test is used to determine if a person has consumed alcohol over a certain period of time. The test works by examining the Ethyl Glucuronide (EtG) and Fatty Acid Ethyl Esters (FAEE) markers in your hair to establish alcohol consumption. Testing hair for alcohol is often used to determine alcohol abuse but it can also be required to show abstinence.

What is hair drug testing?

Hair drug testing can show up to 1 year of drug use, depending on the length of hair; 1cm of hair provides 1 month of drug history. A hair sample will be examined for the drugs analytes - the presence of the analytes in hair is a primary indicator of drug use within an allotted time frame.

The hair can also be segmented into monthly samples to allow a report to show a decreasing use of drugs over a period of time, rather than showing the whole test with a positive result.

What if you have no hair?

There are alternative tests available if your client has no hair. In some cases, if a person is required to undergo a hair alcohol or drug test, they may shave off all their hair. In cases such as these, body hair, fingernail, urine or blood tests can be used.

How much will a hair test cost (prices will vary)?

A drug such as cocaine or cannabis test costs £55 per hair segment. Additional fees such as an expert witness report to interpret the results can be requested separately. The official legal aid rates are charged for any additional expert witnessing if needed (£108 per hour).

How much will a DNA test cost?

A home maternity or paternity testing kit is a simple peace of mind test, which includes everything you need to take a DNA sample in the comfort of your own home. It looks at an up to 68 DNA markers, and tests are run twice for 99% accuracy.

The test starts from £99 for a peace of mind test. The Legal DNA test is £299 which can be used for legal matters such as immigration and change of birth certificates. The chain of custody is preserved throughout the legal DNA test. The test includes the cost of the expert report.

What samples can be tested for drugs and alcohol?

Head hair, body hair, nails, urine, oral fluid and blood are all biological matrices that can be used regularly to carry out laboratory drug testing in humans. As a general rule, the detection time is longest for hair and nail samples, followed by urine, oral fluid, and blood.

Children testing

Children living in homes with drug-addicted parents are in a steady danger of poisoning and may suffer from neglect, maltreatment, and lagging behind in development. Hair analysis could be a suitable way to examine this endangering exposure to drugs. In general, hair from younger children contains higher concentrations than from their elder siblings.

If drug abuse is suspected in families where children are found, the family court can request drug testing for the children to confirm or deny the suspicion. Children drug assessments need to be done over a short period since a child's development is rapid within the first few years of life. Hair analysis can be employed to detect substances including opioids, benzodiazepines, barbiturates, amphetamines, cocaine, new psychoactive substances (NPS) and cannabis etc.

Professionals working in child protection often come under criticism which is why the Children Act 1989 requires proof of significant harm above a minimum threshold. Drug chemical analysis can form such an objective evidence to support their management. In the case reported here, the use of forensic science provided objective evidence within a matter of days. Similar to other forensic tests, the result of the children drug test has medico-legal consequences; therefore, hair or other types of sample analysis such as nails or urine analysis should not be used indiscriminately, and consent should be obtained. In child protection cases, the decision to obtain forensic samples should be based foremost on the child's best interests.

Can I DNA test to see if the child is mine and what consents are needed?

A paternal/maternal legal DNA test or peace of mind test can be conducted on a child to determine if he/she is related to the mother or father.

In order for the test to be undertaken, the birth certificate is required in cases where the instructing party is the father or the mother. If the child is under the local authority supervision/care, then an interim care order (ICO) can be made by the court to determine who has the parental consent. The ICO usually states the local authority or the named social worker to have the consent to instruct such a test.

Can I determine exposure from active use?

Passive exposure may have occurred from the use of the drug during a previous period, especially if the participant is exposed to the drug being in an environment that is contaminated with it. Environmental contamination through passive smoking or drug handling has been shown to contribute to the misinterpretation of results. Appropriate decontamination methods, detecting relevant metabolites and by placing threshold values can potentially minimize misinterpretation. The concern of passive contamination remains a problem. The diffusion of the drug deposits into hair reduces the ability to distinguish between passive exposure and willing ingestion.

Exposure, does not only include the consumption of small and/or infrequent amounts of the drug, but also in some cases different ways of passive exposure such as contamination of hair by the drug, ingestion through food or beverage, exposure through neglected/contaminated environment, passive smoking or drug handling and also previous ingestion before the tested period has shown to contribute to the misinterpretation of results.

The drug can still be traced in the hair when someone stops

COURT & 'FIGHTING' FOR THE CHILDREN

using the drug. This is due to the way hair grows and the different phases of hair growth - in this case, the hair resting phase, where hair stops growing for a period of time but still contains evidence of previous drug use. This inactive hair can last for several months and if any exposure had happened before the testing period, it is likely that it will be detectable at a later stage.

What are cut-offs and why are they used?

For drug testing, a cut-off is a drug concentration that is fixed to minimise the number of false positive results. The cut-off used by the Society of Hair Testing (SoHT) and The European Workplace Drug Testing Society (EWDTS) were found to determine active drug users in adults. In children tests, the cut-off level may vary. The SoHT and EWDTS did not publish cut-off levels for children. It is advisable to report any detected concentration of the tested children samples.

The main purpose of the cut-offs used in the drug hair analysis is:

- to minimise the detection of drugs used in previous periods of time instead of current use;

- to avoid the detection of drugs as a result of external contamination due to environmental exposure.

Crucial points to be aware of in children testing:

In children tests, the cut-off level may vary and therefore the level of the detected drugs were compared to the cut-off levels that are recommended by the SoHT, which determine adult drug abusers. It is important to

take extra caution when interpreting a child toxicology result. The child is usually exposed to the mother's sweat, fluids and other sources, as well as external sources such as shared bedding and pillows or even direct contamination such as the tablet/drug powder being in contact with the hair etc.

That is why, when testing alcohol and drugs in children, it is recommended that paternal and maternal samples are to be tested to minimise and reduce the potential misinterpretations of the results. Moreover, it is advisable that any swabs are to be collected from the environments where the child is exposed to, such as bedrooms and living room.

Analysis of hair and nail washings

The analysis of washings can sometimes provide an indication of whether or not the drugs detected in the hair were as a result of active exposure and/or external contamination (either through sweat or direct contamination such as the tablet/drug powder being in contact with the hair). This step will assist the toxicologist during the results interpretation to determine whether external contamination is likely or unlikely to be considered as the sole reason to explain the presence of the drug in the hair.

Conclusion

In conclusion, I recommend that drug and alcohol findings should not be used in isolation due to many variables and factors that may affect the results - they should be used in conjunction with other evidence from other tests and/or clinical assessments.

In terms of DNA testing, it is always advisable to test more DNA markers especially when the test is not 99% conclusive.

Notes

I've been ordered to attend a SPIP by the court. What should I expect?

About the author

Laura Beech MBACP (Accredited)

Laura is a Relate trained couples, individual and family counsellor practising since 2004. She works with people needing help with relationships, emotions, self esteem, mental health issues, communication difficulties, grief, loss and bereavement. She delivered the SPIP on behalf of Relate for 5 years.

The Separated Parents Information Programme (SPIP) was devised for CAFCASS as part of an ongoing process to enable better co-parenting and to help parents understand separation from the child's point of view. It is not a parenting course and will not teach you how to be a good parent - you already know how to do that. SPIP focusses on your emotions and practical aspects of parenting - it does not cover the legal or financial aspects of being a separated parent.

Parents are either 'directed' by the court to attend a SPIP or they can choose to attend the course themselves independently. If the court orders parents to attend, the course is free.

What happens at a SPIP?

Each parent will attend separately - you will not be expected to attend the same course as your ex. It is hoped that, by attending, you will become clearer about what your children need most from you as children of separated parents, and that you learn and understand the fundamental principles of good communication and how to manage conflict and difficulties between you and the other parent using positive behaviours.

You will be introduced to the 'loss cycle' theory and be asked to reflect on your own emotional journey and responses to the relationship breakup or situation and to realise that your children will also experience loss, even subconsciously, and how that might affect them.

The total length of the course is 4

If I could turn back time, I would push harder for my ex and his family to keep in contact. It is their choice not to be but I wonder if I could have done more.

Lisa, Mum

hours and can be delivered in two, 2 hour sessions or one, 4 hour session with a break in the middle depending on your provider. It is important that you turn up on time or even early as there is a cut-off time which is generally 15 minutes or so from the start time. If you are in a small group of four people or fewer it will be delivered by one trainer; if the group is bigger it will be delivered by two trainers.

It is natural to feel anxious if you have been ordered to attend a SPIP as no one likes to be told what to do and this can make participants' feel defensive or hostile to begin with.

Don't feel alarmed if the course feels very dry to begin with - the trainer has a lot of information

My parents separated when I was 3. I was made to believe at such a young age that it was my fault. That guilt stayed with me for years. Ellie (16)

that they are required to give to you. It is important that the trainer does not stray from the script to ensure that every parent receives the same message wherever they take the course.

There are exercises throughout the day and 2 videos to watch. You will be expected to participate in the exercises and feedback sections of the course; however, if you are struggling with any part, especially if it has triggered strong feelings, you can ask to pass on those parts. If you continue to struggle with your emotions on the day, talk to one of the trainers as they may be able to help you. One of the things they may suggest is that you come on another day when you feel more able to cope.

You will be given a handbook to keep which has all the information covered on the course plus some other useful hints and tips. This handbook can be shared with your friends, family or whoever supports you with your parenting and anyone else who would also benefit from the material.

You are not expected to be experts at the end of the course. You should try to see SPIP as an ongoing process, to improve your communication skills and to realise that the effect of conflict is very damaging to your child's development. It is not the separation that causes the most harm to the children but the level of conflict they experience as a child of separated parents. SPIP invites you to think from other peoples' perspectives so that even if you disagree, you can appreciate someone else's point of view and perhaps understand it.

After the SPIP

You will be given a certificate at the end as proof that you attended - some attendees are required to prove this to the court. Feedback forms will also be given during the session and it is important for your voice to be heard, so, if you have any changes to recommend or experiences you would like to share that you think will be useful, please make sure you do

this. The feedback forms are taken seriously and help to modify future courses.

If you have been ordered by the court to attend the SPIP, the trainers will only report to CAFCASS that you attended unless you have displayed disruptive behaviour or did not participate in any way. They will not report back on your responses.

Most attendees get something useful from the day. Some have said that they felt less alone once they attended the course as they met others in a similar situation. Others have said they can understand different points of view better, and they can identify their strengths as a parent that they already had but had forgotten. Other parents feel better just being able to talk to other separated parents. So, although it can feel daunting attending a SPIP course, go with an open mind and a positive attitude. As the day progresses most people find that they relax and may even enjoy the day!

There are no winners here; we all lose, though the degree of your loss is in your hands.

*Nav Mirza, Dads
Unlimited*

Notes

Resolution

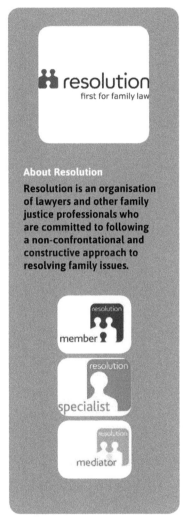

About Resolution

Resolution is an organisation of lawyers and other family justice professionals who are committed to following a non-confrontational and constructive approach to resolving family issues.

Dealing with separation and divorce is difficult. Emotions are high and even if two people agree, the changes can be overwhelming and stressful.

Why should I choose a Resolution member to help with my family issue?

Resolution believes the process of separating, sorting out finances and child care can and should be done in a way that minimises conflict and keeps the best interests of any children at the heart.

Resolution is an organisation of lawyers and other family justice professionals who are committed to following a non-confrontational and constructive approach to resolving family issues.

Resolution members agree to:

- Listen to you, be honest and treat you with respect.

- Explain all options and give you confidence to make decisions.

- Help you focus on what's important in the long term.

- Help you balance financial and emotional costs with what you want to achieve.

- Work with others to find the right approach and best solutions for you.

- Manage stress in what is already a stressful situation.

Resolution has members across the country providing a range of services, from lawyers to financial advisors and family therapists, but everyone agrees to respect our Code of Practice when working to resolve your issues.

Resolution members and associates can be identified by their membership logo. If you are looking for support with your family issue, please use our website to find a Resolution member near you.

OnlyMums and OnlyDads have partnered exclusively with Resolution to provide free consultations with lawyers and mediators through their Family Law Panel. This is aimed at helping you understand your options so you can make the best decisions for your family. All panel members are experienced and sensitive to the issues of domestic abuse, contact and working with grandparents, and many have special skills, including speaking different languages, to ensure you get the best support. In 2018, the Family Law Panel also launched a reduced fees scheme.

Divorce and separation: Finding the best options for your family

There is no one size fits all approach to divorce and separation. As every couple is different, there are also a number of options available, and some may be a better fit than others.

Lawyer negotiations - Both you and your partner appoint family lawyers who focus on your individual interests. The lawyers

Keep in mind a more peaceful resolution. Whatever option, it has to be the one that grants peace for both parents.

Craig, Dad

then negotiate and come to an agreement, with outcomes often depending largely on what the lawyers expect would be the result of any eventual court process.

Mediation - By meeting with both you and your ex-partner, mediators can help identify those issues you disagree on and try to help you reach agreement.

Do it yourself - Negotiating your own agreement, with or without professional support, can be the cheapest way to a settlement and at first glance can seem the easiest. However, it can be a complex process with many aspects you and your partner will need to consider, and so it is not suitable for everyone. This approach can work for couples who have already agreed on how they'd like to divide finances and child care.

Collaborative practice - You and your partner each appoint your own collaboratively-trained lawyer and both partners meet with your respective lawyers to work things out face to face. Both of you will have your lawyer by your side throughout the process and so you will have their support and legal advice as you go.

If you and your ex-partner cannot come to an agreement through the above approaches, you may need to bring your case to court. Alternatively, you could look into **family arbitration,** where you and your partner appoint an arbitrator who makes a final and binding decision on any financial and property disputes, or some child-related issues arising from family relationships.

Common factors that influence people deciding how to get a divorce or separation are:

- Wanting the safest option for you and your children.

- Wanting to be in control of the decision being made about your family's future.

- Whether your financial affairs are complicated and unclear.

- Being up against a powerful personality and not wanting to deal with things on your own.

- Believing you will need support to secure an outcome that is fair.

- Wanting to keep control of costs.

- Not wanting delays or a lengthy battle.

- Wanting an option that will bring certainty and closure

- Wanting the process to be as painless as possible.

- Wanting to understand and influence what is happening.

- Whether you qualify for legal aid.

Ultimately, each approach has its benefits and challenges, but your best option is to speak to a professional who can provide more specific information.

The best thing to do while your parents are splitting up is talk to your parents about how you're feeling, don't leave it all trapped in. Molly (15)

Broken court orders: what can I do?

About the author

**Sarah Wasaya,
Senior Associate,
Stone King LLP**

Sarah advises on all aspects of family law with particular expertise in international and complex financial matters and international cross-border children disputes. She is dedicated to achieving solutions in an amicable and conciliatory way. Sarah is accredited by Resolution as a Specialist Family Lawyer.

Child Arrangements Orders ('CAO') confirm a child's living arrangements and with whom and how often a child is to spend time with their parents and others. It is common for a CAO to include arrangements for birthdays, school holidays and the Christmas period.

If parents cannot agree on the arrangements for their child, an application to the court can be made and a CAO may be ordered by the court. The court's paramount consideration will be the child's welfare having regard to the welfare checklist as contained in section (1)(3)

Children Act 1989 (see Question 55).

Unfortunately, CAOs are not always complied with and this can have significant and long-lasting consequences for the child's emotional well-being.

There are various options for parents in this situation which I set out below.

Mediation/third party involvement

Where a parent fails to comply with or breaches a CAO, it may not be possible for parents to resolve matters between themselves. However, careful consideration should be given to attending mediation or being assisted by a third party mutual family member or friend to attempt to resolve matters relating to the breach, resolve issues between the parties and to agree the next steps. This option can result in a quicker and cheaper resolution than an application to court. If this is not attempted or if it is unsuccessful, the parties can make an application to the court. Mediation may not be appropriate if one parent has been a victim of domestic abuse by the other parent.

CAOs contain warning notices setting out the consequences of failing to comply with them. The notices confirm that a person who fails to comply with a CAO may be made to do unpaid work or pay financial compensation or they may be held in contempt of court and imprisoned, fined or have their assets seized.

The court has a wide range of powers where it believes that a person has failed to comply with a CAO without a reasonable excuse. The court can:

- refer the parties to a Separated Parenting Information Programme (SPIP) or to mediation;

- make an enforcement order (for the person who breached the CAO to undertake unpaid work);

- make an order for the person who breached the CAO to pay compensation for financial loss;

- commit the person who breached the CAO to prison or order them to pay a fine;

- vary the CAO including ordering activity directions, utilising other available resources and amending contact and even living arrangements for the child.

The court will seek to determine the reasons for the breach and the second, third and fourth powers listed above are not frequently used although they are available in cases where it becomes necessary.

The court's powers in relation to a variation of a CAO following a breach are discussed in more detail below.

Activity directions

The court may make a direction for a parent to take part in programmes, classes and counselling or guidance sessions that may assist them in establishing, maintaining or

improving involvement in a child's life or to address a person's violent behaviour to enable or facilitate involvement in a child's life (this is Section 11A (5) Children Act 1989).

Child Contact Intervention

CAFCASS may recommend a referral to CCI where an assessment confirms that a child is not spending time with a parent when it should be. CCI is funded by CAFCASS for up to 12 hours and aims to ensure that the child has a positive contact experience with a parent particularly where there are parental alienation issues or where contact is being reintroduced after a period of no contact. As CCIs are funded by CAFCASS, they may not be available the closer you are to the end of the financial year.

Family Assistance Order

The court can make an order requiring a CAFCASS Officer or an officer from a local authority to advise, assist (and where appropriate) befriend any person named in the order (parents and the child) for up to 12 months (Section 16 (1) of the Children Act 1989). A FAO is not widely granted and requires consent of every person to be named in the order (except the child).

Importantly, a FAO may direct the officer to give advice and assistance in establishing, improving and maintaining contact (Section 16 (4A) of the Children Act 1989). A FAO can also direct an officer to report to the court on such matters relating to an existing CAO and whether it should be varied or discharged (Section 16 (6) of the Children Act 1989).

CAFCASS Monitoring Order

The court can make an order requiring CAFCASS to monitor compliance with a CAO and report to the court for up to 12 months (Section 11H Children Act 1989). The consent of the parties is not required for this.

Joining the child as a party

In complex matters including where a child irrationally refuses to see a parent or where the views and wishes of the child cannot be adequately met by a report to the court, it may be beneficial for the court to join the child as a party to proceedings. A guardian (who is a CAFCASS Officer) is appointed to consider and report on the best interests of the child to the court. The guardian will appoint their own solicitor.

Fact finding hearing

If allegations of domestic abuse are raised as a reason for stopping contact then it is important to request a fact finding hearing as early as possible so that these issues can be dealt with.

Transfer of 'live with' order

A 'live with' order was previously known as a residence order.

It is rare but if there are continued breaches of a CAO, the court may consider that it is in the child's best interests to live with the other parent. In a recent case, the court ordered that a child should move to live with a father after a mother continued to restrict progression of the child's contact with the father (Re C (A Child) [2018] EWHC 557 (Fam)).

There is a presumption that involvement of a parent in a child's life will further the child's welfare unless there is evidence to the contrary (Section 1(2A) Children Act 1989). In the absence of safeguarding concerns, it will always be in the best interests of the child to have contact with both parents.

The courts have a positive duty to attempt to promote contact and these attempts should be stopped only as a last resort and where it is believed that the child will no longer benefit (Re M (Children) [2017] EWCA Civ 2164).

It is important to record all breaches in recitals to orders so that the position is clear to the next Judge who hears the case and the matter can be dealt with appropriately.

It can be more difficult where a breach has been continuing for a significant period of time and in cases relating to older children who oppose the CAO as more weight is likely to be given to the children's wishes and feelings.

If there has been a breach of a CAO without reasonable excuse then you may want to consider without delay which of the above options are appropriate.

It would be beneficial to seek legal advice before and after making an application to the court, even if it is only on an ad hoc basis where full representation may not be affordable. You can receive free help from the Personal Support Unit at court who can help you to complete application forms and go with you to court to take a note of proceedings.

CAFCASS

About the author

Sophie Vessey, Policy and Communications Manager at CAFCASS.

CAFCASS represents the best interests of children in family court cases, acting independently of all other parties. We help to ensure that any risk to a child is identified and assessed at the earliest possible stage, and that from the outset the child's welfare and best interests are at the forefront of the parties' and Judge's minds.

This includes 'private law' (divorce and separation) cases, where parents can't agree on arrangements for their children, such as who the child will live with or who they will spend time with. We also represent children in care proceedings (when a local authority has serious concerns about a child's welfare) and in adoption applications (these are 'public law' proceedings).

We become involved in cases only at the request of the court. In private law, when a parent or carer makes an application to the court, the court will usually refer the case to CAFCASS. We received over 42,000 private law

applications in 2017-2018. The CAFCASS person who becomes involved in private law cases is called a Family Court Advisor (FCA).

There is a lot happening when parents separate - it can be an emotional time with risk of conflict between separating parents. Children may feel caught between their parents, picking up on emotions and feelings. Our role is to provide the court with the information needed for a safe and sustainable decision to be made for the children, which may include assisting the adults to reach a safe agreement.

There are three stages of private law work:

Before the first hearing at court

An FCA undertakes safeguarding checks with the police and local authority to determine whether there are any risks to the children. This is followed, where possible, by separate telephone interviews with the parents where any concerns regarding safeguarding can be discussed. A safeguarding letter reporting the findings from this work will be provided to court at least three days before the first hearing. If the telephone interviews do not take place, the FCA at court will try to speak to the parents before the hearing and provide a verbal update to the court.

At the first hearing

If no safeguarding concerns are identified ahead of the hearing, the FCA will work with the parents to support an agreement to be made without further court proceedings, usually through a parenting plan. This allows the parents to set out any practical difficulties surrounding child arrangements following their separation.

If agreement is possible, a consent order can be made by the court, which makes this agreement binding and ends the court proceedings.

If no agreement can be made or the FCA has concerns about the safety of the child, the court can refer the parties to a range of support services such as mediation to assist in reaching an agreement, or ask us to undertake further work. Most of our cases close at the first hearing with a safe agreement reached by the parents.

After the first hearing

The court orders further work from us in around a third of cases, usually in the form of a 'section 7' report. The FCA will decide what information they need for the report based on what the court has asked them to look into. This may include talking to children about their wishes and feelings, speaking with the parents, and making enquiries with other people such as family members, teachers or health workers. The report will be provided to court for the following court hearing and will

help the Judge make a safe decision for the child.

We recognise that some cases can be safely resolved outside of court proceedings if parents are supported to come to an arrangement that works for their child. We also recognise that, for those cases where our involvement continues past the first hearing, this needs to be tailored to the specific issues in the case.

We are looking at a range of options to continue to improve our services to children in private law. This includes initiatives designed to provide parents with a safe alternative dispute resolution pathway, supporting parents after the first hearing to focus on the needs of the children, and improving the information available for families going through separation.

More information on the role of CAFCASS in the family justice system can be found on the CAFCASS website, CAFCASS.gov. uk.

Only tell children what they need to know. Keep it simple, be honest, they don't need details.

Bridie, Mum

Notes

What records can I keep and can I make secret recordings?

About the author

Shivi Rajput, Solicitor

Shivi graduated with First Class Honours in her LLB law degree and a Distinction in her Legal Practice Course. She qualified as a solicitor in 2012 after being trained by a Deputy District Judge in a Legal 500 firm. She has specialised exclusively in family law since this time.

A frequent cause of frustration within family proceedings is that many disputes take place in private within the confines of the family home, so there is rarely an independent third party present to corroborate your version of events. As a result, it is often your word against your former partner's and it is left to who the Judge or the Magistrates believe. This can be very unsettling.

Without independent witnesses, how does a parent prove that the other is being abusive during handovers, or is inappropriately influencing the children behind closed doors? Often the children themselves are unable to recognise that any manipulation is occurring and even if they do, they may be too young for their account to be given proper consideration by the court.

The temptation can therefore arise for parents to make records, including covert recordings, to gather evidence in support of their concerns. This temptation is heightened by the ever-increasing sophistication of modern recording equipment and the ease with which this equipment is accessible to the public. Almost every parent now owns a smart phone which can easily be used to video incidents. Whilst the desire to collect evidence is understandable, parents should exercise caution when making secret recordings which they later attempt to rely on within children proceedings.

Contrary to popular belief, taking secret recordings for personal or family use is not illegal, but any person who seeks to rely on such recordings in court must first obtain the court's permission to do so, and this is not necessarily an easy task.

Secret recordings of children

In the recent case of M v F (*Covert Recording of Children*) [2016], the father and his current partner had placed recording devices on the child without her knowledge for the purposes of gathering evidence. The father had sewn 'bugs' into the child's clothing, which enabled secret recordings to be made over a number of years.

The Judge stated that it is "almost always wrong" for a recording device to be placed on a child for the purposes of gathering evidence within family proceedings, whether the child knows of its presence or not. In this case, the Judge made a final order for the child to live with the mother, stating that the father's actions in making the covert recordings demonstrated a lack of understanding by him as to the child's best interests and created a secret which was likely to cause the child

Don't keep it bottled up to yourself. I'm not saying everyone must know; they don't need to, but seek advice in another person, it helps! Tyla (15)

emotional harm and adversely affect her relationship with adults in general when she came to learn of it.

This is clearly an extreme example; in other cases, the court has allowed covert recordings into the proceedings as evidence and has relied upon them as a useful corroboration of one party's version of events, but the position remains very case specific.

Secret recordings of handovers

Caution should also be exercised when making secret recordings of the other parent during handovers. In a recent case, the Court of Appeal concluded that video recording handovers amounted to intimidation and could be used in support of an application for a non-molestation injunction.

Secret recordings of professionals

The issues faced may be with professionals involved in the case, such as the CAFCASS officer or social worker, who you believe is inaccurately reporting matters to the court. Whilst CAFCASS have stated that they should have nothing to fear in being covertly recorded and therefore should not object, it is best practice to inform the professional before any recordings are made. Secretly recording anyone is rarely likely to be considered appropriate.

As can be seen above, whilst it is lawful to make covert recordings for personal and private use, there are risks involved, and even if they are allowed into the court proceedings to be used as evidence, the court may consider

that the recordings are harmful to your case. The court may conclude that secret recordings, especially of a child, have led to inappropriate questioning for the purpose of gathering evidence, which can amount to emotional abuse. Secret recording is often regarded as a breach of privacy, regardless of legal principles.

What records can and should be kept?

It is advisable to keep a diary and a handover log, where you contemporaneously note down any issues with handovers, or any other problems, as and when they occur. An up-to-date diary is typically considered to be good evidence, as the entries are made at the time of the incident or shortly thereafter, so the recollection of events is likely to be accurate and detailed, and therefore reliable.

If contact is taking place in a contact centre, you may be able to obtain notes from the contact centre staff, confirming what happened during the contact sessions and if there were any issues or concerns (see Question 20 for more help on contact centres).

Notes

If you're writing something to the other person that you wouldn't want your child to read when they're older, don't write it.

Matthew Richardson, Coram Chambers

Can my ex withhold our child's passport?

About the author

Caroline Young, Clarke Wilmott

Caroline is a Chartered Legal Executive in the family team in Birmingham. She practises in all areas of family law, with particular expertise in complex financial matters arising from divorce and cohabitation disputes.

M ost parents would generally agree that it is in their child's best interests to be able to have the opportunity to enjoy a holiday abroad. However, when parents separate and emotions are running high, people often act out of character and place their own needs before that of the child.

Taking a child abroad

What if your ex-partner has booked a holiday without consulting you and is planning to travel abroad without your permission?

Firstly, it is a criminal offence to take a child out of the UK without the consent of everybody who has parental responsibility unless the court has given permission (see Questions 6, 11 and 13 and Must read article on Page 324 for more information on parental responsibility). However, if an order has been made that a child is to live with a person, that person may take that child out of the UK for up to a month at a time without obtaining permission.

If there are no orders in place or you are the one who has the order, your permission must be sought. If you do not consent to the holiday your ex-partner is entitled to make an application to the court for what is known as a 'Specific Issue Order' to request permission to travel. Unless there is a safeguarding concern or a risk that your ex-partner will not return with the child it is likely that such an application would be granted. It is important,

therefore, that you consider fully the reasons why you are not willing to consent.

Passport disputes

What can you do if your ex-partner is holding your child's passport and is refusing to hand it over to enable you to book a holiday or even to attend a holiday that has already been booked?

If you do not have a 'lives with' order (previously known as a Residence Order) in your favour, then you would need your ex-partner's permission to remove the child out of the UK for a holiday. As stated above you would be able to make an application to the court for permission to take the child on holiday and for the passport to be released.

If the holiday has already been booked and your ex-partner is refusing to hand the passport over then you would have to make an urgent application for the release of the passport. Provided you can show that there is no reason why the child should not be able to accompany you on the holiday and that you plan to return to the country after the holiday, there should not be any issue with securing the order in your favour.

Often in these situations the problem relates to trust, with the party wishing to go on the holiday being reluctant to divulge their plans in any detail and the person holding the passport refusing to release it without having a full itinerary. People should be encouraged to put aside their differences and provide full details of their travel plans to include flight numbers, dates and times and the contact details of the hotel or other accommodation. Arrangements should also be made for facetime/telephone contact during the holiday to provide reassurance that all is well.

If you are concerned that this is going to be a recurring problem, then it is possible for there to be

an order that the passport is held by solicitors and released only for the purpose of a holiday after which it is returned.

If there is a genuine concern that the child will not be returned after the holiday and you are the parent holding the passport it is important that you notify the passport office that the passport has not been lost. There have been cases where, sadly, a parent has indicated that a passport has been lost and obtained a new one enabling them to travel. Once a child has left the UK it can be extremely difficult to secure their return, depending on where they have travelled to.

See Question 92 for more help on securing your child's return if they have been removed from the UK.

Focus on working together. It's easier said than done but you will still need to talk to each other long after this is over. Any issue you can resolve with each other, builds a foundation for your future (and is something you're not having to pay your lawyers to sort for you).

David Lillywhite, Burgess Mee Family Law

Notes

What does supervised contact mean?

About the author

**Juliet Thomas,
Shanahans
Solicitors**

Juliet is a highly
experienced,
compassionate
and friendly family law
solicitor and collaborative
lawyer who will fight hard
to achieve the very best
outcome for her clients. She
is an accredited member of
Resolution as a specialist in
Private Children Law, and a
member of the Law Society
Family Law Advanced Scheme
with the specialisms of Private
Children Law and Ancillary
Relief.

S upervised contact means
that someone will remain
present at all times when a
parent is having contact with his
or her child.

When is supervised contact necessary?

Supervised contact can be an
option when there has been high
conflict between the parents
sometimes witnessed by the
children, where there has been
domestic abuse, where there is a
Family Court injunction order or
a conviction relating to domestic
abuse. Perhaps the parent who

lives with the children has
concerns about the other
parent's parenting skills or
behaviour towards the children
or it may be because there has
been a lengthy gap since the last
contact.

Supervision may be provided by
a family member, for example, by
a grandparent, or by a trusted
friend. It is essential if an
individual is identified as a
potential supervisor, that
individual has the situation fully
explained as supervision is a
responsibility and can be a great
time commitment. After all, the
supervisor is agreeing to be
present each and every time
contact takes place and often
has responsibilities for collecting
and returning the children so
that the parents do not come
face to face. There may also be
conditions the parents agreed on
contact arrangements which the
supervisor would need to
respect.

As supervision is such a
responsibility, parents may not
always be able to identify
someone who can provide
regular supervision. If there is
no-one, another option is to use a
contact centre (to find a local
contact centre go to www.naccc.
org.uk). These centres are usually
staffed by volunteers, have
limited availability and are open
for certain hours during the
week. It is important, therefore,
to find out this information
before using the centre.

Supervised/supported contact

Although contact at a contact
centre is usually called
"supervised" it is more accurate
to call it "supported". Supervised
contact at a contact centre is
one-to-one contact overseen by
a supervisor whereas supported
contact involves the parent and
children being in the centre with
other parents and a staff
member remaining in the same
room but not closely overseeing
the contact.

If contact goes well after a few
sessions, contact may evolve,
progressing to unsupervised
contact. If conflict remains
between the parents, the next
step may be the contact centre
being used as a handover point
only so that the parents do not
need to meet.

Get legal advice, however
"amicable" things are at the
moment.

Colin, Dad

233

Top tips

- Accept at the outset that supervised contact is not a long-term solution. The aim is to initiate contact so contact will evolve to unsupervised contact.

- Decide on the ground rules for supervised contact before the first visit. Are there going to be conditions in addition to supervision? Do's and Don'ts need to be clear to both parents so that contact does not break down because of miscommunication.

- Ask a relative or friend if they are prepared to be a supervisor and for how long and how often. Do not assume. Supervision is a big responsibility.

- Find out information about local contact centres and the centre that best suits your needs.

- Remember the court's view is that children's best interests usually mean having a relationship with both parents so no contact at all is rarely ordered.

- Supervised contact can be helpful to build trust between the parents.

Questions to ask your solicitor

- Is there a contact centre in the area and where is it?

- How long is contact likely to remain supervised?

- What if contact is agreed in principle but you do not want to meet the other parent?

- What if not even supervised contact can be agreed?

- Do I need a court order before contact is supervised?

Notes

What is the law in Scotland?

About the author

**Rachael Noble,
Brodies Solicitors**

Rachael has gained exposure to a wide range of family law issues and runs her own caseload. She became a fully qualified solicitor in April 2015.

ONLY
Mums & Dads

There are many issues which separating parents need to bear in mind under Scots' Law. This article will address some of the most common queries.

Who has parental rights and responsibilities in respect of a child?

A child's mother automatically has parental rights and responsibilities (PRR) in respect of a child, regardless of whether or not she has at any time been married to the child's father. The father of the child will automatically obtain PRR if he was married to the child's mother at the date of conception or at any time thereafter.

The father will also obtain these rights if he is registered as the child's father on the birth certificate - this rule only applies

if the registration took place on or after 4 May 2006.

Where a woman is married to, or in a civil partnership with, the child's mother then she will also automatically have PRR in respect of the child.

An application can be made to the court to obtain PRR in respect of a child by any person with an 'interest'. A genetic or emotional tie to the child would be sufficient to constitute an 'interest'. Any person with an 'interest' in the welfare of the child can also make an application.

What are parental rights and responsibilities?

Those with PRR are responsible for promoting the child's health development and welfare and to provide guidance to the child. Parents must decide where the child is to live and to ensure that contact is maintained with the non-resident parent. They can also act as the child's legal representative. It is important that the child's parents consult with one another in relation to all major decisions affecting the child.

What if there is a dispute in relation to the exercise of parental rights and responsibilities?

Separating parents will often find themselves in dispute in relation to decisions affecting the child. They may, for instance, disagree with each other as to where, and with whom the child should live, how often they see the other

parent, and which school they should go to. Although court is generally seen as the last resort, in those circumstances, it may be necessary for a parent to apply to the court to ask the sheriff or Judge to determine the dispute.

In considering whether or not to make an order, the court has to exercise its discretion. The paramount consideration is the welfare of the child and the court ought not to make any order unless it considers that it is necessary and it would be better for the child that the order be made than that none should be made at all. The test is ultimately what is in the best interests of the child.

The court will allow a child to express a view in relation to the matter in dispute. The court must, however, take account of the child's age and maturity in determining how much weight to give to that view. A child aged 12 or over is presumed to be of sufficient age and maturity to form a view, but consideration can be given to the views of a younger child if the sheriff or Judge is persuaded that they are sufficiently mature.

Courts will generally encourage parents to make decisions about their children. They know their children best after all. If agreement can be reached, this can be documented in a 'contract' signed by both parties. Mediation is also often encouraged.

What happens if one parent wishes to move to another country with the child of the relationship?

It is not uncommon for separating parents to disagree about whether a child should be permitted to relocate with the other parent. In those circumstances, it may be necessary for an application to be made to the court for a 'specific issue order' permitting such a move in the absence of consent from the other parent.

It is unlawful for a parent to remove a child who lives in Scotland outside of the UK unless there is consent from the other parent or an order from the court. Even if a parent wishes to move to another territorial unit of the UK, it is clear from recent Scottish case law (see the case of *GB or L v JC* [2017] CSOH 60) that the appropriate course of action in that situation is for the parent seeking to relocate to seek an order from the court to do so if the other parent will not provide the necessary consent. The matter will require to be litigated in the country where the child is habitually resident, even if the child has already been removed from that country without the other parent's consent.

In considering whether or not to allow a parent to relocate with a child, the court will have regard to a range of factors, including the arrangements in place for the child at the new location, schooling, accommodation, child care, how contact with the other parent will operate, the family ties that the child is leaving behind and the reasons for the move. The child's views may also be considered. The court will ultimately need to consider whether the move is in the child's best interests.

An 'interdict' (an order preventing a course of action) can be obtained to prevent a child being removed from Scotland if a parent is concerned that this may take place without their consent.

What if I want to take my child on holiday abroad?

The consent of both parents is required to take a child on holiday abroad. Details ought to be provided of the proposed trip and if consent is not forthcoming, an application can be made to the court for a 'specific issue order' regulating this.

Who requires to pay maintenance in respect of a child?

Both parents ought to support their child financially. For the purposes of child maintenance, a 'child' means a person under the age of 18 years or a young adult between the age of 18 to 25 who is in full time education. Therefore, the obligation to maintain a child continues if for instance, they attend university. It is therefore open to an individual who is engaged in further advanced education to raise an action against a parent if they do not consider that they are receiving adequate financial assistance.

Where an individual is under the age of 16, or under the age of 20 (if they satisfy certain conditions, for instance if they remain at school or college) then the Child Maintenance Service can regulate maintenance in the absence of agreement. In calculating maintenance, the Child Maintenance Service will take into account the number of nights that a child stays with the non-resident parent. In certain circumstances, it may be possible to apply to the court for a 'top up' of maintenance.

If you require further advice in relation to this, or any other family law issues in Scotland, you should contact a family law solicitor specialising in Scots' Law.

Put your role as a parent first and communicate with each other openly about all issues involving or affecting the children. It may be difficult but it is essential. Showing a united front and providing reassurance to your children is crucial. Make sure they know that, although their parents may no longer be together, they each love them and will continue to be there for them.

Shivi Rajput, Eric Robinson

Parental alienation

Parental alienation is a term generally used to describe complex circumstances where one parent undermines and interferes with a child's relationship with his or her other parent, to the point where the child may reject the other parent. While there is not one single definition, this can take the form of limiting the time the child spends with the other parent and their extended family, and bad-mouthing and belittling the other parent. This section explores the various definitions and descriptions of parental alienating behaviours in more depth and offers guidance on action you and the courts can take to overcome parental alienation.

What is parental alienation?

About the author

Dr Sue Whitcombe
DCounPsych CPsychol AFBPsS
HCPC

Registered Counselling
Psychologist

Sue has 20 years' experience
working with children and
families and is Principal
Psychologist at Family
Psychology Solutions, a not-
for-profit social enterprise
which she founded with the
support of Teesside University.
Sue works with children,
adults and families who
experience life and mental
health difficulties as a result
of relationship issues.

The children need both of
you to be their parents,
especially after you've
separated.

Juliet Thomas,
Shanahans-Law

All children are affected by family breakdown. In most families, both parents work together to help their children adjust to a new way of being, and to minimise the negative emotional impact. In a minority of families, this does not happen. Adjustment to a healthy post separation life can be difficult where there was prior domestic violence, abuse or inadequate parenting by one or both parents. Parental alienation is a particular type of adjustment difficulty where there was no prior exposure to domestic violence, abuse or significantly poor parenting. Other labels which have been applied to this concept including Hostile Aggressive Parenting (HAP), Implacable Hostility, Attachment Based Parental Alienation (AB-PA), Parental Alienation Syndrome (PAS) and the Resist/ Refuse Dynamic.

Parental alienation refers to a situation where a child appears resistant to an ongoing relationship with a parent despite having had a "good-enough", loving relationship prior to the family breakdown. Their resistance is a disproportionate response when the entirety of their experience is considered. This is the child's coping strategy. When one loving, caring parent tells a child that mum or dad is dangerous, nasty or doesn't love them - this causes a psychological tension in the child. This is not their experience. This doesn't make sense - but their parent wouldn't lie to them would they? These conflicting messages are difficult to process

for a young child whose brain development is not yet complete. Children quickly become aware that the less often they see their parent, the less often they feel anxious or upset. This is not usually a conscious process, particularly in younger children. A child will develop a narrative that gives a plausible explanation for not wanting to spend time with their mum or dad. This narrative is created with input - information, stories, non-verbal communication - from the present parent.

Children's brains are wired at birth to ensure they attach to their parents. This attachment is necessary for survival; it ensures that a child has its basic needs met. A child attaches to a caregiver regardless of the quality of care received, even if the caregiver is abusive and neglectful. When a child states they do not wish to see a parent - or they hate them - this is a clear indication that something is amiss. Is this child rejecting an abusive parent? This is known as estrangement and is an adaptive coping mechanism for the child to protect themselves. Or are they rejecting a loving parent due to the alienation process? This would be a maladaptive strategy. When alienated, children may appear to function well. However, continued use of this maladaptive strategy over time means they are likely to have an impaired ability to sustain effective, healthy relationships throughout their life, as well as an increased incidence of mental health and psychiatric disorders and

substance misuse.

Both estrangement and alienation are signs of underlying psychological distress. If we do not understand why a child is resistant to a relationship with one of their parents, we risk the child remaining in a harmful, psychologically abusive environment. Fortunately, with a good understanding of abuse, parental alienation and normal and abnormal child development, it is possible to differentiate between estrangement and alienation.

Children, particularly young children, who experience what is usually considered abuse - physical, sexual, emotional maltreatment - or neglect, rarely reject their parent. In fact, these children crave an ongoing relationship with an abusive parent. They are torn. They are ambivalent. A lack of ambivalence, psychological splitting, where the child idealises one parent and devalues the other, has been shown to differentiate between alienation and estrangement (Bernet, Gregory, Reay, & Rohner, 2017). An alienated child will have an overly close relationship with one parent, while rejecting the other. Often this polarisation extends to the wider family.

Alongside their rejection, a child may appear fearful or overly anxious. They may be verbally or physically abusive, while not demonstrating any remorse or guilt for their behaviour. Children will often suggest trivial reasons

for not wanting to see their parent, insisting that their "decision" is their own, not otherwise influenced. Alienated children may speak with adult language, sometimes with a rehearsed or coached quality. They may talk about matters which should not be in their awareness, such as the financial matters or incidents prior to their birth or cognitive awareness. These symptomatic behaviours and the underlying psychological processes in alienation have been independently identified since the 1980s by researchers and practitioners in social work, law and psychology (Baker & Darnall, 2006; Baker, 2005; Clawar & Rivlin, 1991; Dunne & Hedrick, 1994; Gardner, 1985; Johnston, Campbell, & Mayes, 1985; Kelly & Johnston, 2001; Kopetski, 1998; Wallerstein & Kelly, 1980).

In the alienation process one parent engages in behaviours which foster the fracturing of the child's relationship with the other. These behaviours have also been the subject of much research (Baker & Verrocchio, 2016; Harman, Biringen, Ratajack, Outland, & Kraus, 2016; Verrocchio, Baker, & Bernet, 2016; Verrocchio, Marchetti, & Fulcheri, 2015). Typical behaviours include bad-mouthing a parent, suggesting they are dangerous or have abandoned the child. These messages are reinforced by the removal of photographs and other signs of the absent parent from the home, with no positive

dialogue about the parent or their relationship with the child. Children pick up on these messages; they are attuned to the behaviour and body language of their parents. Parents may withhold affection, exhibit excessive anxiety or distress; all contribute to a child's internalised representation of a 'bad' other parent or a needy, vulnerable aligned parent.

Active alienating behaviours include preventing or frustrating direct and indirect parenting time and communication between the child and parent. There may be overt pressure forcing a child to choose between its parents. Parents may be angry with a child or criticise them if they express love or enjoyment of time with their other parent. False or unsubstantiated allegations of abuse, neglect or domestic violence are common. (Bernet et al., 2015; Fidler, Bala, & Saini, 2012; Gordon, Stoffey, & Bottinelli, 2008; Siegel & Langford, 1998; Stoltz & Ney, 2002).

In assessing a child's rejection of a parent, a full consideration of the historical and current social context of child, alongside their developmental history, behaviour and that of their parents, is necessary. This will enable an understanding of the child's rejection - whether estrangement, alienation, or a combination of both - and inform the most appropriate intervention.

No matter what you think of the other parent please don't influence your child to think the same way that you do about them. Jade (17)

How do I recognise and deal with the first stages of alienating behaviour?

About the author

Alison Bushell, Independent Social Worker

Alison is the founder and director of Child & Family Solutions. She now practices as an Independent Social Worker and Expert Witness in Family Law. She deals exclusively with private law cases but offers consultation on public law matters cases when needed.

When parents separate or divorce, the process can produce very extreme emotions; grief, fear and anger are usually around and if there is also trauma in the birth family of one or both of the parents this complicates matters further as can any mental health or psychological issues.

What I have learned throughout particularly my recent social work practice with separating and separated families is that even the best parents can use some pretty appalling tactics when separating and that previously responsible people will behave in quite dreadful ways when arguably they are needing to be at their most level headed and altruistic.

Children are frequently caught up in hostile communication and care arrangements fraught with stress. This is not good for children and in the long term can cause real damage. Having both loving parents in their life-however flawed one or both of those parents are, by virtue of being human and fallible-is what is proven to be best for children and to maximise their optimal healthy development in all spheres.

Having a parent 'written out' of their life damages their life chances and there is now a wealth of research evidence to support this. It has a seriously detrimental effect on their adult relationships and can lead to substance abuse and self harm.

Parental alienation is now accepted by the UK Court system including CAFCASS as serious emotional abuse of children and thus needs to be remedied in their best interests.

So, whilst almost 90% of couples manage to make arrangements for the children with no court intervention, an increasing number who thought things were sorted out before the decree nisi even came through find that they are encountering issues such as their children resisting spending time with them and behaving in ways that appear hostile or hard to fathom.

There are therapists and certainly social workers who will say this is 'just because the child is caught in the middle of you both' and there are certainly plenty of cases where that holds true. However, those children, if they get good support from their parents, learn to adapt to the situation and things usually resolve in time.

This is not always the case however, and parents can find a child will continue to be distant and hostile and at worst refuse to see them at all. This is perplexing and distressing and parents frequently struggle to manage their feelings and get advice - who do you go to? If you are not in court, having sorted out the care arrangements with a mediator or on your own, then where do you focus your concerns - who do you talk to?

Most parents have no idea how to tackle such difficult or rejecting behaviour and if left unaddressed this can escalate and lead to a breakdown of the relationship between the child and the parent who is not the main carer.

As freelance social workers and family support workers, myself and my team are actively supporting parents on social media, one runs an online support group for parents who are struggling to see their children post separation, one runs a local group for dads and our consultants do assessments when those cases are in court as well as undertaking mediation and therapy, frequently reuniting

PARENTAL ALIENATION

children with estranged and alienated parents.

We are quite literally involved right at the beginning as well as when things have got so bad that court is the only option. We therefore have a good idea of the 'warning signs' of what is known as parental alienation.

Early intervention is key

Some of the child behaviours that parents come to us with which can be the early signs of parental alienation are what we call rejecting behaviours, such as;

- Your child asking you not to attend a school play or an important match.

- Your child's sudden rejection of previously loved family members on your side of the family, including grandparents.

- Your child saying they don't want to see you, see you as much or have staying contact.

- Your child repeating or making allegations against you such as inappropriate chastisement/neglect.

- Your child starting to call you by your name rather than 'daddy' or 'mummy'.

- Your child blaming you for any difficulties in the resident parent's home such as lack of money.

- Your child having too much/ age inappropriate knowledge of financial issues or court proceedings.

- Your child ignoring your behaviour boundaries and authority and refusing to comply when they would previously have done so.

- Your child becoming

withdrawn, reluctant to talk or distrustful of your ability to keep them safe.

- Your child seeming to 'rewrite history' in their newly negative recollections of happy family events.

Some of the difficulties with co-parenting with your ex which might indicate that alienation is present include:

- Difficulties or increasing demands over child support and insistence on having 'their time" even if they are working and won't be spending time with the child themselves.

- A tendency to try to draw other agencies in without telling you, for example going to the school alone to talk about the child's issues. This can set you up as the problem or as disinterested.

- You might feel undermined/ unsupported in terms of setting boundaries regarding screen time, bed times etc.

- You might begin to feel undermined, criticised or completely bypassed in medical or educational decisions, unilateral decisions being taken in these areas by the other parent.

- The other parent might pick up on a perceived weakness in your parenting, your relationship with your child or your home situation and exaggerate its significance to the child, other agencies and the parent.

- This can lead you to defend yourself. You might then send an angry text which is then shared by the alienating parent with others without context to make you seem

> If your former partner does something to upset you, it may be tempting to stop them from seeing your child because you are angry. However, using a child in this way is damaging to the child and, unless there are child safety concerns, it is always considered to be in a child's best interests to have a relationship with both parents.
>
> *Emine Mehmet, Duncan Lewis*

unstable or unsafe. (Sadly your child might then also get drawn into this narrative and be encouraged to support accusations against you).

- In this sense, parental alienation is a form of gas lighting, with the alienating parent seeking to use the child/ren to support them in making the alienated parent seem unsafe or a poor parent, to the point where you as the alienated parent will begin to believe this yourself and lose confidence in setting boundaries etc.

Any of these signs in either area are a cause for concern and if you can identify several in one or both areas you certainly need to get advice and help.

Parental alienation doesn't get better if these issues and this behaviour isn't dealt with quickly. Unhealthy patterns can develop and more importantly you can be reactive or respond as a parent in a way that actually fuels a child's rejecting behaviour.

There are frequently 'triggers' for your child behaving in these ways - we find that this is frequently the arrival of a new partner in one of the parents lives. It can, however, also be a life event in one of the parents lives such as the loss of a parent.

What to do?

If you suspect that your child is being alienated from you or is showing the early signs of this you should try to speak to them about how you are experiencing their behaviour. With pre-teens or teenagers this can be reasonably straightforward but with a young child it can be tricky and it is usually best to try to get professional advice. Saying the wrong thing or making the child feel that they are being told off can make things worse.

Do this in a non-blaming way. Explore possibilities, ask them how they are feeling. Reassure them of your love and support.

Never criticise the other parent to them.

Approach the school or nursery yourself, explain your position. The SENCO or head teacher are the best people to speak to.

Make sure you are 'visible' and involved where your children spend their non-parenting time.

There are sometimes justifiable reasons why a child is resisting contact and this could be linked to feeling, for instance,

frightened by something or unsupported by you at a difficult time or being angry due to an ongoing issue. Maybe you have disciplined them or said no to something they wanted or even broken a promise?

Have you had a sudden change in your life such as a new partner moving in or meeting your child? My practice experience would indicate that children can find it very hard to come to terms with suddenly not having you to themselves and they can also fear the new partner is trying to replace their other parent. This can cause real difficulties for some children and can create complex feelings of resentment and even guilt (if they like your new partner) and disloyalty to mum or dad.

Whilst it might also be the case that the other parent might also be failing to support you or even undermining your parenting decisions or lifestyle choices, it remains the fact that these issues can cause or contribute to contact resistance and it cannot therefore ALWAYS be assumed that it is the negative influence of the other parent.

In trying to resolve this, as well as considering the above, try to speak to the other parent calmly and with a non-blaming approach and if it's too difficult one-to-one, involve a third person, like a godparent or mutual friend.

Seek an appointment with a mediator if this doesn't work.

Make sure they specialise in family mediation.

Get support from online resources, there is so much support and information out there.

Don't worry about feeling that you might need to involve the court - its best to act quickly if mediation isn't successful, as it can take a while to get a hearing.

If you can afford a solicitor find one who from is a 'Children's Panel' firm or who are members of Resolution. Ask for a breakdown of likely costs. Don't overcommit yourself as this can become an additional stress.

If you can't afford legal representation and wish to represent yourself there are some very good paralegals and McKenzie Friends out there. Make sure they have references or a checkable online profile or are qualified. Be prepared to pay around a quarter of what you would pay for a lawyer BUT you'll have to speak in court. This can seem daunting but it gets easier...and again there are many resources to help you.

Finally...ask for support, seek counselling if you feel you can't cope, attend a local support group, join an online forum. There are many parents in your situation and there is a lot of help out there.

Advice to other young people: talk to your parents. Molly (15)

My children don't want to see their dad. What should I do?

About the author

Anthony Jones, O'Donnell Solicitors

Anthony has extensive experience in disputes involving unmarried parties. He represents parents and grandparents in children cases including cases involving international child abduction. He is an Accredited Specialist with Resolution in the areas of complex financial provision and cohabitation.

This is clearly a difficult question to answer as it depends on the reasons as to why the children do not want to see their dad. Children should be encouraged by their mum to see their dad if it is a safe and loving environment.

The starting point is that children should grow up knowing both their parents. If there is an issue as to why they do not wish to go to see their dad then that needs to be explored and resolved. Sometimes it has to be resolved using professionals, whether that be medical or legal professionals.

It is important that children are not ignored. When children reach a certain age and understanding their wishes and feelings will be taken into account. The legislation that deals with children matters is the Children Act 1989 and the court's paramount consideration is always the child's welfare. The court also considers the welfare checklist (a set list of factors) in deciding what is best for the child (see Question 55 for more).

You should try and resolve any dispute regarding contact with each other first. You could use mediation to assist you in doing this which could include the children if they are old enough and understand the situation.

If you cannot resolve the matters, then court proceedings may have to be issued but this should only be seen as a last resort. Many people believe that going to court will resolve their problems but in my experience, whilst the court can make orders in respect of arrangements for children, those issues still need to be resolved so that they do not occur again.

If you are a dad whose children are indicating that they do not wish to see you, it is important to act quickly as any delay is likely to be prejudicial to you. If court proceedings have to be issued then those proceedings will not be resolved overnight - they can take months to resolve and important time will be lost if you do not take action.

There are many solicitors out there that will be able to assist dads in this situation usually by offering a free initial appointment. My advice is to look for a Resolution Member as they adhere to a code of conduct so that your matter can be dealt with constructively and in a non-confrontational way. This will assist in avoiding the situation getting worse.

How you deal with separation can affect your children for years to come. Your relationship as a couple may have ended, but your relationship as co-parents endures for the whole of your lives. Remember: your children love both of you and if you hurt their Mother/Father in words or actions, you indirectly hurt your children.

Amanda Holland, Sydney Mitchell Solicitors

How does the court deal with parental alienation?

About the author

Jeremy Ford, Cambridge Family Law Practice LLP

Jeremy is pragmatic, clear and provides realistic advice with a commitment to client service and the interests of the family's future. He is a highly effective mediator and specialist child dispute arbitrator and is a strong solicitor-advocate, experienced in highly complex children cases.

A child being alienated from one parent by another parent is not a new concept. It has had different guises over the years - whether that be intractable contact or hostility to contact. The term parental alienation is the current and perhaps the most apt description.

It is important for parents not to focus too much on the label but rather to identify the behaviours which are impacting on the relationship between child and parent.

The court, when considering arrangements for children must:

- base any decision on the welfare of the child which is the court's paramount consideration as set out in s1 Children Act 1989 and the welfare checklist in s1(3). The most likely relevant parts of this checklist when considering alienation are:

  - the child's ascertainable wishes and feelings based upon their age and understanding;

  - any harm which the child has suffered or is at risk of suffering;

  - how capable each parent is of meeting the needs of the child;

- consider s2A as inserted by the Children and Families Act (CFA) 2014 s.11 that the court is

  "to presume, unless the contrary is shown, that involvement of that parent in the life of the child concerned will further the child's welfare."

- consider the child's Article 8 right to family life pursuant to the European Convention on Human Rights

- consider Practice Direction 12J, with the obligation to consider when any allegations of harm are raised, whether those allegations will impact upon the ultimate welfare determination the court has to make and if so make a finding as to those allegations.

If a child is refusing to see one parent, the court will have to consider *why* that child is refusing to see that parent. A child is likely to be refusing to see one parent either because of 1) their lived experience of that parent, or 2) their perception of that parent which may be wholly unjustified. If their perception of a parent is wholly unjustified it is important for the court to consider why the child holds such a distorted perception - it may or may not be because of the covert or overt actions (or inactions) of the resident parent.

So rather than run with the phrase 'parental alienation' it is going to be far more helpful to the court to consider the evidence as to *why* a child is exhibiting such negative behaviours towards one parent. If the court finds that these behaviours are a result of the actions of one parent, the court will then need to consider whether those actions are emotionally harmful to the child.

A common misstep in proceedings is for only the child's wishes and feelings to be recorded. The statute is clear that it is the child's *ascertainable* wishes and feelings which are relevant. The question is - why are they saying what they are saying? It may be because of their lived experience of a parent or a narrative they have come to adopt due to parental influence caused overtly or covertly.

Where one parent suspects that the other parent is alienating a child from the other, it is important that the court identifies the issues and makes findings swiftly so that it may then make a decision based upon the child's welfare. Delay is the biggest problem in these types of cases because the longer the children are permitted to believe a false or distorted narrative, the harder it is to rectify those beliefs.

CAFCASS has recently published its Child Impact Assessment Framework with the aim of promoting a consistent approach to how CAFCASS officers identify what is happening in a child's life and whether a child is being alienated or is rejecting a parent due to inappropriate or harmful behaviour. It has a particularly helpful tool on the types of behaviour exhibited by alienated children. This will not eradicate alienation but is a step in the right direction to ensure that there is a consistent approach across the family justice system.

The role of CAFCASS is to report

to the court. CAFCASS is not there to offer therapy, counselling or work with families. It is therefore important for parents to arm themselves with details of experts who are able to assist children and the family members who have been subjected to alienating behaviours for family life away from the court.

The following are examples of what children may say in circumstances where they are being alienated by one parent against the other:

- They hate their parent but can't give any reason or the reasons are trivial;

- The reasons the children give may seem rehearsed;

- They see one parent as completely good and the other as completely bad;

- The child is quick to point out that these are their own feelings and the other parent has not influenced them;

- The child displays an apparent absence of guilt for their behaviour and attitudes

towards the non-resident parent yet in all other respects has a good circle of friends, is performing well at school, and has no problems entering new scenarios;

- The child uses phrases or examples that are very similar to the resident parent or recalls incidents where they would have been far too young to recall them;

- The rejection often spreads to the rejected parent's wider family;

- They start referring to the parent by their first name;

- The child, whilst enjoying contact at a contact centre, refuses to take presents home;

- They become extremely panic stricken over the prospect of visiting their other parent - wide eyed, screaming, sobbing.

When parents separate and there is conflict around the arrangements for their children, I try to impress upon them that one day their children will be adults and will look back at what took place. This helps parents to think about how their behaviour and choices are perceived objectively, rather than being caught up in the moment. It also keeps the focus on resolution rather than accusation or blame. What is important are the memories that are being built for the children, and that the parents and the children themselves can experience a positive future.

Matthew Delaney, Hepburn Delaney

The following are examples of what the resident parent may say or do:

- They are encouraging their children to see their parent but are in fact taking no proactive steps for that to happen;

- It is the decision of the children and they respect that decision;

- They will not force a child to do something they don't want to do;

- Remove children from public school events;

- Use disguised language or behaviour which makes clear to the child that emotional permission is not given for the child to see the other parent;

- Engage the child with a therapist/counsellor with the professional only hearing one side of the story;

- Speaking about the other parent in a derogatory manner in front of the children;

- Refuse to collect the children from the house of the other parent;

- Despite a child enjoying contact at a contact centre will say that the child was distressed following contact;

- Make handovers difficult by either hanging around or being too involved.

It has to be said that on the other side of the equation is the parent who alleges alienation when actually the problem lies at their door but they lack the insight to accept the impact of their behaviour on their child. So parents, practitioners and the court must be alive to the fact that the allegation of alienation may be raised by a parent who is unable to accept the role they have had to play in the presentation of their children.

When parental alienation is raised as an issue it is deeply distressing for the parents and the children as it calls into question what the children are saying. The court deals with evidence and it is important that whichever side of the argument you are on that the court is provided with legitimate examples so that it can make a decision in the best interests of the child.

Notes

Advice to other young people: don't get caught in the middle. Olli (17)

Domestic abuse

R ecognising and acknowledging that you, and your children, are a victim of Domestic Abuse (DA), also referred to as Domestic Violence (DV), can take time. Your expectations are so undermined by DA that a whole new idea of 'normal' develops. But once you separate, patterns of behaviour that were suffered and tolerated before, are seen in a different light. Coming out of a relationship where there was DA will impact on the process of separation. The control, threat and suppression that pervaded the relationship may well increase after separation, leading to sky high levels of anxiety and fear. But this chapter highlights all of the legal structures and emotional support available to you, so that you can feel strong about making the break and starting a new, healthy life.

What are the effects on children who witness domestic violence?

About the author

Dr Angharad Rudkin

Angharad is a Programme Tutor / Child Clinical Psychologist within Psychology at the University of Southampton.

We will never really know how many children and families experience Domestic Violence (DV) as so many of these incidents go unreported. But what we do know for certain is that witnessing DV has an adverse effect on children.

Witnessing DV

Over half of known DV incidents happen when a child is present, and half of these happen when a child is under the age of 6. Most of the time, children are not directly physically hurt during these incidents, but the lasting impact on their development is significant. For example, children who have witnessed DV are more likely to have difficulties in their friendships, find it harder to concentrate at school, do fewer activities outside school, act in an aggressive way and will have symptoms of trauma such as nightmares and flashbacks.

This all makes sense when you think of how children learn. Children, especially younger ones, learn predominantly by observing and imitating. As any parent will tell you, you could tell your child to do something a hundred times and they won't. Show them how to do it and they are far more likely to copy you. Watching your parents physically hurt each other is a terrifying experience for children. The two people you love the most and who guide you through life are doing the very things you know are wrong. These children go back into school the next day and will act out what they've seen. They get into trouble for it, and yet their parents don't. They get into trouble at school and they go home to a house that scares them. There is little wonder they don't blossom.

What does research tell us?

But, research is helping us to understand how we can best support children who have witnessed DV. There are a few clues coming out of studies, with the most significant one being that the child needs a mother with 'good enough' parenting skills and a mother who is functioning as well as she can despite the DV. That is, having a pillar of strength, hope and comfort in the form of a responsive mother can build up the child's resilience to help them get through this period of time (NB: The research has focused mainly on male to female DV as that is still the most common form. It will be interesting to see what is found when researchers begin to study female to male DV). Being a family who is active, sociable and organised is also a protective factor. As you would expect, being exposed to DV for a shorter period of time, and it being the first time it's occurred, will also mean that you are better able to cope with it.

Intervention and support

Given that a child can be buffered from the effects of DV by the continuing care of a 'solid' parent, it follows that any effective intervention should involve the parent as well as the child. Studies have looked at the impact of teaching children social skills as well as coping skills. The main difference in how children did was still determined

My four children became so hard-wired to abuse that they normalised it like toast and honey.

Kitty, Mum

by how their parent was functioning. So again, the message is clear that the more the parent is coping and functioning the more the child will be able to keep going.

Parents need to get all the support they can so that they can in turn be that pillar of strength for their child. Acknowledging and admitting to the DV is the first step. Accessing support and networks is the second. These are difficult to do as DV seeps into the very core of a person's belief in themselves and the future. But, knowing that how you as a parent copes is the biggest determiner of how your child copes may give you the drive you need to change things.

COULD I BE A VICTIM OF DV?

JOT DOWN WHAT BEHAVIOURS YOU THINK ARE ACCEPTABLE OR NOT IN THE FOLLOWING 3 COLUMNS AND ASK YOURSELF IF YOU HAVE EXPERIENCED ANY LISTED IN THE 3RD COLUMN

Behaviours that are acceptable	Behaviours that are acceptable occasionally	Behaviours that are never acceptable

---

For a while I was scared of talking to someone but it really does help. School, teachers, friends, parents and siblings are always great people to turn too. Imogen (11)

Domestic violence: a checklist?

About the author

Beverley Watkins, Watkins Solicitors

As well as being a partner and solicitor in the firm, Beverley is a member of Resolution and The Law Society's Advanced Family Panel. In addition, Beverley is also a member of the Education Law Association.

The Family Court has the power to make a "Non-Molestation Injunction" which is an order of the court usually prohibiting the following:

- Using or threatening violence;

- A person from contacting the applicant;

- A person from going to a home or within 100 metres of a home.

In order to make an application in the Family Court, the Applicant must be "related" in some way, for example married, previously co-habited, parent of a child together, parent, son, aunt, uncle, grandparent etc. Family Non-Molestation Injunctions cannot apply to parties who are not related such as neighbours or former friends.

If there has been a recent serious threat or if there has been recent violence (there is no time limit on what is regarded as "recent"), a party can apply for what is known as an emergency injunction without notice to the other party of the hearing. When dealing with an emergency injunction the court is unlikely to challenge or question the evidence of the applicant. If an order is made there is likely to be a review hearing one or two weeks later when the court will reconsider the matter. This will give the opportunity for the other party to make representations as to why a Non-Molestation Order should not continue. However, at the review hearing often the other party does not attend.

Breach of a Non-Molestation Injunction

Breach of a Non-Molestation Injunction is in itself a criminal offence for which a person could be punished by a term of imprisonment of up to 5 years. The difficulty, however, is that the police seem extremely reluctant to take action in respect of a breach of a Non-Molestation Injunction.

Non-Molestation Injunctions are usually made for 6 months or a year. If, however, there is a breach of a Non-Molestation Injunction during the period when it is in force, it is possible to apply to the court to extend the period of the injunction.

Occupation Orders

Occupation Orders are orders which regulate whether a person can occupy a property when they are entitled to. Often they will prohibit a party from entering or attempting to enter a property even if they are entitled to.

Occupation Orders are often made for 6 months to 1 year. During that period, parties are expected to resolve issues concerning the occupation of property. For example, if parties were married, they are expected to deal with the property and financial matters.

I felt very alone and as if I had nobody to turn to. It knocked my confidence and changed my behaviour. I started messing about at school and not listening in class, but I realised this wasn't the person I wanted to be known as. Cerys (17)

DOMESTIC ABUSE

Legal Aid

Legal Aid is available to apply for a Non-Molestation Injunction. However, it must be remembered that there are tests which an Applicant must meet:

- Disposable needs should be below a certain figure;

- Capital needs should be below a certain figure (equity in a home is taken into account).

Applying for a Non-Molestation Injunction.

There is no court fee payable to make a non-molestation injunction. An application form must be completed and a statement must be signed by the applicant.

The statement should contain the following information;

- Details of the relationship between the parties;

- Details of any children;

> If you (or one of your friends) might want to talk through your options in confidence with a solicitor, the OnlyMums and OnlyDads Panel (www.thefamilylawpanel.co.uk - see Page 32) contains the details of male and female Resolution domestic abuse accredited specialists. Look for the purple ribbon symbol on their profile page.

- Details of where the parties are living;

- Details of the first incident of violence or threats;

- Details of the worst incident of violence or threats;

- Details of the most recent incident of violence or threats;

- Details of any medical treatment, if any;

- Details of witnesses, if any.

The above is not an exhaustive list.

Legal aid and other proceedings

If a non-molestation injunction is granted, it can act as 'gateway evidence' for other legal services such as finance and children matters but an applicant must still be financially eligible.

Notes

The arguing is too much for me and the children. Should I leave?

About the author

Julia Brown, Principal Solicitor at Family Legal Solicitors

Julia has substantial experience of advising and assisting clients in relation to a broad spectrum of family law matters and as an accredited specialist member of Resolution is committed to helping parties to achieve where possible a resolution to their affairs in a non-adversarial and amicable fashion.

The reality of life is that nobody lives in a fairytale relationship these days and, even in a healthy relationship, there are going to be disagreements and at times arguments. If you have little ones, at some point whether you mean it or not, your little one is likely to hear yourself and your partner argue or disagree. Most of us would agree that this is never a positive experience for a child and if you have memories of your own parents arguing you will be able to empathise with the feelings it brings up when this sort of behaviour is witnessed in a household.

Given that it is often said that a healthy argument is part of a healthy relationship, how do we as parents think about dealing with such conflicts in a child-sensitive way?

Effect of arguments on children

A healthy relationship is one where, if the parties argue (and everyone argues from time to time) they are able to do so in a constructive way and come up with positive solutions. However, if you find yourself in a relationship where arguments are a daily feature and this is occurring in front of the children, then this is of course causing not only emotional stress to both the parties but to the children, and their wishes, feelings and welfare should be paramount for any parent.

Don't be fooled into thinking that young children are too small to be affected by witnessing such behaviour as even very small children, babies and toddlers, are able to read emotional cues and can pick up on the fact that Mummy and Daddy are angry or upset. This can have an impact upon their own behaviour and sensitivities leading to both short-term and long-term stress and issues.

Ultimately, if you do find yourself in a relationship where you are being subjected to daily arguments, or even worse, violence, this is something that should not be tolerated.

Domestic violence

When people talk about domestic violence, they often think of physically abusive behaviour but domestic violence covers so much more than this and can be simply just someone asserting control, coercive or threatening behaviour. Quite often, it can be emotional abuse and verbal abuse.

If you find that you are affected by such abuse then you should immediately take steps to seek help for both yourself and for the children if they are witnessing such behaviour. There are a number of charities and organisations out there that can assist, including local Domestic

If you are unsure about the way forward think about what advice you would give to your friend if they were in your situation/dilemma. Courses of action advised to a friend are often more measured than one driven by personal emotion.

Ceri Thomas, KBL Solicitors

Violence Units, the Police, Women's Aid and Local Women's refuges. If you find that you or your children are in any immediate physical danger, then you need to take steps to protect yourself from such abuse, including of course making the appropriate reports to the police.

When considering whether you should leave a relationship, you need to consider carefully whether the relationship is positive for yourself. Often, when people are in these situations they are full of fear; fear that they will have nowhere to stay and fear as to the financial repercussions of a separation.

Alternative accommodation

In terms of finding somewhere else to stay, you should immediately seek legal advice to consider your options: can you stay at home with the children; can you stay temporarily with relatives / friends; or should you seek alternative accommodation by way of a refuge or from the Local Authority housing.

A solicitor will be able to signpost you to relevant help relating to all of these issues. In terms of longer term solutions, your solicitor can give you advice as to whether you need to take further steps to keep your violent partner away from yourself and your children by way of a court injunction known as a Non-Molestation Occupation Order

> Arguments are often just words, and occasionally become physical. The power of words can be underestimated. Children learn to speak long after they have learnt how to understand language. That is, they understand a lot more than we give them credit for! While their little brains are spinning with awareness of the anger, hatred, bitterness and sadness between their parents, they may well just act as normal and look as if they haven't noticed a thing. Children are also acutely aware of sulks and period of furious quiet in the house. You acting 'normal' and pretending nothing has happened is not going to fool them into thinking everything is ok. It's hard to hold in mind our children's needs while we feel trapped in a corner of hate and rage, but just be aware that children are all eyes and ears - that is what they are designed to be as that optimises learning, but it also means they take on board all the adult things around them too.
>
> *Adele Ballantyne*

and will also be able to assist with practical matters such as how to obtain help with housing and various benefits, and how to deal with your long-term separation.

If you decide to leave and the immediate short-term issues are resolved, then a Family Law solicitor will be able to advise you as to the separation process. As part of that process they will be able to assist you with the arrangements for your children and also the arrangements regarding your financial affairs on a long-term basis.

Overall, do not let fear be the reason for staying in a relationship where you are arguing too much in front of your children as this is bound to have a detrimental impact on both

them and on yourself.

On the other end of the spectrum, if you are deeply in love with your partner but unfortunately have issues which you are unable to resolve in a family focused way, it may well be that you need the assistance of some family therapy or counselling - this is something that could be explored between you both.

Whether you leave or not is of course only something you can yourself decide. However, no one should ever stay in a relationship because they are scared. Remember, even if the abusive behaviour is something that you yourself are prepared to tolerate on a personal level, you as a parent have a duty to protect your children from harm.

Talk to your parents. This was one of the hardest things for me but they aren't going to know if something is bothering you if you don't tell them. Brianna (16)

What are the signs of coercive control?

About the authors

Claire Molyneux & Anna Kaznowska, Mills & Reeve

Claire is a family solicitor at Mills & Reeve LLP in Cambridge. She regularly advises separated parents on issues about when they see their children, who their children live with, and relocating with their children.

Anna is a trainee solicitor currently sitting in the family team.

Did you know that, since 2015, controlling or coercive behaviour has been recognised as a criminal offence? This type of behaviour is unfortunately relatively commonplace within families, and often not immediately recognisable to the victim as a form of abuse. Often, the behaviour starts quite subtly and since it can be very broad ranging in nature, the victim may become resigned to it as a 'way of life'. Sometimes a single event tips the balance, and it is only once the victim 'looks back' that they recognise the extent of the abuse. Alternatively, the victim may be very well aware of such behaviour and know that it is wrong but be too frightened or simply not know where to turn or how to get help.

Professor Evan Stark, author of 'Coercive Control, How Men Entrap Women in Personal Life', says that:

"Experiencing coercive control is like being taken hostage; the victim becomes captive in an unreal world created by the partner/abuser, entrapped in a world of confusion, contradiction and fear."

The charity Women's Aid has been instrumental in raising awareness of behaviours that are typically characteristic of controlling and coercive behaviour. They include the following:

An intention to cause fear

Generally, if you experiencing behaviour that is designed to intimidate, frighten or coerce you in any way, it could be controlling or coercive.

"When a victim is frightened of their partner and treads on eggshells out of fear of their reaction, that's a problem," says Women's Aid. *"If they get angry at the slightest things and you're worrying about the consequences of your actions, fearing you will 'set them off', that's abuse".*

The perpetrator is controlling

Control is a significant factor in this type of psychological abuse. It can be subtle and manipulative, such as not letting you go out and visit friends and family, and/or being excessively jealous and possessive. It may also build over time. If your partner is controlling what you wear, say or think, for example, this is another sign. Control of a victim may also be financial, with abusers controlling money, or technology, using tracking software on smartphones and hacking social media accounts.

'Gas lighting'

Gas lighting is when someone exhibits abusive behaviour and either pretends it didn't happen or switches blame on the victim. It can be very confusing and disorientating for victims leading them to doubt themselves and their sense of reality.

On reflection I would have had my ex arrested immediately without hesitation the first time he hit me. My guilt is four children have now normalised domestic abuse. That is my crime.

Kitty, Mum

Perpetrators often make their victims feel guilty about things that did not occur or for which they themselves are to blame. Over the long term, a victim's sense of identity is diminished and it can be very hard to regain a sense of self-worth.

One common element of gas lighting is that perpetrators portray an 'idealised' charming personality to the external world whilst denying any wrongdoing that occurs within the family home.

Personal attacks and criticism

This could be where the wrongdoer tells you that you or your family are stupid, unattractive and that no one else could love them. Abusers also regularly attack their victims in front of family, friends or the general public. Criticism often occurs during daily errands in front of shopkeepers, restaurant staff and professional advisors.

'Using' their victim

In a healthy relationship, both parties appreciate one another's needs and equality is present. They care and support each other and there is an element of 'give and take'. An abuser, however, does not think about their partner and generally puts themselves first.

"With an abuser, there's no consideration that you're upset." says Women's Aid. "They do it because they feel

entitled to behave that way. They believe their partner is there to meet their needs and that they can take whatever they want."

The victim makes up excuses for their partner's behaviour

If you find yourself being evasive in front of friends and family, 'covering up' for your partner's bad behaviour, or making excuses as to why they are not to blame, this could indicate an issue.

One woman said that:

"Although I temporarily separated from him I later felt guilty and went back to him. He was threatening suicide and saying he could not live without me. I was always making excuses for him - that he worked very hard for us, and that having children had put a strain on our relationship" (source: Women's Aid).

It is not an isolated incident

Emotional abuse is not about having one argument which crosses the line (which can easily occur within otherwise healthy relationships). It is an ongoing pattern of systemic behaviour in which one partner is controlling whilst the victim feels a constant sense of fear.

How can I get help?

Any behaviour that is controlling and coercive is entirely unacceptable. It is certainly

harmful for its victim, and is bound to have a direct impact on any children of the family. Remember, the behaviours described above may be criminal offences. If you consider yourself to be in immediate danger, do not hesitate to call 999. To discuss your concerns, you can contact the National Domestic Violence Helpline on 0808 2000 247, which is run in partnership by the charities Refuge and Women's Aid (refuge.org.uk and womensaid.org.uk).

If there has been domestic abuse you may be eligible for legal aid to provide you with free legal advice. You can find a legal aid solicitor by going to thefamilylawpanel.org.

My father was crying. I had never seen him cry. My strong, glamorous father crying? Carol

No one believes me - how do I prove I am telling the truth?

About the author

Jennifer Williamson, Associate at Kathy Webb & Co

Jennifer deals with private children and injunction matters, public law proceedings and social service involvement matters. She is a Resolution Accredited Specialist with a particular specialism in private children law and domestic abuse.

Domestic violence! Bruised, battered, broken women (and men) - pretty self-evident right? But, of course that was never the whole story. Setting aside those perpetrators manipulative enough not to leave physical marks, abuse can be psychological, emotional, financial, or any combination of these. It was in recognition of these equally powerful forms of abuse that the government changed its terminology from 'domestic violence' to that of 'domestic abuse'. A large proportion of victims will have experienced all of the above aspects of abuse and many will find that the psychological and emotional abuse is the worst but usually the most difficult to 'prove'.

It's a sad fact that many victims will not, themselves, realise or appreciate the extent of the abuse they have been subjected to, until they have escaped from that relationship and/or engaged with counselling or support services. An even sadder fact is that, even in this climate of campaign and awareness, the vast majority of victims will not report the abuse that they have been subjected to, out of fear or shame.

Often, a perpetrator of abuse can convince you and perhaps everyone around you, that it is you who is the problem, or even that it is your fault that they are subjecting you to that behaviour, that you deserve it, you drive them to it. Frequently, this can result in disclosures being made by victims and the person whom they have entrusted that information to, not recognising the seriousness of the abuse or not believing the victim. The helplessness a victim of abuse can feel as a result of not being believed can have significant impairments upon a victim's mental health, and further enmesh them in the perpetrator's web. The disbelief or disregard of others reinforces the victims feeling of worthlessness, that they deserve this, that it's normal. It isn't normal and we as a society need to change our thinking; hopefully with campaigns and education this will come about in the longer term, but until then ...

It's extremely difficult to prove you're telling the truth. All you can do is continue to tell the truth. Remember there are two sides to every story, and if you're in court, it's the judge's responsibility to establish proof, either beyond reasonable doubt, or on the balance of probability.

Try to keep calm if others aren't telling the truth and practice calming exercises (e.g. mindfulness). If you feel you're getting frustrated then ask for a recess to calm down, and say why, calmly and clearly.

Mike Flinn

How do you prove that you are telling the truth?

There are various ways in which you can gather evidence to demonstrate that you are telling the truth.

- Consider keeping a diary, thus keeping a chronology of the abusive behaviour; when, where and how it happened. A diary should only be kept if it is safe to do so - think about keeping it electronically on a device, your phone, a tablet, a laptop, where it can be password protected.

- Retain any evidence of domestic abuse that has been perpetrated by way of indirect communication (i.e. text message, letter, voicemail etc.). Don't delete them, no matter how hurtful they are. Use them to show that you are right.

- Consider whether to confide in your GP or seek support through counselling as a way of evidencing through independent professionals that you are suffering abuse. All GP's have training in domestic abuse, and even if they can't help you directly, they can direct you to someone who can.

- Speak to friends and relatives. Have they noticed a change in you? Do they feel you have been isolated from them? Often their views and descriptions will point out things that you have never even noticed.

- Even if you feel that no one believes you, still report the abuse to the appropriate authorities, whether that be the Police or Social Services, should there be children involved in the domestic abusive situation. It is so important that you let people know what is happening to you. Police officers are trained to deal with domestic abuse; even if it seems trivial to you at first, have it recorded.

- Lastly, seek help and support from a domestic abuse support group who will be able to listen but also offer services to help you in dealing with the domestic abuse you have been subjected to. You can find their details online, at your local library, Citizen's Advice or at your GP surgery.

Sometimes you will need protecting. If the police are unable or unwilling to take action, you can use the courts to obtain an injunction. Again, this where victims often feel they won't be believed. The courts are very experienced in dealing with domestic abuse, and very sympathetic to applications.

Legal aid

Legal aid is still available to help you get representation (albeit with some qualifications), and there are specialist solicitors trained in domestic abuse - look for Resolution Accredited Specialists.

It may be worth noting that such an application is made within the family court whereby the burden of proof is on the balance of probabilities. Therefore, even if the domestic abuse is unreported, or disbelieved by friends or professionals such as the Police due to lack of 'evidence', the family court will listen to the evidence you wish to put forward, usually by way of a signed witness statement and oral evidence and decide, on the balance of probabilities, whether the incident has, or has not occurred. Your word is as good as anyone else's - just tell the truth.

The most important way to evidence that you are a victim of domestic abuse is to speak out and to continue speaking out, until someone listens. We are trying to hear you and are here to help.

Don't put the other parent down or argue in front of the kids. It is easy to do - I know, I've been there, done that. In the long run it is better for the kids if you are civil in front of them.

Sarra, Mum

All me and my brother were thinking was this is our fault. Sammie (17)

ONLY
Mums & Dads
parents meet professionals

Organisations

Org

ORGANISATIONS

National Society for the Prevention of Cruelty to Children

About the NSPCC

The NSPCC is the leading children's charity fighting to end child abuse in the UK and Channel Islands.

They help children who've been abused to rebuild their lives, they protect children at risk and they find the best ways of preventing child abuse from ever happening.

The NSPCC is the leading children's charity fighting to end child abuse in the UK and Channel Islands.

We help children who've been abused to rebuild their lives, we protect children at risk and we find the best ways of preventing child abuse from ever happening.

So, when a child needs a helping hand, we'll be there. When parents are finding it tough, we'll help. When laws need to change, or governments need to do more, we won't give up until things improve.

The NSPCC and separation

Separation and divorce can be a challenging and upsetting time for all involved. But although

there may be a lot going on, it's important to make sure children get the support they need.

To support children during a separation and help them with their worries, you should:

- Remind them that they are loved by both parents.

- Be honest when talking about it but keep in mind the child's age and understanding.

- Avoid blame - don't share any negative feelings the adults have about each other.

- Keep up routines such as going to school and specific meal times.

- Let them know they can talk about their feelings with you.

- Listen more than you speak - answering questions will help them to open up.

And if they don't feel like they can talk to you or someone in the family remind them they can always contact Childline anytime, by phoning 0800 1111 or having a 1-2-1 chat online.

Childline is just one of the national services the NSPCC provides to ensure they can be there for every child in their time of need.

Childline

The NSPCC's Childline service has helped young people in need for over 30 years.

Founded by television presenter and journalist Dame Esther

Rantzen, the confidential service is available for young people up until their 19th birthday.

Counsellors are available for young people to speak to 24/7 and can be reached via 1-2-1 chat at www.childline.org.uk or on the telephone at 0800 1111.

The Childline website is packed with advice on a range of subjects, including parents separating and family relationship issues. It also offers moderated discussion boards where children can share their experiences.

Adult Helpline

The NSPCC adult helpline is available 24/7 for any adult that has concerns about the wellbeing of a child.

In addition to its main purpose of allowing adults to report concerns over children, the helpline also exists to offer parents, carers and professionals advice on anything in relation to child protection.

Any adult who has a concern about a child can call 0808 800 5000.

Schools Service

The NSPCC **Speak out. Stay safe.** service teaches primary school children to speak out and stay safe from abuse.

The service aims to visit each primary school across the country once every two years. Through interactive assemblies and workshops trained volunteers help children understand abuse in all its forms and how to recognise the signs. It also explains how they can protect themselves and who to tell when something is worrying them.

Therapeutic services

In addition to our nationwide services, the NSPCC offers a range of therapeutic services through a network of service centres.

Each service is designed to provide therapeutic relief and intervention to children and their families who have suffered, or may be at risk of abuse and neglect.

Our **Letting the Future In** service helps children recover from sexual abuse. The service allows children to express their feelings through play and counselling so they can move on with their lives.

There is also an adapted version of **Letting the Future In** available for children with learning disabilities at some service centres.

Protect and Respect works with children (11-19 years) who have been, or who are at risk of being, sexually exploited.

Sexual exploitation of children is a complicated issue, which is constantly changing. And texting, email and the internet means it can often be hidden. That's why it's vital we help children so they're less vulnerable to sexual exploitation, however it happens. And help those who've experienced it to rebuild their lives.

Parents under Pressure is a 20 week course tailored to the individual needs of a parent who is participating in a drug or alcohol treatment programme to ensure they can deal with their child's needs.

Hear and Now is a new approach which provides therapeutic support to children and young people who professionals have concerns about. They may display worrying signs that something is wrong and sexual harm is a background feature.

Turn the Page helps young people overcome the feelings

and experiences that have made them harm another child sexually.

Baby Steps provides support to new parents who may need additional assistance through pregnancy and the first few months of a child's life.

Young Smiles is a service which builds resilience in children whose parents have mental health issues.

To help the NSPCC be there for more children and aid our fight for every childhood visit:

https://www.nspcc.org.uk/what-you-can-do

Notes

Can I get legal aid?

About the author

**Derek Jordan,
The Family Law
Company by
Hartnell Chanot**

Derek has
extensive
experience in all areas of
family law and since joining
The Family Law Company has
concentrated on the areas
in which he has particular
expertise - Private Law
Children disputes and issues
of domestic abuse.

If you are suffering any form of domestic abuse within or following the breakdown of a relationship, you are likely to feel extremely unsettled, frightened for your future and unsure of your options. An additional concern is very often the thought that to obtain specialist legal advice would be very expensive. The provision of legal aid in England and Wales has changed significantly in recent years but where a person or a relevant child has suffered or is at risk of suffering some form of domestic abuse they may still be able to access legal aid to meet the costs of legal advice and assistance.

Eligibility for legal aid has always relied on satisfying two elements:

- the merits of the case - is there an issue that is sufficiently serious that legal aid should be granted to assist that person? and

- whether they qualify financially for legal aid.

In addition to those elements, however, The Legal Aid, Sentencing and Punishment of Offenders Act 2012 (LASPO) introduced the requirement for there to be either:

- a need for urgent protective orders (Non-molestation Order or Occupation Order), or;

- evidence of previous domestic abuse or a risk of domestic abuse from the other party to the applicant or of abuse of a child in other family law cases such as applications concerning children, divorce or separation and the financial matters arising from relationship breakdown.

There is a range of evidence (known as gateway evidence) that the Legal Aid Agency will accept in applications for legal aid. The evidence can include the fact that the other party has a criminal conviction or formal police caution for a domestic abuse offence or child abuse offence, or that there have been previous protective orders made to protect against the behaviour of the other party.

In addition, evidence can come from assessments by professionals such as social workers or from a medical professional (including GPs, health visitors and midwives) or from domestic violence support organisations or support workers. It is not possible to set out every type of gateway evidence here. For a full list of the acceptable gateway evidence one should go to the Legal Aid Agency's website at www.gov.uk/legal-aid.

The rules and procedure for assessing financial eligibility for legal aid are quite complex and again we would refer you to the Legal Aid Agency's website where guidance can be found on financial eligibility. Essentially, income is assessed on the basis of the total income from all sources and the total income is then reduced by deducting allowable expenses against the gross income. The allowable deductions include housing costs,

My parents told me 'you'll understand when you're older'. Now I'm older I've experienced all the good things about it. Ben (16)

DOMESTIC ABUSE

a fixed allowance for dependents and children, any tax and National Insurance deductions from gross earnings, childcare costs incurred because of working or studying and any maintenance paid for children who do not live with the applicant.

If a person's gross income is in excess of £2,657 per calendar month they are automatically ineligible for legal aid. If the disposable income after the allowable deductions are made is £733 per calendar month or less then they may qualify on the basis of income.

In addition to qualification on income, however, the applicant will also need to qualify on the basis of capital. The capital limit for qualification for legal aid is currently £8,000 although the value of properties can be disregarded in certain circumstances as can the value of any assets that might be in dispute between the parties.

A person in receipt of legal aid is under a duty to inform the Legal Aid Agency of any significant change in their financial position - it is possible that a person begins by qualifying for legal aid but then due to a change of circumstances may find that they move outside of eligibility for legal aid and legal aid will cease. Similarly, a person may not qualify financially for legal aid when they are first assessed but may then become financially eligible.

Legal aid funding is not always completely free. The Legal Aid Agency do apply a sliding scale where a full legal aid certificate has been granted which means that, depending on the income and capital a person has within the overall eligibility limits, they may be required to make a regular contribution from their income during each calendar month the certificate is in force or they may be required to make a one-off payment out of any capital they have. There are also circumstances in which a person who has received the benefit of legal aid will be required to repay to the Legal Aid Agency the fees paid to the person's lawyers. Again, the rules and circumstances under which a person may have to repay the Legal Aid Agency are very detailed.

Broadly speaking, a person may have to make a payment under the Statutory Charge whereby a person who has recovered or preserved any money, property or costs as a result of the case is required to repay the legal costs paid on their behalf or if the legal aid certificate has been revoked. A legal aid certificate may be revoked if the Legal Aid Agency considers that the legal aid funding has been obtained fraudulently by, for example, providing false financial information.

Legal aid funding is therefore very much still available but is subject to rigorous eligibility conditions. Anyone who is dealing with the difficult circumstances of relationship breakdown who has suffered domestic abuse or who needs help to be protected from domestic abuse should always take specialist advice.

Notes

How can I stop my ex from verbally abusing me in public?

About the author

Rose-Marie Drury, Senior Associate at Mills & Reeve

Rose-Marie regularly advises separated parents on issues about when they see their children, who their children live with, relocating with their children and issues relating to legal parentage arising from donor sperm, co-parenting and surrogacy arrangements.

If you are being subject to any form of abuse, whether physical or verbal, you must ensure that you put you and your children's safety first. The guidance below sets out different options for action you can take but you must ensure that you do not do anything that would put you at risk of further abuse. Not all of the options will be suitable for everyone.

If at any point you believe that you are at risk of harm **you must get yourself to a safe place and contact the police to intervene**.

Whatever steps you take you should ensure that you have appropriate support in place for yourself, whether friends or family or through contacting an

organisation which offers confidential support and advice for men and women who are victims of domestic abuse such as the free National Domestic Violence Helpline (0808 2000 247).

Can you safely discuss what has happened with your ex? Would it help to have a third party present (such as someone who knows and gets on with you both or a mediator)?

If you are able to discuss what has happened focus on:

- The impact on your children.

- The impact on you and how that in turn impacts on your children.

- The damage caused to your relationship as co-parents as a result of either of you verbally abusing the other.

- Ground rules for how you will communicate when you see each other, including communication about any issues you disagree on.

- Practical steps to prevent an incident happening again - would it help for handovers to take place in a public place for a period of time or for someone else to assist with handovers?

It may be helpful for you to use a parenting plan (available at cafcass.gov.uk). It may also be helpful for you both to consider attending a Separated Parents Information Programme (SPIP)

which will help you both understand how to manage conflict and difficulties (again, see the CAFCASS website). See Question 71 for more information on SPIPs.

If you feel unsafe or threatened

Sometimes the abuse that you are suffering will mean it is not possible or appropriate to sit down and have a discussion with your ex. If you have a solicitor you may prefer to ask them to write to your ex (or if they have a solicitor, their solicitor) about these issues on your behalf.

If you feel unsafe or threatened by your ex's behaviour, report it to the police. The police will speak to you and your ex separately about the incident and can take a range of actions from giving your ex a warning, issuing a Police Information

Be very careful what you post and comment on in social media because it can be used, even out of context, to damage your case. Think twice or three times before posting!

*Ronan McGuigan,
Fisher & Fisher Solicitors*

Notice (PIN), interviewing them, cautioning them, charging them with a criminal offence, remanding them in custody or applying for bail conditions to be imposed (which might include not to contact you).

Domestic Violence Protection Orders

The police can also issue a Domestic Violence Protection Notice (which is a notice that lasts for 48 hours and which will prohibit your ex from molesting you and may also prevent them from returning to your home if you live together). Once a Domestic Violence Protection Notice has been issued the police can apply to the court for a Domestic Violence Protection Order to be imposed which lasts for 28 days.

Non-molestation Orders

Consider applying to the Family Court for a non-molestation order. This is an order which requires your ex not to harass or pester you. In emergencies the court can make the order at an urgent hearing without giving notice of the hearing to your ex (if the court does so it will then list another hearing with notice to your ex).

Notes

You will need to make an application using form FL401 which is available on the Gov.uk website. How long the order will last for will depend on the circumstances of your case. In most cases the order will last until there is another hearing or for up to 6 to 12 months. If necessary the duration of the order can subsequently be extended by the court .

Breach of a non-molestation order is a criminal offence and so if your ex breaches the order you should report this to the police immediately who should then take steps to arrest your ex.

If there has been domestic abuse you may be eligible for legal aid to provide you with free legal advice. You can find a legal aid solicitor by going to thefamilylawpanel.org or resolution.org.uk.

HOW CAN I EXPECT MY CHILDREN TO REACT?

If your children have seen or heard the abuse, they are likely to be unsettled and worried. If you are the custodial parent then this is likely to be vented on you, usually by the expression of anger. This is a reverse compliment as children, and young adults generally, vent on the parent they feel safe with. They may close down so use these following tips - use open questions and don't push. Listen and show empathy and understanding, even if you don't agree. Have consistent and age appropriate boundaries, and give them appropriate choices. Have a time out system with a safe place where you can express anger safely.

Mike Flinn

ONLY
Mums & Dads
parents meet professionals

Organisations

Org

ORGANISATIONS

Women's Aid

About Women's Aid

Women's Aid is the national charity working to end domestic abuse against women and children.

We believe that no one should face domestic abuse alone and that's why we at Women's Aid are always here for you.

We are a federation of over 180 organisations who provide just under 300 lifesaving services to women and children across England. We run the Freephone 24 Hour National Domestic Violence Helpline on 0808 2000 247 in partnership with Refuge, which gives support and invaluable advice to survivors of domestic abuse.

You can reach out to Women's Aid whenever you feel ready to - it is never too early or too late to get in touch. We are always here to listen to you, believe you and support you.

Pick up the phone

The National Domestic Violence Helpline provides confidential support and information to survivors. It is a Freephone, 24 Hour, 365 days a year support service that responds to the caller's needs which may include for example:

- Signposting survivors to emergency safe accommodation.

- Providing information about legal, housing or welfare rights and options.

- Signposting survivors to face-to-face support via local community based drop-in or outreach domestic abuse services.

- Offering information on getting injunctions or reassurance about reporting to the police.

- Carrying out online crisis and safety planning.

- Signposting survivors to other relevant services.

- Offering emotional support and, if appropriate, signpost to counselling services.

- Sending information packs with a range of help and information leaflets that are available in different languages.

Find support online

Our website (womensaid.org.uk) has a wealth of information and resources on it, including The Survivor's Handbook which provides information and practical support for survivors. It has advice on everything from recognising if you're experiencing domestic abuse and understanding your legal rights through to practical tips on safety planning and accessing the support you need locally.

We also host the Survivors' Forum, a safe, anonymous space for women who have experienced domestic abuse to share their experiences and support one another.

If you're worried about someone knowing you have visited this webpage, please see our safety information about covering your tracks online.

Face-to-face support

The National Domestic Helpline can also help you access assistance from your local service, whether you need somewhere safe to stay in a refuge or support in your community at your local outreach service.

Local outreach services can provide support from one-off information sessions to providing

All me and my brother were thinking was this is our fault. Sammie (17)

a dedicated worker to help you, whether you are thinking about leaving or need support after leaving an abusive partner. They often provide support groups, specialist clinics with services like solicitors, and support and empowerment programmes like the freedom programme. They may also provide activities and support services for children.

You can also find your local service online using our Domestic Abuse Directory where you locate your local service and find out how to contact them directly.

Not all abuse is physical

Domestic abuse is not only an act of physical violence - it can be emotional and psychological too. It can also happen to any woman of any age, class, ethnicity and income. An estimated 1.2 million women experienced domestic abuse last year alone. It is important to recognise that you are not alone and that there is support out there for you, regardless of who you are or what form of abuse you are experiencing.

Domestic abuse is an incident or pattern of incidents of controlling, intimidating, isolating, degrading or violent behaviour, which can include sexual violence. It is usually inflicted by a partner or ex-partner but can also be carried out by a family member or carer. Domestic abuse can take place both online as well as offline and can also continue after the relationship has ended.

Domestic abuse can include, but is not limited to, the following:

- Coercive control. Coercive control is a repeated pattern of controlling, intimidating

and isolating behaviour which the abuser uses to instil fear in the victim and has a devastating impact on survivors' lives. It may include acts or threats of physical or sexual violence but does not always coincide with physical violence;

- Psychological and/or emotional abuse;
- Physical or sexual abuse;
- Financial abuse;
- Harassment and stalking;
- Online or digital abuse.

Protecting yourself after separation

It is important to remember that ending the relationship will not necessarily end the abuse. Leaving an abusive partner can be a dangerous time as abusers can continue to abuse after you have left and in some cases the abuse can even escalate. You can't stop your ex-partner's abuse - only they can do that - but there are some things you can do to increase your own and your children's safety. Find out more information about protecting yourself and your children after leaving an abusive partner in The Survivor's Handbook.

If your ex-partner continues to harass, threaten or abuse you, make sure you keep detailed records of each incident, including the date and time it occurred, what was said or done, and, if possible, photographs of damage to your property or injuries to yourself or others.

If you have an injunction with a power of arrest, or there is a restraining order in place, you should ask the police to enforce

this; if your ex-partner is in breach of any court order, you should also tell your solicitor. If you do not currently have a civil protection order in place, you can apply for a court order to help protect you and your children from further abuse. You may also choose to report the ongoing abuse to the police. In an emergency, always call the police on 999.

Call the Freephone 24-hour National Domestic Violence Helpline, run in partnership between Women's Aid and Refuge, on 0808 2000 247 or visit www.womensaid.org.uk.

Think about the kids needs, not yours. You don't love that person anymore but they do, so be nice! However, also know where to draw the line if contact is being detrimental for your children. Try as hard as you can to keep their relationship but if it's not safe or is damaging the children then know when it needs to stop. But be honest with yourself about it - don't stop it just because you can't stick that person.

Jules, Mum

Can I change the locks on my house to keep my ex from just wandering in?

About the author

Melanie Tubbs, solicitor at Brethertons Solicitors

Melanie qualified as a solicitor in 2008 and has practised family law since 2009. She is a Member of the Law Society Family Law Accreditation Scheme and a Member of Resolution.

When you separate from your partner, spouse or civil partner, and they leave the family home, you may wish to change the locks to stop them coming back.

Can you do this?

It all depends on how you both own or rent the property. If:

- you are renting the property and both names are on the tenancy agreement; or

- you own the property in joint names,

you **cannot** exclude your ex from the home without an order from the court. Your ex is entitled to live in the property and if you do change the locks, they are entitled to break back into the property as long as they make good the damage. This means that they can get a locksmith in or break into the property themselves but they must repair any damage they make and give you a key if the locks are changed.

If your ex is violent or abusive towards you, you can apply to the court for a non-molestation order and an occupation order. You will need to show that you are at risk of being intimidated, harassed or pestered and that you need to be able to enjoy peaceful occupation of your home. It also helps to show that your ex has somewhere else to live whilst the order is in place.

If:

- you rent the property in your sole name; or

- you own the property in your sole name,

you **may be able** to change the locks. However, if you are married or have been living with someone for a long time, they may have rights to live in the property and you must be very careful before stopping them from coming back in. In these circumstances, they could apply to the court to get an order to regain entry to the property and even for an order to exclude you.

There are very limited circumstances in which you can change the locks without any consequences and you should take legal advice if you are thinking about doing this. Changing the locks without having an order in place may mean that your case starts on an aggressive footing and it may stop you being able to deal with other issues in an amicable matter.

Other issues

You may want to think about the other issues that separating from your ex may bring. Are you able to pay the rent or mortgage and bills on your own? What other financial support are you entitled to if you are now living on your own?

It is now a good time to try to talk about Child Maintenance (cmoptions.org can help) and you can look at whether you are entitled to tax credits or other benefits if you are on a lower income or you are working part time.

You can also look at arrangements for your ex to see the children and think about your long-term plans i.e. whether you wish to get divorced and how you might go about separating your assets.

You are still a parent, a daughter, a sister, an aunt... Work on being the best version of you so you can be the best parent you can.

Lisa, Mum

My partner has told me he will take the children away if I report his abuse. What are my options?

About the author

Angela Parsons, Wolferstans

Angela qualified as a solicitor in 2005 and has always practised in family law. Angela is a Resolution member and an accredited specialist in Domestic Abuse and Private Law children.

As a parent you have a duty to safeguard your children from harm.

Being in a home where there is domestic abuse puts children at risk of harm. Whether they are subjected to domestic abuse themselves, or witness one of their parents being violent or abusive to the other parent, children may suffer direct physical, psychological and/or emotional harm, and may also suffer harm indirectly.

You could be seen to be failing to safeguard your children from harm if you do not take appropriate action to protect them from this exposure. However, taking action to safeguard and protect them is understandably difficult when you are scared.

There are some practical steps you can take to protect yourself and the children in the first instance:

- Keep a list of emergency numbers;

- Keep a diary of events;

- Seek medical attention if you have suffered any injury and make a note of the date you visited the GP;

- Keep the police informed; and

- Inform your children's school.

Support

The very nature of domestic abuse can make a person feel that they are isolated, but there are a number of organisations such as Woman's Aid and local Domestic Abuse Services and refuges that can offer practical advice and support.

The details for such organisations can be found online, or your local children's centre, council, health centre, or GP surgery should be able to provide details of such organisations or alternative support.

The family court

It is highly unlikely that a domestic abuser would be able to 'take' your children away if you make an application to court. There are orders that the court can make to protect you and your children. Safeguarding the children will always be the court's paramount consideration.

Children Act Orders

In law, a parent with parental responsibility should be able to see their children providing it is in the child's best interests. The mother who gave birth to the child will automatically have parental responsibility and a father will have parental responsibility if he is named on the child's birth certificate or the parents are married. However,

Don't ever think that your emotions and how you feel aren't valid. Don't ever stay silent. Ensure there will ALWAYS be someone there to confide in. Jess (17)

where there is an allegation of domestic abuse the court will only consider making an order for the child to see a parent who has been abusive if it can be satisfied that the physical and emotional safety of the children and the parent with whom the children are living will not be subjected to further controlling or abusive behaviour.

The court is required to give special consideration to cases in which there are allegations of domestic violence or abuse. In such cases the court must decide whether it is necessary to conduct a fact-finding hearing in relation to any allegation of domestic violence or abuse.

There are a number of factors the court must take into consideration which include the following;

- The views of the parties and CAFCASS;

- Whether any allegations have been admitted;

- Whether there is any evidence available to the court to allow the court to proceed i.e. in non-molestation (injunction) proceedings; and

- The nature of the evidence.

Protective orders

The courts can protect you and the children by making one or more of the following orders:

Non-molestation Order

This is an Order where a party is ordered not harass or intimidate you or your child, not to use or threaten to use violence and in some circumstances it can even limit their ability to contact you or come near you or your home.

Occupation Order

An Occupation Order deals with the occupation of the home and

can for example include the exclusion of the domestic abuser.

Prohibited Steps Order

A Prohibited Steps Order prevents a person from removing a child from a parent's care or from removing a child from their school or nursery.

Costs

If you are a victim of domestic abuse you may qualify for Legal Aid. When you contact a solicitor for advice, they will be able to assess whether you are eligible for Legal Aid and if you are not, then they will be able to provide you with an estimate of the likely costs involved (see Question 84).

If you are concerned about any of the issues raised above, you should seek support and the advice of a solicitor.

Do NOT make negative comments about your ex on social media however tempting this may seem. It will only exacerbate an already difficult situation. Best advice is to resist posting updates and avoid making personal comments at all.

Emma Alfieri, Steeles Law

Notes

What about dads coping with an abusive female partner?

About the authors

Dr Elizabeth Bates & Dr Julie Taylor, University of Cumbria

Elizabeth is a Senior Lecturer in Applied Psychology at the University of Cumbria. Key areas of interest include intimate partner violence and specifically male victims but she also has a keen interest in pedagogic research.

Julie is a Principal Lecturer responsible for Psychology and allied subjects at the University of Cumbria. One of the recurrent themes of her research and practice over the last 25 years has been meaningful stakeholder engagement and seeking to use research and evaluation methods that facilitate this.

From the 1970s onwards, domestic violence researchers have adopted a gendered model of men's perpetration and women's victimisation and have focused on explanations that have their roots in norms of patriarchy. Historically this has excluded male victims from much of the research and consequently the societal narrative. When this issue is explored without a gendered lens, we see a very different picture emerge. Research using more representative samples has revealed not only the extent of men's victimisation but also the bidirectional nature of some violence. The findings reveal that in relationships women can be just as violent as men, and this violence is not motivated purely by self-defence as some would purport.

Whilst there is, relatively speaking, less research exploring men's experiences, our understanding of the prevalence, severity and outcomes for male victims is growing. A study based in the United States utilised data from a national helpline for abused men; of the 190 callers analysed all reported physical abuse included being punched, kicked and choked. A similar study in the Netherlands found the most common kinds of abuse were stabbing with an object, kicking, biting and seizing by the throat. Despite differences that exist for size and strength that lead to the perception that women are unable to injure men, the violence often seen includes the use of a weapon/object, and is often seen to cause injury, for example in a US sample 80% reported injuries with 35% reporting a serious injury (e.g. a broken bone).

There is a tendency within the research to focus on physical aggression as it is seen as more injurious and life threatening. More recently however, there has been increased interest in exploring the impact of coercive control, specifically since the introduction of this into the UK Serious Crime Act (2015). Coercive control (or emotional/psychological abuse as it is often known as) is seen in relationships more commonly than physical aggression. Coercive control can include behaviours such as economic abuse and deprivation, possessive and jealous behaviour, insults and name calling, threats and intimidation, degradation and isolation, and manipulation and control over everyday activities. This has been seen frequently in women's accounts of their abuse, but more recently has been seen in men's experiences. It is seen in the account of men in the aforementioned international studies, but also in a recent UK based study. A non-help-seeking sample was recruited to try and understand men's experience more broadly, the men reported experiences of gaslighting (i.e. the manipulation of someone by psychological means into

doubting their own sanity) and being manipulated through the use of false allegations, coercion around sex and pregnancy, being isolated from friends and family, and a range of threats relating to their children.

Experiencing domestic violence is a traumatic event, and trauma is known to increase the risk of developing mental health issues and psychiatric disorders. Domestic violence is known to have a long-term impact on both physical and mental health; indeed, this has been seen in both men and women who have experienced it. More specifically the literature that has explored men's experience suggests that men typically externalise their psychological distress; men report impacts such as binge drinking, post-traumatic stress disorder symptoms, a loss of self-worth and self-esteem, substance use, and suicide ideation. Despite this, the status of "victim" does not seem to apply to men and women equally. Women's violence and men's victimisation is not construed as serious or in need of intervention. This female to male perpetration is seen as less serious and less in need of support services than any other gender combination. These attitudes are thought to have their roots in socially constructed gender roles, and how synonymous aggressive behaviour is with the male gender role, with women generally being less aggressive in non-intimate contexts. These perceptions have been found to have an impact on men in terms of their well-being and their help-seeking decisions. A recent UK study revealed that experiences of domestic violence coupled with these perceptions

had left men with feelings of anxiety and depression, and also left them reluctant to help seek; indeed, men commented that they felt they were weak and they would not be believed. Furthermore, these men had felt further victimised from services when they had sought help, they commented they had been ridiculed, blamed for their victimisation, and accused of being the perpetrator of the violence.

Whilst there is overlap in men's and women's experiences of abuse, there are also experiences that are unique and gender-based. A specific type of abuse that seems to be experienced overwhelmingly by men is legal and administrative aggression; this is described as the manipulation of legal and other administrative systems in a way that is harmful to the other partner. One particular aspect of this that has been seen in the research is around the use of children. Men described incidents where their female partner has made, or threatened to make, false allegations of either domestic violence or violence towards the children in order to manipulate their parental relationships, or prevent access. This can be a further barrier to leaving the current abusive relationship, or indeed a post-separation experience that can result in parental alienation.

Indeed, there is mounting evidence to suggest that child victims of domestic violence have, like male victims, been silenced by the pervasive social narrative. For many years children have been construed as passive witnesses to abuse and as such have been assumed to be less harmed than the 'direct

victim' (typically identified as the mother). More recent research challenges this construction, suggesting that children are affected directly and indirectly from living in homes where domestic violence is present, and a number of mutually reinforcing negative outcomes may follow such exposure. Unfortunately, the ubiquitous gendered lens and the rudimentary binaries it reproduces have produced support service responses that are partial and fail to meet the needs or safeguard certain victim groups within our communities, in particular, adult male victims and male children aged 13 and above.

For men experiencing domestic violence, there is support available including *ManKind Initiative, Abused Men in Scotland* (AMIS), and *Amen* in Ireland. These organisations are dedicated to supporting male victims and signposting to local support where it is available. For anyone interested in reading more about men's experiences there are several books and papers on this; *Abused Men: The Hidden Side of Domestic Violence* by Phillip W. Cook includes a detailed discussion about the research that exists exploring men's experiences of domestic violence including case studies and interviews with victims. For more information about the research in domestic violence including male victims, women's aggression and the impact on children you can read *Intimate Partner Violence: New Perspectives in Research and Practice* edited by Elizabeth A. Bates and Julie C. Taylor which is due to be released in 2019.

ManKind Initiative

About the author

Mark Brooks

Mark is the Chair of the ManKind Initiative.

The ManKind Initiative is a national charity (based in Taunton) established by both men and women in 2001 and became the first British charity to support male victims of domestic abuse

We have been at the forefront of providing services, support and campaigning for male victims ensuring that they (and their children) receive the support and recognition they need. We have seven trustees (three men and four women,) who play an active role within the charity whilst we have six ambassadors all of whom are domestic abuse survivors. The charity's two Independent Domestic Violence Advisers (IDVAs) run the charity' services and the Chair and

Services Manager are also qualified Domestic Abuse Services Managers.

Our Vision, Mission and Approach

Our vision and aim is to ensure:

- All male victims of domestic abuse (and their children) are supported to enable them to escape from the situation they are in. This includes ensuring there is a support service for men in every town, city and county.

- Recognition and support for male victims is fully integrated and mainstreamed in society's view of domestic abuse and in the statutory and non-statutory delivery of domestic abuse services (gender inclusive).

We view parental alienation and the wilful and continual breach of child arrangement orders as forms of domestic abuse. This is because they are used to psychologically, emotionally and financially control an ex-partner by using the children from the relationship. This is an increasingly common issue based on the calls to our helpline. Whilst it is not legally seen as domestic abuse by the Government and courts, we

firmly believe it should be and are campaigning to make it so.

We take a gender inclusive approach

We also believe that the use of threats and/or false accusations is a form of domestic abuse and should be far more formally recognised. We are concerned about the unintended consequences of changes to legal aid funding for family law matters which is fuelling false allegations of domestic abuse.

The charity does not believe that domestic abuse should be defined as a gendered crime or should be viewed as being gendered in nature - it should be defined as a crime as it is both legally, and, in terms of equality and human rights. This is on the basis that the charity recognises that men and women can be both perpetrators and victims in heterosexual and same-sex relationships. The view that domestic abuse is a gendered crime is old-fashioned and non-inclusive - it does not reflect the diversity of domestic abuse victims in the UK today.

We believe in a gender-inclusive and gender-informed approach to responses, services and support to victims that are able to reflect the gender differences

It was just so lovely to see my parents smile again and I am sure they think the same about us kids. Sian

ONLY
Mums & Dads
parents meet professionals

Organisations

Org

ORGANISATIONS

in the experiences and barriers that some victims face (the majority of experiences and barriers are the same for victims from all genders).

Ultimately, victims of domestic abuse should receive, as the primary consideration, support and recognition based on their individual risk and need. Factors such as gender, race and sexuality are all important but not as important as their primary consideration as an individual.

What we do

We provide a range of services directly to men including an anonymous national helpline that any man anywhere can call us (01823 334244) and a drop in service from our Taunton base which we are looking to expand. On average, we receive 1,800 calls per year. We also receive about 20% of calls from people contacting us on behalf of a male.

We rely solely on donations, fundraising and sponsorships for

our helpline - we receive no public money or grants.

We help other organisations to support men by offering a seven point CPD accredited one day training course, a national conference every November, a national directory of services for male victims (called the 'Oak Book'), information on safe house/refuge provision and deliver presentations at conferences/meetings around the UK. We can also offer advice on how to run communication campaigns to encourage more men to come forward.

We are delivering a two year support service to the welfare staff in the Armed Forces to help them better support male victims.

We can also provide a range of national and local statistics on the numbers of male victims in every area of the country and also UK-wide statistics. For the latest statistics, please visit: http://www.mankind.org.uk/statistics/.

We also give male victims a public voice by campaigning for them by taking part in policy consultations, and sitting on statutory/sector led committees and bodies. This includes our award winning #violenceisviolence campaign video and regularly featuring in the media. Our Trustee Dr Elizabeth Bates also produced a ground-breaking video - 20 Voices.

Alongside sexual violence/abuse charity, Survivors Manchester, the charity worked in partnership with the Crown Prosecution Service on the world's first ever bespoke statement on supporting male victims of these crimes by a prosecuting authority.

Further information

For further information, please contact admin@mankind.org.uk or visit www.mankind.org.uk. Our Twitter feed is @mankindinit.

Notes

It's been suggested I get a Prohibitive Steps Order. What is that?

About the author

Bernadette Hoy, Partner at Garside & Hoy

Bernadette is a specialist on the financial aspects of divorce and separation, and her expertise extends to arrangements for children. She has practiced as a Collaborative Family Lawyer since 2007 and has developed a successful practice using this procedure for couples who want to reach agreement without litigation.

In cases where there is a genuine fear and evidence that someone may take certain action in respect of a child which you would not agree with, you may require the intervention of the court and it is important to seek urgent legal advice.

What is a Prohibited Steps Order?

A Prohibited Steps Order (PSO) is an order of the court providing that certain action cannot be taken by a parent in meeting their parental responsibility (PR) for a child without express permission of the court. In broad terms, the exercise of PR relates to any decisions that are made concerning the welfare, development and upbringing of a child.

Essentially, a PSO restricts the exercise of PR and forbids a person from taking certain steps, such as:

- Removing a child from your care or other approved care giver;
- Taking a child out of the UK;
- Moving the child to another location within the UK;
- Removing a child from their school;
- Bringing a child into contact with certain people;
- Changing a child's name or surname;
- Making decisions in respect of a child's medical treatment, etc.

A court can make a PSO during the course of ongoing family proceedings, in conjunction with another court application (such as a Child Arrangements Order providing for a child to live with you) or as a free-standing application.

Application process

Any parent, person with PR or guardian in respect of a child can make an application for a PSO with the required court fee of £215. The person applying may not have to pay the court fee, or may get some money off, subject to an assessment of their means, for example if you have no or limited savings, if you are in receipt of certain benefits or if you are on a low income. You can find out more about applying for help with court fees at the Gov.uk website.

Before making an application to the court, it is a requirement that you attend a Mediation Information and Assessment Meeting (MIAM), unless you qualify for an exemption from attending (which will often be the case in urgent cases). See Question 40 for more information on MIAMs.

Find someone to talk to in confidence - the turning point for me was going to see a counsellor on my own. I hadn't realised you could do this but it helped me recognise what was happening and gave me the courage to start to take practical steps towards leaving.

Tanya, Mum

Involvement of CAFCASS

After making an application to the court, a Children and Family Court Advisory and Support Service (CAFCASS) Officer will be appointed. CAFCASS will meet with the parties to see if agreement can be reached and prepare a letter to the court setting out the outcome of initial safeguarding checks undertaken as to any potential welfare issues and their recommendations going forward. If welfare issues are highlighted and/or if no agreement can be reached, the court may ask CAFCASS to investigate further and prepare a report (called a 'section 7' report) to the court with their recommendations. This will be considered carefully and given significant weight by the court in making a decision.

Urgent applications

In an emergency, you can apply to the court for an urgent PSO without the other person being given notice of the hearing. In this case, the court may make a temporary or interim PSO and arrange for there to be another hearing when the other person can attend and put their case forward. This will also allow an opportunity for the CAFCASS initial safeguarding enquires to be made.

Welfare of the child is paramount

When considering whether or not a PSO should be made, the court's paramount consideration will be the welfare of the child. In cases where the other party contests the application, the court must have regard to the 'welfare checklist', which is a list of 7 criteria which must be considered before a decision is made (see Question 55 for more information on the welfare checklist):

In addition, the court must have regard as to whether any delay in making a PSO will be prejudicial to a child and it must be satisfied that in the circumstances,

making a PSO would be better for a child than making no order at all. In the event the court decides that a PSO is required, consideration will always be given to the duration of the order and in some cases, an order can be made to last indefinitely.

Notes

Don't let their break-up change any ambition or expectation or goal that you have!
Anonymous (20)

What is a Non-molestation Order?

About the author

Inayat Nadat, Nadat Solicitors

Inayat is a Resolution Accredited Specialist Family Lawyer with specialist areas in children (private law) and domestic abuse.

For years victims of domestic abuse have suffered in silence and have had limited knowledge of the protection that can be afforded to them by the courts (and other authorities).

What is a Non-molestation Order?

In essence, a Non-molestation Order is exactly what the term describes. It is a civil order obtained by a victim of domestic abuse from a Judge (or Magistrates) through the Family Court. The term molestation has a wide interpretation - it can include, but is not limited to, physical, emotional, financial and sexual abuse, and it can also cover coercive and controlling behaviour, intimidating behaviour and harassment. The abuse can be once or over a sustained period of time.

A victim of such abuse can apply to the court for a Non-molestation Order against someone described as an 'associated person'. Such a person(s) can include spouses, ex-spouses, civil partners, ex-civil partners, cohabitees and former cohabitees; it can also include various family members.

The person applying for an order is referred to as the 'applicant' and the person against whom orders are sought is known as the 'respondent'.

By obtaining a Non-molestation Order the court proclaims that the abuser (a perpetrator of the abuse against a victim) cannot do or take certain actions, for example, not to approach the victim, not to act in a threatening manner or use violence or abuse towards a victim (in some cases the child(ren)) or attend any property occupied by the victim. The Non-molestation Order would usually specify that the abuser cannot use or threaten violence but may also prohibit other, more general behaviours, which amount to harassment or cause distress to a victim. An example might be unwanted and frequent contact with the victim by numerous means, through social media and text messages and not just telephone calls. In short, the Non-molestation Order, if granted, prohibits the abuser from 'molesting' the victim.

A Non-molestation Order is time limited and provides protection to a victim. However, a victim can ask for the order to be extended just prior to its expiry if the victim needs to continue with the protection.

Such an order not only provides protection but also empowers a victim with some sense of control in relation to uncalled for actions from their abuser.

Where an order is made by the court and this is breached by the abuser, either by themselves or by instructing any other person to do so, then the victim in such circumstances can contact the Police who can arrest the perpetrator(s) and take them through the criminal justice process. If found guilty of a breach of the terms of a Non-molestation Order the abuser can face charges for a criminal offence and can be dealt with by a fine or up to 5 years imprisonment, although an initial and/or minor breach may not attract a custodial sentence. Any persistent or serious breaches may well do.

The victim also has the option of referring the matter back to the Family Court as well and follow the civil process.

In addition to seeking a Non-molestation Order a victim may also seek to remain in the family home to the exclusion of the abuser. In such circumstances, the option available would be to seek an Occupation Order to maintain some stability for the victim and any child(ren). Such an order is available to an 'associated person' (see above). The court has the power to remove the abuser, for example your spouse or partner, from the family home. There are also

additional powers available to a Judge making an Occupation Order, such as requiring one party to be responsible for maintenance of the home and paying the rent or mortgage and other outgoings such as rates and utility bills affecting the home.

Occupation Orders can in some circumstances be complicated as they affect one party's right to live in the family home and are sometimes considered to be 'draconian' orders. To consider the options of seeking such an order it is important to get the right advice at an early stage for your circumstances.

A court may or may not attach a power of arrest to an occupation order depending on the circumstances. Therefore, an important factor to consider is 'safety' and 'stability', not just for the victim but also for a child(ren).

When would I seek a Non-molestation Order?

In simple terms, you should apply to the court if your abuser falls into the category of an 'associated person' and you are a victim of domestic abuse, as described above.

A victim does not deserve the abuser's conduct or behaviour tantamount to undermining the victim, nor do they deserve to suffer a physical assault or be afraid for their own safety.

It is important that a victim acts expeditiously if there is any risk that the victim (or any child(ren)) will suffer harm through the conduct and behaviour of their abuser.

Research has shown that domestic abuse witnessed by children and young people can cause serious harm to them and is tantamount to child abuse.

Therefore, do not hesitate. The sooner the victim applies for a Non-molestation Order the better, as this will afford some safety to the victim (and the child(ren)) and will control the conduct and behaviour of the abuser as the court will place restriction(s) on the abuser.

Top tips - some do's and don'ts

- Do ensure you understand the terms of the Non-molestation Order, that it adequately safeguards you (and any child(ren)) and provides the necessary protection you seek.

- Do keep a copy of the Non-molestation Order handy in case you should need to refer to it when you are out and about or in case it is breached.

- Do make sure you provide as much detail of the abuse in your application to the court.

- Do make sure your evidence of abuse is in a clear and concise format in your application to the court. Don't be afraid to ask for assistance. Use examples, such as text messages.

- Do use appropriate options to maintain an avenue of communication where there are contact arrangements for children, such as a contact diary.

- Do keep a diary or a notebook with emergency contact details for the Police, Social Services, support agencies and other important contacts. It can also be used to keep a written record.

- Do remember you are worth so much more than having to put up with an abusive relationship and you can move on from it.

- Don't stay quiet.

- Don't continue with being a victim of abuse for yourself and any child(ren)) because you are afraid of what to expect if you move on.

- Don't blame yourself (or the child(ren)). Remember it is not your fault. The abuser is the one at fault.

- Don't dismiss the severity of the abuse or its long-term affect on you (and any child(ren)).

- Don't make an application to gain an advantage on the other party, for example, in contact arrangements or financial & property matters. It should be made to seek protective measures.

- Importantly, don't be afraid to seek help. There are various support agencies and lawyers who specialise in this area of work.

- Finally, do remain positive for you and any child(ren). There is life outside of an abusive relationship.

It is the view of the author that the above article provides some insight into this particular area of the law. It is simply an overview and the author would recommend the reader to seek advice and assistance from a specialist family lawyer who would be better placed to provide advises specific to your own circumstances. However, it is hoped that it provides some valuable information.

Parenting from afar

The natural journey of parenting starts with the close proximity of a baby to their parent, followed by a gradual move towards physical independence in adolescence, where teenagers no longer need their parents to walk them to school or to help them tie their shoelaces. The emotional journey is similar in that it moves from dependence to growing independence, but there is no end point to it. We all need our parents in one guise or another for our whole lives. When this physical and emotional journey is interrupted by parental separation, it is important to remember that being physically far from one another doesn't inevitably mean being emotionally detached. Using social media to stay in touch with children is one way of harnessing the more positive aspects of the complex digital world. The love that a child brings into the world is rarely extinguished through lack of contact, but as a parent, you may well need to be the one who reignites this flame.

My ex is threatening to take our children abroad. What should I do?

About the author

Emine Mehmet, Director at Duncan Lewis Solicitors

Emine is a director of family and childcare at Duncan Lewis and supervises a large team comprising of solicitors, trainees and paralegals. She qualified as a solicitor in 2003 and became a child panel member in 2011. Emine won the coveted Jordan's pro bono lawyer of the year award in 2016.

This area of law is complex so if you are concerned that your child is going to be abducted then you should consult a solicitor immediately.

What is child abduction?

Child abduction is essentially taking a child under 16 away without the consent of the person who usually cares for them (the resident parent) and has parental responsibility (PR) for them.

International child abduction occurs when a person (such as parents, guardians, or anyone with PR for a child) takes a child, or keeps a child, out of the country the child normally lives in without either:

- permission from everyone else who has PR for the child; or

- an order of the court.

This means that if both parents have PR and there are no court orders in place, neither of the parents can take the child out of the UK without the written permission of the other parent.

However, if a Child Arrangements Order has been made by the court stating that the child will live with one of the parents, that parent can take a child abroad for 28 days without getting permission from the other parent, unless a court order says they can't or the holiday coincides with time the child would normally have spent with the other parent.

International child abduction is a criminal offence and anyone found guilty of this offence can be sent to prison or fined or both.

What if I think my former partner is going to take the children away from me?

There are a number of reasons why you may have concerns that your children will be removed from the jurisdiction and practically, if you have these concerns, you should not allow your former partner to remove your children from your care at all. Neither must you provide your former partner with the children's passports until you have had legal advice or have made an application to the court.

If you have these concerns, you can apply to the family court for a Prohibited Steps Order (PSO). A PSO can stop someone removing children from your care or from the jurisdiction without your permission.

Without notice applications

You can make this application without telling your former partner (called a 'without notice' application) if you fear that they may remove the children if they learn of your application before it is determined. Your former partner will then be informed of the application only after the first hearing, and there will be a

> Separation and divorce is scary for children. One of the best things you can do to help is to reassure them that no matter what happens, they still have two parents who love them.
>
> *Vikki Martin, Wolferstans Solicitors*

further hearing which you both attend for the court to decide whether the PSO which was ordered at the first hearing should continue.

If you are making the application on a without notice basis, you will need to explain your reasons for doing so. In an emergency situation, the court can make other directions when a PSO is made such as a port alert to prevent the children from leaving the country. This means that the police will flag the child's name at all UK airports and points of departure.

The court can also issue an order requiring a UK passport to be surrendered which can prevent the Passport Service from issuing a passport or travel document. However, these actions usually require proof that the children are likely to be removed from the UK within the next 24 or 48 hours.

Remember that the court's paramount consideration will be the child's welfare and they will usually allow a child to leave the UK with one of the parents unless there is evidence to suggest the child might not be returned.

HOW TO BUILD A CHILD RELATIONSHIP AFTER YEARS APART

Just having the title "mother" or "father" makes you completely irreplaceable to your child. Your relationship is unique, whether they see you once a day or once a decade.

If you are returning to your child after years apart, it feels as if you're starting from scratch, or even below scratch. Children may react to your reintroduction with anger and fury. They want to let you know how hurt they have felt, but they may also be trying to protect themselves, believing that by pushing you away they are ensuring you can't hurt them again. You will need to resist this with immense patience and compassion.

Don't be afraid to ask their other parent, grandparents or teachers what your child enjoys now. This isn't so that you can impress your child with your encyclopaedic knowledge of their life. It's so that you can enter their world and build up a relationship around their life as it is, rather than around your memories of what it used to be.

Spend time with them and pay attention to them. Remember when their school play is on or what football team they're playing on Saturday (even if you have to write this down once apart from them so as not to forget).

Expect awkward questions and try to answer these as calmly as possible. If you have no answer to their question let them know this. An "I don't know, but I do know how much I missed you" is better than a rambling answer that leaves your child feeling even more confused.

Your relationship with your child won't blossom overnight. It grows and evolves over many years. If you have missed some of these years it doesn't mean you can't have a warm, loving relationship now. You just need to be committed, realistic and content with small steps so that it has space to flourish.

National Association of Child Contact Centres (NACCC)

About the author

Elizabeth Coe, CEO at the NACCC

Having gained her Certificate of Qualification in Social Work, Elizabeth became a Probation Officer before becoming a Family Court Welfare Officer. She has also worked as a Senior Probation Officer, Senior Court Welfare Officer, Guardian ad Litem and has served on the Derbyshire Adoption and Fostering Panel.

More than a million children have no contact whatsoever with one or other parent after separation. Research shows that the negative impacts of separation on children can be reduced, but unfortunately some children experience behavioural problems including antisocial behaviour, distress, unhappiness and both physical and emotional problems. Children may have witnessed domestic abuse, arguments or feel that it is their fault. They can also show a range of behaviours related to the loss they are experiencing.

The NACCC is the only charity in the UK dedicated to solving this problem, by providing safe spaces where children can meet the parents they don't live with. We oversee around 400 contact centres across the UK, run by a network of nearly 4,000 volunteers. NACCC's accreditation of supported and supervised centres is recognised as a standard quality mark for ensuring that child contact centres are run safely for children and their families.

How can child contact centres help?

There are a range of contact services which can be used depending on your situation and the level of risk.

Supervised contact

Is there a potential risk of harm? Supervised contact ensures the physical safety and emotional well-being of children in a one-to-one observed setting.

Supported contact

Supported contact keeps children in touch with parents if trust has broken down or communication is difficult. Parents or family members do not have to meet and several families use facilities at the same time.

Handover service

This is when the centre is used for a short period as a drop off / pick up point. Again, family members do not have to meet.

How are visits arranged?

You will have to apply to go to a contact centre. This application is called a 'referral'. Many centres accept referrals from parents, grandparents and family members direct, but if you prefer your solicitor, mediator, social worker or Cafcass officer can make the referral for you. You and your child/grandchild will be invited to come and see the centre before your first arranged visit. This will help you get to know the centre and the staff, making your first visit easier. Please contact your local centre for more information.

Where is my nearest centre?

Go to 'Find a Centre' on our website, select the type of service and enter your town or postcode. The search will find the local centres in your area. You can then contact the centre direct to set up the referral.

Can you help spread the word about child contact centres?

Please go to our website to find out about our #lostparents campaign.

My ex has moved my two children to France with no consultation. What should I do?

About the author

Gemma Kelsey, Senior Associate at Brethertons

Gemma has a particular specialism in International Children Law. She also regularly instructs in cases involving domestic violence, Child Arrangements Orders, Specific Issues Orders, Prohibited Steps Orders and applications for PR. She is a Resolution Accredited Specialist in Child Abduction Law and Children Law.

As explained in Question 91, a parent who wishes to take their children on holiday or move abroad permanently requires the clear consent of everyone else who also shares parental responsibility for the children. If the consent is not given, then it is necessary to apply to the court to obtain permission. If a parent takes a child abroad without either the other parent's consent or without permission of the court, then it is classed as a wrongful removal and this is unlawful.

If a parent has a Child Arrangements Order ('lives with') then they are permitted to take the child outside England and Wales without the other parent's consent but only for a maximum of 28 days.

If a wrongful removal takes place to a country which is a signatory to the 1980 Hague Convention, then an application can be made for the children's' summary (i.e. immediate) return back to this country. England and Wales is a signatory to the 1980 Hague Convention as is France.

First steps

The first step would be to contact the International Child Abduction and Contact Unit (ICACU) and prepare an application form seeking the return of the children. When completed this is then transmitted to the French Central Authority who will then start the process of issuing Hague Convention proceedings before the French court.

These proceedings should be completed within 6 weeks (although they can take longer) where the French court will have to decide whether there was a wrongful removal and if so whether any of the limited defences under the 1980 Hague Convention may apply. The 1980 Hague Convention proceedings are not a welfare investigation and if a summary return of the children to England is ordered it will then be a matter for the English courts to look into welfare matters such as residence and contact. It is always a possibility that the

was it a blessing or a curse?
That silence.
Did it mask the cracks or make them worse?
That silence.
Abigail (16)

returning parent may, when back, cross apply to relocate with the children lawfully.

In the event of a wrongful removal, it may also be possible to apply to the High Court in England under the Inherent Jurisdiction seeking orders for the return of the children and also orders declaring that they are habitually resident in England and Wales. This approach should however be carefully considered in situations where there is a remedy under the 1980 Hague Convention.

What if the other parent does not have PR?

If you are a parent who does not share the parental responsibility of the children, there is little that can be done after the children have gone. This is because lawfully the parent has not done anything wrong by removing the children if there is no one else who shares parental responsibility for them. If this is the case then as soon as the children's habitual residence transfers to France, any proceedings would need to take place before a French court and it would be French law that applies.

If a parent does not share parental responsibility but has concerns about a child being removed to another country, as with a parent who does share parental responsibility, urgent applications to the court for a Prohibited Steps Order or in some circumstances Location/ Passport Orders, can be made to prevent this happening.

In either circumstance, preventative measures are always better than the aftermath of a wrongful removal.

If there is a proposed move abroad, mediation is always encouraged to see if an agreement can be reached rather than the court determining issues.

Finally, a wrongful removal is also a criminal offence which can carry a custodial sentence if convicted.

Any parent wishing to relocate with children to another country should take specialist advice to ensure that they do not fall foul of the law. Equally any parent concerned about children being taken abroad or finding themselves in a position where a relocation has been proposed but does not agree, should also take specialist advice at the earliest opportunity.

Any parent concerned about an abduction should contact a specialist solicitor in this area, ICACU or Reunite.

Never give up contact and regular visits, no matter how many miles away the children have been moved. They won't ever forget. I did it for 11 years.

Jon, Dad

Notes

Teenagers, young adults and parental separation

About the author

Angela Lake-Carroll

Angela has over 30 years' experience of working with separated families and she has written a range of short guides for separating families. Angela works across the broad range of family law and family dispute resolution as a practitioner and adviser. She has also worked with and contributed to government policy for families, children and young people.

Many parents worry about how older children will deal with the separation of their parents. Adolescents are dealing with a great many things - they are changing physically and emotionally, they are trying to become adults and make their first steps towards independence and they may be starting to have relationships of their own. All these things can affect how they deal with their parents separating. Below are some hints and tips for parents which you may find useful.

Be respectful

Older children and young adults have the right to respect for their feelings. They are often struggling with growing up and may find your separation particularly difficult at a time when they need your attention and support. Try to put yourself in their shoes and not expect that they will be able to put themselves in yours

Think back

You were an adolescent once. Try to think about what that felt like, how you behaved and what would have helped you most - and what you found difficult as far as your relationship with your parents was concerned

Difficult behaviour is not always associated with your separation

Your child may be exhibiting normal adolescent behaviour rather than behaving badly because you are separating. Try not to assume that everything is connected with your separation. Adolescents need to test boundaries, have mood swings, be uncommunicative and spend time alone or with friends

Keep things balanced

It is tempting when you separate to try to make things up to children by being overly generous, allowing changes to well-established routines or providing two very different

models for discipline once separated. Try, wherever possible, to keep a balance. You may not agree on discipline, but you need to ensure that you are delivering a united front to your children, especially to teenagers who need continuing security at a time when they may feel that their life is changing and may be feeling insecure and different. Young adults can be particularly adept at playing their parents off against each other - although this may score some early benefits for them, invariably, they can end up frightened by the sense of power they have and ultimately blamed as the instigator of conflict between their parents. Best not to go there in the first place!

Don't criticise their other parent

Often it can be easy to fall into assuming that an older child or near adult is old enough to understand the differences between you and their other parent and can be an ally or confidante for you. This is very damaging for all children. You are the people whom they love best in the world - they don't want to take sides and may be distressed or angered by your behaviour in trying to get them on side or leaning on them too heavily emotionally

Try not to nag

When you are dealing with a difficult and emotional time yourself, a difficult teenager can feel like the last straw. Try to hold on to the fact that teenagers need to be difficult and to challenge as they struggle to become adults. They may also need extra sleep, time to be alone and to think and they may be uncommunicative. Make sure that they know you are available to them if they want to talk, that you understand how difficult things feel for them and that as their parents, you love them. Acknowledge to them that this is a difficult time for everyone but that you and their other parent will continue to work together to make things as best you can for them and their siblings. If things boil over, make sure you say sorry too - and be honest with them about how, when things are tough for everyone, it is easier to get into arguments.

Risk taking behaviour

Adolescence is a time for experimentation. Be watchful for risk-taking behaviour. Some young people take risks as a means of dealing with unhappiness or insecurity. Others risk take as part of their growing up process. If you think your child is involving themselves in risk taking behaviour. Don't panic. Remember that many young people are going to experiment or take risks as part of a growing up process and don't feel that your child is the only one. If possible, talk to your child, without accusing them, about

your worries and concerns for and about them. Risk taking behaviour includes experimenting with alcohol, smoking, involvement with soft drugs and inappropriate sexual relationships. More serious risk-taking behaviour, which may indicate a need for professional support includes self-harming, eating disorders and regular or heavy drug use. Try to get some sense of whether the child or young person has simply experimented or whether the behaviour is more frequent than a one-off experiment. If you're worried, get professional advice and support (see sources of help and support at the end of this book). Try not to blame yourself - you need to stay confident in your role as their parent in order to help them through a difficult and confusing time.

Someone to talk to

Try to make sure that you keep communications open with your child - keep them informed about what is happening as far as you can and appropriate to their age and understanding. Offer them opportunities to talk to you about how they are feeling by giving them your time. If they are finding it difficult to talk to you, think about to whom, in the family or amongst your friends, may be someone they could talk about their feelings. Make sure that person is someone who can take a neutral

view of the situation and suggest that your child might spend some time with them, or have that person make contact with the child to take them out. Encourage your child to find other ways of dealing with their inability to communicate their feelings - keeping a private journal or computer diary perhaps. If your adolescent child is having difficulty communicating their anger or sadness, think about activities that might help them to discharge some of those feelings - sporting activities, karate, judo, circuit training etc. are good ways of letting off steam

New families

If you are in a new relationship and/or may be forming a new family be careful to talk to your child about how you hope that will work for everyone and seek their views. Do not assume that children from different families will get on and try to put yourself in the children's shoes as to how it might feel to be joined together because of a new parental relationship. For teenagers, privacy is very important - don't assume or expect that they will share their room or belongings easily and try wherever possible to avoid expecting that. Older children can also be very difficult with new partners - this is a normal reaction and you and your new partner will need to work closely

The biggest thing I learned from the whole ordeal was to give my children the missing love that I never had. Oliver (20)

together to agree how you will deal with day-to-day living issues and with discipline. Be aware that your former partner may also find your new relationship very difficult, at least initially, and may resent someone else having a 'parenting' role.

Accepting independence

Young people form social communities of their own. They will want to be with their friends, continue their activities, go to parties or see their boy or girlfriend. This can be difficult when you are sharing time with them. Arrangements that might have worked when they were younger are likely to be less do-able as children get older. Don't insist that they must spend time with you as per an existing arrangement. They will resent you for it and are not likely to be communicative or happy if they have been forced to be with you. As children mature, time spent with either of you should be their choice - not your right. Give them their freedom and they are much more likely to choose to spend time with you, but remember as they grow up they will naturally grow away as they become adults. Be proud that you have raised an independent young adult rather than resentful that you're not getting your quota of time with them.

> "I'd have explained things more clearly and honestly to the children throughout. I didn't always do that and I've caused confusion down the line."
>
> *Kelly, Mum*

Notes

Storybook Dads; Storybook Mums

About Storybook Dads

Imprisoned parents record a story for their children. The recording is sent to the Storybook Dads editing suite in HMP Channings Wood where specially trained prisoners use digital software to remove mistakes and background noises, then add sound effects and music. The stories are burned onto lovely bright child-friendly discs and sent to the family.

It's 8pm, and 7 year old Lola is snuggling down for a bedtime story. "Ok, this one's called The Gruffalo" says her Dad.

It's a typical bedtime scene in homes across the country, but Lola's situation is far from typical. Her dad, Leon, is in Dartmoor prison over a hundred miles away and Lola is listening to his voice on a CD. Leon is taking part in the Storybook Dads scheme which enables imprisoned parents to keep in touch with their children by reading bedtime stories.

"The first time Lola heard the CD, she kept saying 'I love Daddy'" says Leon *"There's not much I can do for her from in here, but she reads along with the CD so at least I'm helping with her with her reading. It's been a hard time for all of us but the stories bring us closer".*

Storybook Dads is a small, award-winning charity operating in over 90 UK prisons (including women's prisons as Storybook Mums). Although the name may indicate otherwise, the scheme is also open to other family members such as grandparents, step-parents and older siblings.

The scheme is simple. Imprisoned parents record a story for their children. The recording is sent to the Storybook Dads editing suite in HMP Channings Wood where specially trained prisoners use digital software to remove mistakes and background noises. Then they add sound effects and music to really bring the story to life. The stories are burned onto lovely bright child-friendly discs

and sent to the family.

The editing process means that non-readers can take part. They simply repeat the story a line at a time after a mentor. The mentor's voice is cut out leaving the parent sounding fluent and expressive.

As well the bedtime story CDs, some prisons allow a DVD option where participants can be filmed reading the story. Music, sound effects, and pictures and animation from the book are added giving a colourful and professional finished DVD.

There is also a 'Me and My Dad' (or Mum) scheme enabling participants to create educational gifts such as memory books, challenge charts and activity sheets - improving literacy and creativity, and encouraging interaction between parent and child.

Storybook Dads helps over 15,000 beneficiaries every year

Over 160,000 children every year are affected by the imprisonment of a parent; even more than are affected by divorce. It can have a devastating effect. Many suffer feelings of abandonment and shame, leading to anti-social behaviour, poor educational performance and increased risk of inter-generational offending. They are three times more prone to mental health problems than their peers.

Contact from behind bars is not easy. Many prisoners, particularly women, are a long way away from their families. Visits and phone calls can be expensive and awkward. In addition, the dehumanising effect of prison means that prisoners may withdraw from their families. The separation can make it difficult to develop the parenting skills necessary for reunification or to form or maintain strong attachments.

In fact, over half of prisoners lose contact with their families. Those that do maintain contact are up to 6 times less likely to re-offend upon release.

Engaging with the project helps parents to realise that reading to a child is the most important thing they can do to help with their child's education. Thus it helps them to develop a positive image of themselves as parents. It also enables them to improve their own literacy and creativity skills.

As well as the educational benefits, the gifts help the children to feel loved and empowers them to self-comfort as they are able to listen to their loved one's voice whenever they need to.

A recent letter from the partner of a prisoner said:

"When Jack's daddy first went to jail, Jack found the separation really hard and he had a few behaviour problems. Since getting the CD and hearing his dad's voice, his behaviour has improved 100%".

Since 2002, over 600 prisoners have been trained in audio or video editing enabling them to create the finished discs for other imprisoned parents. Many start with no real work experience and little confidence in their ability. At **Storybook Dads** they are part of a dynamic, supportive team. They gain valuable work experience, as well as creative and IT skills which are notoriously difficult to teach in conventional prison classrooms.

"Working for Storybook Dads taught me that you can do anything if you put your mind to it. It gives you a sense of normality and responsibility which helps you plan for a life outside prison," says Woody, a prisoner/editor.

When funding allows, the charity provides part-time volunteering or employment to a few editors when they are released. They have use of a laptop to edit stories from home. This enables them the flexibility to explore other avenues of work, education or training.

Storybook Dads is unique. No other organisation in the UK is providing the range of services for prisoners and their children.

For thousands of families dealing with separation, the project provides a lifeline.

Meaning children who couldn't sleep at night are comforted.

And children who felt abandoned, feel loved.

And parents who felt worthless... feel pride.

If you would like to find out more visit www.storybookdads.org.uk or find them on Facebook or Twitter.

Notes

Do I have to do all the driving?

About the author

Chris Fairhurst, McAlister Family Law

Chris has over 20 years' experience specialising in financial and children arrangements following separation, divorce, and relationship breakdown for clients nationwide and living overseas, including complex child abduction as well as national and international relocation cases.

W hen I'm asked this question, I'm reminded of a case I dealt with some years ago where the couple were trying to divide up the equity in the matrimonial home and other assets of the marriage. It wasn't a huge case and the assets were modest but both appeared sensible individuals and had their own jobs which meant there was going to be a clean break on making of a final order. Incidentally, there were no children so it was more straightforward than it could have been, or so I thought.

Although the couple didn't see completely eye to eye, negotiations took place between

solicitors and after a bit of toing in froing a comprehensive agreement was reached in respect to sharing the proceeds of sale and other capital assets and a draft consent order drawn up for submission to court. And then, without any prior notice in any of the prior exchanges, the curveball came: a demand from the other party's solicitor that the whole deal was off unless she could keep the picture over the fireplace. It's value was in the hundreds of pounds when the other assets were in the tens if not hundreds of thousands.

And the deal very nearly collapsed as a result: my client on principle demanding to keep it, as it was one of a pair and therefore there were two to share, the former partner happy to walk away despite the costs incurred to date getting an agreement. It was a case of who would blink first. My advice to my client was to leave it and buy another with the money he would save on my fees for arguing about it. Reluctantly, but eventually, the advice was accepted but not without criticism of me from my client that I hadn't secured the picture and the other lawyer had. I had offered the opportunity of applying to court and letting a judge decide but my client made the sensible decision that the costs of doing so were disproportionate to the value of the picture and there was the uncertainty in any event of what a judge, a stranger to both parties, would decide.

> Focus on the choices you have and the things you can do, because focusing on the other person's reasoning and actions is wasting energy on things you can't know and can't control.
>
> *Matthew Richardson, Coram Chambers*

So, what's this got to do with travel and seeing my children, I hear you ask? Well, the issue of who collects and returns the children after time with a parent is the 'picture over the fireplace' equivalent in child arrangements cases. It is sadly an issue that rears its head more often than it should between parents who don't love each other anymore but clearly love their children and in their own way want the same for their children, that they be happy, even if they have different views about how that might be achieved.

My advice is to follow the course of least resistance.

On many occasions, sometimes at the court door, protracted discussions and agreements can be brought crashing down by an insistence that one parent or another 'do all the travelling if s/he wants to see them' or 'I don't see why I should do it all, s/he has a car as well'. Does it sound familiar?

Faced with that predicament, everything else agreed, what's a court to do? Unfortunately, it's a question of a contested hearing with evidence and submissions from both sides about why the court should favour one parent or another. And yes, if pushed, the court could decide that the travel is shared, or not! You pay your money, you take your chance.

There is no hard and fast rule about any arrangements for children. The family court strives to achieve an order which it believes is in the best interests of any children of the family by applying the welfare checklist which appears in the Children Act 1989 (see Question 55).

However, the law is discretionary and the reality is that no two families and therefore no two cases are alike. Each will turn on its own facts and when dealing with travel arrangements, there is no presumption in favour of one parent or another, nor is the court obliged to share the travel because that is the fair thing to do.

All things being equal of course, 2 parents earning the same, with the same working hours and similar access to transport, or family members to assist, you would hope that arrangements to share the travelling could be agreed without the need of a third party deciding which might not actually satisfy anyone, particularly the children. And it is widely recognised that a child

If both parents drive or have access to a car, could you negotiate one picks up and the other drops off? Or alternate trips? If the ex won't negotiate then it's better that the children see you trying to be reasonable, and just doing the driving. Children almost invariably understand what's happening, and when they are able will voice their views. They will also learn from your actions to be reasonable in the face of unreasonable behaviour. Don't criticise the other parent to them, just try to rise above it all.

Mike Flinn

will benefit emotionally from seeing both parents co-operate and 'be happy', being able to enjoy being taken by one parent to the other and vice versa.

However, real life isn't like that. Parents increasingly work different shift patterns; one parent may earn a lot more or have a car when the other might not.

The starting point must be, however difficult, to try and put yourself in the other parent's shoes. Can arrangements be made that make travel arrangements easier for one or both? Is there someone in the family or close friends that you

both trust that can help you out?

But consider this - is sharing the travel necessary to ensure that the children continue to have a relationship with you, and by the other parent not doing so would that equate to them failing to facilitate the relationship, or is it just a point of principle?

If the former, then if matters cannot be agreed it is something you may want to consider getting legal advice about if mediation, whether formally or with trusted others, cannot assist and as a last resort make an application for a Family Court to decide based upon the circumstances as they apply to you and your family.

If the latter, then you really need to consider the financial and emotional cost of making an issue out of it where all else is agreed. I'm sure it's happened, although I've never dealt with an application, where the family court is asked to simply deal with the sharing of travel and you'll likely have to attend at least 2, if not 3, hearings before a court would even decide one way or another. An expensive exercise if you're paying good money for a lawyer to represent you.

My advice, a bit like to the client with the picture, is to follow the course of least resistance. Do it if you can - if you can make a concession to help the situation then you may find it helps discussions about something else that can't be agreed now or further down the line. If a parent simply says, 'I'm not doing it' you can show you've done everything possible if the need arises.

There were no arguments in front of us, no tears, no slamming doors. I know they did this to protect us. The downside of that silence though was that it was a complete shock to us. Abigail (16)

ONLY
Mums & Dads
parents meet professionals

Organisations

Org

ORGANISATIONS

Reunite International Child Abduction Centre

About reunite

reunite is the leading UK charity specialising in parental child abduction and the movement of children across international borders.

For the last 30 years **reunite** has supported parents and family members dealing with the movement of children internationally, including international parental child abduction. We started life in 1987 as a group of parents who were affected by parental child abduction supporting each other and have since grown into a registered charity that is internationally recognised as a leader in advice, assistance, mediation and research in relation to international parental child abduction and the international movement of children.

In 2017 our advice line handled nearly 19,000 calls and registered 532 new parental child abduction cases involving 730 children, as well as 330 prevention cases involving 468 children.

We appreciate that, as a parent trying to understand the complex legal systems surrounding parental child abduction, it is very easy to feel overwhelmed and isolated while dealing with a situation most people wouldn't even think could happen. However, each year we take thousands of calls from parents going through a similar situation to you; you do not need to go through this alone.

At **reunite** we have two main services for parents: our advice line and our mediation service.

reunite operates the UK's only specialised advice line providing information and support on parental child abduction and the international movement of children. The advice line is available to offer advice on:

- international parental child abduction;
- the prevention of a potential abduction;
- international contact issues; and
- applications for relocation and permission to remove a child from the jurisdiction.

Every call to the advice line is treated confidentiality, and we do not pass judgement on the actions or circumstances of anyone who calls us. We appreciate that every case is different and unique, and so we tailor our advice to your individual circumstances. We offer ongoing, impartial

information and advice to parents, guardians, and family members, and can support you in many situations including:

- your child has been abducted by the other parent;
- you are defending against an accusation of child abduction;
- you fear your child could be abducted by the other parent;
- you live in a different country to your child and you want to set up a contact arrangement;
- you would like to relocate to another country with your child; or
- your child's other parent would like to relocate overseas and you disagree.

We are not lawyers, so we cannot represent you in court, but we can certainly talk you through what options are available to you and point you in the direction of specialist lawyers if needed.

Our advice line is mainly an English language service. However, we do have staff members who can speak Urdu, Gujarati, Hindi, Polish and Spanish.

The advice line is open from Monday to Friday, between 9.30am and 5.00pm UK time. If you have an emergency situation outside of these times, such as an abduction in progress, you can call the advice line and you will be directed to our 24-hour emergency service.

One of our aims is to make information around parental child abduction and the prevention of abduction as easy to access and understand as possible. As a result we have a number of online resources on our website (www.reunite.org) that can be accessed and downloaded for free. One such resource is our series of Prevention Guides, which provide clear and concise information as well as practical steps you can take if you fear your child is at risk of being abducted.

Alongside our advice line we also offer our specialist mediation service. Mediation is a voluntary process that provides parents with the opportunity to speak with specialist mediators in an informal, confidential atmosphere. Parents are helped to identify the issues they wish to resolve and then reach workable solutions that are acceptable to them both and are focused on the best interests of their child. The mediation service can be used in cases similar to those covered by the advice line, namely family cases with an international element.

The mediation process can run alongside court proceedings, so you don't need to choose one over the other. We can also tailor the mediation to suit your situation; such as using interpreters where needed or using online video platforms such as Skype or Zoom if a parent is outside of the UK.

We at **reunite** are here to support you through what can be an incredibly difficult and stressful time, but one which can come to a positive end for yourself, your family, and most importantly your children.

If you'd like to speak with our advice line please call +44 (0)116 255 6234, and if you'd like more information about mediation please call +44 (0)116 255 5345.

SKYPE SESSIONS ARE BEING OVERSEEN BY MY EX

You can't control anyone but yourself. It would be reasonable to ask your ex prior to the session, politely, if they wouldn't mind leaving the children alone whilst they talk to you. Additionally, open up a discussion so ground rules are agreed between you, if you can (e.g. discuss the children's lives and not how they're getting on with your ex). If not then it's better to have some Skype than none, so if none of the above works then just live with it. Remember; you're a role model, so display the behaviour you'd like them to learn.

Mike Flinn

Notes

I am in contact with my child again for the first time in two years. How do I learn to love him again?

About the author

Mike Flinn Dip (Couns), MBACP

Mike has, over the last 20 years, worked mainly with separating families, in schools with both students and staff, and with individual adults and couples. He worked for Couple Counselling Scotland in Dundee and Perth, before moving to Shrewsbury to work with Relate. For the past two years he has worked in private practice.

OK .... The first thing to remember is that you are the adult so it's up to you to role model the behaviours you expect your son to display. If you listen then, generally, so will he. If you stay calm then, generally, so will he etc. It's up to you how this progresses.

Second is that your son, at 8, will have a degree of emotional understanding, which means he will be worried about whether he is good enough for you, whether you will leave him again, and if he can trust you. All of this is

irrespective of the circumstances that led to the 2 year gap. Your comment suggests you might be thinking on similar lines to him, so at least you have an understanding of each other.

You can expect to be seriously tested. He will expect you to leave him so he'll push you very hard. In light of this it's worth you modelling the behaviour you expect him to exhibit.

So listen, check that you've understood by paraphrasing and then reply saying what you think. Then give him the same opportunity. If you get upset or angry, then say so, by using an 'I' statement ... 'I'm getting upset, I'm just taking a 10 minute time out to calm myself down, then I'll be back to listen to you'. Use mindfulness breathing to slow your heart rate down... (in for 5, feel the breath going in through your nose and filling your lungs, then out for 5 through your mouth... I use a 3 syllable word between each number .. ELEPHANT...). This keeps your adrenaline and cortisol levels lower, and if you think of something that makes you happy, you'll increase your endorphin levels, and feel calmer.

Do not say 'You're making me ..... ' because all you'll get is an argument.

It's worth you thinking about why you left your son, and how that

Love your children. Time is fleeting so don't lose these precious moments to feelings of bitterness and resentment.

Lisa, Mum

equates to the way you were parented by your parents. There's a possibility that you were triggered by issues from your own past, and that is worth you exploring with a psychodynamically trained counsellor.

If you are able to communicate with your ex, then talk to them about your son's likes and dislikes, interests and friends. Ask how he's getting on at school, with peers, and what he does in his leisure time. Communicate with school and find out how he's doing from their perspective.

Thirdly, think about how he might feel, what he might like. Try to find things to do together, build up the time you have together, starting with an hour or two, then gradually build it up in one or two hour blocks.

Check how he's feeling and ask him what he'd like to do. If he can't think of anything then go with your instincts.

PARENTING FROM AFAR

You might want to consider where your worry about whether you love him has come from. It might be fear of him rejecting you, which he's perfectly entitled to do, and which will take time and persistence from you to overcome. He will need consistent approaches from you, whether you're rejected or not, to reassure him that you're going to do what you say.

Keep lines of communication open. Listen and show him you understand, whether you agree or not. Children, however smart, can have some very offbeat ideas! Do not tell him he's wrong, just offer him options according to your views.

It's worth thinking about how you show someone you care. Your son knew you for 6 years, so will know this, so do what you used to do. Be ready for rejection and

being ignored. Persist, remembering that actions speak much louder than words. So a touch, a tone of voice, a hug, a card, a message, phone call, all mean a lot to your child, however old. Mine are in their mid 30's and it's still the same!

HOW CAN I REBUILD A CHILD RELATIONSHIP AFTER YEARS APART?

Apologise!

Admit your mistakes.

Tell them you love them, and miss them.

Don't blame anyone else, unless you have proof you tried and were blocked, in which case show what you did but don't blame.

Get ready to deal with their anger. They'll defend the custodial parent. You went once, so you are at risk of going again in their eyes, whatever the circumstances.

Very gently begin to fill them in with your life as it is now. Respond to their questions honestly and age appropriately.

Mike Flinn

Notes

What impact does social media have on personal relationships?

About the author

Mike Flinn Dip (Couns), MBACP

Mike has, over the last 20 years, worked mainly with separating families, in schools with both students and staff, and with individual adults and couples. He worked for Couple Counselling Scotland in Dundee and Perth, before moving to Shrewsbury to work with Relate. For the past two years he has worked in private practice.

Remember the good old days when you had to put pen to paper and stick a stamp on it to share the written word with another? If like me you do, then you'll understand that 'snail mail' wasn't exactly the best form of communication for a quick exchange of pleasantries, or quite so effective as causing instantaneous disagreements that seems to be the case with more modern forms of electronic and other social media.

As the world exploded into the digital age, society had to get to grips with email and texting in short succession. Roll on a generation and we were blessed, or cursed depending on your view, with Friendsreunited, closely followed by Facebook and its ilk, then more recently other social media sharing platforms and more intimate dating apps.

Depending on your generation, they're all different ways of meeting and getting in touch with long but perhaps not forgotten former, or indeed new, acquaintances and a major cause of contributing to relationship breakdown.

What might have previously required attendance at an old school reunion, or a night out on the town, the re-sparking of an old or new flame is now much closer to hand, literally, with mobile phones now accounting for more than half and an increasing share of web browsing and therefore allowing much easier and private accessibility, to getting in touch with others.

The extent to which Facebook and other electronic media are cited in relationship breakdowns

Before you send that angry email or text in reply, stop. Put it in drafts, think about it, make a cup of tea and reflect. Will it help? How would it make your children feel if they read it? If it would make them upset if said in front of them, don't send it.

Peter Burgess, Burgess Mee

and divorce petitions is nothing new. I managed to locate a Guardian article going back to 2004 in researching this article. It's a lot and increasing, but really is just a new way to perform old tricks.

What is perhaps a more modern phenomenon is the electronic footprint, and therefore 'proof' such information leaves, especially if the less technologically adept amongst us aren't quite sure about privacy settings and ability to control what the outside world sees. The number of people suggesting

Realise your bond with each parent could develop in ways you never expected. Bridie (22)

that a partner's private email notification has popped up on the family's iPad is definitely on the increase, meaning that private liaisons are brought literally to the heart of the family.

It therefore follows and is increasingly apparent that individuals are becoming aware, or at least receiving confirmation or a 'tip-off', of their partner's activities through their social media activity, if not directly, via concerned third-party 'friends'. And if settings aren't switched to private then the whole world knows, not just the ones from whom the illicit secret has been kept. 'Airing dirty linen in public' gets a very modern and much wider sharing than might have been the case in days gone by.

What perhaps is not quite as well understood is the extent to which other agencies are able to and do access such publicly available information to inform their own decision making. On more than one occasion I've received

'evidence' from a local authority's social services team within Public Law children proceedings that has consisted of printed pages from an individual's Facebook account, setting out their weekend misdemeanours or referring to their friendship with another as confirmation of a relationship.

It's hard to argue about when presented with such 'facts' and who can blame hard pressed social workers for doing so when they are easily able to from an office computer? Protesting invasion of privacy will fall on deaf ears when the Facebook settings are fixed to Public! Unfortunately, as is usually the case, what might be said in jest isn't necessarily what has happened. But the 'proof' is there and there'll be explaining to do.

There's a lot to be said for putting things in writing in the context of a relationship breakdown. It can help avoid any misunderstanding of the spoken word and ensure what has been

agreed between individuals is in black and white.

But the problem with instantaneous and electronic forms of communication is that people don't really think before they act and then the damage is done. There's no chance to pull back. Unlike spoken words they don't disappear into the air and because they don't, it's a sad fact that in a large proportion of cases, more often than not involving children of the family, evidence is available for production to the Family Court whether that be copies of emails, text message exchanges or printed Facebook pages and the like.

Your personal data says a lot about you and can be used in ways that you wouldn't expect or agree to if you were aware of it. You should protect it.

Children are accepting, unquestioning and observant. These are also characteristics of a good messenger. When you ask your child to pass on a message to their other parent, it is likely they will do it because children believe that adults know right from wrong. But, when you ask your child to pass on a message to your ex, you are misusing the power differential in your relationship with your child. You are counting on your child naively assuming that what you are asking of them is for the best. You are also exploiting their vulnerability to love and be loved by both parents. This all puts your child in a very difficult position. They don't believe you would ever ask them to do something wrong, and yet they feel uncomfortable telling Daddy or Mummy this bit of information. They are desperate for you both to get back together again, and will do anything they can to make that happen, but spying on one and feeding back to another can feel bad. This triangulation doesn't work in any relationship, and definitely doesn't work when children are being asked to carry messages.

Do not ask your child to do anything you wouldn't.

Do not ask your child to do anything you wouldn't ask an adult friend or family member to do.

Use any other method you can to communicate with your ex, be this a home-home book, texts, emails or chats.

Grandparents & the wider family

The ripple effects of a separation can be felt far more broadly than the immediate family. Grandparents, uncles, aunts, cousins who were all closely involved with the family pre-separation can find themselves removed and excluded, a casualty of the separation. This can feel very hurtful for the family members, and the removal of this layer of family contact will also be keenly felt by the children. This chapter explores ways that Grandparents and other family members can still keep their ties to children during and after the emotionally sensitive time of a separation. It is common for grandparents to take sides, to favour their own child, but keeping a balanced view and responding to the needs of the family, will help in maintaining positive relationships.

How can I retain contact with my grandchildren after their parents have separated?

About the author

Alun Jones, Director at Alun Jones Family Law

Alun has specialised exclusively in family law practice since 1996.He is also qualified and experienced in practicing collaborative law and family mediation.

It goes without saying that most grandparents make a positive impact on their grandchildren's lives. They can ultimately help to shape and help to define a grandchild by taking the time to teach, mentor and pass on some of life's most valuable lessons which only come from experience. The time spent together is therefore often treasured on both sides.

Sometimes, however, life can get in the way of this important relationship and the precious tie can sometimes be destroyed. Whether the separation occurs because of a divorce that's ripped the family apart or because of a disagreement that's simply got out of hand, there often needs to be a resolution sought.

This article centres on how contact can potentially be resumed between grandparents and their grandchildren.

Assuming that direct contact has failed at this stage you may now be looking at your other options in order to find a peaceful resolution.

Family mediation

Family mediation can help to resolve differences of opinion and to also potentially find a lasting resolution. Family mediation, however, is often only as effective as the mediator that is involved in the process, so do make your choice wisely. Take your time, speak to your mediator face-to-face and get a sense of whether they are the right person to mediate across both sides. Mediation can be effective at bringing both sides together and working through differences of opinion that are held. It's also worth keeping in mind that family mediation is only effective if both sides enter the process with a willingness to mediate. It is not uncommon at all for one side to not want to participate within the process and dig their heels in from the outset.

What happens if mediation doesn't work?

There are alternate dispute resolution methods available to you. For example, collaborative law can also be attempted. Family mediation and collaborative law are indeed different, but both work on the same principle that both parties want to reach an agreement outside of court. Sometimes, however, one or both sides of the disagreement have no intention of settling matters outside of court amicably. This therefore

without the support of my nan and my boyfriend of now 10 months, I wouldn't have been able to do what I have. Amy (15)

renders both methods of dispute resolution simply unviable. Therefore, the only option is to involve the family courts in certain circumstances.

It is at this stage where it may come as a surprise to some grandparents that they have no automatic right for the courts to intervene and help them regain contact, unless the circumstances are exceptional. Grandparents or their appointed family lawyers will have to apply for permission first in order for the courts to review the case. This does, therefore, add an extra layer of complexity before the case is even accepted or rejected. Grandparents or their appointed advisors must therefore apply to the courts stipulating what they are actually applying for in terms of the type of order that they would like to achieve.

The most common arrangements that are requested are set out below.

Child Arrangements Orders: 'lives with' and 'spends time'

A Child Arrangements Order sets out with whom the children shall live (sometimes referred to as a 'lives with' order) and with whom the children spend time (sometimes referred to as a 'spends time' order). It should be noted that the distinction between a 'lives with' and 'spends time' order can sometimes be so subtle it is almost indistinct.

Like the previous (and now unused) Residence and Contact Orders, no order will be made setting out with whom the children shall live or spend time unless it is necessary to make such an order.

In both instances the court will ask the grandparents to set out what it is that they seek and why they feel it is appropriate.

On some occasions the court may ask a member of CAFCASS to assist by preparing a report. The grandparents' views supported by the report will then be considered by the court.

Special Guardianship Orders

When grandparents want their grandchildren to live with them it is sometimes necessary to consider an alternative type of order that provides greater parenting powers. This is called a Special Guardianship Order. Cases of this nature can be procedurally complicated and emotionally challenging and it is vital that the proper procedure is followed.

To apply for either a Child Arrangements Order or a Special Guardianship Order professional advice should be obtained first, ensuring that you are clear on how to proceed. A family law practice will then be able to pursue the matter on behalf of the grandparents. Applications to court can be frightening - however, when there is no other option but to go to court, most grandparents will agree it's certainly a cause well worth fighting for.

Notes

I don't see my grandchildren. What rights do I have?

About the author

David Kendall, Partner at Wollen Michelmore Solicitors

David is a member of the Law Society's specialist Children Panel and Family Law Panel and undertakes a lot of work on behalf of children, either directly or through a court appointed Guardian. He also represents parents and other carers within care proceedings and private law disputes.

If your relationship with your grandchildren is ended unilaterally then thankfully you don't have to sit there and bear it. There are steps that you can take.

Usually it's not your fault and can happen for many reasons; perhaps where the parents have separated when 'sides' can be chosen, or for some lesser reason or even sometimes when parents feel like their toes are being stepped on.

Making lawful decisions about the children usually requires a concept known as Parental Responsibility (PR). Parents usually get this when their children are born but courts can agree or order this subsequently if it is right for the children. Grandparents can acquire it. Unless you have parental responsibility for the child, you have no automatic rights of access to them. Essentially, this means that as a grandparent, without parental responsibility, you cannot start proceedings for contact through a Child Arrangements Order without first obtaining the courts permission.

However, the law recognises that in certain situations it is in the child's best interests for contact to take place. Grandparents are often seen as not only great babysitters but are fundamental in helping children develop an understanding of their family roots. Grandparents can be and usually are a very valuable and important relationship for children.

To avoid problems with the issue of not having parental responsibility you would need to ask the court for 'leave'. This is permission to seek an order. The court will always consider what is in the best interests for the child first and foremost and each matter is decided on the merits of the case but it will be necessary to prove:

- that you have or at least did have a stable and positive relationship with your grandchild; and

- that a risk of any family fallout or tensions in future (that may be witnessed by the child) is outweighed by the positives a relationship with you will have.

Since you are already at a stage where access has been halted by those with parental responsibility, it is likely that they will contest or oppose any application you make seeking a contact order. Whilst this may prolong the proceedings the court will ensure that there are no unnecessary delays.

Before any application is made you will need to consider or undertake some mediation to try and resolve any issues between you and the parents. If mediation is successful it will mean a more streamlined and less costly way forward.

Sadly, legal aid will almost certainly not be available to fund these applications as they involve private law matters and therefore they will need to be funded privately. But in 2010, Parliament began reading a proposed Bill named the Grandparents (Access Rights) Bill which hoped to ease the overall process. Although Parliamentary time has currently expired and the position remains unchanged at the time being there are groups who are actively petitioning the Government to make changes in this area of law and many grandparents (and lawyers) hope there will be some positive changes in the very near future.

My grandchildren are telling us worrying things and it sounds like neglect. What should we do?

About the author

Kimberley Bailey, solicitor at Woolley & Co Solicitors

Kimberley deals with all areas of family law and provides a holistic and sympathetic approach to reaching solutions that focus on the client's needs, as well as the needs of any children involved. She has considerable experience in complex divorce and related financial issues as well as children cases including international relocation and grandparents rights.

Children say such weird and wonderful things sometimes, don't they? But sometimes they say something which causes real concern and it's then tricky to decide what to do about it, if you should do anything at all. Did they mean what they said? Did you misconstrue it? Should you ask them again for more details?

As a grandparent you've already been there, done that and got the T-shirt parenting your own child. Whether it's occasional visits or whether you now help regularly with childcare for your grandchildren you have a role to play in their life, shaping their understanding of the world around them. You also have a role in keeping them safe, but you don't want to upset their parents who may take your concern as personal criticism, or risk your concern impacting on your relationship.

Abuse isn't just physical harm. It can be verbal, causing emotional harm and impacting on the child's mental health and well-being. Neglect is the ongoing failure to meet a child's basic needs and is the most common form of child abuse. If the children are saying things which mean you think they may be subject to neglect and/or abuse you have to act.

As a rule of thumb, perhaps try to detach yourself emotionally from this being YOUR grandchild and start with health and safety - do you feel that they are being put in danger, even unintentionally? If so, it is time for you to act, however difficult that may be. So, what can you do?

- You can contact the NSPCC for confidential support and advice.

- You can call your local Children's or Social Services department and notify them. You can choose to do so anonymously or by confirming your identity and relationship to the child.

- You can call the police and report your concerns.

Your concerns will then be investigated by the appropriate public bodies and action can be taken, as necessary, to safeguard the children.

If you are concerned that this isn't a matter for the police or social services (or perhaps their enquiries determine that the problem isn't sufficiently serious for them to become involved) and want to do more but you aren't able to discuss it directly with the parents, you can make an application at court to define your involvement with your grandchildren.

There are various court applications which grandparents can make (see Questions 95 to 98 for more information).

It's worrying to take the steps to report neglect, particularly when you are no doubt worried about the impact on your family relationships and the possibility of a false flag, but remember that neglect shouldn't be ignored and your grandchild depends on you for love, support and safety.

We have ended up as parents to our grandchildren. Can we make it official?

About the author

Camilla Fusco, Partner at Anthony Gold Solicitors

Camilla is a Resolution accredited expert in private children law and international European family law. She deals with all aspects of family law and receives instructions nationally and internationally. Camilla is a recommended lawyer in the 2016 and 2017 Legal 500.

Grandparents often play an integral role in their grandchildren's lives providing valuable support. However, in some cases, for example where the parents are unable to look after a child, a grandparent might assume a parental role by caring for the child full time. In such a situation a grandparent would need to have the legal status to be able to make important decisions involved in the child's upbringing. This is called having 'parental responsibility' (PR).

Acquiring PR

A grandparent can obtain PR for a grandchild through the court granting them a Child Arrangements Order (CAO) or by being appointed Special Guardian of their grandchild. Other ways of acquiring PR as grandparents are by obtaining an adoption order or by becoming the child's testamentary guardian. In care proceedings a grandparent who acquires an Emergency Protection Order will be granted limited PR for as long as the order remains in force.

The two main legal options for grandparents raising grandchildren and wishing to formalise the arrangements are:

Applying to the court for a Child Arrangements Order

This is an order made under section 8 of the Children Act 1989 regulating with whom a child will live, spend time or otherwise have contact.

Generally, grandparents do not have an automatic entitlement to apply for a Child Arrangements Order and they must obtain permission from the court before they can apply. There are some exceptions to this such as:

- If the grandchild has lived with them for a minimum of one year immediately before the application (in cases where the grandparent seeks a CAO naming them as a person the child shall live with).

- If the grandparent has the consent of every person who has PR or who is named in a CAO as a person with whom the child lives.

- If the child is in the care of a local authority and the local authority consents.

- If the grandparent is already named as a person in a CAO as someone with whom the child is to spend time.

Otherwise the grandparent must apply for permission. In deciding whether to grant permission the courts consider:

- The nature of the application;

- The applicant's connection

To parents: never make your child choose. To my fellow voices in the middle: you are never to blame for their separation. El (17)

with the child;

- Any risk that the proposed application might disrupt the child's life;

- The local authority's plans for the child's future and the wishes and feelings of the child's parents (in cases where the child is under the care of the local authority).

Even where permission is given this does not necessarily mean that the court will make a CAO providing for the child to live with the grandparent(s). This will depend on what the court considers are the best interests of the child determined in accordance with the Welfare checklist at section 1 of the Children Act 1989 (see Question 55). The court will also bear in mind the need to avoid any delay in reaching a decision.

If the court makes a CAO naming a grandparent as a person with whom their grandchild is to live they will have PR while the order is in force. The order will usually last until the child is 16.

Applying to the court for a Special Guardianship Order

A Special Guardianship Order (SGO) confers PR for the child on the Special Guardian until the child is 18. An SGO is often made where children are being cared for long-term by members of their extended family but adoption is not suitable and the child cannot be cared for by the parents.

The SGO provides the Special Guardian with more secure legal status than being named under a CAO partly because the parent(s) cannot apply to the court to discharge it unless they have

permission to do so. Also, whilst the parents retain PR for the child, their ability to exercise it is limited. In the 2006 case of *S v B and Newport City Council; Re K*, the Judge stated that Special Guardianship allows "familial carers, who are not parents, to have all the practical authority and standing of parents, while leaving intact real and readily comprehensible relationships within the family".

The following people can apply for an SGO:

- A person named in a CAO as a person the child shall live with;

- A person with whom the child has lived for 3 of the last 5 years and within the preceding 3 months;

- A person who has the consent of all those with PR for the child;

- Any person with permission to make the application;

- Foster parents with whom the child has lived for 1 year before the application.

Notice of intention to apply for an SGO must be given to the Local Authority and the applicant will undergo an assessment (similar to a foster carer assessment) so the court can be satisfied that making a SGO will be in the child's best interests. As with a CAO the child's welfare is paramount.

Local authorities are required under the Children Act to make arrangements to provide support for Special Guardians. This may be counselling, advice and information or other services including financial support.

There is a discretionary Special Guardianship Allowance which is

Notes

means-tested and the Special Guardian can also claim child benefit. This is often a crucial factor for grandparents in deciding whether or not to apply for an SGO, or agreeing to be appointed as an SGO in any care proceedings as a 'Kinship Carer'.

Before applying for an SGO or CAO a grandparent will usually need to attend a Mediation, Information and Assessment Meeting (MIAM) to investigate whether mediation may be appropriate (see Question 40 for more).

Whilst it is possible for a grandparent to apply to adopt their grandchild this would not usually be considered the best option as the adoption would sever links with the birth parents.

Money saving tips when employing professionals

Separation and divorce feels like a full-time job, with documents, phone calls and email dominating life. Fortunately, the legal system is moving towards greater flexibility meaning you can do some of the job yourself and buy in legal support for the rest of it. While this takes time it does save money. Research and preparation is the key. But, remember, you are doing this at a time when you may well feel exhausted and wretched. Get all the support from family and friends you can so that the "paper monster" doesn't take over.

How should I prepare for a meeting with a professional to save time and money?

About the author

Ursula Rice, Managing Director of Family First Solicitors

Ursula has practised in the field of family law since 2003. She is warm and passionate about her clients and fights hard for them. Providing practical and accurate legal advice with no messing about is why she set up the firm.

So, you took the plunge and made the call. You have an appointment with a solicitor. How should you prepare?

Remember you are paying money one way or another to meet with this person. Even if the meeting is free there is every chance that you have taken holiday, paid or unpaid, from work, to make the meeting.

Below is a list of the pre-meeting things to find. Of course you can mix and match them according to your circumstances...

If you have divorce and financial issues

- Make a list of your assets. Define those in your name, your ex's name and anything owned jointly. Try and get some broadbrush figures together.

- Date list: when were you married, roughly the length of time you were you together before marriage and how long you were cohabiting if applicable.

- I assume you remember your children's birthdays and full names! Now's the time to check you do!

- Bring any court paperwork if there is any.

If you have domestic violence issues

- If you kept a diary, take it with you.

- Police URN numbers are helpful and any police letters (PIN letters).

- Harassing messages, printed or on your phone are helpful so your solicitor can assess your evidence.

- Any paperwork from social services.

- Any court paperwork if there is any.

If you have Children Act issues

- If your son or daughter was born in late 2003 and you never married the other parent then bring the birth certificate with you (this is to check the situation over Parental Responsibility).

- Bring a selection of emails. No one wants War and Peace, but an indication of the recent communication styles and immediate issue sis helpful.

- Previous or current court paperwork if any.

Trust of Land issues (cohabitation financial issues)

- If there is one, the deed of trust.

- Any paperwork saying or indicating you and your ex

I learnt that there was no need to choose sides. Isaac (15)

were intending to share the property.

- The Land Registry official copy of the property in question.
- Try and remember or dig out some paperwork from the solicitors who dealt with the house.

Generally...

Before you go, arrange flexible child care. Don't be in a rush. Try to leave your children with someone. Kids are awesome, but they shouldn't be privy to the conversation - they will get bored and you might cry. So bringing

your kids is not cool, plus you will only take in half of what is said.

Look up parking and the address before you go.

Have a think about what you want to achieve at the meeting. A basic sense of the law? Something specific answered? A plan of action going forward?

Bring a friend if you can. It's so supportive and helps to have someone to debrief with.

A note book and pen is helpful. Write down those legal nuggets!

Prepare a list of questions before you arrive. What is vexing you or confusing you?

Remember to make a note of costs and don't be afraid to press for a ballpark figure of overall costs.

Immediately afterwards, try and make a note of how you felt about the meeting. This is really helpful if you have lined up a few solicitors to talk to, as you may forget who is who!

Follow the above and you will be more prepared than most to extract maximum value from the meeting.

Notes

How can I buy the best bits of a lawyer?

About the author

Ursula Rice, Managing Director of Family First Solicitors

Ursula has practised in the field of family law since 2003. She is warm and passionate about her clients and fights hard for them. Providing practical and accurate legal advice with no messing about is why she set up the firm.

So, you are thinking about running your case yourself - after all, solicitors cost a fortune and much of the system is having the jargon and the complexity stripped out of it. Why not sail your own boat?

But your ex has a smarty pants lawyer and every document they have sent you reeks of someone who knows what they are doing. Plus, it is really stressful trying to make head or tail of it and you find yourself not quite saying things in the way you want to say them.

If this is you, it might be worth looking into solicitors who are prepared to offer you a piece of themselves, but not a full service. The technical term for this is agreeing an 'unbundled retainer'. This way of delivering legal services is becoming more widespread as legal aid incomes fall and lawyers finally get wise to the fact that not everybody can afford them.

Why would I want one?

An unbundled solicitor will advise you step by step and help you manage the strategy and tactics in your case but you will execute the plan. This saves time and therefore money. Another positive side effect is that it usually decreases delay as you are your only client and get on with things immediately. Receiving unbundled advice will help you put your case in the best way possible and help to steer you in the right direction.

What should I search for?

Look for solicitors using a Google search for 'Pay-as-you-go family law' or 'unbundled family law'. Check their website and Google reviews. Do they have a track record of doing this?

Lots of solicitors offer ad hoc advice, but not as many understand that to offer a good unbundled service, they need to have a proper framework for engaging with clients and helping them get the most out of the system.

I have found a firm that seems to do this - now what?

Call and make your first appointment. At the appointment you need be satisfied with their answers to the following:

- Do they have a named lawyer who you will meet with most of the time?

- How long have they been doing family law?

- How many unbundled clients do they have?

- Is there a clearly set out contract between you and the lawyer that defines how the service will work?

- Can they clearly and in plain English explain to you what it 'feels like' to be in their system?

- Can you switch to full representation if the unbundled service does not work well for you?

- Do they seem able to give you clear answers about costs?

Be very wary if you are offered a trainee solicitor or a newly qualified solicitor to do this work. Miles on the clock really matter with professional legal services. There is a deep contrast between lawyers who have experience and those who do not. The solicitor who is just qualified, but has done five years as a paralegal with a case load of their own is probably very experienced. A 1 year qualified solicitor who became a trainee straight from university and who has only just started having their own clients is actually quite inexperienced.

It pays to ask questions and gauge how confident and experienced people are before trusting them with your work. Ask yourself; does this person seem able to give direct answers to questions? Do they look like they

would be confident advising me in the hot seat if I have a problem?

Making the most of your unbundled session

Each firm will have their own system of working, but a standard way is to offer face-to-face appointments on an hourly rate, by appointment.

At each appointment you need to bring your file of papers (you are in charge of the paperwork so take a look at Question 101). Your appointments will be pre booked usually in line with a natural point in the case, for example to draft an application for a non-molestation order or perhaps to put a Form E together.

You will be paying for and receiving your advice in real time (another good reason to use a very experienced lawyer) so make sure you have a method of capturing that advice. A perfect way is to have a dedicated advice book where you write down the issues, the advice and the 'to do' list that your lawyer should give you.

Collect your niggly little questions so that you can work on them in the session, in one efficient hit.

Make sure you have the means to pay. The advantage for the lawyer is that they get paid there and then. You will not be able to access your lawyer again if you stiff them on their fees. If you have to save up then that is OK.

What kind of work might we do together?

Typical advice might be as follows:

- Formulating a letter before action, or a letter to try and reach an agreement - but you will send it.

- Helping you to fill out an application form like a C100 or Form E - again for you to send.

- Helping you to think about whether you need more disclosure after receiving a form E (and drafting the questionnaire) - you guessed it, you send it!

- Putting a without prejudice offer letter together for you to take to your next mediation session.

- Advocacy - some firms will offer you bolt-on advocacy services for specific hearings.

As can be seen from the above you are buying their brains and experience, not their supersonic photocopier, their admin services or their headed letter paper. You should go away with a to do list that has clear homework for you to get on with.

What kind of cases are suitable for unbundled services?

Generally, if you have one or two family law cases on the go they will work on an unbundled basis.

- Private law Children Act matters (for a Child Arrangements Order) are easy to unbundle, especially if you would like bolt-on advocacy services.

- Special Guardianship Orders.

- Straightforward financial cases where there is a house, 2 incomes, a bit of pension and a bit of cash that people would prefer not to burn up on lawyers.

- Non-molestation Orders, even if they are contested (but see below).

Cases where you would like to mediate are suitable for unbundled services and can really help you focus on the proper issues. It pays to know as early as possible that your aspirations for selling the house are unrealistic, or your refusal to let the kids go on holiday for two weeks to Spain is daft.

What kind of cases do not work on unbundled services?

- Public Law cases under the Children Act i.e. care cases. You need legal aid and you are entitled to it if you are a parent.

- Trust of Land and Appointment of Trustees Act 1996 ('TOLATA') cases. These are complex and most family lawyers like counsel's (i.e. a barrister's) advice when they advise on them. The exception

IT ISN'T YOUR FAULT. It's very easy to believe that your parents unhappiness is because of you, it isn't (I promise). Brianna (16)

is if your lawyer is very experienced in standard civil litigation (which is not always the case with family lawyers) in which case you may be able to unbundle.

- Cases where you have no time to do your part of the work.

- Cases where you feel unable to deal directly with the other party even when you have the help of a lawyer. Sometimes clients seeking Non-molestation Orders are simply unable to put their point across due to the impact of the abusive behaviour. Abuse has a cumulative effect, and the impact on memory, decision making power and cognitive ability shouldn't be underestimated. This can mean that they need the 'shield wall' that full representation services can offer.

- Piece work that is usually fixed fee and impossible for a client to draft - i.e. a consent order. The best option is to switch to a fixed fee after using unbundled services to arrive at the agreement.

Cut to the chase - will I save money?

Yes, compared to the hourly rate. A successfully run unbundled case will save in the region of 30% to 50% of the fees you would normally pay on an hourly rate.

It will also progress things much faster as getting your advice simply depends on how fast you can get an appointment with your lawyer, your ability to pay them in real time and how quickly you finish your homework.

Notes

Unbundled services can be the middle point between crashing around on your own and getting into a tangle, and breaking the bank getting help with things you could have done yourself.

What's the best way of tackling the paper monster?

About the author

Ursula Rice, Managing Director of Family First Solicitors

Ursula has practised in the field of family law since 2003. She is warm and passionate about her clients and fights hard for them. Providing practical and accurate legal advice with no messing about is why she set up the firm.

The waggons of the law run upon the tramlines of well-ordered paperwork. All the orders, case management decisions and judgments that are generated are made after consideration of a body of information, usually in 'the bundle' (the collection of case papers). The papers will be applications, orders made by the court and reports, evidence and sworn statements from the parties.

Paper bundles are used and there is no facility for online bundles at this time.

As soon as your case starts, whether you are the applicant or the respondent, you need to invest in stationery to sort out the papers. The earlier you do this the better. Do not throw away paperwork unless you are sure you won't need it.

Get ready

Must haves:

- Lever arch file - a chunky one! It should be strong enough to hold at least 4 inches thick of paper.
- Hole punch.
- Lined note pad.
- Pens.
- Envelopes & stamps.
- Post it notes large & small.
- File dividers.

Nice to have:

- Photocopier.
- Highlighters.
- Plastic wallets.

How to make your bundle

Divide up your file into the following sections using file dividers or post it notes:

- **Section A** - applications and orders, for example a C100.
- **Section B** - statements. At the beginning this is likely to be empty unless there is a without notice statement (for example in injunction proceedings).
- **Section C** - expert reports, for example CAFCASS letters or reports, or a surveyors report.
- **Section D** - correspondence.
- **Section E** - bills, receipts and other money related stuff.

What's the point of a bundle?

The idea behind a bundle is it creates a book which everybody else has a copy of. It allows the parties and the court to find a document easily, read the same thing at the same time and less time is lost faffing and trying to find the specific piece of evidence that needs to be considered.

There is a difference between your bundle and the court bundle. Your bundle can be a useful place for all your documents and you can choose

Talk to your parents individually and explain how you're feeling. Sophie (16)

what you put in it. The court bundle is the official case documentation and there are rules governing what goes into it. Those rules are found in the Family Procedure Rules 2010 at Practice Direction 27A - you can find it on the justice.gov.uk website.

Note that the Practice Direction does not allow sections D and E in the court bundle unless there is a specific evidential reason, so these are only for your private use.

The key point is that sections A, B and C of your 'private bundle' can also be used as your 'court bundle', so long as you have ordered everything in the right way and followed the practice direction.

TIP - make sure you have only single sided pages in the bundle. Use a photocopier to 'undouble' them if you receive double sided stuff.

How to paginate

The idea behind pagination is that not only does everybody have the same documents in the same section, each page has been given a page number that matches everybody else's page numbers.

Here's how it works:

Take section A. This should have all the applications and orders in it. Write in the top right hand corner the page letter and number. The first page is page A1, second page is A2 and so on. When you get to the end of the section, stop paginating!

Go to section B. The first page is B1, the second page is B2, and so on.

TIP - use a pencil, then you can

rub out if there is a mix up and you need to start again.

Dealing with an index

You may be sent an index from the other party's solicitors. This is a list of all the things that should be in the bundle and it should contain the pagination as well. Cross check that they have included all the documents. It is not uncommon for things to be missing and there are usually 2 reasons for this:

- Either they just didn't realise something existed (pretty common when the solicitors were not involved from the beginning) - politely send them a copy of the document and ask for it to go in.

- Or, they want something excluded from the bundle for tactical reasons. What should you do about this? Firstly, double check the practice direction. Is what you want in allowed? If it is, then tell the solicitors politely that you will ask the Judge to consider whether it should be part of the official bundle at the hearing; then don't forget to ask the Judge!

Dealing with duplicates

One of the most confusing things for those new to the court system is the sheer number of copies that seem to be generated. This happens for a number of reasons. The most common is because people are circulating a draft document, not the final version, to other interested parties. It can also be because a copy of an original document was used to prove a point about something.

The best rule to follow is to keep any drafts but to watch carefully for a court sealed version to

come out. When it arrives remove all drafts from your papers. It's only real if there's a seal!

TIP - the Practice Direction says there should be only 350 pages in the court bundle unless the Judge gives permission for more pages, so it pays to be ruthless with copy documents.

Advantages of being master of the paperwork

Keeping your bundle tidy will make you feel significantly better and in control.

It is far easier for another person to help you if your paperwork is in order.

Court time is severely limited. There is a world of difference between:

"Madam, can I ask you to look at C5 where the CAFCASS officer clearly mentions her concerns over mothers ability to be positive about my sons relationship with me".

and

"err, well I had it here somewhere, let me see *empties plastic bag onto desk* it's something the CAFCASS officer said...".

Collate as much financial disclosure as early as you can and put it in chronological order. It will save your lawyer a lot of time and you a lot of money!

*Fiona Turner,
Weightmans*

ONLY Mums & Dads
parents meet professionals

The family solicitor: a profile

About the author

Emma Palmer, Partner at MSB Solicitors in Liverpool

Emma specialises in international family law and is recommended by the Legal 500 as a solicitor that 'pulls out all the stops for her clients and is excellent at child abduction and care proceedings'.

The role of a family solicitor is varied. We advise clients from all walks of life in respect of divorce, civil partnership dissolution, financial matters on separation, injunctive relief such as non- molestation/ occupation orders and children matters.

The children matters themselves are varied and can include social services involvement, international parental child abduction and disputes from parents when they do not agree on which parent the child should live with and how much time the child should spend with the other parent.

The way we work changes depending on our client's needs and circumstances. Some cases require a more conciliatory stance and may benefit from mediation whereas some cases necessitate a robust stance taken within court proceedings. To get the best outcome for our client we consider each case in its own unique circumstances and tailor our advice accordingly.

We advise clients on the law and what they can do to better their prospects of achieving their aim. We prepare legal documents such as skeleton arguments and prepare client's statements. We manage the case throughout liaising with the other parties/ their representatives and other agencies as appropriate. We represent the client in court by negotiating with the other party and advocating the client's position to the Judge. Where a barrister is used we prepare the documents for the barrister so that they know the client's case before they meet them.

The challenges of the job

When people need a family solicitor it is often because something has gone wrong in a relationship and this

I wish I'd had some support in finding a good solicitor earlier. I was in such a vulnerable state at the time that I felt overwhelmed at the thought of researching solicitors so I went with the first recommendation I was given which turned out to be a poor choice.

Tanya, Mum

understandably brings a great deal of emotional turmoil, stress and anxiety for the future. We always try to be sympathetic and explain things carefully to our clients but inevitably we sometimes have to tell clients things that they do not wish to hear such as a likelihood that a child will spend more time with the other parent than they wanted, or that the child may be taken into foster care.

It is really difficult seeing a client upset and feeling like their world is crashing down around them. Our clients deserve and get from us honest advice and prospects of success but sometimes it is difficult for them to accept that advice.

 It all fell apart. When I came along. Kay (15)

My job is rewarding when...

The job is very rewarding when we get a great result for our client and the client is happy. When we manage to get an outcome which is clearly going to benefit the client and the children there is a great sense of satisfaction. Hearing from past clients months or even years after we have represented them and being told that everything is running smoothly and they are happy is a wonderful boost too.

Tips for parents

Do make sure that you are completely open and honest with your solicitor. It is so much easier to prepare and advise when we know the full facts. It is much harder to resolve something when it comes out unexpectedly in court.

Do make sure that you keep the children's best interests at the forefront of your mind at all times. This will mean that any court proceedings are usually quicker and work out better for the whole family.

Don't send communication to the other parent or their partner in anger. If you receive inflammatory communication from them such as a text or Facebook message, turn your phone off and don't pick it up until the next day.

Don't try and cover up drug or alcohol use by lying about it to a drug or alcohol testing provider - they will find out and the court will realise that not only is there a drug or alcohol problem but also that you cannot be trusted. Trust is a key part of a court order going your way.

Notes

The family barrister: a profile

About the author

Matthew Richardson, Barrister at Coram Chambers

Matthew's areas of expertise include disputes between married and unmarried couples about children and finances, mental health issues, relocation and shared residence, 'parental alienation', children at risk, domestic abuse and surrogacy. Matthew was shortlisted for Junior Barrister of the Year at the 2018 Family Law Awards.

I am a specialist - akin to a consultant in medicine - with expertise both in a particular area of law (in my case family) and as an advocate. I give advice about a case and then help present it, both in writing and in court, in the most persuasive way possible.

Fundamentally the job of a barrister is to take the facts of a particular case, combine them with the applicable law, and arrive at a conclusion about the range of outcomes that can reasonably be expected and pursued. That conclusion - as well as the analysis needed to get to it - needs to be presented to a variety of audiences including my client and their solicitor (with whom a lot of preparatory work is done before a conclusion is reached), the other side and their legal team, and the court. Therefore, a substantial part of my task is to tailor the way the case is presented to the relevant recipient so that that specific person finds it as persuasive as possible.

The challenges of the job

In family disputes, what a parent may instinctively focus on is often not the same as what the court will consider to be central to the case. It is understandable that there is a significant degree of emotional content to a family case and a big part of my job is to help people move beyond their emotional reactions and get to the point of being able to focus rationally and sensibly on the key issues and the steps needed.

This is perhaps the key challenge facing a family barrister - taking account of the emotional content within a case in such a way as to recognise its validity and

> Surround yourself with the right people for you, the right lawyers, right accountants, financial advisors, counsellors and friends. The more of the right people you have for you the easier the process will be.
>
> *James Belderbos, Bird Belderbos & Mee*

significance whilst at the same time not allowing emotions to dictate the approach or to detract from the careful legal analysis that is required, as in any other area of the law, by the court.

In a family case the most important person involved - in terms of the significance of the outcome - is neither my client nor the parent on the other side, but their child or children. An outcome hugely imbalanced in favour of my client may well not be best for the child if it means their relationship with their other parent is significantly undermined. Retaining a healthy degree of objectivity is important for a family barrister because there are times when the person

I'm wiser and more experienced, more realistic and stronger. Definitely stronger. Jess (17)

ONLY Mums & Dads
parents meet professionals

that most needs persuading to change their approach is one's own client.

My job is rewarding when...

...I am able to establish a trusting relationship with my client and therefore find out not just what they want but more importantly why they want it (which is vital to finding workable solutions for the future, because in fact most parents want the same thing - a happy and healthy future for their children) and deliver advice that is both heard and heeded.

... I am able to change someone's mind and influence the outcome in a better direction as a result.

... The future for a family is brighter as a result of the proceedings than it was before. The family justice system is not just looking at what happened in the past and trying to compensate for it - it looks forward, unusually, with a view to making things better after the case is over.

Tips for parents

Do remember the vital importance of evidence. Unfounded allegations are unhelpful and expensive, and people often forget about the need to gather and present proper evidence to prove the things they say. There is an important difference between what is true and what can be proved, and the court can only be concerned with the latter.

Do constantly refer yourself back to the welfare of the child - the key test - and ask whether what you are suggesting is based on it being best for your child or best for you.

Notes

Don't make the mistake of thinking you have to deprecate your former partner's parenting in order to strengthen your own case. Legitimate criticism of poor parenting is one thing, but many people think taking any opportunity for making the other person look bad will make them look better by comparison. Often the opposite is true - focusing on faults can show an inability to see the positives in the other parent and an unwillingness to work with them as co-parents in the future.

Don't forget that, even if you have a poor opinion of your child's other parent, the likelihood is there will always be a relationship of substance between them. The court's starting point is that a child has a right to a relationship with each of their parents and only in the most extreme circumstances will a court completely curtail a child-parent relationship.

Children of separated families can flourish. What can cause harm is unresolved disputes between mum and dad. If your children were here now, what would they say they wanted?

Debbie Wahle, Norfolk Family Mediation

The family mediator: a profile

About the author

Deborah Butterworth, Mediation Dispute Solutions

MEMBER ONLY Mums & Dads

Deborah helps separating and divorcing couples to find fast, practical ways to end their relationship amicably and with less stress. She has had a broad experience in conflict resolution and encourages creative thinking. In parenting plans she helps parents to successfully move forward as separated co-parents.

Mediation is an opportunity to sort out the end of a relationship or marriage with dignity. It provides couples with the space and time to think about the future. People work out the practical arrangements for children as well as create an environment where children feel supported through the changes of their families. Mediation is also a cost-effective way of resolving the financial future when divorcing or separating. The skill of the mediator is to create a trust relationship with each individual to give them confidence in the process. It is also to robustly challenge the proposals to ensure the transparency and practicality of the end result.

Financial mediation allows couples to work out where they will live and check they can afford the day-to-day costs, both at the time of separation and in the future. Mediation is more than making a deal - it's about finding creative solutions to intractable financial conundrums, for example turning a 3-bedroomed house into two 3-bedroomed houses! Financial mediation is also about helping couples through debt management. So many couples find themselves in debt because of the increasing costs of living apart. Finding fast practical solutions can help.

Couples are often so concerned about the day-to-day cost of living apart that they fail to realise they need to include one of the most important family assets - pensions. Mediators help people to find a full and final settlement so both people have knowledge of all the financial assets and how they will be used in the future.

It is the responsibility of parents to include the views of the children in the arrangements for the children. So often parents are caught up in their own view of the separation that children are unintentionally side-stepped. This is not uncommon even when parents say their children are the most important thing to them. The mediator's skill is to bring the children 'into' the room. Some mediators have special training to allow them to have sessions with the children to find out their view.

Separating and divorcing couples should contact a mediator as soon as possible to help sort things out. Even if they been separated for a while or if their case has already gone to court, mediation can still help to resolve things amicably.

Unlike the court system, people can come back to mediation at any time. Sometimes it's beneficial to put interim arrangements in place and come back a few months later to see how they're working. Quite often, improvements or changes can be made to make the arrangements fit in with work commitments, children or the transport system. If your situation changes and the arrangements aren't working, you can go back to the mediator to change the original agreement.

Challenges

One of the biggest challenges for family mediators is getting both parties to agree that mediation is the right option for them. When a couple separate, they can want different things at different times. Finding the right time when they're both ready can be a challenge. When people find out about mediation, they are often are willing to give it a try. During the Mediation Information and Assessment Meeting (MIAM) one of the mediator's biggest challenges is to create an environment where both parties realise they are in control of the process. The important thing to remember is that they will be able to engage with the process and have a direct input into the outcome.

Family law solicitors can play an important role by encouraging their clients to try mediation. Most people going through mediation find it helpful to have legal advice to support them. Clients can arrange this at any time and the mediator may also recommend they do if they are talking about things that relate to legal issues. The mediator can give clients information about local family solicitors and how to choose one. If clients get legal aid for mediation, they may also get free legal advice during mediation.

My job is rewarding when...

- I've helped people who find it difficult to be in the same room as someone they want to be separated from.

- I help people who are nervous and worried about the first joint session to have the confidence to give it a try.

- In the mediation meetings, people re-learn how to talk to each other and put aside the history of hurt and conflict and work towards their independent future.

The best reward I get is to see people talk to each other about their children or how to work out their finances in a way that gives me confidence that they will be able to work things out for themselves in the future, because life has a habit of throwing up problems especially if you have children.

Tips about how to get the most out of a mediation meeting.

Be prepared

- Know and understand the aims of the meeting.

- Bring some ideas for solutions to the problems. Be creative and be realistic.

- Listen to the other party's ideas in full.

- Look to the future, seize the opportunity to move forward.

Use the agenda

- Your mediator will develop an agenda with you about what needs to be discussed.

- If there is something else you want to raise, give as much notice as you can.

- Don't expect answers unless the other party has time to think about your request.

Be guided by the mediator

- The mediator will be able to facilitate discussion, probe and challenge suggestions.

- Each person has the right to be heard - try not to interrupt.

- Write notes on issues to raise when it's your turn.

- Challenge constructively and give reasons why.

- Accept that your suggestions will be questioned, challenged and tested.

Stay focused

- Take time, even a minute, remember you're trying to resolve issues and move on.

- Be mindful that what you suggest may enrage the other party.

- Ask yourself, 'Is what you want to say of benefit to the final outcome?'

- Tell the mediator if you would like someone (including the mediator) to behave differently in the meeting.

- Be prepared to say how the behaviour makes you feel and why you need the change.

Develop understanding

- If you don't understand or accept a proposal, try to listen and question what's said so you can be informed of the other view.

- Realise that you may be misunderstood, be prepared to say more and how you feel.

- Understanding someone's view does not mean you agree with it.

Stay positive

- Remember the reasons why you want to resolve your differences.

- Keep focused on the future.

- Use the time to establish a positive way of communicating.

- Accept you are here because of the past. Mediation can help you to build a new future.

Do I have to put the father's name on the birth certificate ?

About the author

**Bradie Pell,
Partner and
Head of Family
at Graysons
Solicitors**

Bradie deals with
the whole spectrum of legal
issues that affect families,
including divorce, separation,
finances, injunctions and
children matters. She is also
able to advise on pre- and
post-nuptial agreements,
separation agreements and
cohabitation agreements.
Bradie is a member of
Resolution and is also on the
Family Law Panel.

For married parties, the husband is assumed to be the father of the child and therefore, due to existence of parental responsibility, the issue of naming the father on the birth certificate only really becomes significant when you are unmarried.

In summary, parental responsibility is the term used to describe the rights and responsibilities of a person in relation to their children. Parental responsibility is automatically gained by the mother of the child. The father also automatically acquires this if he is married to the mother at the time of birth of the child. However, unmarried fathers only automatically obtain parental responsibility if they are the father of a child born after 1st December 2003 and their name is on the birth certificate. If an unmarried father is not named on the birth certificate, he will not automatically acquire parental responsibility, although he can still obtain parental responsibility by way of a court order (see below).

An unmarried mother of a child can register the birth of a child on her own without naming the father on the birth certificate. Despite this, an unmarried father will still have some rights towards the child and can still gain parental responsibility by doing one of the following:

* **Re-registering the birth**. This can be done with the mother's consent by contacting the local register office and both parents attending. If the father is unable to attend he must fill out a statutory declaration of parentage form, a copy of which can be found at https://www.gov.uk/register-birth/who-can-register-a-birth.

* **Applying for a parental responsibility order**. If the mother does not consent to the re-registering of the birth, the biological father can apply to the court for a parental responsibility order. A parental responsibility order can be applied for at the same time as applying for other court orders, such as a child arrangements order.

* **Applying for a child arrangements order**. This is an order by the courts that governs who a child should live with and have contact with. If it is ordered that the child should live with the father then he will gain parental responsibility.

Ultimately an unmarried mother is not obliged to enter the father's name on the birth certificate. However, as outlined above, not doing so does not mean that the child's father has no rights in respect of the child and it could leave you open to a court application. In reality, the best option for your children is always a harmonious out-of-court agreement. However, if this cannot be achieved there are many provisions in place that prevent either parent from acting in a way that is not in the best interests of the child.

Every bit of damage inflicted on either partner is damage inflicted on the kids, so treat your ex like you treat your kids.

Paul, Dad

How to be successful separated parents

About the author

Angela Lake-Carroll

Angela has over 30 years' experience of working with separated families and she has written a range of short guides for separating families. Angela works across the broad range of family law and family dispute resolution as a practitioner and adviser. She has also worked with and contributed to government policy for families, children and young people.

Very many families today live in situations where children go between their parents rather than living with both - or just one. Being a successful separated parent takes work - and compromise. Listed below are some hints and tips that you may find useful as you plan or begin your changed role as a parent.

Put your child or children first

Whatever has happened that has resulted in your separation as adults is secondary to meeting the needs of your child or children and ensuring their continued and future happiness. Muddling your anger or hurt about the ending of your relationship with what needs to happen to ensure your children's continuing security is dangerous. Ending your relationship is adult business. Raising secure, happy children is your responsibility as their parents.

Continuing conflict between parents causes emotional harm to children that may affect their whole lives

Children caught in conflicts are more likely to have significant problems as they grow up, to under-achieve and to find making adult relationship difficult.

Don't make your child or children take sides

They don't want to. They love you as their parents, it is hurtful and damaging for them to feel that they have to make choices between the two people they love most in the world.

Finding it difficult to be civil to each other?

Think of yourself as partners in a family business - just as sometimes happens in work situations, you may not get on or even like each other, but you have an investment in your children and a task to complete in raising them to adulthood. Keep your communication as parents going - even if it is in a business like way, it will help your children to understand that you remain, as their parents, together and united in your concern for them.

Don't assume that your child or children can't manage living between you

The practicalities that are our responsibility as parents don't affect children and young people in the same way. They can be much more flexible and adapt to sharing their time between you if you provide a secure framework for them.

Think about how you can ensure that neither of you becomes either the 'guest' parent, or the 'hard slog' parent

Children don't differentiate - you are both their parents. They expect you to be in their life, responsible for their day-to-day living, their discipline and to be able to spend time with them. It's important for children to know that their parents agree about them.

Don't think of the time your child spends with you as 'your time' but rather *their* time.

Remember too that older children and especially teenagers need to form their own social circles and grow towards being an independent adult - with your help. Giving them 'permission' to spend time with their friends is an important part of them understanding that you recognise their growing independence.

Think about the language that you use to help your children and you to be reminded that you both remain parents.

Start sentences with 'we speak' e.g.

'Dad/Mum and I hope that', 'have decided that', 'think that'.

Make sure that if you're not sure what the other parent thinks or has said, simply say that you need to check it out with them. 'Hope' is a great word - don't make promises that you may not be able to keep, instead tell your children what you hope might happen.

Think about how it felt for you when your child misbehaved in public

And then think about how it would feel to your child or children if you and their other parent did so at a public event important to them - school plays, sports day, parents' evenings. Your being there at significant events is important to them - as is your civil behaviour together. If you really, really can't manage to attend together, alternate your attendance at significant events.

Happy Birthdays

To a child, a birthday is an exciting occasion - they deserve to have happy birthdays free from worries about an atmosphere between their

parents and free to enjoy their day. They would prefer to spend it with both of you (where it is possible for you to do so) - try to ensure that they will have some contact with both of you, by phone or for a short time at least.

Making their Christmas

Or other significant dates in the calendar means thinking through how you can each compromise to ensure that your child or children can look back at those occasions in their childhood with good memories. Try to think ahead and plan for these events ahead of time - don't make assumptions and don't plan or book things without talking to their other parent, and remember older children and teenagers need to be part of any planning because they too may have things they want to do at significant times of year.

Think about other significant things that happen as children grow up

Typical events could include change or choice of school, medical treatment, problems at school and everyday things such as bedtimes and discipline. Try to think through how you need to ensure that each and both of you know what will happen if and when there are decisions to be made or action to be taken. If you can't do that without help, think about using a mediator to help you set out a framework for

all the important areas of your children's growing up.

Children need families

Don't forget that your children have other family members to keep in touch with - Grand-parents, Aunts and Uncles and family friends. A sense of family and of belonging aids children's feelings of security so ensure that they can continue to spend time with all the family members whom they have previously known and loved.

New partners and friends

Face it - if you haven't already, there's a strong likelihood that you will have a new partner or friend. Just because they are significant to you, do not assume that they will be immediately significant to your child. If they are going to be part of your life for the future, there is plenty of time for them to become involved in your children's lives - don't rush it, children need time to adjust to new arrangements and new people, and your new partner will not thank you for dumping them into a wicked step-parent role!

How would you like to be treated when you have a new partner?

And how would you expect your new partner to treat your children? Whatever that is, apply that to your ex and their new partner.

I sat waiting at the window for hours on end every day waiting for him to turn up but he didn't... Sophie (17)

Help friends and family to know how you want them to help

Friends and family need your guidance to know how they should behave and react. People who love you often want to protect you from hurt or show loyalty. Occasionally and sadly, friends may be acting out their own agendas about past hurts of their own. Be clear with them that you and your ex are trying to work things out together and that is important to you and for your children. Be clear that you want them to support your children - and both of you, no matter what their view about what might have happened.

Remember:

Children learn what they live

Growing up in a situation where things are dealt with through conflict or anger and where there is little or no communication between their parents means that you shouldn't be surprised if your children deal with their relationships with you, their friends and the wider world in the same way - it will be how they think adults behave. Growing up knowing that their parents love and care for them and want them to share their time with each of their parents is a fundamental life lesson for children about relationships, sharing and caring.

Stay confident

When a relationship ends it is easier to feel failure than gain. Remember, however, that no relationship that has produced children is a failure. Try to stay proud of your achievements as parents - and don't lose confidence in your ability to continue to parent well and successfully.

WHEN IS IT APPROPRIATE TO INTRODUCE MY NEW PARTNER TO MY CHILDREN?

The first thing to say here is that your children's thoughts and reactions to a new partner are going to be different from yours.

This is their mum or dad moving on, not their partner.

Age plays a big part in this process. Often younger children will adapt more quickly than say teens, but every child is unique and it's very much dependent on the circumstances surrounding the initial separation as to how they might present a reaction towards a new partner.

Although there are no hard and fast rules, it is a good idea only to introduce a new partner when you are sure (as you can be) the relationship is becoming more committed.

A gradual introduction on neutral territory for a short period of time initially and then building up to more contact is often a good way of introducing children.

Adele Ballantyne

Advice & support

Adfam
Information and support for the families of drug and alcohol users.
www.adfam.org.uk

Advice Now
Plain English information on a website run by a group of organisations including the Citizens Advice Bureau.
advicenow.org.uk

Advocate
A Charity which finds free legal help from barristers.
www.weareadvocate.org.uk

Alcoholics Anonymous
www.alcoholics-anonymous.org.uk

Barnardos
Charity supporting vulnerable children and young people in the UK.
www.barnardos.org.uk

Childline
Confidential help and advice for children.
www.childline.org.uk

Child Poverty Action Group (CPAG)
Information about welfare benefits and tax credits.
cpag.org.uk

Child Protection Resource
Help for anyone involved in the Child Protection (or Child In Need) process.
www.childprotectionresource.org.uk

Children's Legal Centre
Experts in all areas of children's rights.
www.childrenslegalcentre.com

Citizen's Advice Bureau
Public access to advice at branches throughout the country.
adviceguide.org.uk

Civil Legal Advice
Get free and confidential legal advice in England and Wales if you're eligible for legal aid.
www.gov.uk/civil-legal-advice

Dad Info
Service providing separated parents with suggestions about the most successful way to communicate, negotiate and solve problems after family breakdown.
dadinfo.splittingup-putkidsfirst.org.uk/home

Dads Unlimited
Charity offering unbiased and independent advice.
www.dadsunltd.orb.uk

Family Lives
A national family support charity providing help and support in all aspects of family life.
www.familylives.org.uk

Family Mediation Council (FMC)
The Family Mediation Council is made up of 5 national family mediation organisations in England and Wales.
www.familymediationcouncil.org.uk

Families Need Fathers
Charity concerned with maintaining a child's relationship with both parents during and after family breakdown.
www.fnf.org.uk

Family Rights Group
Advises parents and other family members whose children are involved with or require children's social care services because of welfare needs or concerns.
frg.org.uk

Galop
LGBT & anti-violence charity.
www.galop.org.uk

Gamblers Anonymous
www.gamblersanonymous.org.uk/

Gingerbread
National charity supporting single parent families to live secure, happy and fulfilling lives.
www.gingerbread.org.uk

Grandparents Plus
National charity working for grandparents and kinship carers.
www.grandparentsplus.org.uk

LawWorks
Solicitors Pro Bono Group.
www.lawworks.org.uk

Legal Aid Finder
Directory of legal advisers and family mediators who do legal aid work.
find-legal-advice.justice.gov.uk

ManKind
Confidential helpline for men suffering from domestic abuse.
www.mankind.org.uk

Match
Charity offering support and information to mothers apart from their children.
www.matchmothers.org/

Men's Advice Line
Help and support for men experience domestic violence and abuse.
www.mensadviceline.org.uk

MIND
For better mental health.
mind.org.uk

Money Advice Service
Information about financial issues, including sections on divorce and separation.
www.moneyadviceservice.org.uk

Narcotics Anonymous
ukna.org

National Association of Child Contact Centres (NACCC)
Search facility for contact centres by location and type of service. Range of information for families. Helpline: 0800 4500 280 (9.00 - 1.00 Mon-Fri).
naccc.org.uk

National Debtline
A national debt advice charity.
www.nationaldebtline.org

National Family Mediation
NFM is a network of LSC contracted and accredited family mediation services countrywide that offer practical and emotional support to those affected by separation or divorce.
nfm.org.uk

National Youth Advocacy Service (NYAS)
Provide information and advice to children. Act as children's guardians in difficult contact or residence cases.
nyas.net/

NHS Choices
Advice to help you make the best choices about your health and wellbeing.
www.nhs.uk

No Family Lawyer
Wesbsite supporting Lucy Reed's book 'The Family Court Without A Lawyer'.
www.nofamilylawyer.co.uk

NSPCC
UK's leading children charity preventing abuse.
www.nspcc.org.uk

OnePlusOne
Supports parents through separation and co parenting difficulties. It can also be used by parents who are just worried about their relationship.
www.oneplusone.space/the-parent-connection/

Personal Support Unit
Voluntary service helping litigants in person.
www.thepsu.org

Pink Tape
Lucy Reed's family law blog.
http://www.pinktape.co.uk/

Refuge
Support and information about domestic violence.
refuge.org.uk

Relate
Counselling services and relationship advice.
www.relate.org.uk

Respect
Domestic Violence Perpetrator Programmes.
respect.uk.net

Rethink
Advice and helplines for people with issues relating to mental illness.
www.rethink.org

Reunite International
UK charity specialising in international parental child abduction (click on "resources" for a list of signatories to the Hague Convention).
reunite.org/

Rights of Women
A women's charity working in a number of ways to help women through the law. Their site has some really useful free guides to the law.
rightsofwomen.org.uk/get-information/legal-information/

Royal Courts of Justice Advice Bureau
Citizen's Advice Bureau providing free advice to litigants in person, including family law. Able to refer to Bar Pro Bono Unit where appropriate. Appointments line: 0844 856 3534 (or 0300 456 8341 from mobiles).
rcjadvice.org.uk

Samaritans
Confidential non-judgemental emotional support for people experiencing feelings of distress or despair.
www.samaritans.org

Shelter
The housing and homelessness charity.
www.shelter.org.uk

SingleParents
Connecting, supporting and empowering single parents across the UK.
www.singleparents.org.uk

Sorting Out Separation
Government run support service for people going through family breakdown.
www.sortingoutseparation.org.uk

Southall Black Sisters
Empowering BME women to escape domestic violence.
www.southallblacksisters.org.uk

StepChange
National debt advice charity.
www.stepchange.org

Stonewall
Campaigns for the equality of lesbian, gay, bi and trans people across the UK.
www.stonewall.org.uk

Talk To Frank
Confidential drugs advice.
www.talktofrank.com

The Counselling Directory
Help finding counsellors/
therapists and useful information
on website.
www.counselling-directory.org.
uk

Victim Support
Specialist practical and
emotional support to victims and
witnesses of crime.
www.victimsupport.org.uk

Voices In The Middle
A dedicated place for young
people to find help and support.
www.voicesinthemiddle.com

Wikivorce
Advice and support on divorce.
wikivorce.com

Women's Aid
Support and information about
domestic violence.
womensaid.org.uk

Your Rights
Liberty guide to human rights.
Tells you how a conviction
becomes spent.
yourrights.org.uk/

Glossary

Access

This is now called contact. Arrangements for contact form part of a "child arrangements order".

Acknowledgment of service

A standard form (sent by the court with the divorce petition/ matrimonial order application) that the respondent (and any co-respondent) must sign and return to the court to confirm that they have received the petition/matrimonial order application and saying whether or not they agree to the divorce.

Adjournment

In a family law context, this generally means a hearing is postponed to a later date.

Adultery

Sexual intercourse that takes place during the marriage between a spouse and someone of the opposite sex who is not their husband or wife. This is one of the five facts or bases for getting a divorce.

Alimony

See maintenance.

Appeal

The process of asking a higher court to change the decision of a lower one.

Applicant

The person applying to court for an order.

Ancillary relief

This is now called financial proceedings or financial remedy application.

Answer

This is the formal defence to a divorce petition/matrimonial order application, rebutting the evidence. This may be necessary if there are allegations that are unnecessarily offensive, or if those allegations might prejudice discussions about parenting or finances if unchallenged. It is very rare for divorces to be defended.

Arbitration

An alternative to a judge deciding the case introduced in early 2012. The parties can choose an arbitrator to rule on all or just some of the issues in dispute. The arbitrator's decision (called an award) is then made into a binding court order.

Arbitration service

A provider of arbitration services. We have a team of expert arbitrators. You can find out more information about them here.

Arbitrator

An arbitrator is a third party who reviews the evidence in the case (or a discrete issue within the case) and provides a decision that is legally binding on both sides and enforceable in the courts.

Barrister

This is a lawyer who spends the majority of his or her time arguing cases in court. Barristers also use that advocacy experience to work with solicitors in advising on possible outcomes. Also referred to as counsel.

Cafcass

This is the Children and Family Court Advisory and Support Service. A Cafcass officer assists the court with matters relating to children and, in disputed cases of contact or residence for example, may be asked to prepare a report for the court on what orders or action would be in the children's best interests.

Child abduction

The wrongful removal or wrongful retention of a child from his or her place of normal, day-to-day residence in breach of one parent's rights of custody.

Child maintenance

An amount that the parent not living with their child pays to the other parent in order to support the child.

CEV

A cash equivalent value (CEV) is the value of the rights accrued within a pension scheme (previously called cash equivalent transfer value).

Charge on property

This is sometimes used as a means of security if one spouse is awaiting payment of a cash lump sum on a delayed sale of a home. It works like an additional mortgage, but without interest being paid, and is usually expressed as a percentage of the value of the property. It gives the holder of the charge security because they know that they will be paid out of the proceeds of the eventual sale.

Chattels

Legal term for personal effects, usually house contents or personal possessions.

Child arrangements order

This order regulates arrangements relating to with whom a child is to live, spend time or otherwise have contact. It also relates to when a child is to live, spend time or otherwise have a contact with any person. It replaces contact and residence orders and brings together arrangements for both in one order. If you already have a contact or residence order, from April 2014, you will be treated as having a child arrangements order.

Circuit judge

In the family law context, this is a senior judge who deals with the more complicated cases in the Family Court. Appeals from magistrate's or a district judge's decision are heard by a circuit judge.

Civil partnership

The Civil Partnership Act 2004 came into operation on 5 December 2005 and enables a same sex couple to register as civil partners. Being civil partners enables the couple to have equal treatment to a heterosexual married couple in a wide range of legal matters, including on the breakdown of the relationship.

Clean break

An order of the court barring any further financial claims between the divorcing couple. A clean break settlement cannot include spousal periodical payments/ maintenance (it can include child maintenance though). A clean break is only effective if the financial agreement is confirmed within a court order. The court has a duty in all financial proceedings to consider whether a clean break is possible.

Cohabiting/cohabitation

An arrangement in which an unmarried couple lives together in a committed personal relationship.

Collaborative law

An approach to dealing with family law issues such as finances on divorce and children arrangements built on mutual problem solving where the couple and their lawyers pledge to work together to negotiate an agreement without going to court.

Committal to prison

Sending a person to prison for breaching a court order.

Common law husband and wife

This is a common misconception; there is no such thing as a common law marriage. The rights and responsibilities of a couple who live together but are not married differ greatly to those of a married couple.

Consent order

A court order made by a court giving effect to the settlement terms that have been agreed between a husband and wife.

Contact

This was previously known as access. It usually refers to the arrangement for a child to visit or stay with the parent with whom they no longer have their main home. This can be by an order of the court in a child arrangements order or by agreement between the parents. Indirect contact means the exchange of letters, telephone calls or presents. Contact arrangements within a child arrangements order can also be made in favour of others, such as grandparents.

Contact orders

As from April 2014, contact orders no longer exist. They have been replaced with "child arrangements orders" which deal with contact and residence. When a child arrangements order deal with contact, it often orders the person with whom a child mainly lives to allow the child to visit or stay with the person named in the order. See also contact.

Co-respondent

A person with whom the respondent is alleged to have committed adultery. A person should not be named in a matrimonial application unless the applicant believes that the respondent is likely to object to the making of an order.

Counsel

Another name for a barrister.

Counselling

Specialist counsellors, with the right background, are able to help adults or children who are going through a separation. Other help can be provided by psychologists, therapists and family mediators with specialised training in working with adults or children within the family context. These professionals can be referred to as family consultants.

Family consultants can be brought into the collaborative law process to help spouses work out and articulate what they want, and to help and advise on ways to improve communication. Further support can help reduce conflict, help develop coping strategies for dealing with the emotional issues that may affect the family now and in the future and help everyone to move on with their lives following the divorce. Family consultants may also work with children, seeing them separately in appropriate cases, helping them to voice their thoughts, feelings, needs and concerns.

Court

The courts handle all types of family law disputes. From April 2014, there are only two types of court that deal with family law disputes. The Family Court will hear most cases and, depending upon the complexity of the case, the judge might be a magistrate (also called a lay justice), district judge, circuit judge or a High Court judge. Mostly, you will find your local Family Court based at your local County Court. A very few specific types of family disputes will be heard in the High Court.

Court fees

These are the fixed administrative costs paid to the court when making an application. Fees vary depending upon the type of application. If you are in receipt of public funding (legal aid), then the court fees are generally exempt.

Cost order

The court can order one spouse to pay the legal costs of the other. During a divorce, it is quite common for the respondent to contribute towards the applicant's costs. In most financial proceedings, there is a general presumption that each person will pay their own legal fees although costs orders can be made where there is "litigation misconduct", for example a person is dishonest about his or her financial position or ignores court orders.

Child Maintenance Service (CMS)

Replaced the Child Support Agency in November 2013. Its role is to make sure that parents living apart from their children contribute financially to their upkeep by paying child maintenance. It is intended to be used by only those parents who cannot come to an agreement themselves over child maintenance. All new applications for child maintenance made after November 2013 are dealt with by the CMS. There is a child support calculator on the Child Maintenance Options website.

Child Support Agency (CSA)

Replaced by the Child Maintenance Service in November 2013. It continues to administer all applications made before November 2013.

Custody

This is now called residence and forms part of the child arrangements order.

Decree absolute

The final order of the court, which terminates the marriage.

Decree nisi

The interim decree or order of divorce indicating that the court is satisfied that the marriage has broken down irretrievably. Six weeks and one day after decree nisi has been made, the applicant/petitioner can apply to the court to make decree nisi absolute (decree absolute) and the marriage is then terminated.

Directions order

A court order directing how the case will proceed (eg what evidence needs to be filed and what the timetable to trial is going to be).

Disclosure

This is the process of providing complete financial details about a person's capital, income, assets and liabilities. This is either done voluntarily or the court can order it. It is a necessary first step in any discussions about finance, even in mediation or in collaborative law. This is usually done by filling in a Form E.

District judge

A judge who sits in the Family Court. Most family disputes that end up in court are dealt with by a district judge.

Divorce

This is now called matrimonial order proceedings. This is the process which leads to the termination of a marriage. There are two orders: decree nisi and decree absolute.

Domestic violence/abuse

This has many forms including threats of and actual physical aggression, sexual abuse, emotional abuse, controlling or domineering behaviour, intimidation, stalking or passive/covert abuse such as neglect.

Divorce.co.uk

The most comprehensive free resource on the web, provided by the family lawyers at top 50 UK law firm Mills & Reeve. The information provided on the site aims to help families manage their way through relationship breakdown. Find out more at www.divorce.co.uk.

Duxbury calculation

Duxbury calculations are made to assist the decision as to whether or not a clean break is possible. The calculation produces a figure of what level of lump sum payment the recipient needs in order to spend the rest of their life at a certain amount of expenditure each year.

Equity

Refers to the net value of a property after mortgages or other charges are paid off.

Ex parte

This is now called without notice. It most commonly refers to emergency hearings that are conducted with only the applicant present at court. If the court makes an order at the without notice hearing, the judge will ensure that another hearing can be held quickly afterwards in order to hear the respondent's case and then make a final order. Often without notice hearings are used to deal with injunctions.

Family proceedings court

The name given to the division of the magistrates' court that dealt with family law matters. It was abolished on 22 April 2014.

FDA

First directions appointment: this is the first court appointment in financial cases and tends to be mainly administrative (family lawyers sometimes refer to it as a "housekeeping" hearing). The judge will consider what information is needed from both sides in order to progress the case. If the couple is able to agree the directions prior to the FDA then it may be possible to treat it as a financial dispute resolution (FDR).

FDR

Financial dispute resolution appointment/hearing: the second court appointment under the standard procedure in financial proceedings. This is an

opportunity for the parties to negotiate on a without prejudice basis and with the assistance and guidance of a judge. Importantly, the judge who deals with the FDR cannot take any further part in the case if it does not settle at that hearing, other than to give directions for progressing the case to a final hearing. The FDR can, in more simple cases, sometimes be combined with the first appointment (FDA) to save costs and speed up progress.

FHDRA

A first hearing dispute resolution appointment: the first court appointment in a private law children application.

Final hearing

The trial and the final court appearance in all proceedings. A judge will hear the parties and any experts give evidence and will make a binding court order as a result. In limited situations there are grounds for appeal.

Financial proceedings

See financial remedy application. These are generally the court proceedings following a divorce to reallocate the income and capital of a family.

Financial remedy application

This used to be called ancillary relief. This is the application to the court for financial orders following a divorce. The court can make a variety of orders about the finances of a divorcing couple. These are lump sum orders, property adjustment orders, property transfer orders, variation of trusts orders, periodical payments/ maintenance and pension sharing orders.

Five-year separation

One of the five "facts" or bases for getting a divorce, ie, the couple has lived apart for five years (no consent needed).

Form A

The application form sent to the court that begins the process of dealing with the financial claims on a divorce. It puts in place a court led timetable for financial disclosure and also sets a court date, which will either be an FDA or an FDR depending upon how much can be done beforehand.

Form E

This is the court form setting out a person's financial circumstances (called financial disclosure) as well as details about what orders are sought. It is about the same size - and as much fun - as a tax return. It is obligatory to complete and confirm the truth of this form in court led proceedings. It is often also used as a checklist for voluntary financial disclosure and in those cases where the parties are able to come to a financial agreement without needing the help of the court, directly or through mediation or collaborative law.

Form G

This is a simple form sent to the court before the FDA confirming whether or not it is possible to combine the FDA and the FDR hearing.

Forms H and H1

These are forms filed before each court hearing, which provide details of each party's costs and what has been paid towards them.

Former matrimonial home

The house in which the divorcing couple were living together before they separated. If it is owner occupied, it is often one of the biggest assets that has to be dealt with on divorce.

Get

A document made in a Beth Din (a court of Jewish law) dissolving a Jewish marriage following proceedings under Jewish law. It is handed over by a husband to a wife.

Injunction

An order of the court preventing or requiring action, usually made in an emergency.

Interim maintenance

See maintenance pending suit.

Joint tenancy

A form of joint ownership of land in which both parties share the whole title to the property. If one party dies, the survivor will own the entire property (the "right of survivorship").

Judicial separation

A formal separation sanctioned by the court, which enables the court to make orders about money and property but does not actually terminate the marriage.

Leave to remove

An application to the court for permission to remove a child permanently from England and Wales. This is now called permission to remove.

Legal Aid Agency (LAA)

Provides both civil and criminal legal aid and advice to those people who qualify for it. Due to government cuts in the legal aid budget, there are very few family cases which benefit from legal aid. However, you may be able to get legal aid if you have been the victim of domestic violence or if you are using mediation to resolve your dispute.

Legal Services Commission (LSC)

Now called the Legal Aid Agency.

Litigant in person

A person acting on their own behalf without assistance from a solicitor.

Lump sum order

A fixed sum of money paid by one person to another. It may be payable in one go or in instalments. This is one of the financial orders open to the court to make when deciding a financial settlement on divorce.

McKenzie friend

An individual who assists a litigant in person in the courtroom.

Maintenance

A regular payment of money by one spouse to another under a court order or following an agreement. Spousal maintenance refers to maintenance paid from one spouse to another. It is possible to capitalise spousal maintenance by the payment of a lump sum to achieve a clean break. Maintenance can be secured on the assets of the paying party if there is a risk that the order may be breached. Those assets can then be sold to ensure the recipient's claim is satisfied. Those orders are rare. See also child maintenance.

Maintenance pending suit

In financial proceedings, a person can apply for interim periodical payments/ maintenance, which is payable on a temporary basis while the proceedings are ongoing and before they are concluded. It is sometimes called interim maintenance or MPS. This is particularly useful if the financial proceedings are going to take some time to conclude.

Matrimonial order application

This used to be called a divorce petition. This is the document that starts the divorce proceedings. It sets out the basis for the divorce, i.e., whether it is based on unreasonable behaviour or adultery or a period of living apart.

MPS

See maintenance pending suit.

Mediation

The process through which independent mediators try to help a couple reach agreement about the arrangements to be made for children and/or finances following their decision to divorce or separate. It is sometimes wrongly thought to be a discussion about the relationship and whether a reconciliation is possible.

Mediation information & assessment meeting (MIAM)

Before court proceedings can be issued - either about children or about finance - you will usually be required to attend a meeting about mediation to ensure you have information about the process. This is called a mediation information and assessment meeting (MIAM). This meeting can be a useful way of finding out more about mediation, although it is better to have explored the option of mediation before you decide that you want to start court proceedings.

Mediation service/s

A provider of mediation services. We have a team of expert mediators and you can find out more about them here.

Mediator

A third party who assists the parties to reach a negotiated settlement.

MIAM

See mediation information assessment meeting.

Mid-nup

A mid-nuptial agreement: an agreement made during the marriage. See post-nup.

Mirror order

A court order obtained in a foreign court, which reflects exactly the terms of an English court order. Mirror orders are generally obtained to enforce the terms of an English order outside England and Wales.

Mortgagee

This is usually a bank or building society, but it can be anyone who lends you money to buy a property on the security of the property.

Mortgagor

This is the borrower who obtains a mortgage.

Non-molestation order

An order prohibiting a person from molesting another person. The order usually prohibits one person from using or threatening violence or intimidating, harassing or pestering another person. The order can include the protection of children. Once a respondent is aware of a non-molestation order, breaching it is a criminal offence that is punishable by either a fine

or a term of imprisonment. This often goes hand-in-hand with an occupation order or orders relating to the children.

Occupation order

An order regulating the occupation of the family home. A person can be excluded from the family home or from a certain part of it for a set period of time. If the respondent breaches an occupation order, if a power of arrest has been attached to the order, the police can arrest the respondent and bring them back to court.

Offer to settle

Offers to settle may be "open". This means they can be referred to, openly, in court and especially at any final hearing. Offers to settle may also be without prejudice, which means it is not possible to refer to them openly in court except at the FDR and especially not in any final hearing.

Order

A direction by the court that is legally binding and enforceable.

Parental responsibility

If the parents are married, or if the child was born after 1 December 2003 and the father is named on the birth certificate, both parents of a child have joint parental responsibility for that child before, during and after divorce or separation. This term describes all of the rights, duties and responsibilities which, by law, a parent of a child has in relation to that child. Aspects of parental responsibility include decisions about a child's religion, education, name and medical treatment.

Particulars

If a matrimonial order application for divorce is based on unreasonable behaviour or adultery, it has to set out details. This can be upsetting and, in some cases, offensive. It is best to try and agree the particulars before the matrimonial order application is sent to the court.

Pension

Cash and/or an income paid by the Government or a private company or arrangement on a person's retirement. Pension funds can be extremely valuable and may be an important part of any financial settlement, especially after longer marriages. There are three ways of resolving issues around pensions and provision on retirement.

Pension earmarking is arranging that, when a pension comes to be paid, a proportion of it is paid to the other party

Pension offsetting is offsetting the value of the pension against some other asset such as the marital home

Pension sharing is the splitting of the pension at the time of divorce, giving both parties their own pension fund

Periodical payments

The technical phrase for maintenance or alimony.

Permission to remove

An application to the court for permission to remove a child permanently from England and Wales. This used to be called leave to remove.

Petition

See matrimonial order application.

Petitioner

Now called an applicant. This is the person applying for the divorce in the petition/ matrimonial order application.

Post-nup

The aim of a pre-marital agreement is usually to protect the wealth of one or both spouses and, if prepared properly, should be binding. If you are considering a pre-nup you should seek specialist advice immediately. You can also take steps to protect your position after the wedding, which may involve a post-nup/mid-nup. These are the same as a pre-nup, but made at any time after the marriage ceremony.

Power of arrest

This allows the police to arrest a person who ignores or breaks an order of the court. If your partner breaks the order and you call the police, they will ask to see a copy of the order to see if it has a power of arrest. Once the police have arrested that person they must bring them back to court within 24 hours. A power of arrest can only be attached to an occupation order and not a non-molestation order because a breach of a non-molestation order is automatically considered to be a criminal offence.

Prayer

The section of the petition that asks the court to make orders in favour of the petitioner.

Pre-nup

A pre-nuptial agreement (also known as a pre-marital agreement or contract) is made in contemplation of marriage, most commonly setting out the terms which are to apply between the spouses in the event of separation or divorce. Sometimes they can deal with arrangements during the marriage, upon separation/ divorce and upon death.

Parent with care

A term that used to be used by the Child Support Agency for the parent with whom the child had his or her main home. The Child Maintenance Service now refer to the parent with care as the "receiving parent" (i.e. they receive the maintenance on behalf of the child).

Privilege

The right of a person to refuse to disclose a document or to refuse to answer questions on the ground of some special interest recognised by law.

Process server

This is someone employed to serve court papers. To prove that the papers have been served, the process server will normally swear an affidavit, which will be sent to the court.

Prohibited steps order

An order used to prohibit something being done to a child, for example, changing a child's surname or taking the child out of England and Wales.

Property adjustment order/ property transfer order

The court's power to change the ownership of an asset. Usually, but not always, this will be in relation to property.

Questionnaire

A list of questions asking for further details about a person's financial circumstances. This is usually made in response to any gaps or omissions in someone's Form E in financial proceedings.

Relevant child

A child of the marriage, either aged under 16 at the time of decree nisi or aged between 16 and 18 and in full time education or training. A disabled and dependent child of any age will always be considered a relevant child.

Residence

This describes where and with whom a child lives on a day to day basis, or has their primary home. Previously termed custody although the legal consequences are different.

Residence order

As from April 2014, residence orders no longer exist. They have been replaced with "child arrangements orders" which deal with contact and residence.

Request for directions for trial

A specific application to the court which asks for the decree nisi to be made.

Respondent

The person who receives the divorce petition/matrimonial order application or some other application to court, such as in financial proceedings.

Sale of property order

Where a court makes an order for secured periodical payments (see maintenance), lump sum or property adjustment, it may make a further order for the sale of property to satisfy the earlier order.

Seal

A mark or stamp that the court puts on documents to indicate that they have been issued by the court.

Separation agreement

A contractual document that deals with the arrangements between a couple after their separation. Sometimes this is used when a divorcing couple are waiting for the two years' separation to elapse.

Service

The process by which court documents are formally sent to, and received by, the party to whom they are addressed.

Set aside

Cancelling a judgment or order.

Solicitor

A lawyer who advises a client and prepares a case for court. Specialist family law solicitors may also be trained as mediators, collaborative lawyers or arbitrators.

Special procedure

When divorce/matrimonial proceedings are undefended, the decree nisi and decree absolute can be issued without either spouse having to appear at court. Although called "special", in fact this is the normal procedure for most divorces. This is sometimes called a "quickie divorce" by the tabloids.

Specific issue order

An order determining a specific issue relating to a child, for example, which school a child is to attend.

Section 8 order

An order under section 8 of the Children Act 1989: namely a child arrangements order, a prohibited steps order and a specific issue order.

Section 25 factors

The checklist of criteria upon which financial remedy applications are decided.

Statement in support of divorce

This statement poses a number of questions aimed at ensuring that the contents of your petition remain true and correct and that there have been no changes in circumstances that may affect your ability to rely on the fact of (adultery/ unreasonable behaviour/ desertion/ two years' separation with consent or five years' separation) to support the irretrievable breakdown of your marriage. This statement has to be filed at court when you apply for Decree Nisi.

Statement in support of petition

A formal statement sworn on oath to be true by the person making it, usually in support of an application to the court. See also swear.

Statement of arrangements

The document that used to be sent to the court with the petition/matrimonial order application if the divorcing couple had children. As of 22 April 2014, it is no longer necessary to submit this document with your petition.

Statement of truth

A statement or other document containing facts verified as being true by the person making the statement. If the document is false, proceedings for contempt of court may be brought against the person who made the false statement.

Stay

To place a stop or a halt on court proceedings.

Strike out

The court ordering that written material or evidence may no longer be relied upon.

Swear

To declare on oath that what is being said or what is contained in a document is true. This is usually administered by a solicitor, notary public or a member of court staff. It sometimes incurs a small fee.

Talaq

Dissolves an Islamic marriage under Islamic law. It is a unilateral process whereby a husband rejects his wife by saying words to the effect "I divorce you".

Term order

Maintenance/periodical payments for a specified period of time. The term (or length) of the order can either be capable of being extended to cater for something unexpected happening or, alternatively, the court can order that the term cannot be extended.

Tenancy-in-common

This is one way of owning property jointly. The separate shares are agreed (usually when the property is purchased). If one of the owners dies, their share will form part of their estate and will not automatically belong to the survivor, unlike joint tenancy.

Two-years separation

The divorcing couple has lived apart for two years and the other spouse consents to divorce. This is one of the five facts on which a divorce can be based.

Undertaking

An undertaking is a promise given to the court or to the other party. Once an undertaking has been given to the court, it has the same effect as a court order. This means that, if it is broken, it will be seen as contempt of court and (in extreme cases) an application can be made for the person who has broken the undertaking to be committed to prison.

Unreasonable behaviour

This is one of the five facts on which a divorce can be based. Particulars of the behaviour have to be set out in the petition/ matrimonial order application.

Without prejudice

Correspondence or documents that are marked "without prejudice" cannot be shown to the court. The purpose of allowing this is to encourage discussions about settlement. The only time a court can see without prejudice proposals is in the FDR hearing because this is a without prejudice hearing.